Making Sense of Intellectual Capital
Designing a Method for the Valuation of Intangibles

Daniel Andriessen

AMSTERDAM • BOSTON • HEIDELBERG • LONDON
NEW YORK • OXFORD • PARIS • SAN DIEGO
SAN FRANCISCO • SINGAPORE • SYDNEY • TOKYO

Butterworth-Heinemann is an imprint of Elsevier

658.4038
A57m

Elsevier Butterworth–Heinemann
200 Wheeler Road, Burlington, MA 01803, USA
Linacre House, Jordan Hill, Oxford OX2 8DP, UK

Library of Congress Cataloging-in-Publication Data

Andriessen, Daniel.
 Making sense of intellectual capital : designing a method for the valuation of intangibles / Daniel Andriessen.
  p. cm.
 Includes bibliographical references (p. 413) and index.
 ISBN 0-7506-7774-0 (alk. paper)
  1. Intellectual capital—Management. 2. Intangible property—Management. 3. Intangible property—Valuation. 4. Knowledge management. I. Title.

HD53.A49 2004
658.4′038—dc22
                                                                    2003060685

British Library Cataloguing-in-Publication Data
A catalogue record for this book is available from the British Library.

ISBN: 0-7506-7774-0

For information on all Butterworth–Heinemann publications visit our website at www.bh.com

04 05 06 07 08 09 10 9 8 7 6 5 4 3 2 1

Printed in the United States of America

Cover Image: Barnett Newman, *Cathedra*. Reproduced courtesy of Stedelijk Museum, Amsterdam.

Advance Praise for **Making Sense of Intellectual Capital:**

"Weaving a fascinating blend of sharp analysis and story telling, Andriessen describes the journey of a passionate group of experts pursuing one of the most challenging and elusive riddles in modern business—how do intangible resources create value for the firm? This insightful and sweeping exploration of both the underlying questions and their numerous proposed solutions from other contributors in the field offers a wonderfully lucid overview of a complex subject. Andriessen's passion for methodologies that are coherent, rigorous and relevant is contagious. The Weightless Wealth Toolkit draws from the best available intangible valuation tools and methods but takes them to the next level, offering a powerful and original contribution. Whether you are new to the questions around intangibles or already well versed in the field, you will find this an indispensable reference and guide."
—**Verna Allee**, author, *The Knowledge Evolution* and *The Future of Knowledge: Increasing Prosperity through Value Networks*

"Daniel Andriessen deftly walks the fine line between theory and practice. His book is academic enough to provide a fundamental contribution to the science and understanding of the valuation of intangibles. Yet it remains practical enough, with its candor and honesty, to allow for effective implementation of his methods and ideas, manifested in his Weightless Wealth Tool kit. It demonstrates that measurement is not enough, that valuation is paramount in leveraging intangibles for strategic benefit. **Making Sense of Intellectual Capital** is important reading for anyone who considers their intellectual capital to be strategic to their business."
—**Howard Deane**, Chief Knowledge Officer, KMPG LLP, Canada

"A most insightful knowledge navigation book on valuing intangibles . . . Recommended reading for both practitioners and researchers."
—**Leif Edvinsson**, The world's first director of Intellectual Capital; The world's first holder of a professorship on Intellectual Capital, University of Lund, Sweden, 1998 "Brain of the Year"

"In **Making Sense of Intellectual Capital,** Dr. Andriessen has produced one of the most synthesizing books on this important but challenging topic. This book provides a very valuable overview and evaluation of the managerial tools available to managers when it comes to better managing their intangible assets. I highly recommend this book to any manger of a firm that is charged with extracting value from its intangibles."
—**Göran Roos**, Director, Intellectual Capital Services, London

"I strongly believe that **Making Sense of Intellectual Capital** will become *the* compass for the intellectual academic community and *the* comprehensive guide for practitioners in considering intangibles as the main resources to manage in the context of the knowledge economy. Andriessen is a perfect blend of an academic and a practitioner. As an academic he scientifically evaluates the 25 existing methods for managing and measuring intangibles. As a practitioner he also offers in his book his own method for valuing intangibles together with some useful practical applications. Excellent. The book really makes sense in the emerging field of intellectual capital, which currently contains many different contributions of unequal quality and relevance. Andriessen has done a great job that will please both academics and practitioners. This is an inspiring book, mainly of academic nature but with very practical and powerful messages to improve the value of businesses. Andriessen really challenges the Intellectual Capital conventional wisdom with new approaches and contributions."

—**José María Viedma,** President of Intellectual Capital Management Systems and Professor of Business Administration at Polytechnic University of Catalonia

Contents

1

Objective: Valuation and Measurement in the Intangible Economy

2

Methodology: The Science of Designing Practical Methods

3

4

5

6

Lessons Learned: Contributions to Intellectual Capital Research

Preface and Acknowledgments

> "The problem of a painting is physical and metaphysical, the same as I think life is physical and metaphysical."
>
> *Barnett Newman*[1]

On November 21, 1997, a schizophrenic with a kitchen knife slashed Barnett Newman's majestic work "Cathedra" in the Amsterdam Stedelijk Museum. Although this event hardly shocked the world, it did shock me. I had come to love the ultramarine painting, because the vivid blue appealed to my analytical mind, and the physical largeness of the abstract expressionist's painting served as a metaphor for my—at that time, subconscious—ambition to tell my own story. Newman used color, composition, texture, and line to convey *meaning*, not a specific narrative, but a meaning that would be different for each onlooker. The meaning and the beauty of his painting are—like value—in the eye of the beholder. He saw the process of painting as physical and metaphysical, and the result as tangible and intangible: the tangible 8 × 18-foot painting and its intangible conveyance of ideas about the depth of feeling and thought. The schizophrenic not only destroyed a tangible painting, he also destroyed invaluable weightless wealth.

Exactly one year earlier, Professor René Tissen and I met for the first time. Less than two months later we formed KPMG's Knowledge Advisory Services Group. We have made it into a successful group of advisors who work in the area of knowledge management and intangible resource valuation, without disavowing our passion for innovation. I thank René for being my colleague at KPMG, but even more I thank him for suggesting that I pursue my Ph.D. At first I thought the idea was ridiculous. I could not imagine myself spending four years in a dark room sitting behind my computer working on just one subject. In the end, other people helped to change my mind, and that changed my life. René, thank you for keeping your faith in me and defending me. You have been loyal to me, even after I—through my

---

[1] Source: http://209.235.192.90/exhibitions/exhibits/newman/

work as a Ph.D. graduate—discovered I am much more an academic (a philosopher) than a consultant.

Who were the people who changed my mind? Two of them are not aware of it. Arie van der Zwan and Mira Stol–Trip both work for the Ministry of Economic Affairs in The Netherlands. In 1998 they invited KPMG to participate in a pilot project for the valuation of intangible resources. I thank them for their vision, because they provided me with the perfect subject and case material for *Making Sense of Intellectual Capital*.

My brother Bart does know he helped to change my mind. In May 1999 we spent our holidays together in Provence, France. One night we had a conversation about what makes me "tick." During our dialog, I discovered my ambition to work in academia; moreover, I recognized my ambition to gain entry into the academic world: a Ph.D. Bart, thank you for this enlightening moment.

After my holidays I went to see René and told him of my plan. He was delighted and suggested we ask Prof. Mathieu Weggeman to serve as a second supervisor. Mathieu, thank you very much for your support, your knowledge, and your thorough (sometimes ruthless) comments. That is exactly what a Ph.D. student needs.

Six months earlier, I had had the privilege of acting as the aid for Derk Daan Reneman when he defended his Ph.D. thesis at the Free University, Amsterdam. Derk has been a long-time friend and a great supporter of my Ph.D. work. I thank him for his persistent friendship, advice, and encouragement, and I am honored that he was willing to act as my aid at my viva voce.

In 2000, René and I published the predecessor of this book, a book called *Weightless Wealth*. *Weightless Wealth* proposes a method for the identification, assessment, and valuation of intangible resources, which is an earlier version of the method that I describe in this book, *Making Sense of Intellectual Capital*. I thank Jonathan Ellis for his help in writing *Weightless Wealth* and reviewing *Making Sense of Intellectual Capital*. His writing skills and craftsmanship are unprecedented.

Not long after we published *Weightless Wealth*, I met Leif Edvinsson for the first time. At my first visit to the McMaster World Congress on the Management of Intellectual Capital, Leif and I met again, and he gave me the nickname that I still use with pride: IC Challenger. Leif, thank you for your inspiration and for stimulating me to find my own destiny. Your book *Corporate Longitude* motivated me to create a job title that does not say what I do, but describes what I am good at. I am a *sensemaker*, and I help clarify, challenge, and create ideas.

I thank Prof. Nick Bontis and Prof. Christopher Bart who, together with their splendid team of students, organize each year the world's best conference on intellectual capital at McMaster University in Hamilton, Canada. Through your conferences I have found my community, my audience; and each visit convinces me all the more that I need to follow my academic ambition. Through you, I have met many friends from all over the world who I would like to thank for sharing with me a passion for the subject: Verna Allee, Ahmed Bounfour, Jay Chatzkel, James Falconer, Tua Haldin–Herrgard, Clive Holtham, Philippe Leliaert, Darius Mahdjoubi, Bernard Marr, José Maria Viedma Marti, Jan Mouritsen, Joe Peppard, Prof. Ante Pulic, Anna Rylander, and Herman Van den Berg, to name a few. I also would like to show appreciation for Göran Roos, at one time a dear colleague at KPMG, and one of the most inspiring and knowledgeable persons in the field.

A special thanks to my former team members who helped me to create the new method: Jan Blom, Inge van Gisbergen, and Martine Frijlink. I think we were an exceptional team. Each of you brought your unique personality and skills to bear. I also thank my KPMG colleagues Prof. Johan van Helleman, Prof. Willem Dercksen, and Mr. Guus Landheer, who guided us with their wisdom.

I also thank KPMG, a company in which almost everything is possible, that I served with honor for more than 12 years. The firm gave me the unique opportunity to set up a new unit in uncharted territory and to write a book (Tissen et al., 1998). In addition, it enabled me to work on my Ph.D. thesis in parallel with my regular work. A special thanks to the members of the Information Research Center, and especially to Jan Schepers. Without your help in tracing the literature, *Making Sense of Intellectual Capital* would not have been written. Thanks to Frank Lekanne Deprez, my direct colleague, who not only is a walking library, but most of the time happened to have the resources I needed in his possession. I also thank Karima Benaskar, who has been my faithful secretary for many years.

I am grateful for the cooperation of the companies that were willing to serve as guinea pigs for the new method. They did not know what they were getting into when they agreed to work with us, but they had faith that something useful would result (see Chapter 5).

In addition, I thank Karen Maloney of Butterworth-Heinemann. You were kind and brave enough to see through the academic nature of this book and recognize that it contains some very practical and powerful messages to improve the value of businesses.

During the past four years there have been times that I have neglected my duties as a father of two wonderful daughters. Fortunately, there were relatives and friends available who understood my situation and were willing to offer help. Most especially I would like to thank my wonderful mother, Ank Andriessen–Collignon; my in-laws, Hans and Toos Leenders; our neighbors Dioné and Kees Bink; and my fantastic sister Liesbeth for taking care of the children when I was busy writing in the attic.

Lastly, I must thank the three most important people in my life. I express gratitude to my wife, Marian, and to my daughters, Carlijn and Mirthe, for their love, support, and understanding. You provided me with the perfect environment in which to write *Making Sense of Intellectual Capital*. I am sorry for the times I may have placed a heavy burden on you with my ambition. I am grateful and I love you.

Daniel Andriessen
Leiderdorp, The Netherlands
October 2003

Objective: Valuation and Measurement in the Intangible Economy

"And so: he rejected the left horn. Quality is not objective, he said. It doesn't reside in the material world.

Then: he rejected the right horn: Quality is not subjective, he said. It doesn't reside merely in the mind.

And finally: Phaedrus, following a path that to his knowledge had never been taken before in the history of Western thought, went straight between the horns of the subjectivity–objectivity dilemma and said Quality is neither part of mind, nor is it a part of matter. It is a third entity which is independent of the two."

Robert M. Pirsig (1975)

On June 26, 1997, a Dutch member of parliament, Mrs. Voûté–Droste of the Liberal party, petitioned a motion to ask the government for a policy document on intangible resources. The event that triggered this motion was the so-called *techno-lease scandal*. From the beginning of the 1990s, Dutch companies like Philips, DAF trucks, Fokker, and several others were allowed to use this sale and "leaseback" construction to improve their liquidity. Knowledge—mostly in the form of patents—was sold to the Dutch Rabobank and was leased back, leading to considerable tax benefits for the bank and direct cash for the companies. This construction became a political scandal when calculations showed a loss of tax returns of several hundred million Dutch guilders. Voûté–Droste wanted to know the legal possibilities for Dutch companies to capitalize on intangible resources and to what extent these possibilities were used in practice.

On January 21, 1998, the Dutch Minister of Economic Affairs, Hans Wijers, sent a letter to parliament regarding the matter (Ministry of Economic Affairs, 1998a). The letter described the limitations by current rules and regulations on the capitalization of intangible resources. In addition, it provided an overview of the motives found in the corporate world to use or not to use these legal possibilities. It concluded by stating that in The Netherlands "there seems to be some reluctance to use the existing possibilities. This may partly be due to an attitude of risk avoidance on the part of Dutch auditors and partly because of auditors, companies and investors being unacquainted with alternative possibilities" (translated by D. Andriessen; Ministry of Economic Affairs, 1998a, p. 9). The letter then announced a pilot project to allow accounting firms to experiment with new methods for creating transparency in intangible resources.

This letter triggered a chain of events. It led to studies by KPMG, Ernst & Young, PricewaterhouseCoopers, and Walgemoed; an Organisation for Economic Co-operation and Development (OECD) conference in Amsterdam in 1999 on measuring and reporting intellectual capital; a report by the Dutch Ministry of Economic Affairs (1999); and several master's theses. It contributed to the awareness within The Netherlands of the growing importance of intangible resources and it stimulated the search for new methods to help manage, measure, and report this weightless wealth. And it resulted in my first introduction to the *intangible* perspective.

A new use of words creates a new perspective on reality. The viewpoint of intangible resources is such a new perspective. It comes with a motley collection of concepts and phrases like *immaterial assets, knowledge-based assets, tacit knowledge, know-how,* and *intangible assets.* Taking part in the discussion means entering a world full of metaphors, analogies, and figures of speech: There is intellectual *capital* (Edvinsson and Malone, 1997), there are intellectual capital *stocks* and *flows* (Roos and Roos, 1997), and there is knowledge that *travels and changes* in organizations (Bontis, 2002).

As we know from Morgan (1986), metaphors can be powerful tools to help understand complex and paradoxical phenomena like organizations, which can be understood in many different ways: "The use of metaphor implies a way of thinking and a way of seeing that pervade how we understand our world generally" (Morgan, 1986, p. 12). Yet, it is fascinating to see how both academics and practitioners use this new language of intangibles to describe the social world of business as if it were as real as the physical world of everyday life. They sometimes seem to forget they are constructing a social reality, a reconstruction that may or may not be fruitful in explaining and/or improving business performance. This has been a main trigger for this book, which presents a quest for the usefulness of the intangible perspective in improving business performance. I wanted to learn to make sense of intellectual capital and its value.

This book describes my journey into the land of the intangible. The purpose of the journey was to discover new ways to value intangible resources through thorough yet practical research. In this chapter I describe this new intangible perspective, I show that the intangible perspective is able to expose and explain drastic changes in the way the economy and businesses perform, and I indicate that the intangible perspective allows for the definition of specific problems and corresponding solutions. One of these problems is the problem of valuation: How can we put a value on an intangible? I explain the nature of value and valuation, and the differences between a financial valuation, a value measurement, and a value assessment.

I then continue by describing the road map of the journey: the research and design objective, as well as the design problem of my research. I explore the valuation of intellectual capital with my own two feet in the mud. I do not simply criticize the valuation methods others have developed, but experience in practice how difficult it is to design a proper method for the valuation of intangible resources. My ambition was even bigger. I wanted my research to be relevant to practice *and* to science. To achieve this I used a special research methodology that enables the researcher to work according to scientific standards, yet come up with practical results that help improve businesses. This methodology is called *management research practiced as a design science*. But first let us look at businesses from a new perspective.

The Intangible Perspective

The intangible perspective is a resource-based perspective that looks at the economy or at an individual company as a combination of stocks, flows, and transformations of resources. These resources can be tangible, financial, or intangible. The intangible perspective focuses on resources that are not material, and highlights the growing importance in the economy and in companies of this hidden wealth. This perspective brings to light drastic changes that have occurred in the economy during the last 50 years. I briefly describe the history and nature of these changes and the drivers that cause them. I then introduce the intellectual capital community, a group of practitioners and scientists that has helped to promote the intangible perspective and provide tools for valuing and measuring intangible resources.

The Transformation of the Economy

Drucker (1993) calls the change intangibles have induced a process of transformation—a rearrangement of society, its world view, and its basic values. This process has created a society in which the primary resource is knowledge, which he calls the *postcapitalist* or *knowledge society*. In this society, value is created not by the allocation of capital or labor but by productivity and innovation. The leading social group in this society is the knowledge workers, which are comprised of three types: knowledge executives who know how to allocate knowledge to productive use, knowledge professionals, and knowledge employees.

According to Drucker (1993) and Weggeman (1997b) there are three phases in the development toward the intangible economy. The first phase was the Industrial Revolution (1750–1880), during which companies used knowledge to produce tools and products. The second phase was the Production Revolution (1880–1945), during which companies used knowledge to improve labor processes. The third and last phase is the Management Revolution (1945–the present), during which organizations use knowledge to improve knowledge. Managers have become responsible for the application and performance of knowledge.

Seven Characteristics of the Intangible Economy

The intangible economy has seven characteristics that make it fundamentally different from the agricultural and industrial economy. First, knowledge replaces labor and capital as a fundamental resource in production (Stewart, 1997; Weggeman, 1997b), and intangibles like brands create a substantial part of the added value of companies. Nakamura (2003) estimates that private US firms invested at least $1 trillion in intangibles in the year 2000. Gross intangible investments have risen from 3.8% of the Gross Domestic Product (GDP) in 1953 to 9.7% in 2000. Studies have shown the importance of intangibles on future profitability and equity market values of firms. Lev and Sougiannis (1996) have shown the importance of research and development (R&D) capital. Barth et al. (2003) proved there is a correlation between the value of brands and stock returns. Zucker et al. (2003) found that intellectual capital allows biotech enterprises to capture supernormal economic returns. Hall et al. (2001) and Deng et al. (2003) found that the number of patents is associated positively with market value. Seethamraju (2003) shows that the value of new trademarks is associated with the market value of firms. All this evidence proves intangibles are of growing importance for wealth creation.

Second, the knowledge content of products and services is growing rapidly. According to Stewart (1997), the value of the electronic content of a car is more than that of steel. In addition, not only products become more knowledge intensive. Business processes do as well (Jacobs, 1999). Process innovation has become as important as product innovation.

Third, the intangible economy is an economy in which services are as important as products. Not only do products get more knowledge intensive, knowledge itself has become an important product, as shown by the rise of the services industry (Tissen et al., 1998).

Fourth, it is an economy in which the economic laws are different. Lev (2001) explains why the economics of intangibles is different from the economics of physical and financial assets:

1. Intangibles are nonrival assets. They can be deployed at the same time in multiple uses. Although an airplane can be used during a given time period on one route only, its reservations system can serve, at the same time, a potentially unlimited number of customers.
2. In general, intangibles are characterized by large, fixed costs and minimal marginal costs. The development of a software program often requires heavy investment, but distributing and selling it costs very little. Therefore, intangibles are often characterized by increasing returns of scale instead of decreasing returns.
3. Intangibles often profit from network effects. For example, the usefulness of a computer operating system increases with the number of users.
4. At the same time it is often difficult to secure ownership of intangibles, as the widespread violation of copyright law shows. As a result, others may benefit from intangible investments.
5. Innovations in intangibles are often highly risky. R&D, training, and acquiring technologies are often the first steps in the development of new products and services, and therefore have more risk than investments in the later stages of the development process.
6. Often, there is no market for intangibles. They cannot be traded. Markets provide information about the value of goods and services, and this is vital to optimal resource allocation.

The result is that in many industries the traditional economic law of diminishing returns is no longer valid (Arthur, 1996). The assumption behind this law is that companies that are ahead eventually run into limitations, so that equilibrium of prices and market shares is reached. This law no longer holds true. In many sectors, a law of increasing returns has replaced it. Companies that go ahead get farther ahead because of mechanisms of positive feedback.

Fifth, in the intangible economy the concept of ownership of resources has changed. Because knowledge mainly resides in the heads of employees, companies no longer own their most important resource (Weggeman, 1997a). Explicit knowledge can be owned through intellectual property rights, but the enforcement of those rights is becoming difficult. And because knowledge is a nonrival good, it must be appropriated to prevent direct spillover effects to competitors (Soete and Ter Weel, 1999).

Sixth, the intangible economy is an economy in which the characteristics of labor have changed. We have witnessed the rise of the knowledge professional (Tissen et al., 1998). Knowledge workers create most of the value added in companies (Stewart, 1997). They use hardly any physical strength or manual dexterity (Weggeman, 1997a).

Seventh, and lastly, as a result, organizations have changed. The management of intangible resources is fundamentally different from the management of tangible or financial resources. Knowledge is productive only if it is applied to make a difference. Furthermore, it must be clearly focused. It requires the systematic exploitation of opportunities for change and the management of time: the balancing of the long term with the short term (Drucker, 1993). The management of knowledge professionals is more difficult than the management of other employees (Tissen et al., 1998). Weggeman (1992) states that companies cannot control professionals using regulations, procedures, and information systems because they require a natural freedom. More irritatingly, they consider their way of working to be unique. Professionals call for professional organizations with flat hierarchical structures, with managers that facilitate people instead of controlling them, and with professionals that are committed to a team and a task. Organizations have transformed themselves into knowledge companies that handle enormous amounts of information, often diverged from the flow of goods and tangible resources (Stewart, 1997). Knowledge companies are companies that show a limited amount of assets on the balance sheet relative to the added value they produce, because they use less-tangible assets and because they have stripped their balance sheet of fixed assets. According to Lekanne Deprez and Tissen (2002), this process has led to the development of zero-space organizations that are virtual and that use networks to create added value. Knowledge companies also apply different strategies. They no longer compete over minimizing transaction costs but over "shaping and reshaping clusters of assets in the distinct and unique combinations needed to serve ever-changing customer needs" (Teece, 2000, p. 29).

Drivers of the Intangible Economy

The major driver behind the rise of the intangible economy is the combination of three trends into one major discontinuity. The first economic trend is globalization (Hand and Lev, 2003; Houghton and Sheenan, 2000; Weggeman, 1997a,b). There is an increasing interdependence of international flows of goods and services, direct investment, technology, and capital transfers. Competition is becoming increasingly global. As a result, product life cycles are shortened and companies need to minimize costs. They also need to shorten the time-to-market. New products and services require a constant stream of innovation and state-of-the-art knowledge. Companies need to compete by constantly producing new services and products that have more functionality, service, aesthetics, sustainability, and brand recognition (Weggeman, 1997b). If competition can come from anywhere, it becomes increasingly important for companies to be unique. Uniqueness does not come from tangible assets but from proprietary knowledge, special skills, an exclusive way of doing business, and a distinctive image created through "branding."

The second economic trend is the far-reaching deregulation in key economic sectors such as telecommunications, transportation, energy, and financial services (Hand and Lev, 2003; Teece, 2000). Tariff and nontariff barriers have been lowered. Final goods, intermediate goods, services, and resources can flow globally with more freedom than ever before.

The third trend is the exponential growth of technological change, especially the emergence of new information and communication technologies (ICTs). This has resulted in a decline in the price of information processing, in a conversion of communication and computing, and in the rapid growth in international electronic networking (Soete and Ter Weel, 1999). ICT has enabled the global access of information and knowledge.

We can conclude that the intangible perspective is able to expose and explain drastic changes in the way the economy, individual companies, and individuals behave. However, is the intangible perspective also capable of identifying new organizational problems and offering new solutions for management? The intellectual capital community claims that it can.

The Intellectual Capital Community

The intangible perspective allows us to look at companies differently. Chapter 3 describes how various disciplines use this perspective to create a new view of organizations. This new view makes us see things differently and notice different things. It allows for new ways of diagnosing organizations and defining new problems. It also helps in developing new solutions to those problems. The intellectual capital community especially has promoted this perspective, raising the awareness about the importance of intangibles among practitioners as well as academics.

Hudson (1993) quotes the economist Galbraith as the first to use the term *intellectual capital* as early as 1969. Stewart (2001a) claims it dates back at least to 1958. Sullivan (2000) starts his history of the intellectual capital movement with the work of Itami, who in 1980 published a book called *Mobilising Invisible Assets* in Japanese. In the 1980s, the problem of measuring knowledge was addressed on a broader scale by a group of Swedish companies, which Sveiby (2001) calls *the Konrad track*. This group consisted of managers who used primarily nonfinancial indicators to monitor and report intangibles. Sveiby reported their methods in 1989 (Sveiby et al., 1989). The group was called *Konrad* because they met for the first time on November 12, 1987, which is Konrad Day in the Swedish calendar.

The first appearance in the popular press of the term *intellectual capital* was in an article by Stewart (1991) in *Fortune* called "Brainpower." During that same year, Skandia AFS, a Swedish insurance company, appointed Edvinsson as the world's first director of intellectual capital (Edvinsson, 2002a). Later, Stewart (1994) published another article on intellectual capital. A year after that, the first meeting of the Intellectual Capital Management (ICM) gathering took place. Sullivan, Petrash, and Edvinsson brought together people from eight different companies who were all engaged in actively extracting value from their intangible assets (Sullivan, 2000). This meeting boosted the thinking on intellectual capital measurement and knowledge management. Sullivan (2000) wrote: "Representatives involved in this meeting felt as if they had found long-lost relatives. Each had been operating in a vacuum without knowing there were others trying to deal with the same problems" (p. 16). Each of the originators of the ICM gathering would become a well-known author and thought leader in the field.

In 1995, Skandia (1995) presented the first public report on intellectual capital. In 1997, intellectual capital hit the publishing trail

(Edvinsson, 2002a) with the publication of three different books, each entitled *Intellectual Capital* (Edvinsson and Malone, 1997; Roos et al., 1997; Stewart, 1997), as well as a new book by Sveiby (1997). These publications helped to create a large community of both academics and practitioners in the field. From that moment on, there was an explosion of activity, as shown by the overview of literature by Bontis (2002) and Petty and Guthrie (2000).

The questions raised by the intellectual capital community are analogous to the questions often asked about tangible and financial resources: How can we improve the management of intangible resources (Roos et al., 1997; Stewart, 1997)? How can we improve their utilization (Bontis, 2002)? How can we decide whether to invest further in developing an intangible (Sullivan, 1998a)? How can we make better resource allocation decisions (Edvinsson, 2002a)? How can we get information on whether our investments have been productive (Pike and Roos, 2000)? How can we measure intangible resources (Luu et al., 2001; M'Pherson and Pike, 2001a,b)? What is the value of intangible resources (Edvinsson and Malone, 1997; Stewart, 1997)? How should we report intangible resources (Sveiby et al., 1989)?

According to Roos et al. (1997), we can trace the theoretical roots of intellectual capital to two different streams of thought. The first one studies the development and leverage of knowledge. The second one focuses on the development of new information systems that measure the value of knowledge (Figure 1.1).

Over the years, the measurement stream has intrigued me, and I decided to make it the subject of this book. Tissen, Lekanne Deprez, and I (1998, 2000) have covered the other stream in two earlier publications.

Especially within the intellectual capital community, authors seem to be obsessed with the need for measurement. It really is fascinating. The measurement of intangible resources is justified using phrases like "what gets measured gets managed" (Luu et al., 2001); "what you can measure, you can manage and what you want to manage, you need to measure" (Roos et al., 1997); and "in order to manage value creation we need to measure it" (Pulic, 2000b). What is this obsession? Why create a list of 191 indicators of intellectual capital (Liebowitz and Suen, 2000)? Why include more than 160 indicators in an intellectual capital navigator (Edvinsson and Malone, 1997)? Why try to add apples and oranges to create one overall indicator for the value of intellectual capital (Bounfour, 2002; M'Pherson and Pike, 2001a,b; Pike and Roos, 2000; Roos et al., 1997)? I could not make any sense of it.

Figure 1.1

Conceptual roots of intellectual capital (Roos et al., 1997)

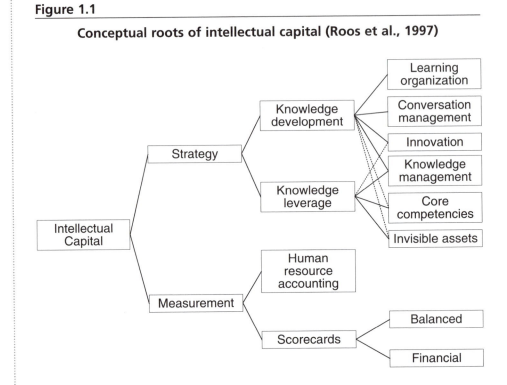

Many of the methods available to measure the value of intangible resources seem to be a solution in search of a cause. (Appendix A contains a description of a sample of 25 methods found in the literature.) To make sense of all the proposed solutions, I decided to study them a little deeper. What are some of the problems that authors try to solve with their methods? What is the underlying problem definition? How robust and useful are these methods?

As we see in Chapter 3, it is possible to group the problem definitions associated with the methods into three categories. The first group focuses on solving internal management problems. This ranges from methods to improve the management of intangibles to ways to progress strategic decision making. The second group concentrates on methods to improve the external reporting of companies. This includes ways to provide additional insight into investments in intangibles, and methods for reporting the financial value of intangibles. The third group of problems relates to transactional or statutory motives for valuation—for example, determining a price for an intangible that will be sold or estimating the value of elements of goodwill when conducting an impairment test.

But I did not only want to study the work of others, I wanted to learn from my own mistakes, too. During the last five years I have developed, together with a team from KPMG, my own method for the valuation of intangible resources. As it turned out, we too have been searching for a cause. This book describes this quest for a new method, from initial conception to its testing at six companies. It describes the brilliant ideas we had and the big mistakes we made. It reconstructs our path from requirements, to design, and to implementation and evaluation. It records what we learned and what we still need to learn.

Valuation and Measurement of Intangibles

I have characterized the exploration of methods for the valuation of intangible resources as a search for the Holy Grail (Andriessen, 2002b). Before we can engage in such a quest, we need to know what we are looking for. What is the nature of value, what do we mean by valuation, and what types of methods for valuation exist?

Value

Nowadays we think about money when we talk about value, but according to Crosby (1997), it was only during the Middle Ages that money developed as a means of quantifying value. Value closely relates to the concept of "values." According to Trompenaars and Hampden–Turner (1997), values determine the definition of good and bad, as opposed to norms that reflect the mutual sense a group has of what is right and wrong. A value reflects the concept an individual or group has regarding what is desired. It serves as a criterion to determine a choice from existing alternatives.

Following the *Longman Dictionary of Contemporary English* (Proctor, 1978) as well as Trompenaars and Hampden–Turner (1997), I define value as *the degree of usefulness or desirability of something, especially in comparison with other things*. I use the term *usefulness* to emphasize the utilitarian purpose of valuation. This is in line with Rescher's (1969) value theory. He states that values are inherently benefit oriented. People engage in valuation "to determine the extent to which the benefits accruing from realization of some values are provided by the items at issue" (pp. 61–62). However, usefulness is not the only aspect of value. Things can be valuable because they are beautiful, pleasing, or in other ways desirable, which is why I included the term *desirability* in the definition. Usefulness and desirability are not mutually exclusive. Things can be desirable because they are useful.

According to Rescher (1969), two questions dominate the discussion about value: (1) Is value a property or is it a relationship linking the item at issue with the valuing subject in some special way? Is it strictly personal or does it have an objective grounding?[1] (2) Is value something to be apprehended only in subjective experience or can it be based on specifiable criteria, the satisfaction of which can be determined by objective examination?

I agree with Rescher (1969) when he states that value is not a property inherent in the item at issue. It depends on the subject's view of usefulness or desirability. In that respect, "value is in the eye of the beholder." Therefore, valuation requires implicit or explicit criteria, or yardsticks for usefulness or desirability. During the Middle Ages, things developed a price, which allowed for the comparison of the usefulness or desirability of any item against any other item. When we use money as a measure of value, it acts as a relative criterion that allows for comparing the usefulness or desirability of things that are very different in nature. This means that when we do *not* use money as a criterion, other criteria or yardsticks need to be present to allow for a valuation.

With respect to the second question, I tend to disagree with Rescher (1969). He states that because valuation is based on criteria, value has an objective basis and can be assessed by impersonal standards or criteria that can be taught to an evaluator through training. The problem is that those criteria may "take account of objective features of the items that are being evaluated" (Rescher, 1969, p. 56), but they may also take account of *unobservable* features of these items. The question is whether all implicit criteria people use in their valuations can be made explicit and can be unraveled into observable criteria. I believe this is often not the case. We cannot always translate value into observable criteria. Some valuations are personal assessments that we cannot make explicit.

Valuation

Rescher (1969) describes valuation (he uses the term *evaluation*) as "a comparative assessment or measurement of something with respect to its embodiment of a certain value" (p. 61). Rescher (1969) describes the importance of values for valuation as follows:

---

[1] This is the same question Phaedrus asked himself with respect to quality in Robert Pirsig's novel *Zen and the Art of Motorcycle Maintenance* (Pirsig, 1975).

> Whenever valuation takes place, in any of its diverse forms...
> values must enter in. It is true that when somebody is grading
> apples, say, or peaches, he may never make overt reference to
> any values. But if the procedure were not guided by the no
> doubt unspoken but nevertheless real involvement with such
> values as palatability and nourishment, we would be dealing with
> classification or measurement and not with grading and valuation
> (p. 71).

Furthermore, he states that any valuation makes use of a *value scale*, reflecting the fact that this value is found to be present in a particular case to varying degrees. This value scale can be an ordinal scale that reflects the varying degrees of value but does not show us the interval between the positions on the scale. Rescher (1969, p. 63) gives the example of a value scale for patriotism that is of an ordinal nature: disloyal → unpatriotic → indifferently patriotic → patriotic → superpatriotic.

A value scale can also be a cardinal scale. Such a scale is of an interval or ratio level (Swanborn, 1981). With regard to an interval level, the interval between the varying degrees of value is known, whereas on a ratio level it is also known what constitutes zero value. We can represent cardinal scales numerically. The advantage of using money as the denominator of value is that it creates a value scale at the ratio level that allows for mathematical transformations.

Four Ways to Determine Value

Valuation requires an object to be valued, a framework for the valuation, and a criterion that reflects the usefulness or desirability of the object. Now we have several options. We can define the criterion of value in monetary terms, in which case the method to determine value is a *financial valuation method*. Or we can use a nonmonetary criterion and translate it into observable phenomena, which I term a *value measurement method*. If the criterion cannot be translated into observable phenomena but instead depends on personal judgment by the evaluator, then I call the method a *value assessment method*.

If the framework does not include a criterion for value but does involve a metrical scale that relates to an observable phenomenon, then I call the method a *measurement method*. Strictly speaking, a measurement method is not a method for valuation, but as we shall see in Chapter 3, this type of method is often used within the intellectual capital community. Swanborn (1981) defines measurement as the process of assigning scaled numbers to items in such a way that the relationships that exist in reality between the possible states of a variable are reflected in the relationships between the numbers on the scale. Measurement methods do not use value scales, but use measurement scales instead.

Measurement has been an important element of management and business ever since the Egyptians used mathematics in their book-keeping more than 3,700 years ago. Italian merchants in the 12th century already knew that good books kept them from "chaos, a confusion of Babel" (Crosby, 1997, p. 203). These merchants started experimenting with double-entry techniques. Two centuries later, in 1494, the Italian mathematician Lucia Pacioli supplied, in print, for the first time a clear, simple explanation of the technique as part of his *Summa de arithmetica geometria proportioni et proportionalità*. Current accounting is still based on these principles. We can trace the origins of nonfinancial measurement as a management method back to the French *tableau de bord*, a measurement tool that dates back to 1932 (Nørreklit, 2000). Another example is the work of the high-level task force on key corporate performance measures installed at General Electric in 1951 (Nørreklit, 2000). During the 1980s, the total quality management movement introduced various quality measures, and in the beginning of the 1990s, measures of customer satisfaction were introduced. In 1992, Kaplan and Norton (1992) published their famous article on the *balanced scorecard*.

In literature, we find all four methods for the valuation of intangibles. The *intangible scorecard* by Gu and Lev (2002) is an example of a financial valuation method. M'Pherson's *inclusive value methodology* (M'Pherson and Pike, 2001a,b) is an example of a value measurement method. The *intellectual capital benchmarking system* of Viedma (1999; 2001a,b; 2002) is a method used to perform a value assessment. In addition, some proposed methods for the valuation of intangible resources are merely measurement methods, because they do not include values. An example is the *Skandia navigator* (Edvinsson and Malone, 1997).

Making Sense of Intellectual Capital looks at all four types of methods, which I summarize as methods for the valuation or measurement of intangible resources. Figure 1.2 shows the relationship between financial valuation, value measurement, value assessment, and measurement.

The decisive factors are the use of values as criteria, the use of money as the denominator of value, and the observability of the criteria or measured variable.

Figure 1.2

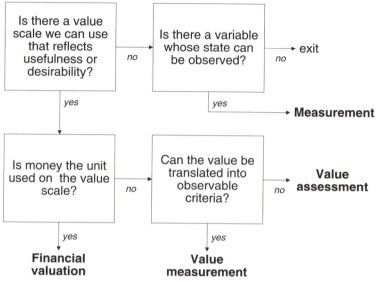

Financial valuation, value measurement, value assessment, and measurement

Objective and Problem

I wanted to design and test a method for the valuation of intangible resources to learn to make sense of the valuation of intangibles. Because I wanted to design and test the method in a scientific way, I decided to base my research methodology on the approach of management research practiced as a design science (Van Aken, 2000). This type of management research is not often practiced and has met with a lot of skepticism within the scientific community. Yet it is unique in the sense that its intention is to help businesses perform better and create scientific knowledge concomitantly. To help develop and promote this methodology, I decided to make acquiring knowledge about this type of management research my second objective. This section describes the fundamentals of my research journey: the objectives of the research, the problems it addressed, as well as its scientific and practical relevance.

My Objectives

My main motivation for my research was to contribute to the scientific body of knowledge of the intellectual capital community.

According to Bontis (2002), this field is in its embryonic stage. He states that the real problem with intellectual capital lies in its measurement (Bontis, 2002). Not only is there confusion about terminology (Bontis, 2001), there are many methods available for financial valuation, value measurement, value assessment, and measurement, and their purposes, strengths, and weaknesses are unclear.

The primary research objective of my research was to contribute to the intellectual capital community by developing knowledge about the valuation of intangible resources. I decided to describe this *research objective* as follows: *To develop knowledge about the valuation of intangible resources, especially about the characteristics and purposes of valuation and the use of valuation methods.*

I developed this knowledge by studying existing literature and by designing and testing a new method for the financial valuation of intangible resources. I deeply believe people learn most when they make mistakes by trying to put theory into practice. My research included a review of 25 existing methods. For each method I analyzed its purpose, strengths, and weaknesses. The results are presented in Chapter 3 and in Appendix A. Chapters 4 through 6 describe the design, testing, and lessons learned of my method, called the *weightless wealth tool kit*. The complete tool kit is contained in Appendix B.

This brings us to the second objective of my research, which was to contribute to the repertoire of intellectual capital methods by designing and testing a method for the valuation of intangible resources. From the literature review it became clear to me that each existing method has its strengths and weaknesses, and that there was room for improvement. I therefore decided to design a method that not only works in the described cases but also works for other cases. The objective of the research was to devise an object and realization design for such a valuation method that had been tested in practice. I described this *design objective* of the research as follows: *To develop and test a method for the valuation of the intangible resources of an organization, and a plan for its implementation.*

A major motivation for this study was my concern about the rigor and relevance of academic intellectual capital research. Academic research in the field of intellectual capital focuses too much on rigor and not enough on relevance. This is probably an overreaction to the fact that "Intellectual Capital research has primarily evolved from the desires of practitioners" (Bontis, 2002, p. 623). On the other hand, there is plenty of practical development of methods that lack proper testing. I wanted to contribute to the reconciliation of the dilemma of rigor versus relevance in intellectual capital research. Therefore, my secondary research objective was to contribute to the methodology of intellectual capital research.

I wanted this contribution to be threefold. First, I wanted to develop further and to codify the various steps of this new methodology of intellectual capital research practiced as a design science. Second, following Weggeman (1995), I wanted to demonstrate that practicing intellectual capital research as a design science can lead to useful results. Third, I wanted to highlight some of the limitations of this methodology and provide suggestions for improvement. I decided to describe this *secondary research objective* as the following: *To develop knowledge about the methodology of intellectual capital research practiced as a design science, its process, its results, and its limitations.*

My objectives are summarized in Figure 1.3.

Problem

Every research project starts with a question. My research started with the following design problem: How can we determine the value

Figure 1.3

Three objectives of my research

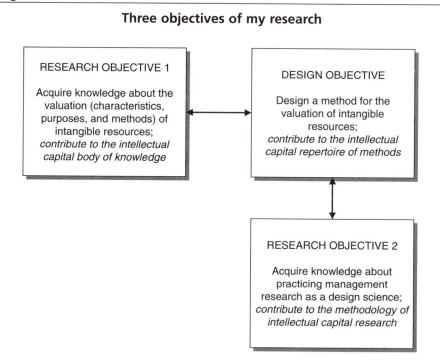

of the intangible resources of an organization in such a way that this information helps to solve organizational problems?

In scientific research it is important to define clearly the key concepts one uses (a glossary of terms is included at the end of this book). I define the key concepts of the problem definition as follows:

Value	The degree of usefulness or desirability of something, especially in comparison with other things
Intangible resources	Nonmonetary resources without physical substance that in combination are able to produce future benefits for an organization
Organization	A group of people involved in a network of subjectively shared meanings that are sustained through the development and use of common language and everyday social interaction, producing goods and/or services by combining financial, tangible, and intangible resources
Organizational problems	Problems of internal management, external reporting, and/or transactional and statutory-related problems
Method	A consistent set of steps to achieve a certain goal
Valuation	A comparative assessment or measurement of something with respect to its embodiment of a certain value
Implementation	The realization of a designed method through a series of interventions

The *practical* relevance of the research lies in the development of a practical method that can help reduce a manager's uncertainty with regard to the value of the company's intangible resources. I wanted to help managers define the problem they intend to solve and help them choose the right tool for the job (see also Andriessen [2002a]). As mentioned previously, there are a number of methods for the valuation of intangibles, the purpose of which is unclear (see Chapter 3). Part of the *scientific* relevance of my research is to clarify the purpose of measuring the value of intangible resources. Why should we want to engage in such an exercise? What is the exact problem we are trying to solve? However, I discovered that defining the right problem to solve turned out to be one of the biggest challenges of my quest.

To make the research manageable, I broke down the design problem into 11 subproblems:

1. What methodology should we use to design a management method in a scientific way?
2. What can we learn from existing methods for the valuation or measurement of intangible resources with respect to the way they define the subject under investigation, the company problems they try to solve, and the quality of the method?
3. How can we define and identify intangible resources?
4. What are the requirements for a new method for the valuation of intangible resources?
5. What is the initial object and realization design of a new method that meets these requirements?
6. What can we learn from implementing the design with respect to the success of the method in solving problems?
7. What changes can we make to the object and realization design to make them more successful?
8. What are the strengths and weaknesses of the new method and how successful is it in solving company problems?
9. How can we improve the method further?
10. What can we learn from the design, implementation, and testing of the method about the valuation of intangible resources and its purposes, limitations, and usefulness?
11. What can we learn from the design, implementation, and testing of the method about the methodology of management research practiced as a design science, its process, its results, and its limitations?

Methodology

A research methodology is a set of rules about the process of scientific inquiry. The choice of methodology depends on the type of research question and the characteristics of the phenomena under investigation (Biemans and Van der Meer–Kooistra, 1994). My research question was a design problem that involved the testing of a draft design of a new management method. This is an example of management research practiced as a design science. In the following section I introduce this type of management research and describe the methodology I used for testing my design.

Practicing Management Research as a Design Science

Management research is the scientific discipline of studying organizations, their environment, and the way they are or ought to be managed. In Chapter 2 I explain that this discipline is scientific and can be practiced in two ways. It can be practiced as an *explanatory science*, studying organizations with the intention of describing, explaining, and predicting their performance. Alternatively, it can be practiced as a *design science*, developing methods to improve the performance of organizations. Both can be done in a scientific way, provided the scientist follows a set of scientific rules (see Chapter 2).

The scientific nature of management research has been the subject of huge debates within the discipline (see the special issue of *Bedrijfskunde* on methodology [1994, 1996] and Van Aken [2000]). The primary debate focuses on the relevance of management theory as developed by the academic community, as well as the rigor of many management theories presented in popular management literature. Having been a practitioner myself for more than 12 years, I see the need for relevant management research. In my work as a practitioner as well as in my work as an academic, I consider it important to help improve the management of organizations. My research is an example of intellectual capital research, which is part of the broader category of management research. In this book I use both terms interchangeably.

Using the Developing Multiple Case Study Method

The testing of the design of a new method for the valuation of intangible resources involved many variables. I was able to control some of them, like the quality of the object and realization design. However, I was not able to control others. Empirical case study research is appropriate for testing hypotheses that have many variables interacting in complex patterns (Biemans and Van der Meer–Kooistra, 1994). However, in empirical research, the application of case studies is limited to situations in which the researcher does not manipulate the independent variables. If it is the intention of the researcher to manipulate variables deliberately, then the appropriate research design is the experiment.

According to Swanborn (1981), during an experiment the researcher should have extensive control over most of the variables. In addition, the allocation of the different values of the independent variables to the group under investigation and the control group should be random. My research had characteristics of an experiment because it was my intent to manipulate variables like the object and realization design. However, my research was not an experiment in the empirical sense, because there was no control group and it turned out to be impossible to control all variables involved.

Van Aken (2000) has extended the use of the term *case study research* to the design sciences. In the design sciences, variables do get manipulated to test technological rules: "The typical research design to study and test technological rules is the multiple case: a series of problems of the same class is solved, each by applying the problem-solving cycle. Design knowledge is built up through the reflective cycle: choosing a case, planning and implementing interventions (on the basis of the problem-solving cycle), reflecting on the results and developing design knowledge to be tested and refined in subsequent cases" (Van Aken, 2000, p. 8).

I followed Van Aken and used *developing multiple case studies* as my methodology. I refined the weightless wealth tool kit as a result of the design knowledge generated from previous cases. This is opposed to the *inventorying multiple case study* methodology, in which the researcher tests the *same* method several times in different cases. When I applied subsequent versions of the method, I got more and more indications and contraindications for the use of the method. In the ideal situation, the method should no longer need adjustments after being tested in x number of cases. At that point it should be clear in what context it can be used, and provisions should be built into the method that allow the user to adjust it to local circumstances. Van Aken (2000) calls this state *theoretical saturation*. My team and I created an initial draft of the method in September 1998 (see Chapter 4) and tested it at Bank Ltd. (see Chapter 5). We used experiences from that test to improve the method. A second test took place at Electro Ltd. To test and develop the method further, we repeated this sequence four times. Testing took place at Automotive Ltd., Logistic Services BU, Professional Services LLP, and Consulting Department (see Chapter 5). As you will see, we did not reach the point of theoretical saturation, but we learned a lot.

Before delving into the specifics of my methodology, and the process I followed to develop it, I present a brief overview of the structure of this book in the next section to assist you in understanding what is to come.

Structure of the Book

In Chapter 2 I refine the methodology of practicing management research as a design science, addressing subproblem 1. This methodology is based on my personal assumptions about the way people view the world, and try to make sense of it. I describe these epistemological postulations and the way they influence my view on scientific research. I show that there are an infinite number of views on the social world that can be equally valid. The task of management research is to test these views and determine whether they are valid in explaining or improving management and organizations. I describe the steps I took and the rules I followed to practice management research as a design science. You will learn that the social reality of organizations is not carved in stone, unlike the physical reality of the outside world. Instead, organizations can be viewed and described in numerous ways. You will learn how to select from these multiple views in a scientific way. If you are a management researcher, you can learn how to practice management research in a way that is scientifically sound and yet produces clear and immediate benefits for businesses. If you are a manager, you can learn to apply multiple perspectives to your own organization.

Chapter 3 addresses subproblems 2 and 3. It looks at 25 different methods already available to value or measure intangibles to learn from them. Each one of these methods uses a different definition of intangible resources, by using terms like *intellectual capital*, *knowledge-based assets*, and *intangible assets*. I explain the differences between these concepts and present the definition of intangible resources that I used. Furthermore, I describe 19 different motives for putting a value on intangibles. This demonstrates that to develop or select a specific method, you should first define the organizational problem you wish to solve. Finally, I look at the solutions proposed. Some of the methods are not rigorous or—despite their intention—do not value intangibles. Others are useful for very specific purposes. I present a comprehensive overview of the most important methods available, and you will learn to define better your own motive for valuing intangible resources and pick the method that suits your problem best.

In Chapter 4, I describe how my team and I developed an initial draft of the weightless wealth tool kit. I prepared this draft as part of a project commissioned by the Dutch Ministry of Economic Affairs. This chapter shows the steps we took in developing the new method by describing the various phases of the project. It describes the requirements for the new method as well as the initial object and realization design, thereby addressing subproblems 3 to 5. You will learn how a major consulting assignment can take place, and will learn some of the common mistakes made by consultants. In addition, this chapter teaches how to define the requirements for a valuation method that is tailored to your needs.

I tested this design at six companies. I describe these tests in Chapter 5, solving subproblems 6 and 7. Each case description presents the context and problem definition we encountered. These often led to specific requirements for the design of the method. I describe the specific design and present how it was implemented. I reflect on the outcome of the method, which led to modification. This adjusted method was used in a subsequent case. This chapter demonstrates some of the difficulties one encounters when trying to implement a method for the valuation of intangible resources, including the lack of sponsorship for the initiative, lack of priority and a shortage of time, missing data, and a lack of implementation skills on the part of the consultants. This is really enlightening stuff.

In Chapter 6, I address subproblems 8 through 11. I summarize the lessons I learned from designing and testing the weightless wealth tool kit. I list the strengths and weaknesses of the method, and describe indications and contraindications for its use. This includes recommendations for the improvement of the method. Furthermore, I describe the hard lessons I learned about practicing management research as a design science. Lastly, I highlight the implications for the intellectual capital community and its attempt to put a value on intangible resources. This summarizes some of the challenges encountered when designing or implementing a method for the valuation of intangible resources. If you are a researcher, you can learn more about how to conduct scientific management research with direct practical relevance. If you are a manager, you can use the findings to judge whether my weightless wealth tool kit is a useful tool for your organization. If it is not, you can learn some of the pitfalls and tricks to select and implement any of the other tools available on the market.

Now let's start our quest by looking at the more fundamental questions of life, reality and truth, introduced by Pippi Longstocking.

Methodology:
The Science of
Designing Practical
Methods

"What did you discover, anyway, Pippi?"

"A new word," said Pippi and looked at Tommy and Annika as if she had just this minute noticed them. "A brand new word."

"What kind of word?" said Tommy.

"A wonderful word," said Pippi. "One of the best I've ever heard."

"Say it then," said Annika.

"Spink," said Pippi triumphantly.

"Spink," repeated Tommy. "What does that mean?"

"If I only knew!" said Pippi. "The only thing I know is that it doesn't mean vacuum cleaner."

Tommy and Annika thought for a while. Finally Annika said, "But if you don't know what it means, then it can't be of any use."

"That's what bothers me," said Pippi.

"Who really decided in the beginning what all the words should mean?" Tommy wondered.

"Probably a bunch of old professors," said Pippi.

Astrid Lindgren (1977)

In May 2000, my colleagues at KPMG and I were preparing a conference on new ways of doing business in a new economy. In one of the meetings we discussed the themes we wanted to address, until my colleague Steven, who was the chairman for the conference, said, "Now I am utterly confused. We are talking about the current economy as 'new economy,' 'knowledge economy,' 'intangible economy,' and 'network economy.' Which one is it?!"

The fact is that all these descriptions of the economic world are probably right. How can that be? How is it possible that we can describe the same phenomena in very different ways? What does this imply for the scientific search for truth? When can we say something is true? I address these questions in this chapter, which presents the foundation for the research methodology I used in my research. The main thing that distinguishes science from practical, everyday work is the rigor of its methodology. This justifies a dedicated chapter on the epistemological fundamentals and methodology of my research.

Practicing science is like building a house. A strong foundation is needed to support claims and conclusions. In the case of my study, this foundation consists of four layers. First, science is about trying to make sense of the world in a rigorous away. I clarify my assumptions about the way this process of "sense making" works. Second, science aims to produce knowledge that is valid and/or successful. I clarify and support this distinction. Third, management research is a special branch of science that is involved in the study of how organizations are designed, how they function, and how they are managed. I explain why management research is a science, by specifying the scientific rules this discipline needs to follow. And fourth, I elaborate on the scientific methodology that I used in my study.

Making Sense of the Social World

It was my intention to generate knowledge. This section explains how people generate knowledge by making sense of the world. I first describe how people make sense by using distinctions. These distinctions guide the way we view the world. I then show how people choose the particular distinctions they use. Finally, I argue that making sense of the social world is different from making sense of the physical world.

Distinctions Make Sense

If we return to the example of my colleague Steven regarding the nature of the changing economy, we may wonder how it is possible that different descriptions fit the same economic world. Yet, it happens all the time. With language, we create distinctions with regard to the world that give us insight, allow us to make predictions, and create the foundation for our actions. This is a process I call *sense making*. People constantly try to make sense of the world by means of interpretation: the process of making distinctions with words and their rules for use. As Maturana and Varela (1987) phrase it:

The act of indicating any being, object, thing, or unity involves making an act of *distinction* which distinguishes what has been indicated as separate from its background. Each time we refer to anything explicitly or implicitly, we are specifying a *criterion of distinction*, which indicates what we are talking about and specifies its properties as being, unity, or object. This is a commonplace situation and not unique: We are necessarily and permanently immersed in it. (p. 40)

Therefore, when we refer to the economy as a *knowledge economy*, we make an act of distinction by distinguishing between economies in which knowledge plays a vital role and economies in which this is not so much the case (like in an agricultural economy).

The World Doesn't Speak

This process of making distinctions can be understood as a two-way process. We interpret phenomena based on previously gained knowledge and experiences embedded in their frame of reference. At the same time, this frame helps us to construct the phenomena we observe. Von Krogh and Roos (1995) say: "The world is brought forth in language. Still, we do not first have a language and then name things with it. Rather, the world and language shape one another" (p. 53). For example, once we chose to describe the current state of the economy as the "knowledge economy," we start to notice specific phenomena, like the knowledge intensity of companies and products, and the rise of the knowledge professional (Tissen et al., 1998). These phenomena do not exist in reality independent of us, but we bring them to light through the words we chose to use. If we choose different words, like *network economy*, we will notice other things, like the growing importance of alliances and partnerships.

Observation of the world is not a passive activity. There is no such thing as an objective reality that speaks out on its own and only needs to be observed. Instead, the only way we can observe reality is by actively using language to create distinctions that separate one array of phenomena from another. Our distinctions guide our observations. The American philosopher Rorty (1989) explains: "The world does not speak. Only we do. The world can, once we have programmed ourselves with a language, cause us to hold beliefs. But it cannot propose a language for us to speak. Only human beings can do that" (p. 4). As a result, when trying to make sense of the world, we do not try to create a representation or picture of the world in our mind. Von Krogh and Roos (1995) add to this: "In fact, the human mind does not represent the world. Rather, it brings forth, or forms the world as a domain of distinctions that are inseparable from the structure of the cognitive system" (p. 53).

We Know According to the Way We Are and the Way We Feel

The making of new distinctions is guided by previously gained knowledge and experiences. "Knowledge enables distinction making and distinctions, in turn, enable (the development of) knowledge" (Von Krogh and Roos, 1995, p. 54). This process already starts when babies are born and are being taught to distinguish between light and dark, hot and cold, up and down, good and bad.

This process of sense making is unique for every individual because every person is unique with regard to the knowledge and experiences gained in life. This is why we often have a hard time understanding each other. In communication, we constantly interpret what is being said by referring to our own domain of distinctions—our personal tradition of previously gained knowledge and experienced feelings. Because this legacy is different from that of any other person, we know we will never have exactly the same insight as the people with whom we communicate. Fortunately, people who share the same culture, organization, or profession often have similar frames of reference. Luhmann (as cited by Reneman, 1998) calls this *Sinn*, a German word describing what makes sense to a system and what does not, and that manifests itself in collective world views, frames of reference, norms, and roles. Von Krogh and Roos (1995) refer to this as *rules:* "The use of words follows certain history-dependent rules that are specific to an institutional setting. Such rules are created and recreated in languaging and form the basis for the social system's knowledge of the world" (p. 99). Communication is possible because of these rules, but the rules do not guarantee that people will understand each other.

A person's choice for using a particular set of distinctions is influenced by cultural background, upbringing, education, and experiences. "Everything said is said from a tradition," says Varela (1979, p. 268). That is why a remark or statement often tells us as much about the person who made it as it does about the phenomenon to which it refers. A person's choice for a particular set of distinctions is often not a purely rational one, but is based on intuition (That word doesn't feel good), normative preferences (I don't like that word), sense of beauty (This distinction produces a nice symmetrical matrix), or goal orientation (Raising attention to this phenomenon is not in my interest). In addition, the array of connotations of a particular set of words plays an important role in selecting them.

For example, in our discussion about the themes for the conference, participants objected to the phrase *new economy*. Some disliked it because it reminded them of commercials for laundry detergent ("NEW! Washes whiter!"). Others felt the distinction between new and old does not create additional insight, other than that the new economy is different from the old one. However, although the additional insight generated by the phrase *new economy* is limited, the impact of the positive connotation of the word *new* on economic life has been enormous. New = better. This must have been one of the reasons why the term *new economy* became popular in 1997. Politicians like former vice-president Al Gore like influential connotations. This is why Gore used the phrase *new economy* to his own benefit. The phrase then led to the distinction between old-economy and new-economy companies, and the "old" ones—like chemical companies or steel manufacturers—felt they had to show their shareholders they were not old-fashioned and could invest in new-economy activities like the Internet. New-economy companies—like Internet startups—benefited from the positive connotation of the word *new* and had no trouble attracting capital. So the simple use of the phrase *new economy* started a battle between the old and the new that generated billions of dollars in investments in information technology and resulted in additional economic growth. Fortunately, or unfortunately, the tide turned. After the crash of the NASDAQ in 2001, the phrase *new economy* acquired a negative connotation and became synonymous with the Internet bubble.

The Social World Does Not Sit Still

So far I have used the phrase *the world* when talking about the phenomena to which a set of distinctions refers. However, we need to differentiate between making distinctions about the physical world and the social world. These worlds are very dissimilar. The biggest difference is that the social world does not exist in the same way as the physical world.

Natural scientists often complain about the lack of scientific rigor in the social sciences. An example is the debate between the members of the Royal Swedish Academy of Sciences about the status of the Nobel Prize for Economics. This debate has continued ever since the prize was established in 1968. A majority of natural scientists has little appreciation for economic science. Economic science is not scientific enough, economic ideas are subject to fashion, there is no clear scientific progress, and a body of knowledge agreed to by everybody hardly exists (Nasar, 1999). However, the kind of scientific progress that exists in natural sciences is impossible in social sciences. Social sciences study an object that does not sit still when being observed, as the physical world does.[1] The object under investigation is the social world: the array of nonphysical phenomena produced by interacting human beings constantly involved in a process of sense making. Sense-making processes, intuition, and feelings guide the behavior of human beings. This process of sense making is unique within every individual. Therefore, the social world does not behave according to general laws, and the interpretation of its behavior is a problem of *equivocality* (Weick, 1995).

Furthermore, human beings continuously recreate the social world. The social world, as such, does not exist. It is created continuously through sense making, communication, and action. It can take almost any shape, depending on how one chooses to look at it. Van Aken (1996) phrases this as follows: "The social world ontologically is the accumulation of people's internalized images of that world" (p. 16, translated by D. Andriessen). Humankind is constructing the social world, putting sense-making systems layer upon layer. These layers include the sense-making systems of economics, law, science, and religion. These systems determine the way we think and act.

Consequently, the social world can be described by an almost infinite number of sets of distinctions, as the history of the social sciences has proved. This is not caused by the immaturity of the social sciences but by the characteristics of its object of study. In the social sciences, including management research, researchers need to construct the phenomena under investigation before they can study them. Social scientists first need to create the social world using certain distinctions. The social world does not exist without them.[2] Which distinctions they decide to

---

[1] Or seems to do so. Quantum theory argues that the physical world changes as it is being observed.

[2] This is why the parable of "the blind men and the elephant" (Morgan, 1986) is not a good metaphor. This poem, written by the American poet John Godfrey Saxe (1816–1887), is based on a fable that was told in India many years ago. It tells the story of six blind men of Indostan who encounter an elephant. Each one feels something different, but together they get a reasonable picture of the beast. Morgan (1986) and De Caluwé and Vermaak (1999) use this poem to stress the importance of using multiple perspectives when looking at organizations. However, although an elephant exists in the physical world, with or without human beings being present, organizations do not. Organizations are not entities waiting to be observed by blind management researchers. Organizations are social constructions, created every time somebody refers to them in a certain way. They are not like elephants, with a fixed shape that merely needs to be defined. Instead, their shape can have any form, depending on how we wish to look at them. This is where the metaphor falls short. The metaphor of the blind men gives the illusion that, if one were to look at organizations from enough different angles, one would see the whole thing. However, the whole thing does not exist.

use depends on personal history, predilection, and context. In response to the critique of the natural scientists, one can argue that practicing social science is more difficult than natural science, because social scientists first need to construct reality before they can study it.

Social scientists who study the social world encounter even more problems. First, almost any direct observation technique used by these scientists will alter the social world.[3] For example, the use of a questionnaire triggers a process of sense making with the interviewee and thereby alters the social world. Second, any social system under investigation is in continuous interaction with its environment. The system and its context are interwoven. Therefore, when scientists study causal relationships in the social world, it is difficult for them to separate the context variables from the variables under investigation.

Social Science

This section describes the way social sciences make sense. I explain two ways of practicing science by making a distinction between explanatory sciences and design sciences. Each type of science uses a different approach to testing propositions. The approaches can complement each other in a fruitful way. I then argue that a social scientist needs to choose carefully the correct test when testing propositions and apply a specific set of scientific rules when doing so.

Anything Goes?

If we continuously shape the world as we experience it by selecting our own preferred distinctions in a rather subjective way, does that mean that "anything goes" (Feyerabend, 1993)? Is any set of distinctions as good as any other? Obviously, this is not the case. However, how can we decide which set of distinctions is better? The answer depends on the purpose for which we want to use the distinctions. In science, we can use distinctions for two rather distinct purposes[4] (based on Van Aken [2000]): First, we can use a set of distinctions to create theories that describe, explain, and predict the world. This is the purpose of the *explanatory sciences*, such as the physical sciences and

---

[3] Except when they use unobtrusive measures of precipitated behavior.

[4] A set of distinctions can also be used to build systems of propositions that are "empirically void" but internally logical and consistent. This is what is happening in the *formal sciences* like mathematics. This application is not relevant for the purpose of this study (Van Aken, 2000, p. 5).

major sections of the social sciences. Second, we can make use of the same set of distinctions to diagnose a situation, define the problem, and design practical methods to improve the situation. This is the purpose of the *design sciences*, such as the engineering sciences, medical science, and modern psychotherapy.

We can use a particular set of distinctions to various degrees for either one of the two purposes (or for both at the same time). We can use a set of distinctions to create *empirical propositions* that *describe, explain, or predict* the world. In addition, we can apply the same set to create *practical propositions* that *diagnose situations, define problems, or offer practical methods and solutions* to improve the world. The extent to which a set of distinctions is able to produce propositions for descriptions, explanations, and predictions, I call the *empirical claim* of that set. The extent to which a set of distinctions is able to produce propositions to diagnose a situation, define a problem, and design practical methods, I call the *practical claim* of that set.

It is important to notice that a set of distinctions can serve both claims at the same time and to various degrees. Take, for example, the phrase *knowledge economy*. It creates the distinction between knowledge economies and nonknowledge economies. We can use this distinction to make an *empirical proposition*, claiming that today's economy is more knowledge intensive than previous economies (description), because of developments in technology, customer demands, and complexity (explanation) (Tissen et al., 2000). If these factors continue to grow, the knowledge intensity of the economy will continue to increase (prediction).

We can use the same distinction between knowledge economies and nonknowledge economies to create a *practical proposition*, claiming that the main driver of the economy is knowledge and when there is a lack of knowledge in organizations (diagnosis, problem definition), companies need to invest in innovation and knowledge management (solution). It is important to note that the empirical or practical claim of a set of distinctions is not related to whether a claim has been tested in practice. Untested empirical or practical claims are hypotheses. Falsified empirical or practical claims are claims that have turned out to be untrue. With the division between empirical and practical claims, we can show that it is possible to use a set of distinctions to create several kinds of propositions (Figure 2.1).

First, if a set of distinctions allows us to make an empirical claim, then we can use it to describe a situation and create an *empirical theory* that, with the help of causal relationships, provides explanations and predictions. Second, if a set of distinctions allows us to make a practical claim, then we can use it to diagnose a situation and design

Figure 2.1

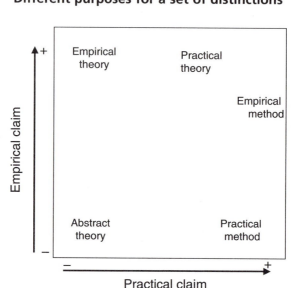

Different purposes for a set of distinctions

practical methods that, with the help a series of consistent steps, create solutions for improvement problems. Third, if a set of distinctions allows us to make an empirical claim and a practical claim, then we can use them to create a practical theory/empirical method. A practical theory is a theory that can help solve problems. This is the case if the causal relationships as specified by the theory can be used to influence the social world for the better. An empirical method is a method to solve problems in the social world that is based on known heuristic rules of the following type: If you want to achieve Y in situation Z, then something like action X could help. Fourth, if a set of distinctions does *not* allow us to make an empirical claim and a practical claim, we can formulate theories that neither provide explanation nor provide practical methods. These are often experienced as *abstract*. An example is the distinction I make between three building blocks of knowledge, also known as I^3, or information, interaction, and intellect (Tissen et al., 2000). This is an abstract theory.[5] Without the help of

---

[5] However, we need to keep in mind that the extent to which a proposition provides explanations and/or practical methods varies with the sense maker that is using it. We have seen that when interpreting propositions, a sense maker continuously refers to previously gained knowledge and experiences. As a result, a proposition that one person experiences as abstract can give somebody else enormous inspiration on how to describe and explain or diagnose and improve a situation.

further distinctions and argumentation, this theory cannot be used to describe and explain phenomena or diagnose and solve problems.[6]

So we have seen that a set of distinctions can have two purposes: to produce empirical propositions and/or to produce practical propositions. We can now test whether a particular set of distinctions is useful. Science is all about testing empirical and/or practical propositions. However, the scientific test is different for each of the two sets.

How to Test an Empirical Proposition

We use an empirical test to test empirical propositions. The scientific testing of empirical propositions follows a procedure called *the empirical cycle* (Swanborn, 1981). This cycle contains the following steps (see the left side of Figure 2.2).

We use a set of distinctions to observe phenomena and to create empirical propositions resulting in a research question. Then we use a set of distinctions to create an empirical theory by means of induction, and we deduct testable hypotheses. These hypotheses contain predictions about the expected state of these phenomena. We can falsify these hypotheses by research. To test the hypotheses we choose a research design (for example, statistical testing using data gathered through questionnaires). The variables contained by the hypotheses need to be made observable and (in many research designs) measurable before we can test the hypotheses. This step is called the *operationalization of the variables*. We need an operationalization theory to underpin the validity of the operationalization. Then we can make observations to measure the state of the variables. We evaluate the findings and draw conclusions about the validity of the theory and the usefulness of the empirical proposition.

At first glance, this procedure undisputedly leads to validation, but closer inspection shows it does not. There is a hole in this empirical cycle, especially when we apply it to the social world. This hole sits in the operationalization phase. We cannot prove the validity of the operationalization theory. We can never decisively prove that we

---

[6] This division also shows that Kurt Lewin's well-known adagio, "There is nothing quite so practical as a good theory" (Lewin, 1945, p. 129) is not automatically true. For theory to be practical, it needs be able to create practical claims. Therefore, additional requirements need to be fulfilled:

1. Good theory needs to provide angles that can be used to diagnose a situation.
2. Good theory must contain independent variables that can be manipulated.
3. Good theory needs to provide information about the context in which changing the independent variables can produce the required results.

Figure 2.2

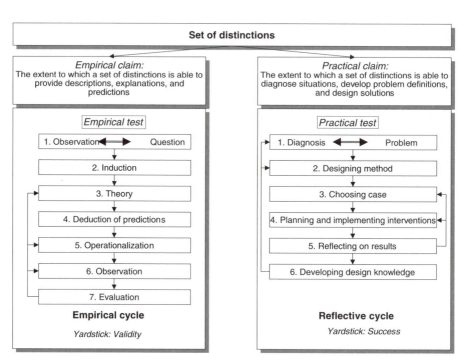

The empirical and the reflective cycles

accurately measure what we want to measure. If we find that the results of an observation are different from what was expected, it follows from the empirical cycle there are three possible causes (see the feedback arrows in the left side of Figure 2.2):

1. We have falsified our hypotheses and therefore need to alter our empirical theory.
2. We have failed to measure what we wanted to measure and therefore need to alter our operationalization theory.
3. We made errors in our observations and need to correct them.

The problem is that we will never know beyond a doubt which mistake was made. The best we can do is to have a group of scientific practitioners agree on the validity of the operationalization and the accuracy of the observations so we can falsify (or not) our theory. Therefore, the best we can do is to use a *consensus theory* of truth with regard to the validity of the empirical proposition of a set of distinctions. For example, if we apply this to the testing of empirical propositions based on the term *knowledge economy*, it would lead to the following: Based on the distinction of knowledge economy we could state that the current economy is more knowledge intensive than all previous ones. To test this hypothesis we would need to operationalize the variable knowledge intensity and measure it throughout history. If we find that today's economy is not the most knowledge-intensive economy, then there are three possible conclusions:

1. Our empirical hypothesis is not valid.
2. We didn't measure knowledge intensity correctly and therefore need to alter our operationalization theory.
3. There are errors in our data (for example, because of a lack of appropriate historical data) and we need to make better observations.

It is impossible to conclude decisively which conclusion is correct.

How to Test a Practical Proposition

We use a practical test to test practical propositions. The *reflective cycle* (Van Aken, 2000) is the process for the scientific testing of practical propositions (see the right side of Figure 2.2). Let me briefly explain each step in the cycle: We use the set of distinctions to diagnose a class of situations and to define a class of problems. Then we design a practical method to provide a general solution for the class of problems. At this stage, the solution is context independent. To test the solution, we need to translate the method in the context of a specific case. Therefore, the next step is to select a case in which we use the method to solve the case-specific problem, applying the problem-solving or regulative cycle. According to Van Aken (2000), "This cycle consists roughly of: defining the problem out of its 'messy' context, planning the intervention, applying the intervention and evaluating" (p. 6). We use this cycle to plan and implement interventions that help solve the problem in this specific case. The next step in the reflective cycle is to reflect on the results of the case. This leads to the development of so-called *design knowledge* (in other words, knowledge that we can use in designing solutions to the class of problems [Van Aken, 2000]). This design knowledge may lead to improvements in the method, to alterations in how we diagnose the class of situations, or to changes in the way we define the problem. The evaluation may also lead to the conclusion that the problem in this specific case was not part of the class of problems for which we designed the method. We use the reflective cycle several times, generating indications and contraindications for the success of the method. In this way, we develop further knowledge about the application domain of the method: the class of problems and the class of contexts for which the method needs to provide a solution.

The reflective cycle also contains a "hole." The conclusions we draw from the evaluation of the tests are ambiguous. When the results of an implementation are different from what was expected, there are four possible causes (see the feedback arrows in Figure 2.2):

1. We made the wrong diagnosis and defined the wrong problem.
2. We designed an unsuccessful method.
3. We picked cases outside the application domain of the method.
4. We did not implement the method correctly.

In most cases, it will be difficult to find out what the mistake was.[7] For example, if we apply this to the testing of practical propositions based on the term *knowledge economy*, it would lead to the following: Let's use the distinction to develop a *practical proposition* about the knowledge intensity of companies. Let's state that the main driver for success for companies is knowledge, and when there is a lack of knowledge, companies need to invest in knowledge development and knowledge management. To test this hypothesis, we need to diagnose the knowledge intensity of a number of companies and design an intervention method to improve the knowledge intensity (for example, through implementing knowledge management techniques). Then we must find a number of cases for which a lack of knowledge is a useful problem to solve. In each case, we need to make a design for knowledge management and its implementation, considering local circumstances. As a result, each design is unique. We then implement the designs. An evaluation of each case shows whether the intervention was successful. Because the practical proposition was that knowledge drives business success, business success is the dependent variable that we must use to judge the success of the intervention. If we find that our interventions did not improve the business success of the companies involved, there are four possible conclusions:

1. Knowledge intensity is not an important independent variable for business success.

---

[7] In management research, we have the advantage that we can ask the object under investigation about his or her experiences. This creates insight into the particular organizational and context variables that influence the success of the intervention. However, this often does not lead to a decisive and compelling conclusion.

2. Knowledge management is not a good method to improve knowledge intensity.
3. In the cases studied, knowledge intensity was not a problem, so the cases were not part of the application domain of the method.
4. In the various cases, we did not design or implement knowledge management properly.

It will be impossible to conclude decisively which conclusion is correct.

Bringing the Two Together

The purpose of the explanatory sciences is to produce tested empirical theories that are valid. The purpose of the design sciences is to produce tested practical methods that are successful in solving problems. Therefore, an important difference between the two scientific approaches is the yardstick that we use for finding truth.

The debate about the nature of truth has been going on for more than 2,000 years. Dominant in the western way of thinking is the *correspondence theory of truth*, which states that the criterion for truth is "correspondence with reality" (Koningsveld, 1976). This theory presupposes a reality with certain characteristics that speak for themselves, and allows for collation with our representations. This theory of truth cannot be reconciled with the view described earlier, in which the social world as we experience it is continuously shaped by the distinctions we decide to apply to it.

The concept of empirical versus practical tests provides us with two alternative criteria for truth that are applicable to the social world. The first criterion of truth I name the *contextual validity criterion*. This is an alternative reading of the correspondence theory of truth. According to this criterion, an empirical proposition of a set of distinctions about the social world is true if observations based on that same set validate predictions derived from the proposition. The term *contextual* acknowledges the fact that we can only observe the validity via the distinctions we have used to construct the proposition. If we used other distinctions, we would notice other things. The validity is contextual because we first construct the phenomena as a context using our distinctions before we test the validity of our propositions. The social phenomena we try to explain only exist in the context of the distinctions we have used to identify them.

The second criterion of truth I name the *contextual success criterion*. This is an alternative reading of the pragmatic theory of truth. According to this criterion, a practical proposition of a set of distinctions about the social world is true if action based on that proposition leads to success as defined by the proposition. The term *contextual* acknowledges the fact that we can only define the success via the distinctions we used to construct the proposition. The success is contextual because we first construct the phenomena as a context using our distinctions before we test our propositions. We construct a problem using these distinctions and then we try to solve it. The problems we try to solve only exist in the context of the distinctions we have used to define them. If we used different distinctions we would define different problems.

These two criteria for truth are my genuine attempt to reconcile the correspondence and pragmatic theory of truth in the social sciences. There should be room for both definitions of truth. The scientific status of scientific research does not depend on whether it is aimed at testing the validity of a proposition using a correspondence theory of truth. We can consider testing the success of propositions by applying a pragmatic theory of truth to be equally scientific, provided the researcher obeys certain scientific rules.

The explanatory sciences and the design sciences have an important thing in common. They both involve the use of cause-and-effect statements. We can describe theory, as used in the empirical cycle, as "a set of interconnected general and specific statements, of which at least some are statements predicting certain events under certain conditions" (Swanborn, 1981, pp. 89–90, translated by D. Andriessen). Therefore, a theory includes a number of cause-and-effect statements. Some of them are formulated as predictions or hypotheses that can be tested through observation. A practical method is based on means–end statements that provide guidelines about a finite number of acts to be performed to reach a specific end. As mentioned earlier, their general form is as follows: If you want to achieve Y in situation Z, then something like action X could help. Means–end statements are a specific type of cause-and-effect statement. According to Kuypers (1984), *means* are chosen causes and *ends* are intended effects. Van Aken (2000) uses the terms *technological rule* and *heuristic rule*. For Van Aken (2000), design sciences are about the systematic testing of technological rules.

This is where the two approaches complement each other. Explanatory sciences can provide causal models that we can use in the design sciences to ground means–end statements. Design sciences can, by testing which means–end statements are successful in practice, provide an indication for the validity of cause-and-effect statements, give information about the specific context in which these statements are valid, and point toward independent variables that are missing in the empirical theory.

Figure 2.3

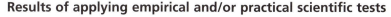

Results of applying empirical and/or practical scientific tests

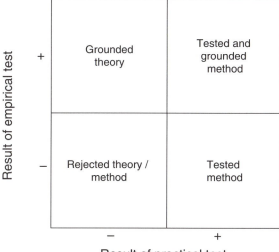

Figure 2.3 can help to explain the relationship between empirical and practical propositions and the results of applying empirical and practical tests.

If an empirical proposition in the form of an empirical theory passes the empirical test (see the top left corner of Figure 2.3), we can say it is grounded. If that theory is used to create a practical method and that method turns out to be successful in solving problems, then the practical method is a tested and grounded method (see the top right corner of Figure 2.3). However, to create practical methods it is not necessary to use tested and grounded means–end relationships. Practical methods can be very successful whereas the causal relationships on which they are based are unclear, untestable, or different in each case. If a practical method is successful in solving problems and is not based on grounded causal relationships, it is a tested method (see the bottom right corner of Figure 2.3). Chinese medicine (Van Aken, 2000) and homeopathic medicine are examples of systems of very powerful, tested means–end relationships that are not based on scientifically grounded causal relationships.

Science Follows Its Own Rules

I wanted to make a contribution to the science of management research in general and the science of intellectual capital research in particular. Science is a specific way of making sense that is different from ordinary sense making because it follows its own rules. "The system of science brings forth its own world of scientific exploration and proof" (Von Krogh and Roos, 1995, p. 63). The sets of distinctions that scientists use are the building blocks for creating theories, formulating hypotheses, drawing conclusions, or designing methods. There are as many different views about the rules of scientific method as there are scientists. Yet, common to these views is that the scientific process of sense making should be somehow structured, internally consistent, and aimed at testing the validity of its conclusions. I decided to apply the following scientific rules to my research. They are derived from the epistemological theory laid out in this chapter:

1. The scientist needs to use an internally consistent set of distinctions with clear definitions of the key concepts because management research is about making sense of the world scientifically using sets of distinctions.
2. Scientists need to make their assumptions explicit, including those on epistemology, because sense making is based on personal assumptions.
3. The distinctions steer the questions scientists ask and the findings of the research. Therefore, scientists need to formulate a clear research question and deliver precise answers.
4. Science is all about testing propositions to determine their validity or their success, so scientists need to test the propositions using the appropriate empirical or practical test.
5. Scientists need to use a structured, stepwise, explicit methodology for testing that can be replicated, which will make it possible to check the reliability of the conclusions.

Management Research

Management research is a social science. It studies the social world of organizations and management. I decided to design my research as a management research study in the field of intellectual capital. In this paragraph, I define management research by identifying its subject of investigation. I show that we can practice management research both as an explanatory science and as a design science using the epistemological principles described in the previous section.

The Subject of Management Research

Management research is the scientific discipline studying organizations, their environment, and the way these organizations are or should be managed. Organization and management are both examples of phenomena in the social world. They do not exist unless we refer to them that way. What we refer to depends on our definition of organization and management. Therefore, the subject of investigation studied by management research depends on one's definition of organization and management. I show the effect of choosing a particular definition on the subject under investigation by presenting three common definitions of organizations. Then I introduce the definition I used in this study.

Some definitions of organizations include the notion of coordinated activities, such as the one used by Barnard (1938): "An organization is defined as a system of consciously coordinated personal activities or forces" (p. 81). This definition creates a set of distinctions by discriminating between coordinated and noncoordinated activities, consciously coordinated and unconsciously coordinated activities, and personal versus nonpersonal activities. We can use these distinctions to create various empirical and practical propositions. An empirical proposition that may follow from this definition is that in every organization there is consciously coordinated activity. We can test this proposition using an empirical test. A practical proposition that could follow from this set of distinctions is that an organization performs better if activities are coordinated. In a particular situation, an organizational diagnosis based on this proposition may lead to the conclusion that there is a lack of coordination. A method to solve this problem may involve a new organizational structure. We can test this practical proposition using a practical test.

Some definitions include goal orientation. For example, an organization is a group of people who cooperate to achieve a common goal. This definition distinguishes between goal-oriented and nongoal-oriented behavior, and between common goals and other goals. Empirically this definition states that every organization has a common goal, which is something we can test in practice. Practically this definition points to the need for clear and common goals. We can test this proposition by designing a method that creates clear and common corporate goals, and by testing whether it is successful (for an example of such a method, see Weggeman [1995]).

There are also definitions of organizations that include the notion of sense making as described above. Walsh and Ungson (1991) define an organization as "a network of intersubjectively shared meanings that are sustained through the development and use of common language and everyday social interaction" (p. 38). Empirically this definition focuses on the occurrence of meaning sharing through communication. Organizations are entities developed and maintained only through continuous communication activity. "If the communication activity stops, the organization disappears" (Weick, 1995, p. 75). Practically, this definition points toward the improvement of communication and the sharing of meaning—for example, through techniques like dialog (Isaacs, 1999).

My research looked at the intangible resources of organizations from the viewpoint of sense making. Therefore, I decided to include the concept of sense making into my definition of an organization. I followed Walsh and Ungson (1991), and defined an organization as *a group of people involved in a network of intersubjectively shared meanings that are sustained through the development and use of common language and everyday social interaction, producing goods and/or services by combining financial, tangible, and intangible resources.* When we study organizations, we can identify attempts to manage this network. I defined management as *the process of allocating—and in the case of intangible resources, also nurturing—the resources. It involves sense making, decision making, and communicating.* It follows from my definitions that I think that management research studies people who are engaged in interactions to combine resources. This view does not presuppose coordination, although coordination may help in achieving certain goals. It also does not assume goal orientation, although having a common goal will probably make an organization more successful. What it does presume is the availability of financial, tangible, and intangible resources, and the existence of language and communication.

Companies are social constructions and so is their social environment. This environment consists of many sense-making systems that have been created by humans to regulate human activities. These sense-making systems have helped to counter chaos and to create wealth. The legislative system, the economic system of the capitalistic world, and the accounting system are examples of sense-making systems in the company environment that have been created by humans.

What these systems have in common is that they use words with meanings that are often well defined. The rules of use of these words are common across the globe. In the case of law and accounting, the mechanisms of these sense-making systems are to a large extent codified. In the case of economics, the mechanisms seem to be well understood. However, the unique aspect of the economic sense-making system is that this system acts as a self-fulfilling prophecy. People behave according to the rules of these systems because they believe these rules to be true. Although humans created these rules and can therefore change them, the rules have become a set of laws from which no company can escape. The legislative, economic, and accounting worlds require companies to act in accordance with a social rationality that cannot be ignored, although it is socially constructed (Strikwerda, 1994). For business people there seems to be a social reality that can be as ruthless as the physical world. Yet, if we take a closer look, we see that these three sense-making systems provide degrees of freedom: that regulation requires interpretation, that we can challenge or change economic laws, and that accounting involves judgment and choice.

The Scientific Nature of Management Research

The scientific nature of management research has been the subject of huge debates within the discipline (see, for example, the special issue of *Bedrijfskunde* on methodology [1994, 1996] and Van Aken [2000]). The debate focuses on the relevance of management theory as developed by the academic community, as well as on the rigor of many management theories presented in popular management literature. Schön (1983) describes this debate as the dilemma of "rigor or relevance":

> This dilemma of rigor or relevance arises more acutely in some areas of practice than in others. In the varied topography of professional practice, there is the high, hard ground where practitioners can make effective use of research-based theory and technique, and there is the swampy lowland where situations are confusing "messes" incapable of technical solution. The difficulty is that the problems of the high ground, however great their technical interest, are often relatively unimportant to clients or to the larger society, while in the swamp are the problems of greatest human concern. Shall the practitioner stay on the high, hard ground where he can practice rigorously, as he understands rigor, but where he is constrained to deal with problems of relatively little social importance? Or shall he descend to the swamp where he can engage the most important and challenging problems if he's willing to forsake technical rigor? (p. 42)

The dilemma between rigor and relevance can be reconciled. Trompenaars and Hampden–Turner (1997) describe reconciliation as a process of "be ourselves but yet see and understand how the other's perspective can help our own" (p. 199). The process combines the strength of the two extreme positions of a dilemma to create synergy. It involves thinking not in terms of either/or but through/through: improving relevance through rigor and improving rigor through relevance. Trompenaars and Hampden–Turner (1997) describe three steps in the reconciliation process. The first step is to become aware of the differences. The next step is to respect these differences. The third step in reconciliation is to find ways by which both approaches can reinforce each other.

Applying this approach to the rigor–relevance dilemma in management research means we need to become aware that there are two approaches to management research. One approach focuses on generating rigorous results. However, this approach often produces results that have no direct application in solving everyday problems. The other approach focuses on important everyday problems, but lacks the rigor that scientific research requires.

To respect these differences we need to see that there is room in management research for both approaches. As we have discussed, we can practice social sciences in two ways, each of which qualify as scientific. The same goes for management research. Management research qualifies as a scientific discipline when we practice it in a rigorous way that involves testing of empirical and/or practical propositions. We can practice management research as an *explanatory science*, studying organizations with the intention of describing, explaining, and predicting their performance. For this type of research, the yardstick is validity, using the contextual validity criterion of truth described earlier. Alternatively, we can practice it as a *design science*, studying organizations with the intention of developing methods to improve performance. For this type of research the yardstick is success, using the contextual success criterion of truth described earlier. We can do both in a scientific way, provided we follow certain scientific rules.

The third step in reconciliation is to find ways by which both approaches can reinforce each other. Both approaches can contribute to and learn from each other, especially in the area of theory building and testing. Management research practiced as an explanatory science can provide causal models that we can use in the design sciences to ground means–end statements. Design sciences can, by testing which means–end statements are successful in practice, provide an indication for the validity of cause-and-effect statements, give information about the specific context in which these statements are valid, and point toward independent variables that are missing in the empirical theory.

My Study

In this chapter we have moved from the broad issue of making sense of the social world, via the specific sense-making process of the social sciences, to one particular discipline of the social sciences, called *management research*. The next step is to describe my study as a particular application of management research: intellectual capital research practiced as a design science. I define the type of research that my study involved and describe the methodology I used. In addition, I explain the methodology of reconstructed logic that I used for this study and elaborate on the specific methodological consequences of the context in which this study took place.

The Reflective Cycle Used in This Study

The objective of my scientific journey was to develop a method for the valuation of the intangible resources of an organization, as well as a plan for implementing this method. To do this I used the reflective cycle to generate design knowledge about the new method. Figure 2.4 shows a more detailed overview of the reflective cycle.

The reflective cycle starts with a general diagnosis and description of the problem I want to address: the problem of how to determine the value of the intangible resources of an organization in such a way that this information helps to solve organizational problems.

Figure 2.4

The reflective cycle

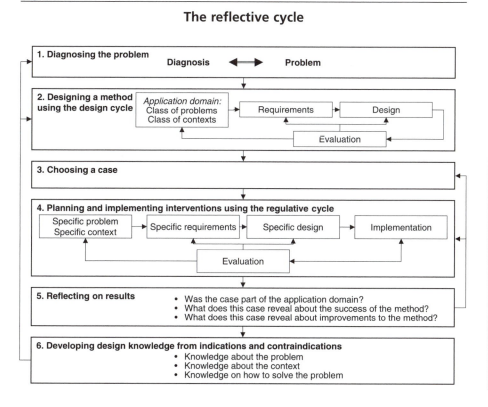

The second step in the reflective cycle is designing a first draft of a method that helps solve the problem: the weightless wealth tool kit. For this I used the *design cycle*, which consists of the following four activities. First, a general diagnosis and description of the problem gives us an impression of the application domain of the method we want to design. The application domain describes the class of problems the weightless wealth tool kit needs to address and the class of contexts to which it needs to be applied. Second, the class of problems and the class of contexts, as well as demands from clients, from users, and from the environment provide input for the requirements for the weightless wealth tool kit. Third, based on these requirements and on available theories, we create a first draft of the design for the new method. Fourth, we check whether this design meets the requirements. This evaluation led to changes in the design, but also to changes in the problem definition and the requirements. According to Van Aken (1996), a researcher should continue this process until an adequate design is created.

The third step in the reflective cycle is the selection of a case to test the draft method. The specific problem of the case has to fit the class of problems for which we design the method. In addition, the specific context of the case has to match the criteria describing the class of contexts for which the weightless wealth tool kit was designed. In practice, every context is unique and therefore every problem is unique. When researchers start to test the method they may discover that the specific problem in that specific situation is different from the ones for which the method was designed. If this is true, the researchers cannot use that case to test the method.

The fourth step in the reflective cycle is to use the weightless wealth tool kit to solve the case-specific problem using the *regulative cycle*. The regulative cycle consists of five activities. First, we diagnose the specific situation to define the problem in its context. Second, this often leads to specific requirements that supplement the general requirements. Third, this frequently forces us to make amendments to the method. Fourth, we implement the method. And fifth, we evaluate the outcome of the method. This evaluation leads to further modifications of the design, but also to changes in the way we perceive the problem and sometimes to changes in the set of specific requirements.

The fifth step in the reflective cycle is to reflect on the results using three evaluation questions:

1. Was the case part of the application domain?
2. What did this case reveal about the success of the method?
3. What did this case reveal about improvements to the method?

As a sixth step in the reflective cycle, we develop design knowledge in three areas. First, we develop knowledge about the class of problems for which we designed the weightless wealth tool kit. This leads to further refinement of the problem definition. Second, we develop knowledge about the class of contexts for which the method is applicable. The indications and contraindications demonstrate under what circumstances the method produces proper results. They are the conditions for success that need to be fulfilled. Third, we develop insight into the means–end relationships that we use to solve the problem.

In my study I decided to use the contextual success criterion of truth as my yardstick to assess the quality of my method. I defined the success of the method as the extent to which the method was able to solve organizational problems. In each case I needed to determine the extent to which the method led to solving the specific problem of that company as defined in step 1 of the regulative cycle.

I chose to apply the reflective cycle using the methodology of *developing multiple case studies*. This meant that I went through the cycle a number of times. Each time, I refined the weightless wealth tool kit based on the design knowledge that I generated during the previous case. In this way I acquired more and more indications and contraindications for its use. In the ideal case, the method should no longer need adjustments after being tested in x number of cases. At that point its theoretical saturation (Van Aken, 2000) is reached. It should be clear in what context the method can be used, and provisions should be built into the method that allow the user to adjust it to local circumstances. Unfortunately, I never reached this point, although I learned plenty on the way.

Difficulties in Applying the Reflective Cycle

In this section I describe three difficulties researchers encounter using the reflective cycle. I describe how I coped with these difficulties in my study.

The first difficulty is the problem of finding the cause of a failing method. This relates back to the "hole" in the reflective cycle described earlier. The second problem has to do with the impact of external variables on the outcome of the method. How can one isolate the effect of the method from other factors? The third difficulty arises when the researcher and the designer/implementer of the method is the same person. In this circumstance, it may be difficult for the researcher to keep an independent view of the process and its results.

The first difficulty is that many errors that we make along the way may cause a method to be unsuccessful. The feedback arrows in Figure

Figure 2.5

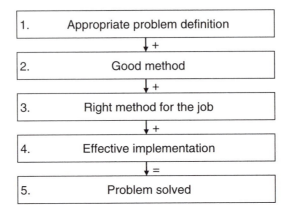

Necessary conditions for a successful intervention

1.	Appropriate problem definition

↓ +

2.	Good method

↓ +

3.	Right method for the job

↓ +

4.	Effective implementation

↓ =

5.	Problem solved

2.4 indicate these errors. If we find the problem is not solved, it could be that we did not diagnose the situation correctly and we have identified the wrong problem. It could also be that the case did not match the application domain of the method. In other words, we selected the wrong tool for the job. Another possibility could be that we implemented the method poorly. A final error is the one for which we are looking: We used a poor method that was unsuccessful and we need to fix it. Figure 2.5 summarizes the errors, redefined as necessary conditions for a successful intervention.

The numbers in Figure 2.5 refer to the phases in the reflective cycle (see Figure 2.4). Of the four errors, three are of interest. We may gain knowledge about the way we wrongly diagnosed problems using the method (error 1), we may learn that the method in practice is not successful in solving problems (error 2), and we may learn that in some situations it is not the right method for the job (error 3). The one factor we want to eliminate is the quality of the implementation. We need to find a way to check whether poor implementation (error 4) influenced the outcome of the method. Poor implementation may have caused the method to be unsuccessful.[8]

During my study, a team of external consultants implemented my method. To check the quality of the implementation, I used the work of De Caluwé and Stoppelenburg (2003) regarding the effectiveness of

---

[8] The opposite could also be true. Effective implementation may compensate for a poor method (Gable, 1996). Weggeman (1995, p. 284) refers to this effect as the *placebo effect*.

consultancy. They make a distinction between three types of criteria for the effectiveness of external consultants: formal criteria, criteria regarding content, and process criteria. The first two reflect the extent to which a predefined problem is solved. Based on literature research they identify 13 criteria that fall into these categories. The last criterion reflects the quality of the implementation. De Caluwé and Stoppelenburg (2003) identify six process criteria. These process criteria are especially relevant for this study. De Caluwé and Stoppelenburg (2003) studied the effectiveness of external consultants working for the Dutch government by studying 56 assignments. They asked clients and consultants which criteria they found important in assessing the effectiveness of consultants. Table 2.1 shows the results. It is interesting to see that two criteria in the "top four" are process criteria. Governmental clients in The Netherlands see the level of involvement of the consultant and the client system as well as the intensity of the communication as important criteria for the effectiveness of a consultant assignment. The other four process criteria rank lower on the scale: the degree to which the approach is being developed along the way, the extent to which the consultant provides concrete directions to the client system, the level of equivalence between the consultant and the client system, and the extent to which a specific method was used.

The process criteria are indicators of the quality of the consulting process, from the perspective of both the client and the consultants. De Caluwé and Stoppelenburg (2003) did not test whether these factors influenced the success of the engagement, yet we can assume that process elements considered essential by both clients and consultants will be important intervening variables. They will be necessary (although probably not sufficient) requirements for success. I used these six process criteria to check the quality of the implementation of the weightless wealth tool kit. I determined whether the conditions for success where fulfilled to identify any intervening influence from the quality of the implementation on the success of my method.

The second problem with the reflective cycle is that it may be difficult to separate the four errors from external factors that influence solving the problem. If, for example, we design a method to improve the sales capability of a company and we find that sales indeed go up, it may be that this is caused by a change in the environment and not by the implementation of the method. To cope with this problem I used the work of Phillips (2000). He presents eight methods to isolate the effects of a consulting intervention from other factors (see Table 2.2).

In my study it was not feasible to work with control groups, trend line analysis, or forecasting techniques. Neither was it possible to

Table 2.1

Ranking of Importance of Criteria for the Effectiveness of Consultants		
Rank	**Criterion**	**Type**
1	Level of goal achievement	Formal criterion
2	Level of involvement of the consultant and the client system with the assignment	Process criterion
3	Intensity of communication between the consultant and the client system	Process criterion
4	Degree to which a solution was found for the problem	Formal criterion
5	Level of expertise provided by consultant	Formal criterion
6	Extent to which the client system came closer to making a decision	Content criterion
7	Degree to which the client system learned from the assignment	Content criterion
8	Level of participation by the client system in the assignment	Formal criterion
9	Extent to which the client system has broadened its way of thinking	Content criterion
10	Degree to which actual project budget equals the budget originally estimated	Formal criterion
11	Degree to which actual time requirements equal the time originally estimated	Formal criterion
12	Extent to which cooperation and communication has been improved	Content criterion
13	Degree to which the approach is being developed along the way	Process criterion
14	Extent to which the consultant provides concrete directions to the client system	Process criterion
15	Level of equivalence between the consultant and the client system	Process criterion
16	Extent to which the client system improved its effectiveness	Content criterion
17	Degree to which all agreed tasks were executed	Formal criterion
18	Extent to which the required resources were used	Formal criterion
19	Extent to which a specific method was used	Process criterion
From De Caluwé and Stoppelenburg (2003), translated by D. Andriessen.		

Table 2.2

	Methods to Isolate the Effects of a Consulting Intervention from Other Factors	
	Method	**Description**
1	Control group of similar companies	Use a control group of similar companies where no consulting intervention took place
2	Trend line analysis	Do a trend line analysis. Any improvement of performance after the intervention over the levels predicted by the trend line can be reasonably attributed to the intervention
3	Forecasting method	Similar to the trend line analysis; however, this method forecasts the influence based on a trend line of external factors
4	Use the participants' estimate of the impact of the intervention	Participants in the process are asked to determine the impact of the consultant.
5	Ask managers for an estimate	The same technique but with the use of managers
6	Solicit input directly from customers	Ask customers whether they have noticed any changes
7	Calculate the impact of factors other than consulting	Calculate the impact of factors other than consulting that influence a portion of the improvement and credit the intervention with the remaining portion
8	Ask an external or internal expert	Ask for the opinion of an expert
	From Phillips (2000).	

solicit customers, isolate other factors, or ask experts. The method I used in three cases was to ask the managers of the organizations involved about the impact of the method on their organization. In one case, I asked participants. In two cases I was not able to use any of the methods suggested.

The third difficulty with the reflective cycle arises when the researcher and the designer/implementer of the method are the same person. In this circumstance, it may be difficult for the researcher to keep an unbiased view of the process and its results. Researchers may have a tendency to underestimate or overestimate the method's level of success. They may underestimate or overestimate the importance of the quality of the implementation as an intervening variable between the method and its level of success. To mitigate this problem I built in safeguards. First, the implementation of the method was a team effort. A team of between two and four consultants was involved during each implementation process. Second, in the case of Electro Ltd., I was only partially involved, and at Logistic Services BU, I was not involved with the implementation. Third, I was able to evaluate four of the six cases approximately two years after the implementation. During these evaluation sessions, I asked specific questions regarding the role and quality of the consultant to determine the way this may have influenced the results.

The Use of Reconstructed Logic

In his criticism of the empirical cycle (which he calls the *hypothetico-deductive method*), Kaplan (1964) introduces the concept of reconstructed logic. He states that the empirical cycle is a poor reconstruction of how scientists work and their actual logic-in-use: "The 'hypothetico-deductive' (re) construction fails to do justice to some of the logic-in-use, and conversely, some of the reconstructed logic has no counter-part in what is actually in use" (p. 10). Kaplan's (1964) first criticism is that this reconstruction hides some of the most important aspects of science: ". . . the most important incidents in the drama of science are enacted somewhere behind the scenes" (p. 10). His second criticism is that no scientist acts purely logically: "Second, a reconstructed logic is not a description but rather an idealization of scientific practice. Not even the greatest of scientists has a cognitive style which is wholly and perfectly logical, and the most brilliant piece of research still betrays its all-too-human divagations" (p. 10).

This last remark is especially true for my study. My project for the development of a method for valuing intangible resources was not set up as a scientific project. In this book I use reconstructed logic to reconstruct my project as if it were a developing multiple case study that uses the reflective cycle. There were three main differences between this reconstruction and the actual logic-in-use. First, the diagnosis of the situation and the problem definition tended to shift throughout the project. In fact, both did not become clear until the very end. Second, the requirements for the new method did not fully crystallize until the method was completely designed and tested. Third, some of the cases took place in parallel and not in succession. Therefore, I was not always able to refine a design based on the design knowledge generated from the previous case. The impact of using reconstructed logic is especially apparent in Chapter 4. In that chapter I list the requirements of the new method and describe the design by reconstructing and describing the thinking process that took place within the design team. This shows how the team's understanding of the problem definition and the solution evolved. The reconstruction helps to identify the implicit problem definitions and requirements the design team used. Before I do that, let us first determine what we can learn from existing methods for the valuation of intangible resources.

Legacy: Methods for the Valuation and Measurement of Intangibles

"Are you ready to give it to us?" urged Loonquawl.

"I am."

"Now?"

"Now," said Deep Thought.

They both licked their dry lips.

"Though I don't think," added Deep Thought, "that you're going to like it."

"Doesn't matter!" said Phouchg. "We must know it! Now!"

"Now?" inquired Deep Thought.

"Yes! Now . . ."

"Alright," said the computer and settled into silence again.

The two men fidgeted. The tension was unbearable.

"You're really not going to like it," observed Deep Thought.

"Tell us!"

"Alright," said Deep Thought. "The answer to the Great Question . . ."

"Yes . . . !"

"Of Life, the Universe and Everything . . ." said Deep Thought.

"Yes . . ."

"Is . . ." said Deep Thought, and paused.

"Yes . . . !"

"Is . . ."

"Yes . . . !!! . . . ?"

"Forty-two," said Deep Thought, with infinite majesty and calm.

It was a long time before anyone spoke.

Out of the corner of his eye Phouchg could see the sea of tense expectant faces down in the square outside.

"We're going to get lynched aren't we?" he whispered.

"It was a tough assignment," said Deep Thought mildly.

"Forty-two!" yelled Loonquawl. "Is that all you've got to show for seven and a half million years' work?"

"I checked it very thoroughly," said the computer, "and that quite definitely is the answer. I think the problem, to be quite honest with you, is that you've never actually known what the question is."

Douglas Adams (1979)

On January 17, 2001, I visited for the first time the Canadian McMaster World Congress on the Management of Intellectual Capital and Innovation, and I was hooked. Never before had I encountered such a passionate community of people sharing a mutual interest in the fundamental changes in the economy. I was astonished by the size and productivity of this community. The astonishment regarding the drastic changes in the way the economy works has triggered many scientists and practitioners to create new sets of distinctions and to develop new management tools. The increase in the number of publications follows an exponential curve. In this chapter I present an overview of some of the existing methods for measuring and valuing intangibles. I studied a sample of 25 different methods to determine how they worked and what problems they intended to solve. Appendix A contains a description of the methods in the sample.

The purpose of this analysis was to learn about the valuation of intangibles from previous attempts to value or measure intangible resources. I wanted to learn about the way the authors define the concept of intangibles to gain a better understanding of these phenomena. I wanted to analyze the way these authors define the problem they intend to solve. This gave me insight into the array of problems associated with the management of intangible resources. Finally, I wanted to learn about the various ways to approach the problem of valuing intangible resources. I analyzed the strengths and weaknesses of these approaches, and this helped me in defining the requirements for my own method.

These issues coincide with the first three steps of the reflective cycle described in Chapter 2 (Figure 3.1).

I analyzed each method using three questions:

1. *What* is the subject under investigation and what distinctions and definitions do the methods use to bring this subject to the surface?
2. *Why* have the authors developed a method? What is their problem definition and what are some of the consequences of this problem?

Figure 3.1

The what, why, and how of existing methods for the valuation of intangibles

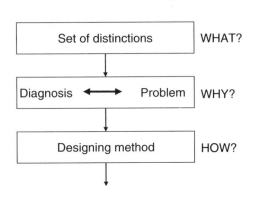

3. *How* do they value intangibles? What is their solution and what are the results of the method?

The subject of intangibles is addressed by various disciplines, including accountancy, information technology, sociology, psychology, human resource management, training and development (Bontis, 2002), and management research. Following Bontis (2002) and Bontis et al. (1999), I made a selection of relevant streams of thought. I decided to focus on five communities (Andriessen, 2002a). Each stream is a set of distinctions that can be used to define specific problems and develop specific solutions.

The *intellectual capital community* builds on the work of people like Thomas Stewart and Leif Edvinsson and offers various models for valuing and measuring intellectual capital. The *accounting community* is struggling with a decrease in the relevance of traditional financial information and is working on ways to recognize intangible assets in financial statements. The *performance measurement community* has adopted the concept of intangibles to add credibility to its approaches for measuring performance. The *valuation community* is creating more and more sophisticated tools for coping with the highly uncertain nature of intangible value, using concepts like real options. Within the *human resources community* there is a revival of the human resource accounting (HRA) techniques that date from the 1960s and 1970s.

Table 3.1 presents 25 methods that came out of these communities. This selection is based on the work of others (Bontis, 2001; Bontis et al., 1999; Luthy, 1998; Petty and Guthrie, 2000; and Sveiby, 2002) and on additional research.

Table 3.1

	Sample of 25 Methods for Valuing and Measuring Intangibles	
Section in Appendix A	**Method**	**Community**
A.5	Holistic value approach (HVA) (Pike and Roos, 2000)	Intellectual capital
A.7	Intellectual capital audit (Brooking, 1996)	Intellectual capital
A.8	Intellectual capital–index (Roos et al., 1997)	Intellectual capital
A.9	Inclusive Value Methodology™ (M'Pherson and Pike, 2001b)	Intellectual capital
A.10	Intangible asset monitor (Sveiby, 1997)	Intellectual capital
A.12	Intellectual capital benchmarking system (Viedma, 2001b)	Intellectual capital
A.13	Intellectual capital dynamic value (Bounfour, 2002)	Intellectual capital
A.14	Intellectual capital statement (Mouritsen et al., 2001c)	Intellectual capital
A.16	Konrad group (Sveiby et al., 1989)	Intellectual capital
A.19	Skandia navigator (Edvinsson and Malone, 1997)	Intellectual capital
A.20	Sullivan's work (Sullivan, 1998abc)	Intellectual capital
A.24	Value-Added Intellectual Coefficient™ (VAIC) (Pulic, 2000a,b)	Intellectual capital
A.2	Calculated intangible value (Stewart, 1997)	Accounting
A.3	Citation-weighted patents (Hall et al., 2001)	Accounting
A.11	Intangibles scoreboard (Gu and Lev, 2002)	Accounting
A.15	iValuing factor (Standfield, 2001)	Accounting
A.17	Market-to-book ratio (Stewart, 1997)	Accounting
A.22	Tobin's Q (Stewart, 1997)	Accounting
A.25	Value chain scoreboard (Lev, 2001)	Accounting
A.1	Balanced scorecard (Kaplan and Norton, 1992, 1996a,b, 2001)	Performance measurement
A.4	Economic Value Added™ (Stewart III, 1994)	Performance measurement
A.18	Options approach (Dixit and Pindyck, 1998)	Valuation
A.21	Technology factor (Khoury, 1998)	Valuation
A.23	Valuation approaches (Reilly and Schweihs, 1999)	Valuation
A.6	Human resource accounting (Sackmann et al., 1989)	Human resource

The allocation of methods to the various communities is somewhat arbitrary. My allocation is based on five criteria derived from the following characteristics:

1. Authors within the intellectual capital community tend to use intellectual capital as their main concept, publish in the *Journal of Intellectual Capital,* and attend the yearly World Congress on the Management of Intellectual Capital at MacMaster University, Hamilton, Ontario, Canada.
2. Authors from the accounting community tend to focus on issues around external reporting of companies. They search for methods to measure the value of intangible assets using publicly available data. They also have a strong tradition in testing these measures using statistical analysis.
3. Authors from the performance measurement community do not focus on intangibles per se, but look for ways to measure company performance.
4. Authors from the valuation community look for ways to value individual intangible assets using either a cost, market, or income approach. Their motives for valuing intangibles often involve a transaction of some sort (selling or licensing of patents or trademarks, taxation compliance, litigation).
5. Authors from the human resources community focus on human-based intangibles and try to raise the profile within companies of human resources and the human resource function.

What: Distinctions and Definitions

The problem with intangible resources is that they are intangible. *Longman's Dictionary of Contemporary English* (Procter, 1978) describes the term *intangible* as "which is hidden or not material, but known to be real," but also as "which by its nature cannot be known by the senses, though it can be felt," and "which is difficult to understand" (p. 582). Each of the three descriptions matches the subject of this book. Therefore, a key problem is how to identify something that is hidden or not material. As we have seen in Chapter 2, science demands we make clear distinctions using comprehensible definitions.

The intellectual capital community primarily use the term *intellectual capital*. The accounting and the valuation community and key members of the performance measurement community (Kaplan and Norton, 2001) use the term *intangible assets*, whereas the human resource community uses the terms *human resources* or *human assets*. Table 3.2 provides an overview of the main distinctions used by the 25 methods.

Table 3.2

	Main Distinctions Used by 25 Methods		
Section in Appendix A	Method	Community	Distinctions
A.4	Economic Value Added™	Performance measurement	None
A.17	Market-to-book value	Accounting	None
A.18	Options approach	Valuation	None
A.22	Tobin's Q	Accounting	None
A.23	Valuation approaches	Valuation	None
A.6	Human resource accounting	Human resource	Human resources
A.1	Balanced scorecard	Performance measurement	Intangible assets
A.2	Calculated intangible value	Accounting	Intangible assets
A.10	Intangible asset monitor	Intellectual capital	Intangible assets
A.11	Intangibles scoreboard	Accounting	Intangible assets
A.15	iValuing factor	Accounting	Intangible assets
A.21	Technology factor	Valuation	Intangible assets
A.25	Value chain scoreboard	Accounting	Intangible assets
A.5	Holistic value approach	Intellectual capital	Intellectual capital
A.7	Intellectual capital audit	Intellectual capital	Intellectual capital
A.8	Intellectual capital–index	Intellectual capital	Intellectual capital
A.9	Inclusive Value Methodology™	Intellectual capital	Intellectual capital
A.12	Intellectual capital benchmarking system	Intellectual capital	Intellectual capital
A.13	Intellectual capital dynamic value	Intellectual capital	Intellectual capital
A.19	Skandia navigator	Intellectual capital	Intellectual capital
A.20	Sullivan's work	Intellectual capital	Intellectual capital
A.24	Value-Added Intellectual Coefficient™	Intellectual capital	Intellectual capital
A.16	Konrad group	Intellectual capital	Know-how capital
A.14	Intellectual capital statement	Intellectual capital	Knowledge
A.3	Citation-weighted patents	Accounting	Patents

Intellectual Capital

Bontis (2001) complains that in the intellectual capital community many distinctions exist that are merely labeled differently (for example, structural capital = organizational capital = internal structure). He believes the reasons for this to be that the field is still in its embryonic stage, and he states that no one is willing to give up their own nomenclature and build on each other's work. Figure 3.2 provides an overview of the various classification schemes used in the intellectual capital community.

Most authors use the term *intellectual capital*. Stewart (1997) defines it as "packaged useful knowledge" (p. 10). Sullivan (1998c) defines it as "knowledge that can be converted into profits" (p. 4). Both limit intellectual capital to knowledge. Other authors include additional intellectual intangibles. Roos et al. (1997) define intellectual capital as "the sum of the knowledge of its members and the practical translation of this knowledge into brands, trademarks and processes" (p. 37) Edvinsson and Malone (1997) define it as "the possession of the knowledge, applied experience, organizational technology, customer relationships and professional skills that provide a company with a competitive edge in the market" (p. 44)

A third group of authors "look beyond the brain" (Andriessen, 2001) and include more than just pure brain-based capabilities. Brooking (1996) defines intellectual capital as "the combined intangible assets, which enable the company to function" (p. 23). Viedma (1999, 2001a,b, 2002) sees intellectual capital as equal to a company's core competencies.

The Konrad group (Sveiby et al., 1989) and Sveiby (1997) take a special position. The Konrad group (Sveiby et al., 1989) talks about know-how capital; Sveiby (1997) prefers the term *intangible assets,* which he defines as "invisible assets that include employee competence, internal structure and external structure" (p. 11).

The word *capital* is derived directly from the Latin *capitale,* with the adjective corresponding to the noun *caput,* meaning head. It originally referred to the head part of a debt, as distinguished from the interest. Over the centuries, the meaning of the word broadened until not only interest-bearing sums of money were considered capital, but all sorts of other collections of wealth were considered capital, provided only that it was possible to link them as the embodiment of interest-bearing sums of money—that is to say, as "money at work" (Böhm–Bawerk, 1959).

What is interesting is that the intellectual capital movement broadened the meaning of the word capital even further to include

Figure 3.2

Overview of Intellectual Capital Classifications

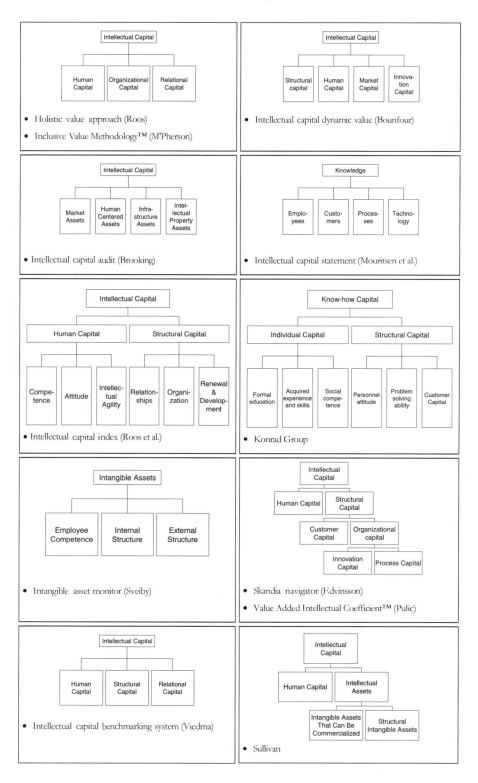

nonmonetary sources of wealth creation. By adopting the connotation of the word capital, the intellectual capital movement created a new perspective on companies. The use of the term *capital* makes one see new things because capital has value. It can be measured. It is a "stock" that involves input and output, and it needs to be managed.

When it comes to classifying types of intellectual capital, members of the intellectual capital community discuss the number of "roots" of the intellectual capital tree (Edvinsson and Malone, 1997). One of the discussions is whether relational capital (also referred to as *customer capital, external structure, relationships*) is part of structural capital or is a separate root. Roos et al. (1997) use only two roots—structural and human capital—because they want to highlight the difference between nonthinking and thinking resources. The reason for making this distinction is that the two types of resources need very different management methods. Others create a third root to highlight the importance of the external environment in their models.

Some authors want to stress the importance of innovation, renewal or development (Bounfour, 2002; Roos et al., 1997; Edvinsson and Malone, 1997). Others emphasize intellectual property (Brooking, 1996) or assets that can be commercialized (Sullivan, 1998a,b,c). Therefore, in my view, the reason that authors are not willing to give up their own nomenclature is that each author wants to convey a specific message that he thinks is important.

Mouritsen et al. (2001c) have commented on the intellectual capital classification schemes. They claim classification is problematic because the categories are related and even integral to each other. People (human capital) work through technology (structural capital), and customers (relational capital) get services from people (human capital). In addition, the classifications do not provide any guidelines for handling issues or solving problems. Finally, the mere fact that an indicator is classified into one of the types of intellectual capital does not mean it refers to or measures that type of intellectual capital. Their argument is supported by the fact that the same indicator can sometimes fall into two categories at the same time (for example, employee training in technology [human capital or structural capital?] or customer satisfaction with employee service [relationship capital or human capital?]).

Intangible Assets

One of the clear advantages of the accounting profession is that it uses well-defined concepts. The International Accounting Standards Board defines an intangible asset as "an identifiable non-monetary asset without physical substance held for use in the production or supply of goods or services, for rental to others, or for administrative purposes" (International Accounting Standards Committee, 1998, p. 984).

An asset is defined as "a resource controlled by an enterprise as a result of past events and from which future economic benefits are expected to flow to the enterprise" (International Accounting Standards Committee, 1998, p. 984). Therefore, to meet the definition of an intangible asset, an item needs to be identifiable, a company needs to have control over this item, and the item must be able to generate future economic benefits.

This accounting approach to intangibles is more narrow than the concept of intellectual capital. Intangible assets are restricted to the structural part of intellectual capital and they exclude human capital. Usually an enterprise has insufficient control over the expected future economic benefits arising from people to consider that these items meet the definition of an intangible asset.

Intangible assets do not cover all the structural capital components included, for example, by Edvinsson and Malone (1997). According to the International Accounting Standards Committee (1998), an enterprise has insufficient control over the economic benefits from customer relationships and loyalty to consider that customer capital meets the definition of intangible assets. The main category of intangibles that *does* meet the criteria is intellectual property. This includes patents, trademarks, and copyrights.

According to the International Accounting Standards Committee (1998), an item can only be recognized as an intangible asset if it meets the definition *plus* it is probable that the future economic benefits that are attributable to the asset will float to the enterprise *and* the cost of the assets can be measured reliably. Otherwise, the item should be treated as an expense. As a result, many intangible resources cannot be recognized on the balance sheet because they do not meet the definition, or their benefit and cost cannot be measured reliably.

Another common term in accounting is *goodwill*. Goodwill is defined as the excess of the cost of an acquired company over the sum of identifiable net assets. The Financial Accounting Standards Board (FASB) of the United States recognizes that goodwill meets the definition of an intangible asset. In FASB statement no. 142 (Financial Accounting Standards Board, 2001a), goodwill is treated as an asset that, if it has an indefinite useful life, will not be amortized but will be tested at least annually for impairment.

According to the FASB (1999), the two main components of goodwill are the fair value of the going concern element of the acquired entity's existing business and the fair value of the expected synergies from combining the acquiring entity's and the acquired entity's net assets and businesses. Therefore, the term *goodwill* is a much broader concept that *does* include intangible resources that do not meet the definition of an intangible asset. However, goodwill only occurs when an acquisition takes place, which is why it can be recognized as an asset in the transaction-based accounting system. Internally generated intangible assets and goodwill are not recognized on the balance sheet.

This leads to the conclusion that the accounting profession takes a limited view of intangible resources. Because the whole accounting system is based on transactions and on reliable identification and measurement, it focuses on acquired, recognizable intangible assets and acquired goodwill.

Lev, Professor of Accounting and Finance at the Stern School of Business, takes a broader view of intangibles. He defines an intangible asset as "a claim to future benefits that does not have a physical or financial embodiment" (Lev, 2001, p. 5). He distinguishes between innovation-related intangibles, human resource intangibles, and organizational intangibles (Lev, 2001). He argues that accountants in principle adopt this broad definition, but in practice subject the definition to an array of ambiguous and nonoperational conditions of reliability and verifiability. He promotes the adoption of his economic definition of an asset. In one of his proposals to improve external reporting (see Section A.11 in Appendix A), Lev suggests the creation of a complementary economic asset-based accounting system that recognizes all assets (investments, internally created and externally created assets) that are claims to expected benefits.

Human Resources and Human Assets

Core to the human resources community is the concept of *human resources,* or the people who are employed by the company. The human resource community founds its work on the premise that people are valuable organizational resources and therefore ought to be managed as such (Sackman et al., 1989). Tissen (1991) shows there has been a transition in the way organizations view the role of people. Until the beginning of the 1980s, the dominant view was that people had to adapt to organizations. Since the 1980s, the view has changed and managers have begun to see people as creative and vital resources.

To express the fact that people are vital sources of wealth, some authors use the term *human assets.* The purpose of this distinction is to indicate that people should be treated as assets that are as important as tangible and financial assets. However, this term has evoked criticism because the term *assets* has the connotation of ownership. In accounting terms, an asset is controlled by the enterprise, and people clearly are not. Therefore, authors argue against treating people as assets on ethical grounds (Johanson et al., 1999).

Reflection

There seems to be a "confusion of tongues" when it comes to defining intangibles. Some voices say that the field desperately needs to shape up and get its basic vocabulary right. I do not agree. As we saw in Chapter 2, the distinctions that we chose to use guide what we see. Or, phrased the other way around, authors that want to tell their readers a specific message use specific distinctions. For example, because Sullivan (1998a) wants to convey a message about the importance of commercializing intangibles, he uses the term *intellectual assets* for intangibles that are codified and can be commercialized. For the same reason, he uses the term *structural capital* to describe all the supporting infrastructure (intangible and tangible resources!) needed to commercialize intangibles. If we were to ask him to change his vocabulary and submit to a common standard, he would have great difficulty expressing his own message.

My personal preferences when it comes to the vocabulary of intangibles are based on three messages I think are important to pass on:

1. There is more to life and business than knowledge.
2. The term *capital* can sometimes be misleading.
3. We need to look at the synergy of combining intangible resources and not at individual ones.

Let me explain in more detail what I mean.

Look Beyond the Brain

The intellectual capital community highlights the intellectual activities and characteristics of companies. The community focuses on knowledge creation, intellectual skills, and explicit knowledge. It tends to overlook intangibles that are nonintellectual or right-side-of-the-brain oriented but that can be equally important for future success. Two examples may help to clarify this (Andriessen and Tissen, 2000).

The pop singer David Bowie has maintained his position for three decades in an industry that is known for "here today; gone tomorrow." Much of this, of course, is the result of his musical skills.

However, he also has a feel for the mood of the times. The transformations he has undergone—from Ziggy Stardust to the White Prince—show an ability to recreate an image in line with the changing tastes of the market. This proved to be of market value: He became the first person in the entertainment industry to float a personal bond issue. Ownership of the bonds entitles investors to a share in not only the income from royalties on the singer's past material, but also on the receipts of future live concerts. The investors obviously thought it was a good deal. The entire issue was sold within one hour for a total cost of more than $50 million (David and Meyer, 1998). Should we consider Bowie's unique talent "intellectual capital?" To me, his skills are more right-side-of-the-brain than left-side-of-the-brain.

Many companies enjoy success because their employees share collective values and norms. I do not consider these resources "intellectual." At Microsoft, the culture is so closely knit that secretaries who, thanks to their shares in the company, are millionaires, still come in to work every morning. General Motors, in contrast, has never had such an open exchange of information. In fact, until recently, the information culture within General Motors' concentrated mainly on financial information and the personality of the person presenting any new information. A strong product manager was thought to be able to convince the market of a new model, even if market research had shown otherwise. In addition, some observers believe that this is one of the root causes for General Motors' being unable to harness its full potential as a designer and manufacturer of automobiles. The former chief executive officer (CEO), Jack Smith, was able to change this culture, and now the emphasis lies more firmly on operational and quality information (Davenport and Prusak, 1998).

Therefore, the intangibles of companies include intangible resources that are all very different by nature. Some we can describe as intellectual or knowledge assets—products of the left side of the brain. Others, like corporate culture, the charisma of leaders, and many of the talents of employees, are found more on the right side of the brain and in the hearts of people, and should not be labeled "intellectual." The problem is that the word *intellectual* has many connotations and associations, including rationality, intelligence, and reason. In stating that the success of companies depends on their intellectual capital, the intellectual capital community shows a rationalist view of organizations; a view that has often proved to be incorrect or, at the very least, incomplete.

For example, Edvinsson (2000) promotes "the systematic transformation of human capital into structural capital as a multiplier, with much more sustainable earnings potential for the organization." This approach is "very much focused on the packaging of knowledge into recipes to be shared globally and rapidly" (p. 12). The idea is that human capital can only work a limited number of hours a day whereas structural capital works for you 24 hours a day, and thus is at least 50% more efficient. Unfortunately, we can only turn a limited part of human talent into structural capital. It is the part that is intellectual in nature, but only that part of human knowledge that can be structured and made explicit. This often is not the part with the most benefit with regard to the future success of companies (Tissen et al., 2000).

The Undesirable Connotations of Capital

The word *capital* has proved to be useful in creating awareness about the importance of intangibles. The word resonates with chief financial officers, CEOs, and the financial community. Capital is good (and more is even better), it is nice to own, it has monetary value that can be measured, it is additive by nature, it is a stock, and of course it needs to be carefully managed and thus needs to be measured.

I argue that selecting the word *capital* to create the concept of *intellectual capital* has added tremendously to the proliferation and acceptance of the concept, but we need to be aware of its limitations. In the case of intellectual capital, more is not always better. Accumulating knowledge can be very costly. According to Tissen et al. (1998), companies do not need more knowledge but they need value-adding knowledge.

There are more limitations to the use of the word capital. Companies can own capital, whereas many intangibles that contribute to company success cannot be owned. Human resources are an obvious example, but also relationships with customers, suppliers, and alliance partners cannot be owned. This is where the accounting concept of assets also falls short. It requires companies to have full control over the asset before a resource meets the definition of an asset. Blair and Wallman (2001) call these intangibles level 3 intangibles. They distinguish between three levels. Level 1 intangibles can be owned and sold (patents, copyrights, brands, and trade names). Level 2 intangibles can be controlled but not separated out and sold (R&D in process, business secrets, reputational capital, proprietary management systems, and business processes). Level 3 intangibles may not be wholly controlled by the firm (human resources, organizational capital, and relationship capital).

Furthermore, valuation of intellectual capital is not as straightforward as the valuation of other types of capital. Yet this assumption is often being made, for example, when it is stated that intellectual capital is the difference between market value and book value. As we see later, this statement is problematic.

If intellectual capital is capital with monetary value, then why don't we simply put it on the balance sheet? See, for example, Pulic (2002), who promotes human capital to be recognized as an asset on the balance sheet. Moreover, if intangible capital is an intangible asset, then there must be intangible liabilities (Caddy, 2000). As we saw in Chapter 1, it is not that simple. The unique characteristics of intangibles mean that it is impossible to fit them into the transaction-based accounting system (Webber, 2000).

Capital is a stock. Treating intellectual capital as a stock offers interesting perspectives on the potential of firms. It allows us to look at the way companies create future wealth using their unique capabilities. This perspective is similar to the resource-based theory of the firm (Bontis, 2002). However, the intellectual capital stock is an accumulation of historical flows and it is a source of future flows of wealth. It is not only the stock that is important, but also the ability to use this stock and the resulting flows (Rylander et al., 2000). Roos and others (Roos and Roos, 1997; Roos et al., 1997) have been some of the first to acknowledge the importance of intellectual capital flows. The concept of intellectual capital stocks and flows creates an interesting new perspective on organizations. We can describe organizations as a dynamic system of financial, tangible, and intangible stocks and flows. We can even model this system using system dynamics simulation software like I Think™ (see, for example, Sveiby et al. [2002]). Yet, when trying to model these processes, we rapidly trip on the limitations of the stock and flow analogy. As opposed to financial capital, the unit of measurement of intellectual capital is not uniform, and most of the time it is problematic. What unit do we need to use to measure a stock of knowledge? The best we can do is to try to find proxies that reflect some of the characteristics of these stocks. Furthermore, as we have seen, intangibles are nonrival assets and nonadditive by nature. A stock of knowledge can create a flow of wealth without the stock diminishing. As a result of these problems, the system dynamic model created by Sveiby et al. (2002) requires so many assumptions about the transformation of stocks measured in different units that the accuracy and usefulness of the final model becomes questionable. Therefore, although the stock–flow analogy is useful to emphasize the transformation processes in companies, we should not take it too literally.

A final problem with the use of the term *capital* has to do with measurement. As we will see later in this chapter, the mere fact that intellectual capital is labeled as capital is not sufficient to claim that it needs to be managed or measured. This claim requires a more precise problem definition and an explanation of assumptions about the way measurement and management work.

Reunite the Pieces

The problem with the intellectual capital classification schemes is that the schemes seem to miss the essence of wealth creation. Only a *combination* of intangible resources can create wealth. The value of intangible resources lies in their combined strength and not in their individual characteristics. Companies become unique and successful by combining various types of intangible resources. By separating human capital from structural capital, customer capital from organizational capital, and innovation capital from process capital, we lose track of the correlation and synergy between the categories. It is this synergy between intangibles that creates uniqueness and wealth, not the individual resources. The use of classification schemes that break down the total capital of a company into its contributing parts hampers us in seeing the forest for the trees and identifying the effects of combining different types of intangibles. We look at each intangible in isolation when, in truth, the strength of intangibles is cumulative.

Another problem is that, because we use the same classification scheme for different companies, every company starts to look the same. On the one hand, this is a good thing, because it allows for benchmarking. However, when it comes to making strategic management decisions on how to improve or sustain company success, this method has its shortcomings.

An even more important problem arises once we start to look for indicators for each of the categories. Liebowitz and Suen (2000) have shown the enormous array of possible measures for the various categories of intellectual capital. However, the problem with most intellectual capital reports based on these classification schemes is that there is little or no connection between the various indicators. Without information on the relationships between the categories, we do not know what it means when, for example, the share of employees with advanced degrees goes up, and the partner satisfaction index goes down.

Synthesis: Intangible Resources

These reflections about distinctions and definitions led me to the following conclusions. To identify important intangible drivers of company performance, we need to "look beyond the brain" and include nonintellectual activities and capabilities. This is why I prefer the term *intangible* to *intellectual*. The term *capital* has too many connotations that do not fit the intangible nature of the subject under investigation. The term *asset* is associated too much with control and ownership. This is why I prefer the term *resources*. Therefore, I use the concept of intangible resources, which I define as nonmonetary resources without physical substance that in combination are able to produce future benefits for a company. This definition is broad enough to include nonintellectual resources, it stresses the importance of the synergy between resources, and it avoids the requirement of ownership. However, this does create a demarcation problem: Which resources belong to the company and which do not? Chapter 4 describes how I solve this problem.

Why: Problems and Consequences

The 25 methods address a wide variety of problems. We can group them into problems involved with improving internal management or those involved with improving external reporting (Andriessen, 2002a). There are also statutory or transactional reasons to analyze the value of intangible resources, which creates a third group of problems. A fourth group of problems deals with the accuracy and reliability of national accounts (see, for example, Gröjer and Johanson [2000]). This fourth group of problems is beyond the scope of this book. My analysis of the 25 methods shows that they address different types of problems. Table 3.3 provides an overview of the types of problems dominant in each of the 25 methods.

Improving Internal Management

Some authors refer to improving internal management as *improving management accounting* (Stewart, 2001b) and *management control* (Gröjer and Johanson, 2000). According to Eccles (1991), the use of nonfinancial performance measures to improve internal management dates back as far as 1951, when General Electric installed a high-level task force to identify key corporate performance measures. The French *tableau de bord* is a measurement tool that dates back to 1932 (Nørreklit, 2000). During the 1980s, the total quality management movement introduced various quality measures. In the beginning of the 1990s, measures of customer satisfaction were introduced. In 1992, Kaplan and Norton (1992) published their famous article on the balanced scorecard.

The issue of improving internal management is a wide one. Various problem definitions fall into this category. Table 3.4 gives an overview

Table 3.3

	Overview of Problems Addressed by the 25 Methods		
Section in Appendix A	**Method**	**Community**	**Problem Addressed**
A.18	Options approach	Valuation	All three
A.23	Valuation approaches	Valuation	All three
A.25	Value chain scoreboard	Accounting	External reporting
A.16	Konrad group	Intellectual capital	External reporting
A.3	Citation-weighted patents	Accounting	External reporting
A.1	Balanced scorecard	Performance measurement	Internal management
A.15	Valuing factor	Accounting	Internal management
A.21	Technology factor	Valuation	Internal management
A.7	Intellectual capital audit	Intellectual capital	Internal management
A.12	Intellectual capital benchmarking system	Intellectual capital	Internal management
A.13	Intellectual capital dynamic value	Intellectual capital	Internal management
A.4	Economic Value Added™	Performance measurement	Internal management and external reporting
A.17	Market-to-book value	Accounting	Internal management and external reporting
A.22	Tobin's Q	Accounting	Internal management and external reporting
A.6	Human resource accounting	Human resource	Internal management and external reporting
A.10	Intangible asset monitor	Intellectual capital	Internal management and external reporting
A.11	Intangibles scoreboard	Accounting	Internal management and external reporting
A.20	Sullivan's work	Intellectual capital	Internal management and external reporting
A.24	Value-Added Intellectual Coefficient™	Intellectual capital	Internal management and external reporting
A.5	Holistic value approach	Intellectual capital	Internal management and external reporting
A.8	Intellectual capital–index	Intellectual capital	Internal management and external reporting
A.9	Inclusive Value Methodology™	Intellectual capital	Internal management and external reporting
A.14	Intellectual capital statement	Intellectual capital	Internal management and external reporting
A.19	Skandia navigator	Intellectual capital	Internal management and external reporting
A.2	Calculated intangible value	Accounting	Statutory and transactional

Table 3.4

Overview of Internal Management Problem Definitions	
Category	Problem Definition
1. "What gets measured gets managed"	What you can measure, you can manage and what you want to manage, you need to measure (Roos et al., 1997). If an asset or process is to be managed properly, it must be measured (M'Pherson and Pike, 2001a,b). Because intellectual assets are the most important assets within any business, they must be measured and managed according to the most objective means possible (Standfield, 2001). We become what we measure (Edvinsson, 2002a). What gets measured, gets managed (Luu et al., 2001). To manage value creation we need to measure it (Pulic, 2000b).
2. Improving the management of intangible resources	Improve low status of human resources and the human resources management function within companies (Sackman et al., 1989). Enterprises do not know what their intangible assets are, what they're worth, or how to manage them (Brooking, 1996). How better to manage and measure knowledge and other intangibles in the company (Roos et al., 1997) Measurement is a means of focusing managers on intangible assets and allowing them to monitor their assets (Sveiby, 1997). Help companies to apply knowledge management techniques systematically and comprehensively (Mouritsen et al., 2001c). There is a need for tools to improve management of intellectual capital (Stewart, 1997). Adding to the long-term sustainability of the organization and nurturing the roots of sustainable cash flow generation (Edvinsson and Malone, 1997). Making decisions whether to invest further in developing an intangible, to continue holding it, or to sell it (Sullivan, 1998a). Better manage intellectual capital to obtain the corporate vision, strategy, and objectives (Luu et al., 2001; Sullivan, 2000). Preventing making decisions that damage the intangible asset stock of the company (Bontis et al., 1999). Seeking better ways to utilize organizational resources (Bontis, 2002). Improve incentives for knowledge workers and entrepreneurs (Leadbetter, 2000; Luu et al., 2001).

Table 3.4 *continued*

| Overview of Internal Management Problem Definitions ||
Category	Problem Definition
3. Creating resource-based strategies	Create a balanced view on drivers of future financial performance (Kaplan and Norton, 1996a). Do we have the requisite resources for our strategy (Roos et al., 2001)
4. Monitoring effects from actions	Create a balanced view on results of action already taken (Kaplan and Norton, 1996a). To give feedback information showing whether actions are working (Pike and Roos, 2000). Having a metric for assessing success and growth (Brooking,1996). To know as much as possible about the company so that it can monitor its progress and take corrective action when needed (Sveiby, 1997). Difficulty of comparing investments in R&D with their outcomes (Webber, 2000). To measure progress toward goals (Stewart, 1997). Assessing the effectiveness of investments in intangibles (Luu et al., 2001).
5. Translating business strategy into action	How to implement new strategies (Kaplan and Norton, 2001). Translating strategic intent into actions (Pike and Roos, 2000).
6. Weighing possible courses of action	Making trade-off decisions (Roos et al., 1997). How should a corporate manager facing uncertainty over future market conditions decide whether to invest in a new project (Dixit and Pindyck, 1998; Luerman, 1998a,b) Make better resource allocation decisions (Edvinsson, 2002a).
7. Measuring income in a reliable way	Periodically matching costs with revenues to measure income and assets in a reliable way (Webber, 2000).
8. Enhancing the management of the business as a whole	Preventing poor management decision making that destroys shareholder wealth (Stewart III, 1994). Manage the whole company, and not just its visible part, integrating the need for a complete measurement system with the need for a holistic management strategy (Roos et al., 1997). Facilitate the process of learning from the best competitors (Viedma, 2001a). Establish a link between inputs, processes, the build-up of intangible assets, and company performance (Bounfour, 2002). Incorporating market value risks in decision making (Standfield, 2001). Improve management accounting information to be more relevant to managers' planning and control decisions (Johnson and Kaplan, 1987).

of problem definitions regarding internal management used by the authors of the 25 methods in addition to other authors in the field. The problem definitions can be grouped into eight categories of problems:

The first category of problem definitions is the popular notion that management requires measurement or that measurement leads to better management. A typical example is Standfield's (2001) motivation for measuring intangibles: "As intellectual assets are the most important assets within any business, they must be measured and managed according to the most objective means possible" (p. 316). If we compare this with the following statement, "Because food and drink are the most important means for any human being to stay alive, they must be measured and managed according to the most objective means possible," it becomes clear that the importance of intangibles is neither a necessary nor a sufficient condition for measurement. Moreover, measurement is neither a necessary nor a sufficient condition for management. Stewart (2001) calls the phrase "you cannot manage what you cannot measure," ". . . one of the oldest clichés in management, and it's either false or meaningless. It's false in that companies have always managed things—people, morale, strategy, etc.—that are essentially unmeasured. It's meaningless in the sense that everything in business—including people, morale, strategy, etc.—eventually shows up in someone's ledger of costs or revenues" (p. 291). Therefore, we need a more detailed problem definition to justify the measurement of intangible resources.

We find a second, more valid group of problem definitions in the intellectual capital and HRA literature. This category is based on the belief that intangible resources are not managed properly, that they deserve more management attention, and that they need to be managed differently than other resources. This has been the driving force behind HRA, and has inspired intellectual capital authors like Roos, Sveiby, and Edvinsson. Sveiby, for example, has made it his task to supply managers with a toolbox to help them in managing knowledge-based companies. Included in this category of problem definitions are problems regarding the lack of awareness about the importance of intangible resources. Awareness is a requirement for management.

Yet, improving the management of intangible resources is not a very specific problem definition. Kaplan and Norton (1992) are more concrete, and they identify a third category of problems. Their aim is to complement financial measures of company performance with operational measures to create a balanced view of results of action already taken and drivers of future financial performance. This means they want to create insight into the value drivers: the vital resources that determine future success. These resources are often intangible, and are the basis for creating resource-based strategies. To help develop these strategies they use a tool called a *strategy map* (Kaplan and Norton, 2001). Roos et al. (2001) also use the intangible perspective to help create resource-based strategies.

The second aim of the method of Kaplan and Norton (1996a)—the balanced scorecard—is to measure performance in a balanced way as a feedback mechanism for management actions. This fourth category of problems lies at the core of the performance measurement community but also plays an important role in the intellectual capital community. The accounting community also adopts this perspective, but is specifically interested in monitoring the effects of investments in intangibles to be able to calculate some form of return on investment (Webber, 2000).

After working with their method for a couple of years Kaplan and Norton (2001) found it addresses a more fundamental problem: how to link a company's long-term strategy with its short-term actions. Therefore, their problem definition shifted from measuring performance to strategy implementation: "But we learned that adopting companies used the Balance Scorecard to solve a much more important problem than how to measure performance in the information era. That problem, of which we were frankly unaware when first proposing the Balanced Scorecard, was how to implement new strategies" (Kaplan and Norton, 2001, p. viii). This leads to a fifth category of problems. Pike and Roos (2000) describe this category as translating strategic intent into actions.

Roos has been one of the strongest advocates of methods that allow for making trade-off decisions. According to Roos et al. (1997), this is where the early intellectual capital models (which they referred to as *first-generation models*) fall short: "Intellectual capital systems have long lists of indicators with no prioritization, thus making it impossible for managers to evaluate trade-off decisions" (Roos et al., 1997, p. 7). The sixth category of problems is especially concerned with making trade-off decisions. This requires a method that consolidates different indicators into one measure of value.

A seventh group of problem definitions originates from the accounting community. Although the accounting community is primarily concerned with the quality of corporate reporting, it does address elements of internal management because information that is reported externally is also used to make internal decisions. The accounting community is struggling with intangible assets because intangibles frustrate the important accounting concept of periodically matching costs with revenues. For example, R&D investment in product and process innovation is immediately expensed in financial reports as if no long-term benefits are expected from it. This interferes with the accounting concept of periodically matching costs with revenues. This concept is crucial in measuring income and assets in a reliable way.

The last category of problems looks at the business as a whole. An example is the method of Economic Value Added™ (EVA, a trademark owned by Stern Stewart and Co.). EVA is not a method specifically designed to measure the value of intangibles. Its aim is much wider. The problem EVA addresses is poor management decision making that destroys shareholder wealth. According to EVA advocates, poor decision making is often a result of using the wrong indicators of wealth creation, like return on investments or return on assets. The problem with most traditional indicators is that they are based on accounting-derived earnings instead of cash flow, and they do not include the cost of capital in the equation. EVA was developed to correct this.

It is clear from this overview that authors in the field of measuring the value of intangible resources use many different problem definitions when it comes to improving internal management. They range from clichés like "what gets measured gets managed," to the general problems of managing intangibles, to the specific problem of matching costs with revenues.

Improving External Reporting

Within the accounting profession, the problem of intangibles is often described as one of "relevance lost" (Johnson and Kaplan, 1987). This includes a loss of relevance of the financial statements to managerial decision making, and a loss of relevance of financial reporting to external stakeholders. In this section I focus on financial reporting to external stakeholders. Since the earlier 1990s, the study of the problems associated with financial reporting has intensified. In 1991, the American Institute of Certified Public Accountants formed a special committee on financial reporting, also known as the *Jenkins Committee*. Its aim was to offer recommendations to improve the value of business information and the public's confidence in it. The committee based its findings on a detailed study of user needs for information. It studied the needs of professional investors and creditors, and their advisers. The committee found that to meet users changing needs, business reporting must

- Provide more information with a forward-looking perspective, including management's plans, opportunities, risks, and measurement uncertainties

- Focus on the factors that create longer term value, including non-financial measures indicating how key business processes are performed
- Align information reported externally with the information reported to senior management to manage the business (American Institute of Certified Public Accountants, 1994, p. 5)

Interestingly the committee identified accounting for intangible assets as a "low-priority issue." In 1998, the FASB (2001b) formed a steering committee to study then-current practices for the voluntary disclosure of certain types of business information that users of this reporting may find helpful. The basic premise underlying this study was that improving disclosures makes the capital allocation process more efficient and reduces the average cost of capital. One of the findings was that additional data regarding intangible assets would be beneficial.

That same year, Mavrinac and Siesfeld (1998) published their groundbreaking study of investors' information needs. The study included a survey of 275 portfolio managers of institutional investors in the United States. They found that the top five of the most valued nonfinancial measures were

1. Execution of corporate strategy
2. Management credibility
3. Quality of corporate strategy
4. Innovativeness
5. Ability to attract employees

The Brookings Institution published a report in March 2001 (Blair and Wallman, 2001) that was the follow-on to an earlier conference on intangible assets sponsored by the United States Securities and Exchange Commission. The Brookings Institution identified the following problems associated with external reporting:

- An increased cost of capital and reduced perceived fairness of the capital markets to individual investors
- The decreasing usefulness of common performance measures like return on equity
- The problem of information asymmetry between informed and uninformed investors
- The misallocation of resources

- The problem of identifying a fair, useful, and feasible basis for assessing tax liabilities and collecting taxes (Blair and Wallman, 2001, p. 23–31)

Table 3.5 gives an overview of problem definitions regarding external reporting used by the authors of the 25 methods in addition to other authors in the field. I clustered the problem definitions into five categories:

The first category has to do with the notion that we need to close the growing value gap between book and market value. However, is this the case? Is the financial statement becoming less and less relevant because of this value gap? A discussion about the relevance of financial statements for external stakeholders must start with the objectives of financial reporting. FASB concepts statement no. 42 describes three objectives:

1. Financial reporting should provide information that is useful to external stakeholders in making rational investment, credit, and similar decisions.
2. It should provide information to help users in assessing the amounts, timing, and uncertainty of prospective net cash inflows to the enterprise.
3. It should provide information about the economic resources of an enterprise, the claims to those resources, and the effects of events on those resources (Upton, 2001, p. 60).

So, contrary to popular belief, it is not the objective of the balance sheet to approximate the market value of a company (Rutledge, 1997; White et al., 1997). Upton (2001) phrases this misunderstanding as follows: "If accountants got all the assets and liabilities into financial statements, and they measure all those assets and liabilities at the right amounts, stockholders' equity would equal market capitalization" (p. 60). This fallacy underlies the widespread statement that the difference between book value and market value represents intangibles or intellectual capital (see, for example, Edvinsson and Malone [1997], Stewart [1997, 2001b], Sveiby [1997], and Roos et al. [1997]).

Not only is there no need to make book value equal market value, it is also impossible. Comparing the gap between market value and book value of companies with intellectual capital is like comparing the difference between an apple and an orange with a banana. The book value represents the historic value of the assets of a company not yet amortized. The market value is equal to the perceived present value of the future cash flow of the company (Figure 3.3).

Table 3.5

Overview of External Reporting Problem Definitions	
Category	**Problem Definition**
1. Closing the value gap between book and market value	Real value of companies cannot be determined by traditional accounting measures only (Edvinsson and Malone, 1997; Luu et al., 2001). Accounting methods prevent financial statements from accounting two thirds of the real value of organizations (Batchelor, 1999).
2. Improving information to stakeholders about the real value and future performance of the enterprise	Communicate the attributes of value to shareholders outside the company (Pike et al., 2002). Give stakeholders a better understanding of the real value of a company (Roos et al., 1997). Allow an accurate assessment of returns on investment in intangibles (Rylander et al., 2000). How to describe the company as accurately as possible so stakeholders can assess the quality of management and the reliability of the company (Sveiby, 1997). Investments in intangibles are not visible in most financial statements, which results in a complete lack of transparency (Lev, 2001). How to report operations of know-how companies so that external stakeholders can get their answers (Sveiby et al., 1989). Permit company-to-company comparisons (Stewart, 1997). Traditional financial data as presented in the annual report are no longer leading indicators of future financial performance (Edvinsson and Malone, 1997). Capturing the half-hidden information now hidden in the footnotes of the balance sheet (Edvinsson and Malone, 1997). Traditional financial data as presented in the annual report do not show the real value of companies (Edvinsson and Malone, 1997). Companies wishing to convey information that fully informs about their value (Sullivan, 2000). Predict current and future income (Luu et al., 2001). Providing nonfinancial performance data that are relevant to shareholder evaluations and investment decisions (Lim and Dallimore, 2002; Mavrinac and Siesfeld, 1998). Preventing overvaluation by investors (Leadbetter, 2000).

Table 3.5 *continued*

Overview of External Reporting Problem Definitions	
Category	**Problem Definition**
	Allow more effective and efficient allocation of resources on the capital market (Luu et al., 2001). Corporate governance (Gröjer and Johanson, 2000). Investor decisions (Gröjer and Johanson, 2000).
3. Reducing information asymmetry	Reducing the information asymmetry gap (Pike et al., 2002). There is information asymmetry between the general public and those who do have access to information on investments and returns regarding intangibles (Lev, 2001). Providing nuanced, dynamic information to the small investor (Edvinsson and Malone, 1997, p. 8). Diminishing the risk of insider trading (Leadbetter, 2000). Diminishing information inequality (Luu et al., 2001). Insider gains (Gröjer and Johanson, 2000).
4. Increasing the ability to raise capital	Help new knowledge-intensive businesses acquire loans (Stewart, 1997). Improve ability to raise capital (Pike et al., 2002). Creating a basis for raising a loan (Brooking, 1996). Lowering the costs of capital (Leadbetter, 2000; Lev, 2001; Luu et al., 2001). Attract investors and financiers for new knowledge-intensive organizations (Luu et al., 2001). Credit decisions (Gröjer and Johanson, 2000).
5. Enhancing corporate reputation and affecting stock price	Enhancing external reputation and market valuation (Pike et al., 2002). Influence stock investments (Sackman et al., 1989). Communicate corporate identity (Mouritsen et al., 2001a). Illustrate the value of the company (Mouritsen et al., 2001a). Decrease volatility of market values (Leadbetter, 2000; Lev, 2001). Decrease in the bid–ask securities spread (Leadbetter, 2000; Lev, 2001). Conveying information that positively affects stock price (Luu et al., 2001; Sullivan, 2000).

Figure 3.3

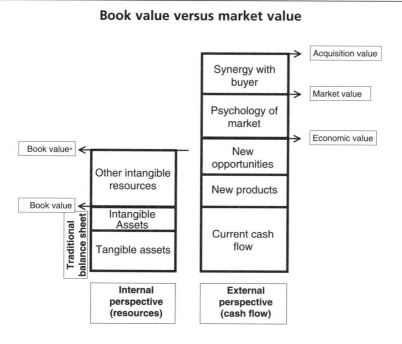

Book value versus market value

Using the concept of book value implicates taking an internal perspective on the company and listing its resources: tangible, intangible, and financial. Using the concept of market value implicates taking an external perspective on the company. It means looking at cash flows that will be generated by current products, new products, and new opportunities. It also involves the psychology of the market, including puffery or pessimism. These two perspectives, by definition, cannot be subtracted.

Pike et al. (2001) add another argument by stressing the fact that all resources of a company combine and interact with each other. The equation Market Value = Book Value + Intellectual Capital is incorrect because the variables are not separable, as required by the equation. For example, book value depends partly on retained earnings, which derive from operations, which involve intellectual capital (M'Pherson and Pike, 2001b).

The second category of problems addresses disseminating poor information to stakeholders regarding the real value and future performance of the enterprise. This problem is at the root of the other types of problems mentioned in Table 3.5. Lev (2001) and Lev and Zarowin (1999) show there is a deteriorating usefulness of financial reports. From 1980 through 1996, the association between corporate earnings and stock price changes has diminished. The same diminishing pattern of association exists between stock prices and returns, and key financial variables such as cash flow and book (equity) values. Traditional financial data as presented in the annual report are no longer leading indicators of future financial performance.

This leads to the third category of problems concerned with the growing information asymmetry between the public and those who have access to information on investments and returns regarding intangibles. According to Lev (2001) this asymmetry leads to

- Abnormal gains to informed investors

- Increased volatility of market values resulting in a lack of confidence of investors

- An increase in the bid–ask securities spread (Traders quote this price differential for buying or selling a security. This may result in a market shutdown).

- An increasing cost of capital (pp. 93–95).

Lev (2001) is concerned about the uninformed investors—typically, private investors. He draws attention to "the democratization and the externalization of decision-making processes both within organizations and in capital markets" (p. 107). Democratization points toward the increasing role of individual investors in capital markets. They have less access to inside information than analysts and investment fund managers, which creates an uneven playing field. Externalization points toward the fact that increasingly important decisions that managers need to make are shared with entities residing outside the company. This increases the scope of information required. Therefore, Lev (2001) argues, there is a need "to provide the needs of the emerging constituencies—primarily individual investors and the myriad partners to the networked corporations—enabling these constituencies to make and execute decisions at the level of professional investors and managers" (p. 109). Edvinsson and Malone (1997) share Lev's concern. They are looking for ways to provide nuanced, dynamic information to the small investor. They also state that the asymmetry leads to a misallocation of capital: "As a result, too many deserving companies are underoptimized and undercapitalized, and thus sometimes are unable to complete their destiny. Meanwhile, other, troubled firms are artificially propped up until they collapse, pulling down shareholders and investors with them" (p. 8). The misallocation of capital, in the end, produces social costs like unemployment, reduced productivity, and even diminished national competitiveness.

A lack of transparency of intangibles makes it difficult for companies that lack tangible assets to raise money from investors or banks. The fourth category of problems focuses on the difficulty companies have in raising capital. Banking regulations may be biased against lending to companies with few tangible assets, which can be used as security (Leadbetter, 2000). This may especially disadvantage young, high-tech companies with little record of accomplishment.

This lack of transparency also leads to undervaluation of companies that are intangibles intensive. Lev (2001) found that investors systematically undervalue companies with a high growth rate of R&D expenditures. Failing to identify and assess the value of intangibles and the lack of information on intangibles in financial statements is likely to lead to the mispricing of companies (Cañibano et al., 1999). This leads to the fifth category of problems. There is strong interest among intangibles-intensive companies to report their intangibles to influence stock price. The motive for reporting intangibles may not only be increasing a company's market value, but also its reputation. Mouritsen et al. (2001a) found that many companies joining the pilot of the Danish Agency for Trade and Industry (2003) on creating intellectual capital statements did so to increase their reputation. The statements were used as a means of communicating corporate identity to improve recruitment and to attract new customers.

Authors working on improving external reporting are more thorough in the way they describe the problem than those working on improving internal management. At the heart of the external reporting problem is the notion that there is no transparency in reporting intangible resources. This leads to a whole range of problems on both the micro and macro levels, ranging from the difficulty in raising capital to diminished national competitiveness.

Lev (2001) provides an interesting analysis of why it is so difficult to change financial reporting standards to solve some of these problems. Under the heading "the politics of intangibles," he identifies three major players in the debate about improving external reporting and their reluctance to changes: managers, accountants, and analysts.

Managers will be reluctant to capitalize, for example, on acquired in-process R&D because the amortization will be a heavy burden on future reported profitability. Analysts see the mandated expensing of acquired R&D as a one-time item with practically no consequence for the company stock price. So, the manager gets the best of both worlds: no price hit at the time of expensing and a significant boost to future reported profitability. Furthermore, if the acquisition fails and the in-house R&D had been recognized as an asset on the balance sheet, then the company would have to plead guilty and publicly write off the investment.

Accountants want to stay away from risky assets on the balance sheet that may draw lawsuits from irate shareholders.

Analysts earn part of their position and benefit from the information they obtain from managers. Through channels not available to the public, they obtain information about a firm's innovation activities. Public disclosure of such information may harm their position.

Statutory and Transactional Issues

Literature on methods for the valuation of intangibles (Lee, 1996; Reilly and Schweihs, 1999; Smith and Parr, 1994) provides additional statutory and transactional reasons for valuing intangible resources. Statutory provision, administrative ruling, or regulatory authority can mandate a valuation. Alternatively, valuation can be discretionary in the case of a transaction. Table 3.6 gives an overview of both types of motives.

The first category of motives focuses on transactions. Transactions involving intangible resources include the purchase, sale, or license of

Table 3.6

Overview of Statutory and Transactional Reasons	
Category	**Type**
1. Transaction pricing and structuring for the sale, purchase, or license of an intangible asset	Discretionary
2. Financing securitization and collateralization for both cash flow-based financing and asset-based financing	Mandatory
3. Taxation planning and compliance, with regard to all sorts of possible deductions, tax compliance, and estate planning	Mandatory
4. Bankruptcy and reorganization, including the value of the estate in bankruptcy and the assessment of the impact of proposed reorganization plans	Mandatory
5. Litigation support and dispute resolution, including infringement of intellectual property rights and breach of contract	Mandatory and discretionary
6. Impairment testing of goodwill as required by FASB statement no. 142 (Financial Accounting Standard Board, 2001a)	Mandatory
Based on Reilly and Schweihs (1999).	

an intellectual property right. Gröjer and Johanson (2000) call this the *tradability motive*. This category of problems also includes the sale or acquisition of a business, of which intangible assets are an important component (the merger and acquisitions motive [Gröjer and Johanson, 2000]). A valuation may be used to negotiate the transaction deal price.

The second category of motives covers the issue of financing securitization. Many financial institutions require an independent appraisal of intangible resources that are pledged as collateral against loan commitments or lines of credit.

The third category looks at tax issues. Many tax jurisdictions allow for the periodic amortization of the cost of acquired intangible assets. Special tax regulations relate to the transfer of intangible assets between subsidiaries of the same parent company. Many international conglomerates transfer intangible assets and use intangible asset royalty rates to shift taxable income into countries with lower income tax rates. The sale and leaseback construction used at the beginning of the 1990s by Dutch companies like Philips, DAF trucks, and Fokker is an example of using intellectual property to create tax benefits.

The fourth category of motives evolves around bankruptcy and reorganization. A valuation of the intangible assets of a debtor in possession may be necessary for bankruptcy-related accounting and taxation considerations. Bankruptcy judges are empowered to authorize the sale of intellectual property rights to outside parties because of reorganization.

The fifth category looks at litigation support and dispute resolution. Litigation may require the quantification of economic damages related to breach of contract and intellectual property infringement.

Finally the valuation of intangibles became relevant for external reporting with the introduction of FASB statement no. 142 (Financial Accounting Standard Board, 2001a). This statement from the FASB states that goodwill and intangible assets that have indefinite useful lives will no longer be amortized but instead will be tested annually for impairment. This means that their fair value must be compared with their recorded amounts. This requires estimating a fair value of certain types of intangible assets.

Reflection

It is interesting to see how adopting an intangible perspective can result in as much as 19 categories of problem definitions. Yet, not all of them are adequate or precise enough to guide us toward solutions. This leads to the "jumping to solutions" problem. Others lead us to very specific solutions. This underpins the notion covered in Chapter 2, that the way we define a problem directs our solutions. Let me show you what I mean.

Inadequate Problem Definitions

Some categories are insufficient in justifying the need for the valuation of intangible resources. Measurement is neither a necessary nor a sufficient requisite for management. The existence of a value gap between book value and market value is in itself not enough to justify the valuation of intangible resources.

Improving the management of intangible resources in itself is a noble cause but the leap to measurement is still big. The argument is that if we start to measure the value of intangibles, they will receive more management attention and this will improve the way they are managed. This hypothesis needs further testing. The question is whether measurement is the first place to start if we want to improve the management of intangibles.

Internal Management Problem Definitions

When we look at the remaining internal management problems, we see they can be grouped further into two types of problem definitions. One type looks at the retrospective problem of measuring the results of past events by monitoring the effects of action or measuring income in a reliable way. Another type looks at the prospective problem of improving company strategy by creating resource-based strategies, translating these strategies into action, and weighing the effects of alternative actions. This is a rather distinct difference, so any designer of management methods will probably need to make a choice: Do I want to improve monitoring or do I want to improve strategy development and execution? Both types of questions will probably lead to different functional requirements and will require different solutions. Still, as discussed later in this chapter, many authors claim their method is a cure to many diseases. There is little empirical evidence for this claim.

External Reporting Problem Definitions

The problems around the external reporting of intangible resources are a rather different set of problems. This group is less diverse and there is a strong relationship between the underlying problem definitions. Also, there is more empirical evidence regarding the nature and consequences of these problems. There is empirical proof that the usefulness of financial information is deteriorating, that this leads to a lack of transparency (especially in the field of innovation), that this leads to information asymmetry and mispricing of companies, and that this makes it more difficult for certain types of companies to raise capital. These problems again lead to a different set of requirements and probably require different solutions.

Statutory and Transactional Reasons

Statutory reasons for valuing intangible resources are the result of situations in which it is mandatory to carry out a valuation exercise. In some of these circumstances, the method that needs to be used is specified. FASB statement no. 142 (Financial Accounting Standard Board, 2001a), for example, states the kind of fair value assessment required to perform impairment testing. In the case of litigation, the court demands that the valuation be carried out according to professional standards (Reilly and Schweihs, 1999). In this case, the requirements for the valuation method are given. The next section shows that the methods that fulfill these requirements are already available. When the motive for valuation is a transaction, the trader is free to use a method of choice. In many cases, a standard financial valuation, using a cost, market, or income approach (discussed in the next section), or a combination of these, is sufficient.

How: Solutions and Results

I have grouped the 25 methods, using the distinction between financial valuation methods, value measurement methods, value assessment methods, and measurement methods as presented in Chapter 1 (Table 3.7). The decisive factors are the use of money as the denominator of value, the use of values as criteria, and the observability of the criteria or measured variable.

HRA is a label for a number of methods. It encompasses financial valuation methods, value measurement methods, and measurement methods (see Appendix A, Section A.6). Therefore, HRA appears three times in Table 3.7.

Twelve methods are financial valuation methods that use money as the denominator of value. The other 15 do not use money. As we saw in Chapter 1, values are a prerequisite for valuation. Of the 15 methods, six contain values that act as yardsticks. Five of the methods that contain yardsticks use measurement to determine value. Only Viedma's (2001) intellectual capital benchmarking system relies on expert judgment. His method is an example of a value assessment

Table 3.7

The 25 Methods Grouped by Type			
Section in Appendix A	Method	Community	Type of method
A.2	Calculated intangible value	Accounting	Financial valuation
A.4	Economic Value Added™	Performance measurement	Financial valuation
A.6	Human resource accounting	Human resource	Financial valuation
A.11	Intangibles scoreboard	Accounting	Financial valuation
A.15	iValuing factor	Accounting	Financial valuation
A.17	Market-to-book value	Accounting	Financial valuation
A.18	Options approach	Valuation	Financial valuation
A.20	Sullivan's work	Intellectual capital	Financial valuation
A.21	Technology factor	Valuation	Financial valuation
A.22	Tobin's Q	Accounting	Financial valuation
A.23	Valuation approaches	Valuation	Financial valuation
A.24	Value-Added Intellectual Coefficient™	Intellectual capital	Financial valuation
A.1	Balanced scorecard	Performance measurement	Value measurement
A.5	Holistic value approach	Intellectual capital	Value measurement
A.6	Human resource accounting	Human resource	Value measurement
A.7	Intellectual capital audit	Intellectual capital	Value measurement
A.9	Inclusive Value Methodology™	Intellectual capital	Value measurement
A.12	Intellectual capital benchmarking system	Intellectual capital	Value assessment
A.3	Citation-weighted patents	Accounting	Measurement
A.6	Human resource accounting	Human resource	Measurement
A.8	Intellectual capital–index	Intellectual capital	Measurement
A.10	Intangible asset monitor	Intellectual capital	Measurement
A.13	Intellectual capital dynamic value	Intellectual capital	Measurement
A.14	Intellectual capital statement	Intellectual capital	Measurement
A.16	Konrad group	Intellectual capital	Measurement
A.19	Skandia navigator	Intellectual capital	Measurement
A.25	Value chain scoreboard	Accounting	Measurement

method. Nine methods do not use values, norms, or other yardsticks and we therefore cannot consider them valuation methods. They are merely measurement methods.

The holistic value approach and the Inclusive Value Methodology™ combine indicators and financial attributes into one "value space," making them hybrid methods. I include them with the other value measurement methods because their focus is on indicators. The technology factor method uses nonfinancial criteria to help calculate a financial value. I include it in the financial valuation methods.

Lev (2000, 2001) and Lev and Zarowin (1999) have developed three proposals for changing and complementing current accounting practice to improve external reporting. These suggestions fall outside the scope of this book but are worth mentioning. Their most modest proposal is to improve the generally accepted accounting principles (GAAP) by mandating the capitalization of intangible investment when the project passes successfully a significant technological feasibility test. In this way, certain investments are recognized as assets the moment there is more certainty that they will produce future earnings. A second, more radical proposal is to restate financial statements from previous years when the earnings of investments or reorganizations become evident. The third and most radical proposal is to develop a complementary accounting system that recognizes all investments that meet the economic definition of an asset, without any reliability or verifiability restrictions. This economic asset-based information system is maintained in the double-entry manner along with GAAP.

Financial Valuation Methods

Table 3.8 provides an overview of the financial valuation methods. The methods focus on different problems and have different scopes. Most of them attempt to cover all types of intangible resources. Others only look at intellectual property, technology, or human resources. Three use the market-to-book ratio as a basis for their calculations. Four apply an income approach using retrospective income data. Four others apply an income approach using prospective income data. I review the most important approaches here, but reviews of all approaches can be found in Appendix A.

Table 3.8

Overview of Financial Valuation Methods

Section in Appendix A	Method	Community	Problem Definition	Scope	Approach	Time Span
A.15	Calculated intangible value	Accounting	Internal management	N/A	Market-to-book ratio	Retrospective
A.17	Market-to-book value	Accounting	Internal management and external reporting	All intangibles	Market-to-book ratio	Retrospective
A.22	Tobin's Q	Accounting	Internal management and external reporting	All intangibles	Market-to-book ratio	Retrospective
A.24	Value-Added Intellectual Coefficient™	Intellectual capital	Internal management and external reporting	All intangibles	Income and cost	Retrospective
A.2	Calculated intangible value	Accounting	Statutory and transactional	All intangibles	Income	Retrospective

A.20	Sullivan's work	Intellectual capital	Internal management and external reporting	Subset: intellectual property	Income	Prospective and retrospective
A.11	Intangibles scoreboard	Accounting	Internal management and external reporting	All intangibles	Income	Prospective
A.18	Options approach	Valuation	Internal management	All or subset	Income	Prospective
A.21	Technology factor	Valuation	Internal management	Subset: technology	Income	Prospective
A.6	Human resource accounting	Human resource	Internal management and external reporting	Subset: human resource	All	Prospective and retrospective
A.23	Valuation approaches	Valuation	All three	All or subset	All	Prospective and retrospective

General Introduction to Valuation

In the literature on valuation methods (Lee, 1996; Reilly and Schweihs, 1999; Smith and Parr, 1994), one can find three approaches to financial valuation:

1. Cost approach
2. Market approach
3. Income approach

The *cost approach* is based on the economic principles of substitution and price equilibrium. These principles assert that an investor will pay no more for an investment than the cost to obtain an investment of equal utility (Reilly and Schweihs, 1999). Thus, the price of a new resource is commensurate with the economic value of the service that the resource can provide during its life.

The problem with the cost approach is that in many cases cost is not a good indication of value. Many of the most important factors that drive value are not reflected in this approach. These factors include (Smith and Parr, 1994):

- The amount of benefits associated with the resource
- The trend of the economic benefits (increasing or diminishing)
- The duration over which the economic benefits will be enjoyed
- The risks associated with receiving the expected economic benefits

Furthermore, all relevant forms of obsolescence of the subject resource have to be identified, quantified, and subtracted from the cost of the resource to estimate the value. The cost approach is appropriate to value intangible resources when setting transfer prices, royalty rates, or when estimating the amount of damages sustained by the resource owner in an infringement or other type of litigation.

The *market approach* is based on the economic principles of competition and equilibrium. These principles assert that in a free and unrestricted market, supply and demand factors will drive the price of any good to a point of equilibrium (Reilly and Schweihs, 1999). In the market approach, an analysis is made of similar resources that have recently been sold or licensed. The market data are used to estimate a market value. The market approach can only be used if data are available on the transaction of intangible resources that are similar to the subject resources. When the subject resources are unique, which is often the case, this approach is not appropriate.

The *income approach* is based on the economic principle of anticipation. The value of intangible resources is the current value of the expected economic income generated by these resources. When applying an income approach the following requirements must be fulfilled:

1. Income projection requirement
2. Income funnel requirement
3. Income allocation requirement
4. Useful life estimation requirement
5. Income capitalization requirement

Income Projection Requirement

The income approach is based on a projection of economic income and thereby on somehow predicting the future. Therefore, it always contains a level of uncertainty and subjectivity. "All income approach analyses are based on the premise that the analyst can project economic income with a reasonable degree of certainty. . . . The term reasonable degree of certainty is, by its very nature, subjective" (Reilly and Schweihs, 1999, p. 182).

Income Funnel Requirement

Intangible resources generate not all the income produced by a business enterprise. Tangible resources and networking capital also contribute to the income generated. The problem is how to assign the overall enterprise income to the constituent components of the business enterprise, including all tangible and intangible resources. This requirement is referred to as

> a funnel of income adjustment because all of the income that is generated by a business enterprise can be analogized to the top (or wide) end of a funnel. For analytical purposes, we are only interested in that portion of the total enterprise income that gets down to the bottom (or narrow) end of the funnel—that is, that relates directly to the subject intangible asset. The adjustment is often necessarily in order to avoid double-counting or over-estimating intangible asset values (Reilly and Schweihs, 1999, p. 177).

This adjustment should include a fair return on the investment of all the resources used in the production of economic income, especially investments in tangible assets and networking capital.

Income Allocation Requirement

The economic income that is left after the funnel of income adjustments can be attributed to the intangible resources of the business enterprise. The next problem is how to allocate this income among the various (bundles of) intangible resources. This allocation should take into account the synergy of the combined intangible resources within the company.

Useful Life Estimation Requirement

Crucial in any income approach analysis is the estimation of the remaining useful life of the intangible resources. This is also referred to as the *forecast period* (Copeland et al., 1990), the *projection period* (Reilly and Schweihs, 1999) or the *cash flow duration* (Smith and Parr, 1994). There are at least eight different ways to look at the remaining useful life of intangible resources:

1. "Economic life, depending on the ability to provide a fair rate of return
2. Functional life, depending on the ability to continue to perform
3. Technological life, depending on changes in technology
4. Legal or statutory life
5. Contractual life
6. Judicial life, as a result of a court rule
7. Physical life
8. Analytical life, as a result of an analysis of similar intangible resources" (Reilly and Schweihs, 1999, p. 241)

Income Capitalization Requirement

To come to a current value of future income, the economic income generated by the subject intangible is divided by an appropriate rate of return. This discount rate reflects

- The expected growth rate of the income stream generated by the subject intangible
- The cost of capital appropriate for an investment in the subject intangible
- A compensation for inflation
- The degree of risk associated with an investment in the intangible

The income approach is often the best alternative compared with the cost and market approach but requires assumptions on income projection, income funneling, income allocation, useful life estimation, and income capitalization. According to options theory, the problem with the income approach is that it assumes that the investment decision cannot be deferred. The possibility of deferral creates two additional sources of value (Luerman, 1998a):

1. If we can pay later, we can earn the time value of money on the deferred expenditure.
2. While waiting, the world can change and the value of the investment may go up (or down).

Furthermore, the decision to make an irreversible investment means we cannot put this money into other possible investments. Options are lost, which is an opportunity cost that must be included as part of the cost of the investment. In addition, the value of creating other options should be taken into consideration. An investment may look uneconomical but may create other options in the future that are valuable. To incorporate these sources of value in the decision-making process, options theory draws from the research that has been done on the valuation of financial options. Options theory adds an additional metric to the current net value matrix, which Luerman (1998b) calls the *volatility metric*. This includes the uncertainty of the future value of the assets in question and how long a decision can be deferred. If we then allow investment options to influence other future options, we can use "nests" of options upon options to depict investment strategies and to calculate the value.

The Problem with Market-To-Book Ratios

Methods based on the *market-to-book ratio*, like market-to-book value as proposed by Stewart (1997), Tobin's Q (Stewart, 1997) and the iValuing factor (Standfield, 2001) are widely criticized. As we saw earlier, comparing book value with market value is like comparing apples with oranges. Book value is the reported stockholders' equity (less the liquidating value of any preferred shares), which represents the difference between assets and liabilities, both of which are most often valued at historic costs. Market value is equal to the perceived current value of the future cash flow of the company.

That the residual between market and book value contains more than only intangibles becomes clear when we look at the underlying theory of the market-to-book ratio. According to White et al. (1997), in theory they are the same. Market value equals the sum total of the discounted expected cash flows. For an infinite and constant cash flow this is

$$Value = \frac{CF}{r}$$

where *CF* is the cash flow and *r* is the expected rate of return. *CF* is equal to

$$CF = r^* B,$$

where B is the book value of the firm and r^* is the actual rate of return. If we assume that the firm earns the required rate of return r ($r^* = r$), then CF is rB and value = B.

If we assume that the actual rate of return does not equal the required rate of return, the equation can be transformed into

$$Value = B + \frac{(r^* - r)}{r} B$$

The component $\frac{(r^* - r)}{r} B$ is a measure of the firm's economic good-will—the excess of market value over book value. Firms with growth opportunities will have an actual rate of return that is bigger than the expected rate of return. Their market value will be higher than their book value. Therefore, the difference between market value and book value is in part the result of expected growth opportunities and not only of intangible resources.

Rutledge (1997) offers additional explanations of the growing difference between market value and book value since 1981. Falling inflation has shifted enormous amounts of capital from investments in tangible assets such as real property into securities. This growing demand pushed the bond prices higher, raising the market value of companies. In addition, companies have gotten rid of their tangible assets on the balance sheet by selling operating assets and renting them back.

Another problem with the market-to-book ratio is that book values most often are valued at a historical cost basis. This is not correct. When we want to subtract market value and book value, we need to reduce both types of value to the same denominator. However, in doing so we must be careful not to be caught in a circular approach. Subtracting book value and market value requires the need to transform the book value of the assets and liabilities into a type of value equal to a value that comes out of a market valuation. This means we need to revalue each asset and liability using a new definition of value—a definition in line with a definition of value of the company as a whole as determined through the stock market. This definition includes a proper premise of value and standard of value (see Chapter 4). The market value of a company is the value under the premise of "value in continued use." This means the assets and liabilities need to be appraised under the premise of value of "value in continuous use, as part of a going concern business enterprise." The proper standard of value to adopt would probably be market value. Reilly and Schweihs (1999) define market value as "the most probable (or most likely) price that an asset would bring in a competitive and open market under all conditions requisite to a fair sale, including the condition that the buyer and seller are each acting prudently and knowledgeably, and assuming the price is not affected by undue stimulus" (p. 60). If we ignore the problem that this definition of value is still quite dissimilar from value as determined by the stock market (because that market also includes buyers and sellers who are not acting prudently and knowledgeably), then it still is difficult to estimate market value for all assets and liabilities. It becomes even more difficult if we then add the requisite of applying the correct premise of value. This implies we need to appraise all assets and liabilities at market value under the premises of continued use. This means we cannot use, for example, the market price of a piece of machinery, but we need to determine the "price" of that piece of machinery as it is in use as part of the business enterprise. There is only one market that can give us such a price, and that is the stock market. So, to revalue all assets and liabilities at market value we need to use the stock market value of the company as a whole and subtract all intangible value—the value not related to the assets and liabilities. However, we cannot do this because the intangible value was what we were looking for in the first place. Therefore, we are caught in a circular approach.

Retrospective Income Approach Methods

The valuation methods within the sample that use an *income approach* can be divided into two types. The calculated intangible value as proposed by Stewart (1997), the VAIC (Pulic, 2000a,b, 2002), and EVA (Stewart III, 1994) are retrospective methods that use historical financial figures to calculate economic income. The intangibles scorecard (Gu and Lev, 2002; Lev, 1999; Webber, 2000), the technology factor (Khoury, 1994, 1998) and Sullivan's (2000) method for determining the purchase price for an acquired company are prospective methods that use financial forecasts to calculate economic income.

The calculated intangible value method is based on the assumption that the premium on a company's value is a result of its intangible resources. This can be a premium in market value, a premium compared with normalized earnings, or a premium return on assets. The calculated intangible value uses the latter method. It calculates the current value of the premium earnings after taxes if earnings are compared with the industry average return on assets. The calculated intangible value does not reflect the value of all intangible resources. It only calculates the contribution of unidentified intangible resources to premium earnings. Intangibles that contribute to normal earnings are not included. Therefore, calculated intangible value does capture some of the value of intangibles, but how much is unknown. This problem surfaces once we try to determine the calculated intangible value for a company that performs below industry average. In this case, calculated intangible value is a negative value, which would indicate a negative value of its intangibles. This cannot be true.

The VAIC calculates economic income (which Pulic [2000b] calls *value added*) in a special way because it treats labor expense as an asset, not a cost. The consequences are fourfold:

1. In calculating the value added of a firm, Pulic (2000b) excludes all labor expenses.
2. Labor expenses are treated as an asset that Pulic (2000b) calls *human capital*. The value of human capital can be expressed by the expenditures for employees.
3. It is possible to calculate the efficiency of this asset by computing how much value added one unit spent on employees creates (Pulic, 2000b).
4. Labor expense should no longer be an item on the profit and loss account; instead, it should be recognized as an asset on the balance sheet (Pulic, 2002).

Pulic (2000a) calculates value added and the value of three types of intellectual capital: human capital, structural capital, and capital employed. According to Pulic (2000b), the value of human capital can be expressed by the labor expense. The value of structural capital is equal to value added minus human capital. The value of capital employed is equal to the book value of the net assets of the firm (Firer and Williams, 2003). Pulic (2002) then sets out to calculate the ratio between each of the three forms of capital and value added, resulting in capital employed efficiency (CEE), human capital efficiency (HCE), and structural capital efficiency (SCE). To come to an overall measure of efficiency, Pulic (2002) adds the three efficiency measures:

$$VAIC = CEE + HCE + SCE$$

The approach looks interesting because it uses publicly available data and allows for comparison between companies and even regions and countries (International Business Efficiency Consulting, 2003). However, we can seriously question the assumptions on which it is based. Consequently, the method produces some very dissatisfying results.

First, the VAIC method does not properly separate expenses from assets. Labor expenses may include expenses that provide future benefits (like training expenses or labor on R&D), but a large part of labor expenses will provide immediate benefits, and this part should *not* be treated as an asset.

Second, what is puzzling is that the method confuses stocks and flows. Value added is a flow indicator. Labor expense is a flow indicator, but the VAIC method treats it as a stock. If we were to accept that labor expenses yield future benefits, then we still would need to treat it as a flow, in this case as an *investment* into human capital, not as the value of human capital itself.

Third, the aim of the VAIC method is to calculate the efficiency of the three types of intellectual capital. However, simply calculating ratios does not provide information about the *contribution* of these types of intellectual capital to value creation. What we need is insight into the causal relationship between these types of capital and value added.

Fourth, the method ignores the fact that value added is not only the result of human capital, structural capital, and capital employed individually, but it is also the result of the synergies between these three.

Finally, the solution to add all efficiency indicators to come to one overall indicator is an interesting idea but produces some strange results. When a company has little net assets (for example, because of some big liabilities), capital used would be small to zero, and as a result CEE and VAIC become very big. So, big liabilities can result in very positive VAIC scores, which is another dissatisfying result.

The third retrospective financial valuation method is EVA. According to Stewart III (1994), management decision making must be focused on allocating, managing, and redeploying scarce resources to maximize shareholder value. Stern Stewart & Co. developed EVA to help do this. EVA allows managers to calculate the current net value and thus the shareholder value that results from their decisions. In its basic form, it is calculated by subtracting the operating expense (including tax) and the financing expense (cost of capital × capital) from sales. The result is the economic value that has been added, taking into account the cost of capital needed to create that value. The crucial point is that EVA is charged for capital at a rate that compensates investors for bearing the firm's explicit business risks.

It has never been the intention of the EVA method to measure the value of intangible resources. Yet, EVA is on many lists of intellectual capital measurement methods (Bontis, 2001; Bontis et al., 1999; Sveiby, 2002; Van den Berg, 2003). However, EVA is not a stock but a flow indicator. It therefore cannot be a measure of the value of intangible resources. At most, it indicates the added value of a resource. But does it measure the added value of intangible resources? There are two arguments in favor of this. One is what Bontis et al. (1999) call the *implicit argument*. This argument states that effective management of knowledge assets will increase EVA. Therefore, EVA can be used as an indicator to measure the performance of managing knowledge assets. However, this argumentation has two limitations. First, EVA states explicitly that the management of resources is not important, but implementing projects that create more value than their cost of capital is important. In many cases the aim to create more value than the cost of capital leads to decisions that result in low-risk cash flow in the short to medium term. These decisions may not add to the long-term sustainability of a company's knowledge assets.[1] The second limitation is that besides the management of knowledge assets there are many other factors that influence EVA. Consequently, we cannot contribute changes in EVA solely to knowledge assets.

Strassmann (1998, 1999) uses a different argument for employing EVA as an indicator for the value of intangibles. His term for EVA is *knowledge value added*. This is the value added by a firm's Knowledge Capital[TM] (a trademark owned by Strassmann, Inc.). Strassmann (1998) defines Knowledge Capital as the employees' accumulated knowledge about a company. According to Strassmann (1998), EVA is the net surplus economic value created by the firm, because the suppliers, the tax authorities, and all labor and shareholder expenses are already fully accounted for. He states:

> The creation of management value-added is something that defies the laws of conservation of energy. These laws state that the output of any system in the universe can never be greater than its input. Delivering a positive management value-added must be therefore an act of creativity that springs forth from something that is intangible, as if it were an artistic conception. The source of this creative energy is Knowledge Capital. This ephemeral element can be quantified only indirectly by observing how much management value added it yields. (Strassmann, 1998, p. 5).

---

[1] However, EVA does include adjustments to encourage managers to give proper considerations to the long term as well.

To come from EVA as an indicator of knowledge value added to the value of Knowledge Capital Strassmann simply divides EVA by the price of knowledge capital (using the interest rate a firm pays for its long-term debt) because "the value-added is the interest rate earned from an accumulation of knowledge residing in the firm" (Strassmann, 1998, p. 5).

This argument is limited in three ways. First, economic value added is not produced solely by intangibles. Tangible assets can also produce added value above the cost of the capital needed to acquire the assets. This is why companies that are low knowledge intensive can still create added value. Therefore, an unknown portion of EVA is attributable to tangible assets and not to "an act of creativity." Second, knowledge capital is not the only form of intellectual capital. Structural and relationship capital also contribute to value added. Therefore, an unknown portion of the intangible part of EVA is attributable to structural and relational resources. Finally, EVA is not the interest earned from a particular resource base; it is the other way around. EVA is the result of using a resource base with a certain rate of efficiency. If one would like to calculate the value of this resource base, one would need to divide the value added by a rate of return on these resources instead of an interest rate. This rate of return is unknown. Therefore, one cannot calculate the value of intangible resources using the EVA method.

Prospective Income Approach Methods

According to Lev (as cited in Webber, 2000), the main problem with EVA is that it is purely based on history. It is a method for accounting in the past whereas one should look at knowledge's potential for creating future earnings. Gu and Lev (2002) have created the intangibles scoreboard. The scorecard calculates future earnings that are created by intangible resources, and uses these intangible-driven earnings (IDEs) to calculate intangible capital (Gu and Lev, 2002). The method starts by looking at company earnings. Because earnings tend to fluctuate over time and only reflect the past, Gu and Lev (2002) calculate an average based on three years of historical data plus earnings forecasts for one, two, and three years. The result is an estimate of annual normalized earnings. To come from these normalized earnings to IDEs, Gu and Lev (2002) calculate the expected rates of return on tangible and financial assets. Using a normal rate of return (7% for physical capital and 4.5% for financial capital) and the current value of these assets (based on adjusted book values), they calculate the earnings linked to tangible and financial assets. Subtracting these from normalized earnings results in IDEs. Lastly, they forecast the series of IDEs over three future periods based on a three-stage valuation model. For future years one through five, they use financial analysts' growth forecasts. For the next five years, they converge this forecast into the long-term growth of the economy (3%) and from year 11 to infinity, they use a 3% growth rate. Then they use a discount rate that reflects the above-average risk of these earnings to calculate the current value of these earnings, the value of intangible capital. The intangibles scoreboard is based on the idea that tangible, financial, and intangible resources produce earnings. IDEs are the residual after a fair return for tangible and financial capital has been subtracted.

What is interesting is that Lev (1999) uses the result to develop seven additional ratios that can help to shed light on the knowledge intensity and efficiency of companies:

1. Intangible capital margin (IDEs/sales)
2. Intangible capital operating margin (IDEs/operating income)
3. The ratio of intangible capital to book capital, to indicate the degree to which a company is knowledge based
4. The intangible capital margin (intangible capital/sales)
5. The comprehensive value (intangible capital and book value)
6. Market-to-comprehensive value (A 1 : 1 ratio would indicate that market value is mostly derived from past performance and short-term earnings forecast.)
7. The return on investment of R&D (intangible capital/investments in R&D)

There are two limitations to this approach. First, Gu and Lev (2002) calculate a fair return on the tangible and financial resources used, which is not the same as the contribution of these resources to earnings. The actual contribution can be lower or higher. More troublesome is a second limitation that is that, in fact, the earnings are the result of *combining* tangible, financial, and intangible assets. This synergy produces value. This makes it difficult to funnel part of the earnings to each of the capital types. However, Gu and Lev's (2002) thorough statistical analyses show that IDE and intangible capital are superior measures in explaining company performance. We can calculate these measures using publicly available data. They allow for comparison across industries and over time. We can us them to distinguish between overvalued and undervalued stocks.

The technology factor method attempts to calculate the fair market value of a specific technology. This can be a group of patents, individual patents, know-how, a copyright, or a trade secret. It uses a discounted cash flow (DCF) approach to calculate the net present value (NPV) of the incremental cash flow derived from the practice of a specific technology within a specific business. The technology factor method consists of two parts. Part 1 is the calculation of the NPV of the incremental business. This is a straightforward income approach to valuation (see Section A. 23 in Appendix A). Part 2 is the estimation of a technology factor between 0 to 100% that approximates how much of the total incremental cash flow can be attributed to the specific technology. The technology factor is based on a qualitative assessment by a multidisciplinary team of experts. This team looks at utility issues and competitive advantage issues. The utility issues include

- Usefulness of the technology to the company
- Usefulness of the technology to others
- Capital required for implementation
- Time required for implementation
- Useful life of the technology
- Other

The competitive issues includes questions like

- Does the technology allow competitive differentiation?
- Are there alternative technologies?
- What is its legal strength?
- What is the anticipated competitive response?

Each issue is assessed using −, 0, or +. The minus sign signals negative impact on value and the plus sign signals creation of value. Then for the utility issues and the competitive issues an overall assessment is made, resulting in a low, medium, or high value for the technology factor range (low, 0–30%; medium, 30–50%; high, 50–75%). Both assessments are then combined into an overall range, and an overall technology factor score is estimated. This score is multiplied by the NPV to calculate the value of the technology.

The technology factor suffers from double counting. When we look at the various issues listed under utility and competitive advantage, we see that these issues address elements that already have been covered when calculating the NPV. For example, the issue of "usefulness" is an issue that has already been covered when solving the income projection problem of the NPV calculation. The issue of "capital required for implementation" is estimated when calculating projected cash flow. The issue of "useful life of the technology" is incorporated into the useful life estimation, which is also part of the NPV calculation. The issue of "legal strength" is incorporated as a risk component in the discount factor. Thus, some of the issues are addressed twice: as part of the calculation of the NPV and again as part of the technology factor. This will most likely result in a lower total value. Surprisingly, the problems of income funneling and income allocation are not addressed in the checklist. The technology factor does not calculate which part of the cash flow can be attributed to the technology. To summarize, the technology factor solves problems that (should) have been resolved when calculating the NPV. At the same time, it does not address the problems that it should address.

Value Measurement Methods

Sveiby (1997) describes why we need measurement methods instead of valuation methods for measuring intangible resources: "Still there exists no comprehensive system for measuring intangible assets that uses money as the common denominator and at the same time is practical and useful for managers. Depending on the purpose for measuring, I do not think such a system is necessary, either. Knowledge flows and intangible assets are essentially non-financial. We need new proxies" (p. 156).

Table 3.9 provides an overview of the value measurement methods in the sample. The methods focus on different problems and have different scopes. They have in common that they include values that are used as yardsticks to determine a nonmonetary value of intangible resources. Three of the methods attempt to cover all types of intangible resources. HRA looks only at human resources. Two attempt to combine indicators into one overall measure.

Balanced Scorecard

The French *tableau de bord* was probably the first tool to monitor company performance with the help of indicators. It dates back to 1932 and is often regarded as the predecessor of the balanced scorecard (Bourguignon et al., 2001). In its original form the *tableau de bord* was a set of physical performance measures covering various production statistics. When Kaplan and Norton (1992) introduced

Table 3.9

Overview of Value Measurement Methods

Section in Appendix A	Method	Community	Problem Definition	Scope	No. of Indicators
A.1	Balanced scorecard	Performance measurement	Internal management	No intangibles	>1
A.7	Intellectual capital audit	Intellectual capital	Internal management	All intangibles	>1
A.5	Holistic value approach	Intellectual capital	Internal management and external reporting	All intangibles	1
A.9	Inclusive Value Methodology™	Intellectual capital	Internal management and external reporting	All intangibles	1
A.6	Human resource accounting	Human resource	Internal management and external reporting	Subset, human resources	Diverse

their balanced scorecard in the United States, the use of indicators to supplement accounting information became popular. The scorecard translates the vision and strategy of a company into objectives and performance measures in four areas: the financial perspective, the customer perspective, the learning and growth perspective, and the internal perspective.

Although the balanced scorecard is often considered a tool for measuring stocks and flows of intangible resources (Bontis et al., 1999; Luthy, 1998; Sveiby, 2002; Van den Berg, 2003), it is questionable whether it actually does. The scorecard identifies objectives within each of the four perspectives and measures the level of goal attainment using indicators and targets. In a later publication, Kaplan and Norton (2001) use the concept of intangibles extensively, but it is not essential to the way they define the problems they intend to solve or the solutions they propose. Leaving out the term *intangible assets* would not make any difference. In fact, the balanced scorecard does not measure the value of intangible resources, not even in the learning and growth perspective. What *is* measured in the learning and growth perspective is the level of goal achievement in specific improvement areas. These improvement areas have to do with competencies, technology, and corporate climate. The scorecard does not measure the size or value of stocks of intangibles, nor does it measure flows from one type of intellectual capital to another. Some of the indicators used may measure aspects of intangible resources (for example, customer satisfaction). However, they are selected because they are key success factors within the overall strategy, not because they represent important intangible resources. Kaplan and Norton (2001) state that today's economy "calls for tools that describe knowledge-based assets" (p. 2). However, the balanced scorecard does not do that. Sveiby (2001) makes a similar point when he states that the balance scorecard is not a stock flow perspective, whereas his intangible asset monitor is.

Intellectual Capital Audit

Brooking's (1996) intellectual capital audit is one of the few well-documented methods to audit various types of intangible resources. Brooking (1996) describes 30 ways to audit various aspects of intangibles and provides 158 questions touching on a range of issues (Van den Berg, 2003). Each aspect is, in fact, an indicator of some kind. The audit is a value measurement approach because the method includes yardsticks for the optimal state of each aspect of each asset. The intellectual capital audit gives a comprehensive overview of the strengths and weaknesses of all intangible resources.

Brooking (1996) recommends that companies undertake a six-step intellectual capital audit:

1. Step 1 is understanding the transition the company needs to go through as well as the goal of the audit, its domain, and its constraints.
2. The second step is to identify the company's intangibles and to determine the set of aspects of each asset.
3. The third step is to determine the optimal state of each aspect of each asset. The optimal state functions as a yardstick for the audit.
4. Step 4 requires choosing the appropriate audit method for each type of asset. Brooking (1996) describes 30 different methods for the four types of intellectual capital.
5. The fifth step encompasses the actual audit of each aspect of each asset.
6. During step 6, this information is documented in a database. The current state of each aspect is compared with the target value and is indexed on a scale from 0 to 5 points, with 5 points indicating the optimal state. The scores are plotted on a target. The size of the dots (large or small) reflects the importance of the assets. This provides an instant overview of the strengths and weaknesses of intellectual capital.

However, Brooking (1996) does not provide much help for the most difficult steps in the audit process: how to identify relevant intangibles to audit, how to determine what aspect to audit, and how to set a target for each aspect.

Holistic Value Approach and Inclusive Value Methodology

Both M'Pherson and Pike (2001a,b) and Pike and Roos (2000) developed a method that consolidates measures of value into one indicator of value. Pike and Roos (2000) developed the holistic value approach; M'Pherson and Pike (2001a,b) developed a similar tool called the Inclusive Value Methodology.

The problem with the consolidation of separate indicators of value is that is requires consolidating both apples and oranges. M'Pherson and Pike (2001a,b) have made a tremendous contribution to the field of value measurement by developing an extensive list of requirements for the proper consolidation of multidimensional value measurement based on measurement theory. When a method meets all the requirements, it can add apples and oranges in a methodologically sound way.

For example, when translating objectives or key success factors into indicators, there is the requirement of completeness: The indicators must cover the full meaning of the objective as understood by the stakeholder. This ensures that the overview of indicators represents all the important intangible resources. The requirement of normalization demands that for each indicator a lowest acceptable value and a highest achievable value are determined. These values act as yardsticks for value measurement. A third requirement states that when combining the various normalized indicators, the appropriate combinatory rule must be used. According to M'Pherson and Pike (2001a) the additive rule (1 + 1 = 2) that is often used (for example, by Roos et al. [1997] and Bounfour [2002]) is an exception.

The holistic value approach and Inclusive Value Methodology™ result in one nonfinancial measurement of value. This solves the problem associated with measurement methods like the Skandia navigator, which often contain long lists of indicators (Roos et al., 1997). These lists make it difficult to discern the forest from the trees. Moreover, it makes it difficult to make trade-off decisions. A management decision may result in five indicators going up and three indicators going down. Is that better than if they all remained the same? The holistic value approach and the Inclusive Value Methodology are especially suited to help making trade-off decisions, especially in situations in which the interests of various parties need to be considered. The downside is that it is rather complicated to implement them. Companies will need probably specialist help.

Value Assessment Methods

In my sample of methods for the valuation of intangible resources, only one method can be considered a valuation assessment. This is Viedma's Intellectual Capital Benchmarking System (ICBS). Another example not included in the sample is Edvinsson's IC Rating™[2]. A valuation assessment does contain values as yardsticks; however, it does not rely on measurement to determine value because these yardsticks are not translated into directly observable phenomena. Instead, the method depends on personal judgment by the evaluator.

Viedma's (2001b) primary concern is the competitive gap that exists between a company and its world-class competitor. He states that "[k]nowing the causes that produce the competitive gap between the company and the international market leaders in the same business activity is the key issue in order to increase company competitiveness"

---

[2] See www.intellectualcapital.se.

(p. 5). This gap exists in every business unit. For every business unit, the world-class company against which to benchmark can be different. By benchmarking each business activity, Viedma (2001b) tries to gain insight into how to manage intellectual capital in an efficient way and to facilitate the process of learning from the best competitors.

The intellectual capital benchmarking system method uses a general model of business excellence to identify the factors to benchmark. This general model is a normative model describing "the foundations which all companies inevitably have to rely upon if they want to achieve high standards in that extraordinary competitive context of today's global markets" (Viedma, 1999, p. 7). There is a general model for operational processes, one for innovation processes and one for social capital. From this general model, Viedma (2001b) creates specific models for the specific business units of a company. These models include normative criteria for excellent performance. From these models, a set of questions is developed to measure whether these criteria apply to the company under investigation and to the world-class competitor. The criteria are measured on a scale from −5 to +5, indicating whether the company is doing worse or better than a competitor. All questions of the questionnaire have a response precision box that indicates the accuracy of each answer using a scale from 0 to 100 points. These measures are consolidated in a reliability index of the overall assessment. The results are presented as a *balance sheet*. Under the "assets" heading, all factors are placed on which the company is doing better than the competitor; the "liabilities" heading includes all factors on which the company scores worse. The factors are weighted and added, creating a weighted average.

The intellectual capital benchmarking system suffers from the same weakness as other value assessment methods. The assessment depends solely on the judgment of an assessor. This judgment has a strong impact on the outcome of the assessment. Viedma (2001b) acknowledges this problem, and it is the reason why he added the reliability index. Another weakness is that it is problematic to develop a general model of business excellence that is valid in all industries and all contexts.

Measurement Methods

Table 3.10 provides an overview of the remaining methods in the sample. A surprising 36% of the methods in the sample do not incorporate any values as yardsticks to determine value. We cannot consider these methods to be valuation methods. They are merely measurement methods. Yet, some authors of measurement methods

Table 3.10

Overview of Measurement Methods

Section in Appendix A	Method	Community	Problem Definition	Scope	No. of Indicators
A.19	Skandia navigator	Intellectual capital	Internal management and external reporting	All intangibles	>1
A.10	Intangible asset monitor	Intellectual capital	Internal management and external reporting	All intangibles	>1
A.14	Intellectual capital statement	Intellectual capital	Internal management and external reporting	Subset: knowledge management	>1
A.6	Human resource accounting	Human resource	Internal management and external reporting	Subset, human resource	>1
A.16	Konrad group	Intellectual capital	External reporting	Subset, human resource	>1
A.25	Value chain scoreboard	Accounting	External reporting	Subset, innovation	>1
A.3	Citation-weighted patents	Accounting	External reporting	Subset, patents	1
A.8	Intellectual capital–index	Intellectual capital	Internal management and external reporting	All intangibles	1
A.13	Intellectual capital dynamic value	Intellectual capital	Internal management	All intangibles	1

claim their method intends to measure value. Edvinsson and Malone (1997) state that their intellectual capital navigator fulfills the task to "[l]ook upward toward more sweeping measures of value" (p. 70). Roos et al. (1997) state that their intellectual capital–index "can help the company signify to the market its hidden value creation process, and thus help the market make a better assessment of the company's value" (p. 91).

Leaving out values that could act as a yardstick makes it difficult for managers and stakeholders to interpret the results (Andriessen, 2001). Yardsticks help to give meaning to a measurement by turning it into a valuation. Without the yardsticks, looking at the indicators in, for example, Skandia's intellectual capital supplements leaves you with a feeling of "so what?" Two hundred sixty-nine contracts per employee (Skandia, 1994), is that good or bad?

In the following paragraphs, I review seven of the nine measurement methods. Reviews of the citation-weighted patents method and HRA are included in Appendix A.

Skandia Navigator, Intangible Asset Monitor, and Intellectual Capital Statement

The Skandia navigator is the best-known example of a measurement method for measuring intellectual capital. It was developed by Edvinsson (Edvinsson and Malone, 1997), former corporate director of intellectual capital at the Swedish insurance company Skandia. The navigator consists of five groups of indicators, each of which focus on a different area of attention (Figure 3.4). The financial focus records the financial results of the company and looks at the past. The customer, human, and process focuses look at the present, whereas the renewal and development focus looks at the future.

Edvinsson's work is by no doubt the biggest contribution to the field of intellectual capital measurement. It is probably the most widely cited example of an intellectual capital measurement tool. It has added significantly to the general awareness about the importance of intangible resources and the shortcomings of traditional reporting. Edvinsson has developed the Navigator further into the IC Rating^{TM} method (Lundqvist, 2000), which has been applied to over 200 companies in Sweden, and a method to forecast the growth of IC using a mapping tool called the "digital IC-landscape" (Edvinsson, 2000).

Sveiby's (1997) intangible asset monitor is a framework for indicators that measure both levels and trends. His framework consists of a 3×3 matrix (see Table 3.11 for sample indicators). For each type of intangible asset, there should be indicators of growth and renewal, efficiency, and stability. Management should select one or two indicators for each cell.

Sveiby (1997) raises special attention to the issue of comparison. "As in all measurement systems, it is the comparisons that are interesting. A measurement tells nothing at all unless it is compared against a yardstick of some kind: another company, a previous year, or a budget, for example" (p.164). This is why he recommends measuring intangibles for at least three measurement cycles before attempting to evaluate the results.

A problem with the Skandia navigator is the long lists of indicators it contains (Roos et al., 1997). These lists make it difficult to see the forest for the trees. In addition, it makes it difficult to make trade-off

Figure 3.4

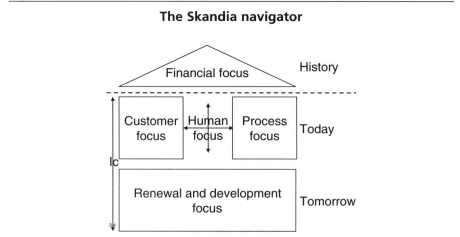

The Skandia navigator

Table 3.11

Intangible Asset Monitor			
Perspective	**Competence**	**Internal Structure**	**External Structure**
Growth and renewal	No. of years in the profession	Investment in information processing systems	Profitability per customer
Efficiency	Proportion of professionals in the company	Sales per support person	Satisfied customer index
Stability	Average age	Rookie ratio	Proportion of big customers
From Sveiby (1997).			

decisions. Another weak point with the Skandia navigator (as well as Sveiby's intangible assets monitor) is that it is difficult to interpret cause and effect. When two indicators go up, how do we know whether the first causes the second? Without insight into cause-and-effect relationships, it is difficult to diagnose a situation and develop corrective actions.

The intellectual capital statement described by Mouritsen et al. (2001a,c, 2002) intends to help companies apply knowledge management techniques in a systematic and comprehensive way. The intellectual capital statement uses three ways to indicate relationships between indicators. First, each statement contains a knowledge narrative describing the strategy of the firm, its ambition level, and the area in which the company and its employees must excel to create value. It contains management's finality relationships packed in a compelling story. Second, each intellectual capital statement contains a set of indicators. Mouritsen et al. (2001c) call this set an *intellectual capital accounting system*. This system consists of indicators that describe resources, qualifying activities, and the effects of the activities (Figure 3.5). The third element consists of so-called *sketches;* visualizations, for example, like the house-shaped figure of the Skandia navigator. What is interesting is that Mouritsen et al. (2001b) consider the indicators and their causal relationships unimportant for monitoring and

Figure 3.5

Intellectual capital accounting system

Management arena	Monitoring of effects	Qualification management	Portfolio management
Modality	Competencies	Qualifying activities	Portfolio
Areas / Domain	Effects	Activities	Resources
Employees	• • • •	• • • •	• • • •
Customers	• • • •	• • • •	• • • •
Process	• • • • •	• • • • •	• • • • •
Technology	• • • •	• • • •	• • • •

diagnosing situations. The indicators primarily demonstrate serious-ness on the part of top management. They allow inquiry into whether management is serious about implementing the strategy. "Indicators create seriousness because they are published. Stories create compre-hensiveness of the strategy proposed although it cannot be defined in its details. Sketches, which visualize the relations in the story, produce and suggest the connectivity in the indicators reported" (Mouritsen et al., 2001b, p. 418).

Konrad Group and the Value Chain Scoreboard

The three methods described in the previous section intend to improve internal management and external reporting using one method. The Konrad group (Sveiby et al., 1989) and Lev (2001) focus on improving external reporting only. The Konrad group proposes a list of 35 indicators that know-how companies should report, grouped into four categories:

1. Know-how capital, which includes mainly human resources indicators
2. The return on know-how capital, which includes indicators that focus on value added and profit per employee
3. The stability of the business, which includes indicators that focus on potential risks around business stability
4. Financial stability, which includes indicators on solvability, interest cover and liquidity.

According to Lev (2001) the information that is most relevant to decision makers concerns the value chain, or business model, of the enterprise. He describes this value chain as a process of innovation, starting with discovery and learning, passing through implementation, and culminating in the commercialization of new products and services. For each of these three phases of the value chain, Lev (2001) proposes three boxes of indicators (Figure 3.6). This model represents a broad cross-section of industries. Specific companies use specific subsets of indicators.

The framework does need some additional fine-tuning. For exam-ple, it is not clear why box 6, Internet, is in the implementation phase. The Internet can be a source of renewal (when used as a channel for receiving customer feedback), in which case it is part of the discovery and learning phase. It can also be the channel for commercialization or a means to increase brand value, in which case it is part of the commercialization phase. This may be the reason why "on-line sales" is in box 7, Customers, and not in box 6.

Figure 3.6

The Value Chain Scoreboard

Discovery and learning	Implementation	Commercialization
1. Internal renewal • Research and development • Work force training and development • Organizational capital, processes	**4. Intellectual property** • Patents, trademarks, and copyrights • Licensing agreements • Coded know-how	**7. Customers** • Marketing alliances • Brand values • Customer churn and value • On-line sales
2. Acquired capabilities • Technology purchase • Spillover utilization • Capital expenditures	**5. Technological feasibility** • Clinical tests, food and drug administration • Beta tests, working pilots • First mover	**8. Performance** • Revenues, earnings, and market share • Innovation revenues • Patent and know-how royalties • Intangibles-based earnings
3. Networking • Research and development alliances and joint ventures • Supplier and customer integration • Communities of practice	**6. Internet** • Threshold traffic • On-line purchases • Major internet alliances	**9. Growth prospect** • Product pipeline dates • Expected efficiency savings • Planned initiatives • Expected breakeven and cash-burn rate

Further testing of the framework is needed to determine whether it is generic enough to cover all industries. In the financial services industry, for example, intellectual property and technological feasibility play a minor role, leaving the implementation phase almost blank. It may be necessary to expand box 6 to include more indicators that show how service-oriented companies turn innovation into value.

A final comment is that, as with any measurement method, the value chain scoreboard does not include yardsticks. This makes it difficult for the user of the information to interpret the results.

Intellectual Capital–Index and Intellectual Capital Dynamic Value Method

Roos et al. (1997) developed their intellectual capital–index and Bounfour (2002) his intellectual capital dynamic value method to cope with the problem of too many indicators. Both combine several indicators into one overall indicator. Unfortunately, their approach for consolidating indices is not methodologically sound. Their approaches do not fulfill all requirements for consolidation as described by M'Pherson and Pike (2001a). The selection of indicators does not fulfill the necessary and sufficient measuring requirement that states that the total selection of indicators should be necessary and sufficient to describe the value that needs to be measured. This means they need to be complete, distinct, independent, minimal, observable, and measurable. Furthermore, the indicators are not normalized in the correct way. Finally, indicators are combined using the additive combinatory rule, whereas it could very well be that a different rule is more appropriate.

Reflection

To come to an overall appraisal of the 25 methods, I tested them against five criteria. First, we have seen that some methods contain logical flaws. It is important for any method to be methodologically sound. So the first criterion is: Is the method methodologically sound? I have tested all methods against this criterion using logical analysis (see appendix A).

Second, we have seen that some methods that authors present as methods for the valuation of intangible resources value something else or value more than just intangibles. Because I was looking for a method to value intangible resources, I included this criterion in my appraisal. This second criterion is: Does the method value or measure intangible resource?

Third, in Chapter 1 we saw that valuation always includes the use of certain values or yardsticks. If these yardsticks are missing, the method is not valuing intangibles but is measuring intangibles. Some methods in my sample do not include values. The aim of my study was to find a method for the valuation of intangibles resources. Therefore, the third criterion is: Does the method include values as yardsticks or is it merely a measurement method?

Fourth, as we saw earlier in this chapter, my definition of intangible resources includes a wide range of nonmonetary and nonphysical resources. I wanted my new method to be able to cover this wide array of intangibles. Some of the methods described in the previous section value only a limited number of intangible resources, like patents, human resources, or innovation. So the fourth criterion is: Is the method able to value a wide array of intangible resources?

Fifth, we have seen that financial valuation methods can be retrospective or prospective. Because I have defined value as the degree of usefulness or desirability, it is a forward-looking concept. For businesses, usefulness of resources is equal to their usefulness for future wealth generation. Therefore, the method should be forward looking. It should be prospective instead of retrospective. So the fifth criterion is: Is the valuation method prospective?

I tested each of the 25 methods against these five criteria using logical analysis. To come to an overall appraisal, I looked at the level of compliance of each method with the five criteria. Table 3.12 provides an overview of the appraisal of the 25 methods in the sample. The methods that met all five criteria were marked + in the right column; the others were marked −. This table is a useful tool to help you decide which method is a good candidate for solving the specific problem at your organization.

Five methods contain methodological flaws that limit the usefulness of the methods. The intellectual capital–index and the intellectual capital dynamic value method do not fulfill all requirements for proper multidimensional value measurement. They both combine indicators without proper normalization and weighing, using only the additive rule. With the iValuing factor it is totally unclear why the market-to-book ratio is an indicator of risk. The technology factor suffers from double counting. The VAIC method mixes stocks and flows, and confuses ratios with correlations.

Six methods that are often listed as methods for measuring the value of intangibles fail to do so. The balanced scorecard measures goal attainment, not intangibles. The valuation methods that are based on market-to-book ratios (iValuing factor, market-to-book value, and Tobin's Q) do measure value, but only an unknown portion of that value is attributable to intangible resources. That is also the problem with the EVA™ method, whereas calculated intangible value, on the other hand, does not reflect all the value of intangible resources—only a premium.

When indicators are used to measure the value of intangible resources it is important that the method include values that act as yardsticks to determine value. Many of the classic intellectual capital methods like the Skandia navigator, the intangible asset monitor, the intellectual capital–index, and the work of the Konrad group do not include yardsticks. This explains why Rylander et al. (2000) found that users in Sweden were not satisfied with the information on intellectual capital as it is presented in annual reports. "The link to value creation is unclear and the information is therefore perceived as difficult to interpret and does not provide deep enough insights to deliver any real value to users" (p. 723). Only the holistic value approach, the Inclusive Value Methodology, the intellectual capital audit, some HRA methods, and Viedma's intellectual capital benchmarking system include values that act as yardsticks.

Table 3.12

Review of 25 Methods for the Valuation or Measurement of Intangibles

Section in Appendix A	Method	Purpose	Means	Methodologically sound?	Measuring intangibles?	Yardsticks or benchmarks?	Wide range of intangibles?	Prospective?	Overall Appraisal
A.1	Balanced scorecard	Internal management	Measurement	+	–	+	n/a	n/a	–
A.3	Citation-weighted patents	External reporting	Measurement	+	+	–	–	n/a	–
A.5	Holistic value approach	Internal management and external reporting	Measurement	+	+	+	+	n/a	+
A.6	Human resource accounting	Internal management and external reporting	Measurement	+	+	–/+	–	n/a	–
A.7	Intellectual capital audit	Internal management	Measurement	+	+	+	+	n/a	+
A.8	Intellectual capital–index	Internal management and external reporting	Measurement	–	+	–	+	n/a	–

Code	Name	Type							
A.9	Inclusive Value Methodology™	Internal management and external reporting	Measurement	+	+	+	+	n/a	+
A.10	Intangible asset monitor	Internal management and external reporting	Measurement	+	+	-	+	n/a	-
A.12	Intellectual capital benchmarking system	Internal management	Measurement	+	+	+	+	n/a	+
A.13	Intellectual capital dynamic value	Internal management	Measurement	-	+	-	+	n/a	-
A.14	Intellectual capital statement reporting	Internal management and external	Measurement	+	+	-	-	n/a	-
A.16	Konrad group	External reporting	Measurement	+	+	-	-	n/a	-

Table 3.12 *continued*

Review of 25 Methods for the Valuation or Measurement of Intangibles

Section in Appendix A	Method	Purpose	Means	Methodologically sound?	Measuring intangibles?	Yardsticks or benchmarks?	Wide range of intangibles?	Prospective?	Overall Appraisal
A.19	Skandia navigator	Internal management and external reporting	Measurement	+	+	–	+	n/a	–
A.25	Value chain scoreboard	External reporting	Measurement	+	+	–	–	n/a	–
A.2	Calculated intangible value	Statutory and transactional	Valuation	+	–	n/a	n/a	–	–
A.4	Economic Value Added™ reporting	Internal management and external	Valuation	+	–	n/a	n/a	–	–
A.6	Human resource accounting	Internal management and external reporting	Valuation	+	+	n/a	–	–/+	–
A.11	Intangibles scoreboard	Internal management and external reporting	Valuation	+	+	n/a	+	+	+
A.15	iValuing factor	Internal management	Valuation	–	–	n/a	n/a	–	–

A.17	Market-to-book value	Internal management and external reporting	Valuation	+	−	n/a	n/a	−	−
A.18	Options approach	All three	Valuation	+	+	n/a	+	+	+
A.20	Sullivan's work	Internal management and external reporting	Valuation	+	+	n/a	−	+	−
A.21	Technology factor	Internal management	Valuation	−	+	n/a	−	+	−
A.22	Tobin's Q	Internal management and external reporting	Valuation	+	−	n/a	n/a	−	−
A.23	Valuation approaches	All three	Valuation	+	+	n/a	+	+	−/+
A.24	Value-Added Intellectual Coefficient™	Internal management and external reporting	Valuation	−	+	n/a	+	+	−

n/a = not applicable.

Seven methods have a limited scope, looking only at human resources, knowledge management, innovation, technology, intellectual property, or patents.

Of the 12 valuation methods, only four are forward looking, not including the general income approach described as part of Section A.23 in Appendix A and forward-looking methods within HRA.

When we look at all the nonfinancial methods, we see that only the holistic value approach, the Inclusive Value Methodology, the intellectual capital audit, and the intellectual capital benchmarking system score positive on all five criteria. Only the first one is aimed at improving internal management as well as external reporting (Rylander et al., 2000). The other three are designed to improve internal management. The holistic value approach and the Inclusive Value Methodology produce one overall indicator of value, making them suitable for monitoring and for making trade-off decisions. The other two provide a range of indicators. A limitation of the intellectual capital benchmarking system is that the benchmark depends solely on the judgment of an assessor. Actual measurement of indicators does not take place, making this value assessment method unsuitable for monitoring purposes. However, it offers practical starting points for improving the management of intangibles, as does the intellectual capital audit.

When we look at the valuation methods, we see that only Gu and Lev's (2002) intangibles scoreboard scores positive on all five criteria. The valuation approaches and the options approach also score positive, but contain generic tools that need to be tailor made to valuing intangible resources. The intangibles scoreboard uses an income approach to calculate the current value of future IDEs. It is a prospective method that looks at all intangible resources. Its outcome has proved to be highly significant in explaining market value.

There seems to be room for the further development of value measurement methods that can help improve external reporting and financial valuation methods that can help improve internal management. The holistic value approach can be a good candidate for the former (see Rylander et al. [2000]), although a first application to improve external reporting still has to be developed. The intangibles scoreboard may contain all the ingredients for the latter. The kind of prospective-looking information on the value of intangible resources that this method produces would be especially helpful with the prospective problem of improving company strategy by creating resource-based strategies, translating them into actions, and weighing the effects of alternative actions. In Chapter 6 I elaborate on this idea.

Implications for the Requirements of a New Method

In this chapter I explained what I've learned from previous attempts to value intangible resources. The lessons learned contain important implications for the design of my new method, the weightless wealth tool kit. The first lesson is that it is important to define the concept of intangibles in a precise way using the correct terms in order not to omit important sources of wealth. I decided to use the concept of intangible resources, which I defined as nonmonetary resources without physical substance that in combination are able to produce future benefits for a company. This broad definition creates a demarcation problem because it includes resources that are not totally controlled by the enterprise. Chapter 4 shows how I solve this demarcation problem.

Second, the valuation of intangible resources can be the solution for many problems. Many existing methods for the valuation or measurement of intangible resources can be characterized as a solution in search of a cause. It is important to define clearly the problem the new method tries to address. However, it may be difficult to do so in advance. I must confess that I have made the same mistake. I started to develop my method without a proper understanding of the specific problem I wanted to solve. It was not until the end of my research that I found out the best purpose of my method. However, before you start to develop or select a method, it is useful to define the problem you want to tackle. At least make a distinction between improving internal management and external reporting. When it comes to improving internal management, you need to decide whether the method aims at improving the monitoring of intangibles or at improving strategy development and execution. Statutory or transactional motives require specific and often predefined approaches. I excluded these motives from my study.

Third, there is a clear difference between valuation and measurement. Valuation includes values that are used as yardsticks. Because I wanted to develop a valuation method, I decided that it should include those values. During the development of the weightless wealth tool kit, I decided to use money as a denominator of value, and that a prospective income approach was the most appropriate. I made many more of these far-reaching decisions during the development of the method. In Chapter 4 I discuss the hurdles I needed to overcome and the unknown territory I needed to explore to design my weightless wealth tool kit.

Design: Draft of a New Method

"To boldly go, where no man has gone before."
Star Trek, The Man Trap, *September 8, 1966*[1]

On Monday May 10, 1998, a letter arrived at KPMG from the Dutch Ministry of Economic Affairs. It contained a request for proposals inviting accounting firms in The Netherlands to participate in a pilot project for the valuation of intangible resources. The letter ended up on my desk because I was one of the founders of the KPMG Knowledge Advisory Services Group, an innovation unit focusing on knowledge management. This letter set into motion the design of the weightless wealth tool kit.

This chapter presents how my design team used the design cycle to develop a preliminary version of the method. The design cycle is the second phase of the reflective cycle introduced in Chapter 2 (see figure 2.4). Our team went through the design cycle four times to produce a final draft. This process took place from May through September 1998. Each iterative step produced a further detailing of the method, and I describe these iterations in detail in four separate sections.

As we saw in Chapter 2, I make use of reconstructed logic to describe this design process. The process took place before I had the

---

[1] The first use of the phrase occurs in *Introduction to Outer Space,* a report prepared for President Eisenhower by the Science Advisory Committee, in which the phrasing is "to go where no one has gone before." Source: *Congressional Quarterly Weekly Report,* 4 April 1958:421. Available at:
http://www.fas.org/spp/heavens/03/03a.htm#N_1_

intention to study it scientifically. While reconstructing it, I identified the various elements of the design cycle. What was the problem definition we used and how did it shift over time? How did we demarcate the application domain of the method? What were the implicit and explicit requirements we used? What did the various drafts of the method look like and what inspired us to design them as such?

This reconstruction provides an insider's behind-the-scenes look at the development of a consulting method. It shows the wild ideas we had, the brilliant ideas we dropped along the way, and the mistakes we made that ended up in the final draft. This reconstruction allows me to indicate how our personal tradition (Varela, 1979) affected the design. Our intuition, normative preferences, sense of beauty, and goal orientation all influenced the design process.

To distinguish between what actually happened and the reconstruction, I describe each iteration in two parts. Part 1 is a factual description of the way the thinking of the design team evolved with regard to the problem and its solution. Part 2 is an evaluation of the result. This evaluation is based on hindsight, using knowledge acquired during the testing of the method and the writing of this book.

During each evaluation, I highlight the four steps of the design cycle. I have named these steps 2.A through 2.D to indicate they are substeps of the reflective cycle introduced in Chapter 2 (see Figure 4.1). The design cycle describes the process of designing management methods. Step A of the design cycle is defining the application domain. During discussions with the Ministry of Economic Affairs and among members of the team, we gradually developed an understanding of the class of organizational problems we were trying to address. We introduced different sets of distinctions and various ways to diagnose the situation. My design team and I developed a further understanding of the contexts in which the method should be applicable.

Step B of the design cycle is to create a list of requirements for the new method. There are four types of requirements (Van Aken, 1996; Weggeman, 1995)[2]:

1. *Limiting conditions* define the requirements the environment places on the method when applied.

---

[2] To illustrate this distinction, Van Aken (1996) gives the example of the design of a television set. The functional requirements will say something about the sound and picture quality of the TV. The operational requirements will say something about its ease of use. The limiting conditions provide information about the electric current (220 V/50 Hz), and one of the design limitations may be that the new model must be based on the same chassis as the other models.

Figure 4.1

The design cycle

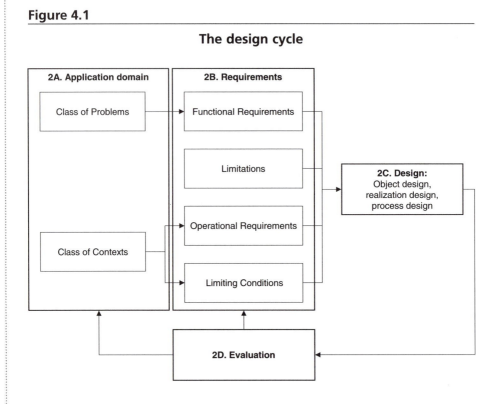

2. *Functional requirements* define the results the method needs to produce. These requirements follow primarily from the problem definition and the demands from the client.
3. *Operational requirements* define the ease of use of the method as defined by the users of the method.
4. *Design limitations* set the boundaries for finding solutions to the design problem. The designer of the method often sets these boundaries.

Our design team used implicit as well as explicit requirements. The available budget was an explicit limiting condition to the design, as was the availability of company resources to implement the method. Some of the functional requirements came directly from the Ministry of Economic Affairs; others were a logical consequence of the problem definition. The Ministry also provided some of the operational requirements because it had specific ideas about which companies should be able to use the tool. The fact that the implementation team was limited in size also led to specific limitations.

Step C is designing the new method. Based on the requirements, a solution is designed called an *object design*. This is the design of the intervention or artifact (Van Aken, 2000). The solution is implemented using a *realization design*: the plan for the implementation of the intervention or for the actual building of the artifact. A method is the combination of an object design and a realization design.[3] We worked on both designs simultaneously.

Step D of the design cycle is evaluating the design. This may lead to further modifications to the application domain, to the set of requirements, or to the design itself. In practice, this evaluation often remained implicit. Each brainstorming session and each session with the client led to further modifications.

Request for Proposals

Request

As mentioned, in May 1998, the Dutch Ministry of Economic Affairs invited accounting firms in The Netherlands to participate in a pilot project for the valuation of intangible resources. The initiative was based on the observation that the Dutch economy was evolving rapidly into a knowledge-based economy, in which companies create added value using intangible resources like knowledge, creativity, technology, quality management, and market relationships. According to the Ministry, a lack of information on these resources in annual reports results in a lack of insight into the economic potential of companies.

> Because of a lack of common definitions and of problems of valuation, these intangible means of production are underrepresented in annual reporting. This results in a lack of insight into the true economic potential of companies. This may have a negative effect on, among others, the ability to acquire outside capital on moderate terms. The Ministry of Economic Affairs wants to stimulate the development of practical methods for companies that will enable them to make transparent and, if possible, value their intangible means of production in a scientifically based and socially acceptable way. (Ministry of Economic Affairs, 1998b, p. 1; translated by D. Andriessen)

---

[3] Van Aken (2000) further distinguishes a *process design*, which he defines as the method used to design the solution to the problem. This *process design* is reflected in the design cycle itself, which is part of my research methodology.

This project was unique because the Ministry gave several accounting firms the opportunity to develop their own distinctive approach in parallel and to test this in practice with a number of their own knowledge-intensive audit clients. The Ministry asked participating firms to produce a draft supplement on intangible means of production for the annual report of their clients, as well as a detailed description of the method developed and the lessons learned. The request stipulated that participating clients should be knowledge-intensive clients (more than 20% of employees with a higher education), they should be interested in explicating their hidden strengths (both as an internal management tool and as an external reporting tool), and they should employ more than 50 employees.

Evaluation

The Ministry described the class of contexts of the new method as knowledge-intensive companies with more than 50 employees. The problem definition of the Ministry can be summarized as follows: How can companies make transparent and, if possible, value their intangible means of production in a scientifically based and socially acceptable way, and produce a draft supplement to their annual report?

The phrase "intangible means of production" played a key role in the problem definition of the Ministry. This phrase was used to make a distinction between tangible and intangible means of production. This distinction led to the observation by the Ministry that there is much less information on intangible means of production in annual reports than tangible ones, which indicates that the Ministry was focusing on problems regarding external reporting. The Ministry mentioned the problems that companies have in raising capital, which supports an external focus.

According to the Ministry's problem definition, two causes for this underrepresentation are a lack of common definitions and difficulties regarding financial valuation. This implies that the solution is to be found in developing common definitions and solving the valuation problem. Indeed the accounting firms were stimulated to value intangibles if possible. Strangely enough, they were also invited to develop their own approach and develop their own definitions, without taking into consideration the approaches of their competitors. In the planning of the project, the Ministry made provisions for discussions between the participating firms to work toward a common approach. In practice, none of the firms was willing to share their full insights during these meetings or to adjust their approach. As a result, no common definitions were created.

The problem definition continued by stating that this underrepresentation of intangibles in annual reporting results in a lack of insight into the economic potential of companies. The letter used the phrase "annual reporting" (*jaarverslaggeving*) to focus on a particular type of company information: information that is reported in the balance sheet, profit-and-loss statement, and other elements of the annual report. This implies that changing annual reporting will help to improve insight. This ignored other sources of company information like corporate brochures, Web sites, press releases, and personal contacts. The Ministry tried to find the solution by creating an appendix to the annual report.

The problem definition was not very precise regarding the consequences of a lack of insight. The only consequence mentioned was a possible negative effect on the ability to acquire outside capital. The fact that the Ministry left this part of the problem definition open gave participating accounting firms the opportunity to create their own problem definition. It will come as no surprise that all four participating firms found different solutions for different problems.

Finally, the problem definition provided some initial functional requirements for the design of a new method. The Ministry was deliberately vague about the requirements so as not to influence the firms too much in developing solutions. The request indicated that the method should create transparency, and it should do so by putting a financial value on intangibles "if possible." The Ministry was not clear about the meaning of the word *transparency,* nor did it clarify the benefits of a financial valuation. These turned out to be important questions, and the cause of huge debates within our own team and between the participating firms.

Iteration 1

Our design team was a multidisciplinary team consisting of people with a background in accounting, economics, administrative science, and electrical engineering. A team of experts (the Xpert Team) supported us, consisting of a number of university professors working in the field of business administration, social–economic policy, and valuation. In this section I describe our initial ideas about the new method. These ideas were captured in the KPMG proposal to the Ministry. I then evaluate the proposal, looking at the problem definition, the application domain of the new method, its requirements, and some initial elements of the design.

Design

In the proposal to the Ministry, we laid down the foundations of a new method. Our team approached it from the perspective of the emerging knowledge economy. The team considered that with knowledge becoming the most important means of production, both internal management information as well as external reporting are lacking in providing insight into the development and added value of knowledge within companies.

We rephrased the problem as: How to create, in a meaningful way, insight into the development, value and potential of the intangible resources (especially knowledge) of companies" (KPMG, 1998, p.3; translated by D. Andriessen). In the proposal, we raised the difficulty of providing meaningful data to various stakeholders, each with different information needs. The proposal also stated that companies should not try to capture as much knowledge as they can, but should instead focus on value-adding knowledge (this was based on Tissen et al. [1998]).

As for the class of contexts, we decided to develop a method for middle-size knowledge-intensive companies with 50 to 1,000 employees. This would include companies that produce products that contain knowledge as well as companies that sell knowledge. In addition, we wanted the method to be applicable to all industries.

During this first version of the object design, the first module was a strategic knowledge map. We proposed to develop such a map for each company involved. A strategic knowledge map is a map of all knowledge domains important to the future success of a company. Each domain on the map was broken down into smaller knowledge links and knowledge segments. The idea was that the implementation team could use this map to focus on value-adding knowledge.

As we saw in Chapter 3, one of the problems with measurement methods is how to interpret cause and effect. Which measures measure causes and which measures measure effects? What is the strength of these causal relationships? To solve this problem, we introduced a knowledge value chain. The idea was to measure the investments in knowledge accumulation and maintenance, the size of the knowledge stock, and the application of this knowledge in the company's value creation process. This value chain would show how the various input, stock, and output measures relate. This approach is similar to the value chain scoreboard as developed by Lev (2001).

One of our objectives was to design a method that would help to improve the way intangible resources are managed. We suggested using a knowledge management scan that assessed the maturity of the knowledge management efforts. It would be based on an instrument called the *value enhancer* (Tissen et al., 1998). This tool assesses the way a company manages its knowledge. It produces a variety of scores that can be used to benchmark a company against the competition.

The proposal suggested a three-step approach as the process design for the method. During the first step, a panel of experts would develop a framework for intangible resource reporting. This framework would include suggestions on what information to report externally in a supplement to the annual report. It would provide guidelines for the information needed to report to various stakeholders, the methods to use to gather this information, and the format of the report. During step 2, the implementation team would implement the method, gathering and analyzing the data and reporting to the individual companies. During step 3, we would collect the lessons learned and report them to the Ministry.

Evaluation

In this section I look at three elements of the design cycle: the problem definition, the class of contexts, and the requirements for the new method.

Shift in Problem Definition

This first version of the method shifted the problem definition in four ways compared with the Ministry's request for proposals. First, we narrowed the problem down to knowledge, because we considered this to be the most important intangible. This was because most members of our design team worked for the Knowledge Advisory Services Group of KPMG. We further limited the problem definition to include only the problem of measuring value-adding knowledge.

Second, we tried to define the Ministry's concept of "making transparent intangible means of production" by stating that we wanted to create insight into the development, value, and potential of intangible resources. Although the Ministry treated intangibles primarily as a static asset, we wanted to provide information on the progress in knowledge development and the potential of knowledge resources.

Third, we broadened the scope of the problem to include the improvement of both external reporting and internal information management. The Ministry seemed to focus only on external stakeholders, because the request for proposals specifically mentioned the lack of access to outside capital for knowledge-intensive firms.

Fourth, we wanted to challenge companies to improve the management of their knowledge. This was a further stretch of the problem definition. The Ministry never mentioned improving knowledge management as a goal. This ambition was clearly triggered by the consulting background of most members of our design team. We were not only interested in pure information gathering, we wanted to help improve the performance of companies. We had a deeply held belief that most companies do not manage knowledge well. Moreover, members of our team thought this might provide KPMG with commercial opportunities in the future for selling knowledge management work.

These modifications resulted in the following version of the problem definition: How can companies create, in a meaningful way, insight into the development, value, and potential of their intangible resources (especially knowledge) for the benefit of internal management and external stakeholders, and produce a draft supplement to the annual report?

In hindsight, I think it was a mistake that we did not study the causes and consequences of a lack of insight into intangibles at this stage. Neither did we include steps in the process design to identify the information needs of the various stakeholders. This omission would turn out to be a hindrance for obtaining a proper understanding of the problem at hand.

Defining the Class of Contexts

This first version of the method demarcated the application domain of the method in three ways. It focused on medium-size companies only because of pragmatic reasons. We thought that larger companies, especially if they were multinational companies, would be too difficult to embrace. We focused on knowledge-intensive firms, defined as firms with more than 20% of staff with a higher education. And we wanted the method to be applicable to enterprises in all industries, ranging from companies that sell products to companies that sell knowledge or services.

Some Implicit Functional Requirements

The object design reflected three implicit functional requirements. The use of a knowledge map reflected the requirement that the method had to be able to demarcate value-adding knowledge from other types of knowledge within a company. The use of the knowledge value chain reflected the requirement that the method had to be able to identify relationships between various leading and lagging indicators. The suggestion of a knowledge management scan reflected the requirement that the method should be able to improve the management of knowledge. These three requirements continued to play a major role in the further development of the weightless wealth tool kit.

Iteration 2

When the Ministry granted us the assignment, we developed the principles of the new method further and created a second version. We held a brainstorming session and outlined a number of building blocks for the new method. During the first part of this section I describe the results of this session. During the second part I evaluate the consequences for the problem definition, the list of requirements, and the various elements of the new method.

Design

In preparation for an initial discussion with the Xpert Team, we held a brainstorming session and produced a list of 12 building blocks for the new method.

Building Block 1: Look Beyond the Brain

Our design team concluded that the weightless wealth of companies consists of intangible resources of a very diverse nature. Some can be described as knowledge; products of the left side of the brain. Others, like corporate culture, the charisma of leaders, and many of the talents of employees, are found more on the right side of the brain and in the hearts of people. These should not be labeled *knowledge*. We felt that both types of intangibles needed to be the subject of investigation of the weightless wealth tool kit. The new method needed to be able to identify and assess not only knowledge, but other intangible resources as well.

Building Block 2: Focus on the Core

When developing a method to define the true economic potential of a company, it is not sufficient simply to list all its intangible resources. The new method needed to produce *relevant* data on intangibles. This required distinguishing between relevant and irrelevant intangible resources. We defined relevant resources as those resources that provide substantial added value to the company and those that are of strategic importance.

Figure 4.2

Decision tree to focus on core intangible resources

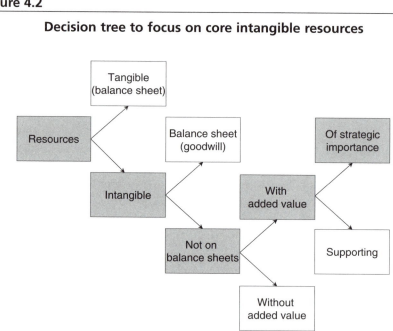

Figure 4.2 presents the decision tree that we used to focus on these core intangibles. Of all the resources in a company, some are tangible and others are intangible. Some of the intangibles may be on the balance sheet. We were interested in those that were not on the balance sheet, and especially those that have added value for the company. However, we wanted to focus even more. It was only interested in intangible resources that are truly important for the future success of the company.

To clarify the difference, take, for example, the skills of an employee working at the company restaurant. His skills can be considered intangible resources that undoubtedly have added value for the company. However, they are, in most cases, not of any strategic importance. We did not want to include these kinds of skills in its inventory of intangible resources.

We used the phrase "of strategic importance" to distinguish intangibles that have a profound influence on the future course of a company from those that are important but play a more supporting role. Take, for example, the skills and knowledge that reside within the accounting department of a company. Although most of these are very important and should not be missed, they play only a supporting role in making the company a success. We were aware of the fact that this decision tree excludes many intangible resources from the analysis that other methods might include, yet we decided this focus was necessary to be able to produce meaningful and useful results.

Building Block 3: Past, Present, and Future

Some methods for valuing or measuring intangible resources are focused on the past (see Chapter 3). We were not so much interested in the past, but in the current management of intangible resources within a company and the future potential of these intangibles. Therefore, we decided to look at past, present, *and* future aspects of intangible resources.

Building Block 4: Stock, Stewardship, and Potential

The reason our design team was interested in the past, present, and future was that it wanted to design a method that could provide information about the existing stock of intangible resources within a company, the way this stock is managed, and its future potential. In Dutch, this produces a catchy phrase "*bezit, beheer en belofte,*" which can (rather poorly) be translated into "stock, stewardship, and potential" of intangible resources.

Building Block 5: Money, Zero to Ten, and Percent

The distinction between stock, stewardship, and potential gave us further clues regarding the kind of information the method should produce. We felt the method should say something about the size of the stock of intangible resources within companies. A valuation of the stock would provide this kind of information. Furthermore, we wanted the method to produce insight into the quality of the stewardship of intangible resources using some form of report mark. In the Dutch school system, this is a mark between zero and ten. Lastly, to express the potential of intangible resources, we considered the use of some form of growth figure expressed, for example, as a percentage. The relationship between building blocks 3, 4, and 5 is shown in Figure 4.3.

Building Block 6: Select Strategically Important Intangibles Using the Concept of Core Competence

During the summer of 1995, under the mission "Vision 2000 Reinventing KPMG," 100 directors and employees were challenged to use all their knowledge, skills, and creativity. The goal was to study new opportunities for KPMG in its endeavor to become the most

Figure 4.3

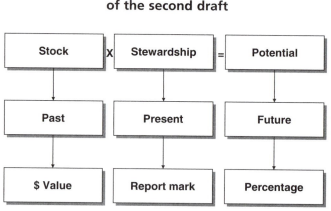

Relationship between building blocks 3, 4, and 5
of the second draft

client-oriented advisory firm in The Netherlands. The 100 directors and employees met regularly over a three-month period before publishing an in-depth study. They sketched the most complete possible outline of future developments in society, information technology, culture, politics, and economy, as well as the way in which these elements would influence one another. A detailed picture emerged of 18 discontinuities that would have an effect on the market, clients, and on KPMG. The 100 directors and employees created an inventory of the portfolio of services based on David Maister's "3 E-theory" (Maister, 1993). This resulted in a matrix of KPMG services clustered according to efficiency, experience, and expertise. They produced a summary of all KPMG's core competencies and latent competencies, plus a description of the skills underlying them. They also identified the existing and the desired culture within KPMG. Attention was also paid to the possible models that could be used to achieve cultural changes in KPMG. The result was a strategic architecture. It determined the direction of KPMG's future development. There was also a goal—a strategic intention—that not only lay in the realization of the growth directions, but also in the developments that KPMG wanted to make in the field of organization culture. Six new business opportunities (of which the KPMG Knowledge Advisory Services Group was one) showed the value that the strategic architecture of KPMG and the Vision 2000 process had for everyday practice.

The experience of Vision 2000 had a profound influence on the way two of my design team members view organizations. They had been part of the Vision 2000 project and had worked in close relationship

Figure 4.4

The little egg

with Stratogos, the consulting firm of Gary Hamel. They experienced the power of the core competence concept. During the process of developing the new method, we realized that a core competence is in fact a bundle of various types of intangible resources. During the Vision 2000 project, two of my team members had worked extensively with a model designed by Van der Wal, a colleague at KPMG. The model was known as "the little egg" or *het eitje*. This egg was used to create visual representations of KPMG's core competencies. It originally looked like Figure 4.4, and was adapted from the work of Leonard–Barton (1992, 1995).

Leonard–Barton (1995) describes core capabilities as bodies of knowledge that comprise four interdependent dimensions. Employee knowledge and skills, and physical technical systems are the dynamic knowledge reservoirs. Managerial systems create the channels through which knowledge is accessed and flows, and values and norms serve as knowledge-screening and control mechanisms. Van der Wal changed the dimension of physical technical systems to *technologies and technical systems,* because the latter description is less bound to physical equipment. This makes it applicable to companies that—like KPMG— do not use a lot of physical equipment. He also changed managerial systems to *management processes,* because he saw management more as a process than a system. He added a fifth dimension, which he called *assets and endowments,* that stood for all intangible resources inherited from past activities, like brand, the installed base of customers, and networks of suppliers. This helped to make the model applicable to service companies that strongly depend on their brand and relationship with clients.

To use this model to select strategically important intangibles, we needed to broaden some of the categories even further. We realized that in many companies technology is not the key component of competitive advantage. So we expanded the category *technologies and technical systems* to include explicit knowledge. Especially in the service sector, the central element of core competencies is often not technology, but tacit and explicit knowledge and company culture. We also struggled with the management processes category. We considered that the way primary processes are designed and implemented also adds significantly to a company's competitive advantage, and decided to include these processes as well. Furthermore, we did not look at this category as a dimension aimed purely at creating the channels through which knowledge is accessed and flows. We saw management and primary processes as intangible resources that can be identified independently. The same is true for the values and norms dimension. Leonard–Barton (1995) includes this dimension because values and norms serve in her model as knowledge-screening and control mechanisms. With the mantra "look beyond the brain" in mind, our design team included this dimension because it saw values and norms as powerful resources for competitive advantage. A company can identify and leverage these resources independently of other types of intangibles. Finally, we had a lively discussion on the assets and endowments category. In the original model, this category also included tangible assets. Because it was our intention to use the model to identify only intangible resources, we excluded the tangible ones. Exclusion was justified because many core competence definitions found in the literature name only a combination of intangibles. Where tangible assets play a role in core competencies, they are often buildings, such as an office network. Such property then contributes to the core competencies, but does not constitute an essential part of them (KPMG, 1999a).

The use of the little egg model resulted in the following categories of intangible resources (Figure 4.5; see also Andriessen and Tissen [2000]).

Building Block 7: Unraveling Core Competencies to Identify Strategically Important Intangibles

We realized that the concept of core competence provided a tool to identify intangible resources, demarcate which ones are important, and

Figure 4.5

Five categories of intangible resources

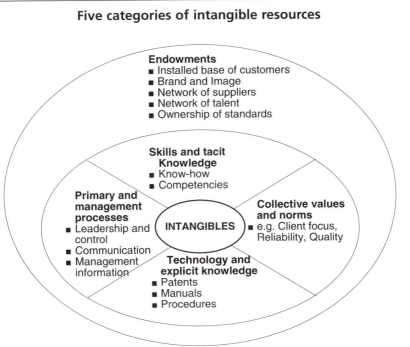

spot their combined strength. Hamel and Prahalad (1994) define a core competence as "a bundle of skills and technologies that enables a company to provide a particular benefit to customers" (p. 199). By expanding the scope of a core competence so that it not only includes skills and technologies but also collective values and norms, business processes, and endowments like brands we constructed a classification scheme that could be used to identify intangibles. Furthermore, we could build on the available literature on core competencies to construct the tools necessary to identify intangible resources in a reliable way.

One of the innovative features of the core competence approach is the distinction between core and noncore capabilities.

> Of course, there is nothing very novel in the proposition that firms "compete on capability." The subtlety comes when one attempts to distinguish between those competencies or capabilities that are "core" and those that are "noncore." If one produced an inventory of all the "capabilities" that are potentially important to success in a particular business, it would be a long list indeed—too long to be of any great managerial usefulness. Senior management

can't pay equal attention to everything; there must be some sense of what activities really contribute to the long-term corporate prosperity. The goal, therefore, is to focus senior management's attention on those competencies that lie at the center, rather than the periphery, of long-term competitive success (Hamel and Prahalad, 1994, pp. 203–204).

The distinction between core and noncore allowed us to identify those intangible resources that are of strategic importance to companies, based on the premise that all strategically important intangibles will somehow be part of a core competence. Identifying all core competencies will then automatically produce an inventory of strategically important intangible resources.

The core competence approach also focused the attention on synergies between intangible resources. The value of intangible resources lies in their combined strength and not in their individual characteristics. A core competence is, by definition, a combination of intangibles, reinforcing each other to produce an extraordinary capability. Core competencies, therefore, provide clear insight into the way individual resources produce synergies that add to company success.

Building Block 8: Using the Core Competence Community to Value the Human Component

At this stage of development of the new method, we began to think about ways to do a financial valuation of intangible resources. The idea was that if we could value the core competencies of a company, we would automatically value the underlying strategically important intangible resources. We recognized that any core competence consists of a human component (skills and tacit knowledge, and collective values and norms) and an organizational component (technology and explicit knowledge, processes, and endowments). We figured that each of the two components would require a different valuation approach.

We produced an initial idea on how the valuation might work. For the human component, the unit of analysis would be the individual employees that contribute to a specific core competence. We named this group *the core competence community.* If we could value the group of individuals, we would have valued the human component of a core competence. We came up with a four-step approach. Step 1 was to identify all members of the core competence community. Step 2 was to value each member using a cost, market, or income approach. Step 3 was to apply a synergy factor S to account for the value of the synergy between the members. This factor would be a function of the number of relationships between the members, which is equal to $\frac{1}{2} * n(n-1)$, where n is the number of members in the core competence community. Step 4 was to apply a diversity factor D to account for the level of diversity between the community members. The result was the following formula for the value of the human component of a core competence (*hccc*). We did acknowledge the fact that it would be difficult in practice to estimate the value of the parameters of the formula:

$$Value_{hccc} = \sum Value_{members} * S(\tfrac{1}{2} * n(n-1)) * D$$

Building Block 9: Valuing the Organizational Component

We then suggested valuing the organizational component by esti-mating the value of the individual elements—technology and explicit knowledge, processes, and endowments—using a cost, market, or income approach. At this stage, we did not know how to do this in practice, and did acknowledge the fact that it would be difficult.

Building Block 10: the Sum of the Core Competencies = the Total Value of the Intangible Resources

The next building block was the notion that if the values of the indi-vidual core competencies were added, the result would be the total value of all strategically important resources. We did recognize the fact that this does not include *all* intangible resources. The ones that are not important, or those that play a supporting role, are not part of any core competence. Because we had decided we were only interested in the value of important intangibles, this formula fit our purpose.

Building Block 11: Assessing Core Competence Stewardship

Building blocks 1 through 5 were concerned with the existing stock of intangible resources in companies and their identification and valuation. However, we also wanted the new method to be able to assess the quality of the way these intangibles are managed. We sug-gested a checklist for proper intangible resource stewardship, which we defined as

- Ensuring that a core competence does not dilute or disappear
- Making sure a core competence is maintained
- Protecting core competencies
- Continuously looking for ways to leverage a core competence
- Developing core competencies for the future

Building Block 12: Stock × Stewardship = Potential

The final building block brought all other blocks together in one overall philosophy. The potential of a company is the result of the available stock of intangible resources and the quality of the way they are managed. By assessing both, we would be able to draw conclusions about the economic potential of companies: stock × stewardship = potential (*bezit × beheer = belofte*). We did acknowledge the fact that, in this formula, economic potential is not equal to future success. The success of a company also depends on the external environment. We decided to exclude these external factors from the analysis.

Evaluation

Next I reflect on these 12 building blocks by looking at the shifting problem definition, the additions to the list of requirements, and the central role of core competencies as cornerstones of the object design. I conclude by highlighting two mistakes that we made and that have haunted us for a long time.

Another Shift in the Problem Definition

The second version of the new method produced another major shift in the problem definition. Our design team went back to the broader concept of intangible resources and deliberately steered away from a narrow focus on knowledge. Looking back, I realize that the female members of the team especially put this point forward. They thought the focus on knowledge was much too narrow. This is a clear example of how even gender can influence a person's choice for using a particular set of distinctions. We decided to broaden the discussion about the weightless wealth of companies to include the whole range of intangible resources: intellectual and nonintellectual.

We limited the object under investigation to strategically important intangible resources to prevent information overload and to ensure the results of the new method were relevant. We extended the problem definition to include information on the existing stock of intangible resources, the way they are managed, and their future potential. These modifications resulted in the following revised version of the problem definition: How can companies create, in a meaningful way, insight into the financial value of the stock of strategically important intangible resources, the quality of the way they are managed, and their future potential for the benefit of internal management and external stakeholders, and how can they produce a draft supplement to the annual report?

The way the design team composed this second version of the method clearly shows the interaction between defining the problem, listing requirements, and designing the elements of the method. The new problem definition led to a number of requirements that I summarize here as the *identification requirement,* the *demarcation requirement,* the *financial valuation requirement,* and the *management assessment requirement.* In addition, the introduction of the core competence concept as a key element of the new method led to the identification of additional requirements, especially the *synergy requirement.* I describe these requirements next in further detail.

Identification Requirement

An important requirement for the new method was that it needed to be able to identity intangible resources. As we saw in Chapter 3, the issue is how to identify something that is hidden or not material. The identification requirement stated that the method needed to include a definition of intangible resources, a classification of different types of intangible resources, and tools that allow the user to identify intangible resources within a company in a reliable way. Reliable means the tools needed to yield the same results when used by different users.

Demarcation Requirement

The problem definition looked at the problem of creating insight into all intangible resources that reside within a company, whether human or structural by nature. Underneath this is a strong belief that the success of a company lies as much in the implicit and the non-intellectual skills and attitudes of people as in its structural intangible resources. However, by including the human-based intangible resources, we created a problem of demarcation. What part of the skills and knowledge of an employee is part of a company and what part is not? Which intangible resources fall within the "organizational domain" of the company?

Two examples may illustrate this issue. If one of the employees of a company loves to go fishing over the weekend, is her knowledge about trout fishing important if the company manufactures wheelchairs? Probably not. However, what if the company manufactures fishing rods? Does that make these skills part of the intangible resources of the company? As a second example, let's say a manager enjoys horse riding. Would he use these horse-riding skills (like the ability to lead, to be patient, to give commands) in his managerial work in the office? Probably yes. Does that mean these skills are part of the intangible resources of the company?

We figured the answer would be a gliding scale: some skills are more important for the company than others. Therefore, we rephrased the demarcation problem as "how to determine which intangible resources are important for the future success of a company." This question already surfaced in the KPMG proposal that stressed the importance of focusing on value-adding knowledge. The weightless wealth tool kit needed to answer this question by providing criteria that help to decide whether a specific intangible resource is important.

This demarcation requirement should not be confused with the question of ownership. I agree with Edvinsson and Malone (1997) that a company never has ownership over its human capital. Consequently, no company can own the implicit knowledge and the skills that reside within an employee. Hence, a company does not own all of its intangible resources. Some intangible resources are not owned but do fall within the organizational domain of the company. They are important to add value and to create future success, yet they are not owned.

Financial Valuation Requirement

From this second version of the weightless wealth tool kit it is clear that we were aiming at a financial valuation. The problem definition required a financial valuation of the existing stock of strategically important intangible resources of a company. When we constructed this version of the method, we did not yet have a clear understanding of the nature of this requirement. This became more clear in the final version. However, our goal was to find a method to put a monetary value on intangibles. I named this the *financial valuation requirement* of the new method.

Management Assessment Requirement

The problem definition also implied an assessment of the way a company manages its intangible resources. This was the management assessment requirement. This requirement was not present in the request for proposals.

Synergy Requirement

The synergy requirement stated that the method needed to be able to identify the combined strength of intangible resources. As we saw in Chapter 3, it is a combination of intangible resources that creates sustainable wealth. The weightless wealth tool kit needed to be able to identify the synergies between the intangible resources that make companies unique and create added value.

Core Competence as the Core of the Object Design

The second version of the design included cornerstones of the new object design. It comprised new ideas and abandoned some of the old ideas. The central element in the new object design of this second draft was the concept of core competence. It helped to meet a number of requirements.

We used the core competence approach to help meet the *identification requirement*. We transformed the classification of the five elements of a core competence into a classification of intangible resources. Furthermore, the core competence approach gave access to a variety of techniques that exist to identify core competencies, which could be used to identify intangible resources within a company in a reliable way (see, for example, Hamel [1994], Hamel and Prahalad [1994] and Leonard–Barton [1995]).

The distinction between core and noncore helped to meet the *demarcation requirement*. The question here was which intangible resources fall within the organizational domain. Because a core competence is a bundle of intangible resources that enables a company to provide a particular benefit to customers, it follows that the intangibles that constitute the competence fall within the organizational domain. Unraveling the core competencies of a company produced a list of strategically important intangible resources that reside within a company.

In addition, the fact that a core competence is a combination of intangibles helped to identify synergies between intangible resources, thereby meeting the *synergy requirement*. The core competence approach helped to look at intangibles not in isolation, but as bundles that create a particular ability. The approach showed for each subject intangible resource how it contributes to a particular core competence, and thus how it contributes to current or future company success. The approach also showed how individual intangibles are supported by other intangibles in creating added value. The second version did not yet provide ways to meet the valuation requirement, the management assessment requirement, or the potential requirement.

Core Competence Approach Replacing Knowledge Tools

With the introduction of core competencies, we no longer needed the knowledge tools that were present in our proposal. The "egg" model of core competencies replaced the strategic knowledge map as an aid to focus on value-adding intangibles. The knowledge value chain was replaced by the notion of investing in, managing, and exploiting core competencies. A checklist for intangible resources stewardship replaced the knowledge management scan.

Mistakes in the Second Version

The second version of the weightless wealth tool kit introduced a couple of persistent mistakes that remained part of the method until the tool kit was first tested. First, the resource category assets and endowments in the core competence model included assets. At the time of the second draft, we did not notice that this produced an inconsistency. A core competence is a bundle of various types of intangible resources or assets, yet in the model one of the types of assets was called *assets*.

Second, we did not yet acknowledge there was a problem regarding the synergy between core competencies. We did solve the problem of identifying synergies between intangible resources. However, by introducing core competencies, we created the issue of possible synergy between core competencies. Combining core competencies may produce a value that is higher than the value of the contributing parts. The method did not account for this additional value.

Iteration 3

We constructed a third version of the new method after further deliberations with the Xpert Team and with representatives of the Ministry of Economic Affairs. In this section I describe the key issues we discussed and the changes we made to the design. Then I evaluate these changes with regard to their impact on problem definition, context, requirements, and design.

Design

The discussion at the first meeting of the Xpert Team focused on two issues: financial valuation and reporting formats. The discussion on valuation focused on the two rather different perspectives on company value represented by book value and market value. So far, the Ministry and the design team had been focusing on intangible resources as resources that are missing on the balance sheet. This internal perspective views a company as a stock of assets, with a value equal to the sum of the value of the individual assets (tangible, financial, and intangible). This internal perspective led to the conclusion that the team needed to find ways to value this missing link and "repair" the balance sheet.

The Xpert Team had a rather different view on value. One of its members was an expert in mergers and acquisitions. He provided an external perspective, looking at future cash flow that is generated by existing products, new products, and new opportunities. The value of a company from an external point of view is equal to the present value of its future cash flow. We recognized that this external perspective is more fruitful than the internal perspective when the aim is to identify the potential of intangible resources. This stimulated us to look for ways to value intangible resources based on an external perspective.

The Ministry's request was to develop a draft supplement to the annual report. The accountant on the Xpert Team initiated a discussion on the exact reporting format. The format would influence the way the company auditor is involved. In the Dutch situation, there are six options (Table 4.1). It was reconfirmed to go for option 2 and to produce a supplement to the annual report that would not require an audit statement and would not be limited by rules and regulations.

At the first meeting with the Ministry of Economic Affairs, we presented the requirements and building blocks of the new method. The Ministry's main concern was the ease of use of the proposed method. The civil servants explained that the purpose of the project was to create tools especially for middle-size companies. They stressed that they wanted to focus on knowledge-intensive startup companies, but that the tools needed to be applicable to other companies as well. These tools needed to enable companies to provide insight into their true

Table 4.1

Overview of Reporting Options			
Option No.	Format Option	Rules and Regulations?	Auditor Involvement?
1	Separate report	No	None
2	Supplement to annual report	No	None
3	Part of the letter of the board	No	Marginal audit
4	Part of the additional information section	Yes	Full audit
5	Supplementing balance sheet in addition to traditional one	Yes	Full audit
6	Incorporated in balance sheet	Yes	Full audit

value to outside investors. The Ministry hoped that this would lower their cost of capital. Therefore, the tools needed to be transparent and easy explained, standardized, and explicit, which would allow companies to use them without the help of outside experts. The Ministry admitted it was concerned that the proposed method was too complicated and would be too big a leap for most middle-size companies.

When we discussed this concern with the experts, they suggested incorporating tools that smaller companies already use. They recommended assessing the quality of the stewardship of intangibles using the European Foundation for Quality Management (EFQM) model. They shared the concern that the core competence framework that was proposed would be challenging for middle-size companies, but pointed out that economic developments are forcing these companies to think and act more strategically. They felt that this stretch that the method would provide to companies was not a bad thing.

The valuation expert initiated a further discussion on the valuation of core competencies. He strongly suggested trying to develop a financial valuation method using an income approach. As we saw in Chapter 3, the income approach is the best alternative when the market approach is not feasible. It provides a better indication of financial value than a cost approach. However, as we also saw in Chapter 3, a number of requirements need to be fulfilled before the approach yields reliable results. We decided to use an income approach, but to keep two other options in reserve. If the income approach turned out to be unfeasible, a cost approach would be used. If this second approach was not feasible, we would try to develop a valuation measurement method instead. Although the goal was to create a financial valuation method, we expected to end up with a mix of approaches, depending on the available data. This mix was expected to vary from company to company.

We also decided to make reliability part of the problem definition. The Ministry had explicitly asked for a method that could determine value "in a scientifically based and socially acceptable way." We translated this requirement into the requirement of reliability. The reliability of a financial valuation is the extent to which the valuation produces a stable result, independent of random variables like the person who is using the valuation method (see also Swanborn [1981]).

By the end of September 1998, we put together all the building blocks and additional considerations, and created a third version of the new method. The object design included various tools, combined in four distinct steps (Figure 4.6).

Step 1 would be an analysis of the company's surroundings and potential future. It would answer questions about current and future

Figure 4.6

Object design of the third draft

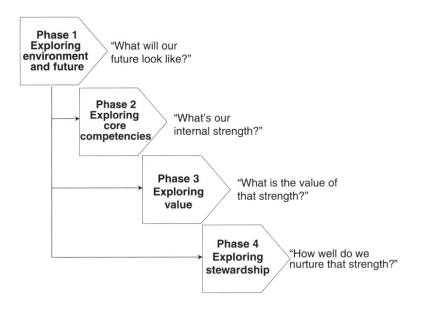

markets, customers and competitors, opportunities and threats, and future product/market combinations. The tools proposed were market analysis, competitor analysis, and discontinuity analysis. Step 2 focused on the internal strength of the company. Using a core competence approach, this step was intended to answer questions about uniqueness and excellence, customer appreciation, and the economic engine of the company. Estimating the value of this uniqueness was the purpose of step 3 of the method. Using an income approach, a cost approach, or a value measurement method, this step was supposed to explore the value of the company's intangible resources. Step 4 would assess the quality of the company's stewardship over its intangible resources. To achieve this, the EFQM method, elements of competence management assessments and general organizational audit approaches would be combined.

To implement the object design, we designed a stepwise approach. It involved a number of iterations using brainstorming sessions and interviews. It started with gathering information on the company, its competitors, and its environment. Then, four to six interviews would be held with key players within the company. This information would be used to conduct a first workshop with three key players and to have an initial brainstorming session on the core competencies of the company. This would undoubtedly lead to the need for additional information. This newly gathered information would be used at a second brainstorming session. The result of this meeting needed to be a list of competencies and a proposal for the estimation of their value. The next step would be to make an initial calculation of the value of the core competencies and an assessment of the level of stewardship. These results would then be presented to the key players for evaluation. After that, a final report would be written. The report needed to include an action list for further improvement of the method.

We sensed that companies would defer with respect to their level of involvement. Some companies would be willing to invest substantial time and effort into the implementation; others would have limited resources available. Therefore, we designed three different modes of company involvement (Table 4.2). This was based on an assessment of the time and resources the client would need to assign.

Mode I, with limited involvement from the client, would be possible if there was already a substantial amount of data available. Less interviews and brainstorming sessions would be needed. If the amount of available data was limited, more client involvement would be necessary and mode II would be used. Additional feedback sessions and interviews with customers would be required. We also designed a client collaboration mode in which the analysts and members of the client organization would form a joint team and implement the object design together.

We decided to take this version of the new method to the first client because time was running out. We acknowledged the fact that the method still had some major omissions, but we had the faith that we would be able to fill these gaps when working with the client.

Evaluation

I evaluate the changes in this third version of the weightless wealth tool kit with regard to their impact on problem definition, context, requirements, and design.

Further Specification of the Problem Definition and the Class of Contexts

The discussion on the reporting format helped to clarify that the main deliverable of the new method was a supplement to the annual report. This supplement would not require an auditor opinion. The accountant of the Xpert Team proposed this point. Being an auditor, he was concerned with a possible obligation for auditors to audit the

Table 4.2

Modes of Client Involvement for the Implementation of the Method		
Mode I: Most Data Available	**Mode II: Limited Data Available**	**Mode III: Client Collaboration**
Four two-hour interviews with key players Two three-hour brainstorming sessions with three key players Disclosure of financial, human resource, information technology, and other information One two-hour session with key players One contact person for day-to-day contact between client and analysts	Six two-hour interviews with key players Two to three three-hour brainstorming sessions with three key players Bilateral feedback session with key players Active client support on disclosure of financial, human resource, information technology, and other information Client interviews One two-hour intermediary feedback session with key players One three-hour end presentation for key players One contact person for day-to-day contact between client and analysts	Creation of joint team with members of the client organization and analysts Collaborative scan of company surroundings and future developments Joint interviews with four key players Two three-hour brainstorming sessions with three key feedback players Joint gathering of financial, human resource, information technology, and other information Client interviews One two-hour intermediary feedback session with key players One three-hour final presentation for key players Estimated time needed from members of client organization: two days a week for eight weeks

valuation of intangible resources. Because he sensed that this information would be at least partly subjective, he wanted to refrain from having to pass judgment. This addition resulted in the following version of the problem definition: How can companies create a supplement to the annual report that provides insight in a reliable way into the financial value of the stock of strategically important intangible resources, the quality of the way they are managed, and their future potential, for the benefit of internal management and external stakeholders?

The discussion with the Ministry clarified the scope of the class of context for the method. The Ministry made it clear that the target audience for the new method was medium-size companies.

Reliable Financial Valuation

The discussion on company value helped to specify further the requirements that followed from the decision to do a financial valuation. We decided to develop a method for the financial valuation of core competencies. We also decided to use a prospective income approach to financial valuation. This is in line with Chapter 3, in which we saw that a prospective income approach is desirable because it looks at the potential of intangibles.

These decisions led to a number of additional requirements for reliable financial valuation. There is the requirement to define carefully the appropriate standard and premise of value. We called this the *value definition requirement*. Any valuation requires first the selection of the appropriate standard of value. This standard provides an answer to the question: Value to whom? Reilly and Schweihs (1999) list ten different standards, including fair market value, market value, acquisition value, owner value, and insurable value. Then proper valuation requires selecting the appropriate premise of value. "The premise of value is the assumed set of intangible asset transactional circumstances under which the subject intangible asset will be analysed" (Reilly and Schweihs, 1999, pp. 61–62). Often the highest and best use for an intangible resource is selected as the premise of value. This premise states that the use of the resource is legally permissible, physically possible, financially feasible, and aimed at maximum profitability.

In addition, the choice for an income approach led to the following additional requirements for reliable financial valuation as described in Chapter 3:

- Income projection requirement
- Income funnel requirement
- Income allocation requirement
- Useful life estimation requirement
- Income capitalization requirement

Ease of Use

The Ministry explained that the new method needed to be transparent and easy to clarify to companies. When companies understood the method, it would be easier for them to accept and use the results. Therefore, the method needed to consist of a number of logical steps. Every step needed to result in a clear deliverable that was of immediate use to the client. A modular setup would be even better because it would allow clients to select those elements from the method that interest them most. Use of the method needed to be user independent. This required a complete standardization of steps and tools. Each step and tool needed to be documented to the extent that it could be used without extensive training and without help from the developers of the method.

Applicability

The method needed to be applicable to a wide range of medium-size companies. The problem of a lack of insight into intangible resources is perhaps the most significant in startup companies. They do not have any record of accomplishment and they often start with not much more than a good idea. The method needed to work for both startups and mature companies.

Analyst–Client Cooperation

We knew that initiatives in the field of performance measurement and intellectual capital often are time-consuming for the subject company. In many instances, management does not have much time to invest in these kinds of initiatives. Therefore, the method needed to allow for both limited and heavy client involvement. More client involvement would most likely reduce the capacity needed from outside consultants.

Budget Limitations

The way the Ministry's project was structured and planned, and the budget that was available, created a number of limitations to the design. First, there was the limitation of time available. The method could take a maximum of three months to implement. Second, there was a budget constraint. For a medium-size company it needed to take a team of no more than five analysts, who spend a maximum of 200 hours, to apply the method. We felt that it needed to take members of the subject company no more than 100 hours to gather data, complete questionnaires, attend workshops, and give interviews.

Object and Realization Design Still Contained Gaps

Figure 4.7 shows our estimation of the level of completeness of each of the tools suggested in the third draft of the method.

Figure 4.7

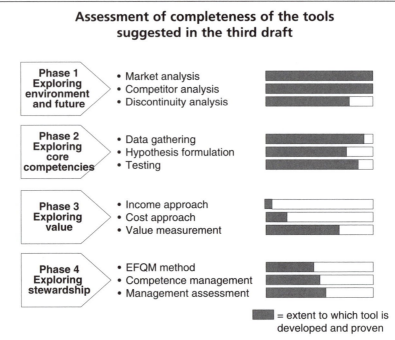

Assessment of completeness of the tools
suggested in the third draft

Phase 1 Exploring environment and future	• Market analysis • Competitor analysis • Discontinuity analysis
Phase 2 Exploring core competencies	• Data gathering • Hypothesis formulation • Testing
Phase 3 Exploring value	• Income approach • Cost approach • Value measurement
Phase 4 Exploring stewardship	• EFQM method • Competence management • Management assessment

■ = extent to which tool is developed and proven

Although we took this version of the method to the first pilot client, the design still contained some gaps. We did not know how to value the identified core competencies using an income approach and how to meet the requirements for reliable financial valuation as described earlier. Therefore, we included as a fallback option the possibility of using either a cost approach or a value measurement method. The management assessment requirement had also not yet been met, and we had not yet developed the EFQM method for assessing the management of intangibles. However, we were confident we would solve these problems along the way.

Iteration 4

As seen in the previous sections, the problem definition, the list of requirements, and the design itself changed substantially over a period of three months. In this section I summarize the results of this evolution and describe the version of the method that was tested at six companies.

Table 4.3

Changes in the Problem Definition During the Design Process	
Version	**Problem Definition**
Request for proposals	How can companies make transparent and, if possible, value their intangible means of production in a scientifically based and socially acceptable way, and produce a draft supplement to their annual report?
Iteration 1	How can companies create, in a meaningful way, insight into the development, value, and potential of their intangible resources (especially knowledge) for the benefit of internal management and external stakeholders, and produce a draft supplement to the annual report?
Iteration 2	How can companies create, in a meaningful way, insight into the value of the stock of strategically important intangible resources, the quality of the way they are managed, and their future potential, for the benefit of internal management and external stakeholders, and how can they produce a draft supplement to the annual report?
Iteration 3	How can companies create a supplement to the annual report that provides insight in a reliable way into the value of the stock of strategically important intangible resources, the quality of the way they are managed, and their future potential, for the benefit of internal management and external stakeholders?
Iteration 4	How to produce a supplement to the annual report that provides in a reliable way insight into the value of the stock of strategically important intangible resources and the quality of the way they are managed for the benefit of internal and external stakeholders?

Problem Definition

The problem definition changed significantly during the design process (Table 4.3).

When we compare the first and the last problem definition, we see that the latter contains a number of specifications. First, it limits intangible means of production to strategically important intangible resources. The aim of the method was to focus on intangible resources that are important for the future performance of the company. This is the group of intangibles that provide substantial added value and are of strategic importance. This focus helped to produce relevant results. The final problem definition specified transparency as insight into a stock of intangible resources and the quality of the way they are managed. This specification clarified the kind of insight the method needed to produce. It needed to provide insight into financial value, and it needed to value the stock of existing intangible resources, leaving intangible flows out of the analysis. It needed to provide insight into a company's efforts to manage this stock, and it needed to include a yardstick to assess the quality of management. The problem definition translated the Ministry's phrase "scientifically based and socially acceptable" as "reliable." The reliability of a financial valuation is the extent to which the valuation produces a stable result, independent of random variables like the person who is using the valuation method. The problem definition specified the target audience for the method as both internal management and external stakeholders.

The method tried to cover two of the three types of problem definitions described in Chapter 3. It was aimed at solving problems regarding improving internal management of intangibles. Specifically, it addressed the problem of improving the management of intangible resources (category 2 in Table 3.5). In addition, it aimed at improving external reporting.

Requirements

This section summarizes the requirements we defined for the weightless wealth tool kit. This summary is based on the literature review in Chapter 3 and the reconstruction of the design process in this chapter. Requirements can be categorized into limiting conditions, functional requirements, operational requirements, and limitations. Categorizing them in some cases is arbitrary (Weggeman, 1995). The numbers in parentheses in the following text refer to Table 4.4.

Limiting Conditions

The Ministry wanted to have a method especially for knowledge-intensive (1.1) middle-size companies (1.2) in every industry (1.3). The Ministry wanted to focus on startup companies, and the tools should be applicable to mature companies as well (1.4).

Functional Requirements

Chapter 3 described the difficulty of identifying and demarcating intangible resources. It also showed how intangible resources create synergy when they are combined. The method needed to contain tools to identify intangible resources (2.1), demarcate which ones are of strategic importance to the company (2.2), and show how they create synergy (2.3). The requirements for reliable financial valuation based

Table 4.4

Overview of Requirements	
Type of requirement	**Requirement**
1. Limiting conditions	1.1 Knowledge-intensive companies 1.2 Middle-size companies 1.3 Applicable in every industry 1.4 Startup and mature companies
2. Functional requirements	2.1 Identification requirement 2.2 Demarcation requirement 2.3 Synergy requirement 2.4 Value definition requirement 2.5 Income projection requirement 2.6 Income funnel requirement 2.7 Income allocation requirement 2.8 Useful life estimation requirement 2.9 Income capitalization requirement 2.10 Management assessment requirement
3. Operational requirements	3.1 Transparent and easy explainable 3.2 Standardized and explicit 3.3 Stepwise and modular
4. Limitations	4.1 Maximum of 200 hours of analyst time 4.2 Maximum of three months to complete 4.3 Maximum of five analysts 4.4 Maximum of 100 hours client time 4.5 Heavy and limited client involvement

on a prospective income approach follow from the valuation theory described in Chapter 3. This theory requires a definition of the standard of value and the premise of value (2.4), the projection of future income (2.5), a funneling of part of this income to the intangible resources (2.6), and the allocation of the remaining income over the subject intangible resources (2.7). It also requires a useful life estimation of the subject intangibles (2.8) and a capitalization of the income to calculate a present value (2.9). A third element was the wish of the design team to assess the quality of the way intangibles are managed (2.10).

Operational Requirements

The Ministry wanted companies to be able to use the method without outside assistance Therefore, the method needed to be transparent and easy to explain (3.1), standardized, and explicit (3.2), which would allow companies to use the method without the help of outside experts. Our design team added that the method needed to have a modular setup so companies could choose those elements that interested them most (3.3).

Limitations

The limitations came from budget and capacity restraints and from previous experiences by the design team in consulting to middle-size companies. The budget limited the available time to spend with each client to 200 hours (4.1). The timeline of the total project allowed for a maximum of three months lead time per client (4.2). The available team for the implementation had a maximum size of five consultants (4.3). From our experience in working with middle-size clients, we knew that to get their cooperation, the method required limited time from the client side (4.4). We also knew other clients would like to get involved more heavily (4.5).

Design

The final draft of the method contained two phases. Phase 1 aimed at identifying strategically important intangible resources of a company by defining the company's core competencies. Phase 2 aimed at putting a financial value on these core competencies using a prospective income approach.

Phase 1: Object Recognition

Defining core competencies is like taking bearings. You need to look at it from several angles to get a clear picture. The design of the weightless wealth tool kit contained four different angles (Figure 4.8).

First, it looked at the company's markets and market strategy by determining its market goals, the opportunities and threats, and the existing product/market combinations. This provided background information on the company's current strategy and the markets in which it wants to operate. Then it searched for unique competencies by looking at the company's economic engine (where does the company make money now and in the future), the way customers look at the company, the factors critical to the company's success, and finally by trying to identify individual intangible resources that may contribute to core competencies.

Combining this information led to the formulation of a number of hypotheses for core competencies. We defined a core competency as "the ability to. . . ." Using this structure helped avoid the mistake of putting forward a product or service as a core competence. We also

Figure 4.8

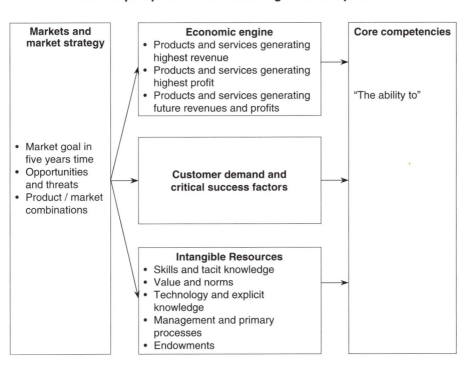

Different perspectives for defining core competencies

demanded that the customer benefit be included in the definition. This helped to prevent too much of an internal focus.

Then the method broke down each of the core competencies into its contributing intangible resources using the distinction between skills and tacit knowledge, norms and values, technology and explicit knowledge, processes, and endowments. The result was a list of the strategically important intangible resources.

As a next step, the method contained a test to help determine whether the competencies identified were truly core competencies instead of supporting competencies or basic competitive requirements. According to Hamel and Prahalad (1994), a competence is core or it is not. They use three criteria: a core competence must make a disproportionate contribution to customer-perceived value, it must be competitively unique, and it must have potential by being extendable to an array of new products or services. The test that was part of the method was based on the so-called *champagne test*, which members of the design team had used during KPMG's Vision 2000 project to determine whether a KPMG competence identified passed as a core competence. The test was named the champagne test because a bottle of champagne was awarded each time a KPMG core competence passed the test. The test consisted of 27 statements grouped around five main tests:

1. Definition test: Does this core competence deliver exceptional customer value, and how does the customer perceive this?
2. Sustainability test: How difficult is it to imitate this core competence?
3. Reality test: Do we master this core competence better than the competition?
4. Status quo test: How critical is this core competence with respect to our current position in the field?
5. Future test: How critical will this core competence be for us to become the leader in our field?

The champagne test clearly was based on the three criteria of Hamel and Prahalad (1994). The definition test covered the criterion of customer benefit, the reality test addressed the criterion of uniqueness, and the future test explored the criterion of extendibility. Added to these three criteria was a criterion regarding the extent to which a core competence can be copied, and a criterion testing the importance of the core competence to current operations. We felt that one dimension was missing. Whether a competence is core also depends on its vulnerability. If a core competence depends, for example, on the skills and expertise of a very limited number of people, there is a severe chance a company will lose it. So we decided to include a core competence robustness test that reviewed the extent to which the competence was anchored within the organization. Furthermore, we felt that the status quo test was not relevant for assessing whether a competence is core. A core competence will provide a company with a powerful ability to . . ., regardless of whether this ability is already used. Therefore, we decided to exclude this test from the assessment tool. This resulted in the following tests for determining whether a competence is a core competence:

1. Added-value test: Does the competence provide added value to customers?
2. Competitiveness test: Is the company better in this specific competence than its competitors?
3. Potential test: Does this competence provide opportunities to create new products and services in the future?

4. Sustainability test: How difficult is it for competitors to imitate the competence?
5. Robustness test: How well is this competence anchored within the organization?

Phase 2: Financial Valuation

Any financial valuation requires defining the proper standard and premise of value. The weightless wealth tool kit needed to determine the value of intangible resources of a company to its current owner, given the owner's current use of the intangible resources and given current capabilities for commercially exploiting the intangible resources. In this situation, the appropriate standard of value is owner value. Reilly and Schweihs (1999) describe owner value as follows: ". . . the question that is usually answered through an owner value analysis is: What is the value of this intangible asset, given the owner's abilities (or inabilities), given his or her sources of capital (or lack of sources of capital), given his or her commercialization plans (be they brilliant or incompetent) and so forth?" (p. 60). It is this kind of information that we wanted to report to both internal and external stakeholders.

The premise of value explains under what conditions the valuation is taking place. The weightless wealth tool kit needed to report value in a going concern, given the company's current commercial strategy. The corresponding premise of value is value in continued use, as part of a going concern business enterprise. "This premise of value contemplates the contributory value of the subject intangible asset both to the other assets (both tangible and intangible) of a business enterprise, and from the other assets (both tangible and intangible) of a business enterprise" (Reilly and Schweihs, 1999, p. 63).

On October 16, 1998, when my implementation team and I were already working on the first pilot company, we had an internal meeting with the KPMG team that did the audit for Bank Ltd. We discussed the intermediate findings and the next steps to take. When we discussed the options for valuing core competencies, we suddenly realized that the five criteria for a core competence as described in the previous section provide the key to solving the valuation problem. We became conscious that the value of a core competence correlates to its score on the core competence test. After all, the higher the customer benefits, the more valuable the competence; the longer the sustainability, the higher the value, and so forth. Every test provided an indication of the value of a core competence, as shown in Figure 4.9.

Figure 4.9

The relationship between the strength and value of
a core competence

OF LITTLE VALUE		OF GREAT VALUE
No value added to the customer	**Added-value test**	Clearly value added to the customer
Poorer or equal to the competition	**Competitiveness test**	Better than the competition
Soon to be commonplace	**Potentiality test**	Creates new opportunities
Easy to imitate	**Sustainability test**	Difficult to imitate
Vulnerable	**Robustness test**	Securely anchored in the organization

Because all five factors are essential for the value of a core competence, we decided that the total value of a core competence could be
determined by multiplying the five indicators:

$$\text{Value of Core Competence} = \text{Added Value} \times \text{Competitiveness} \\ \times \text{Potential} \times \text{Sustainability} \times \text{Robustness}$$

In words, this formula indicates that the value of a core competence
(its degree of usefulness) equals the added value of the core competence for the customer, given the current competitive relationships; the
growth that can be expected in the coming years (potential); and the
number of years for which it can be exploited (sustainability). This was
then corrected by a factor showing whether there is a risk that the
company will lose the core competence prematurely (robustness).

A financial valuation requires a way of determining the potential,
sustainability, and robustness of a core competence as well as finding
a proxy for the added value of the core competence for the customer,
given the current competitive relationships. We decided that the
income generated by a core competence can act as proxy for the added
value it provides for a customer given the competition in the industry.
A customer is willing to pay more when the added value is higher and
when there are fewer alternatives available in the marketplace.

This formula incorporated the criteria used by Hamel and Prahalad
(1994) and Leonard–Barton (1995) to identify core competencies.

Each criterion was used as an indication of the value of a core competence. Furthermore, the formula was used to meet all requirements for a proper financial valuation using an income approach. Using this basic idea, all requirements for financial valuation could be met. We had cracked the code! Next, I briefly highlight each requirement.

Income Projection Requirement

Intangible resources themselves do not generate any income. Selling of products and services generates income. Therefore, in the case of intangibles, the income projection requirement is the problem of projecting into the future the income stream generated by the products and services to which the subject core competence contributes. The first question to answer was: What measure of income are we going to use? There are many measures of economic income. Reilly and Schweihs (1999) list a "top ten" and note that this is not an exhaustive list. In choosing a measure, we had two considerations. We wanted the estimated value of intangible resources to reflect the future earning potential of the intangibles without a distortion by the way the company is organized, financed, and taxed. In addition, we wanted the measure to be as simple as possible. We decided to use a contribution margin, defined as net revenue less cost of goods sold and other direct costs. This contribution margin reflects the income stream a product or service generates without the figure being distorted by overhead costs or other costs that are the result of the way the company is organized, financed, and taxed. Of course, the contribution margin is not equal to the cash flow that results at the end of the day. As a result, the valuation can be higher than if a net cash flow after tax measure is used.

We developed a list of questions to help determine the contribution margin (Table 4.5). The list was based on the distinction between past, present, and future, as described earlier. The idea was that it is easier to predict the future contribution margin if the prediction is based on historic figures and forecasts. This is the same method used by Gu and Lev (2002). In addition, a question was added to check whether the contribution margin is a proper reflection of the added value of the core competence to customers. This is not the case, for example, when a new company does not yet make a positive contribution margin. In this case, adjustments are necessary.

The second question to answer was how to project this economic income into the future. Again, because we wanted the method to be as simple as possible, we decided to use an indicator based on the potential test described in the previous section. We developed a list of questions to help determine this indicator (Table 4.6). The list was

Table 4.5

Questions to Help Determine the Contribution Margin			
Element	**Past**	**Present**	**Future**
Contribution margin	What were the net revenues, cost of goods sold, and other direct costs for year $t - 1$, $t - 2$, and $t - 3$?	What is the forecast for the net revenue for the current year?	What is the forecast for the net revenue for the year $t + 1$ and $t + 2$?
Corrections	Are there any identifiable reasons that explain why the contribution margin is not a proper reflection of the added value of the core competence to customers? Do we need to make an adjustment?		

Table 4.6

Questions to Help Determine the Potential Factor			
Element	**Past**	**Present**	**Future**
Established applications	What was the growth rate of the contribution margin between year $t - 1$, $t - 2$, and $t - 3$?	What is the expected growth rate of the net revenue for the current year?	What is the expected growth rate for the net revenue for the year $t + 1$ and $t + 2$?
Logical extensions	Which new products has this core competence helped to produce in recent years?	Which new products are currently in the pipeline?	Which new products can be expected in coming years?
Opportunities and threats	What developments have created opportunities for leveraging the core competence in the past or have posed a threat?	What are the implications for the current situation?	What developments will create opportunities for leveraging the core competence or pose a threat?

based on the distinction between past, present, and future, and it used a distinction between established applications of the core competence and logical extensions. The list also asked for further opportunities and threats.

Income Funnel Requirement

A product or service is not produced solely through intangible resources, but is also produced with the aid of tangible and networking capital assets. Therefore, the method needed to isolate a portion of the economic income that is a fair rate of return for these other assets. This was especially true in this case, because the method used an economic income measure that is on a gross level of income and therefore does not yet include a provision for a return on tangible assets and networking capital. We decided to estimate the value of all tangible assets and networking capital by looking at their accounting book value. This was a pragmatic choice because it would have been too complicated to estimate the market value of these assets. The method then estimated a fair rate of return for these assets. Ideally, this would be done using a weighted average rate of return based on an assessment of the blended risk of all assets. To make the method more easy to use, we decided to use a simple risk-free borrowing rate as represented by the yield on a government bond of 5%.

Income Allocation Requirement

Next, the method needed to allocate the contribution margin of the products and services to the underlying core competencies. The contribution of a core competence to the realization of a product varies. The core competence can make an essential, substantial, or supporting contribution, but also may not contribute at all. To estimate this contribution, the method used a competence–product matrix. In each cell of the matrix, the contribution each competence makes to the product was assessed using a simple scoring mechanism: 0, no contribution; 1, supporting contribution; 2, substantial contribution; 3, essential contribution. When the various columns were added, relative weights could be calculated. The method used this information to allocate the contribution margin of each product to each of the core competencies (Figure 4.10).

Useful Life Estimation Requirement

The next problem we needed to solve was the problem of estimating the useful life of the intangible resources. We decided to estimate

Figure 4.10

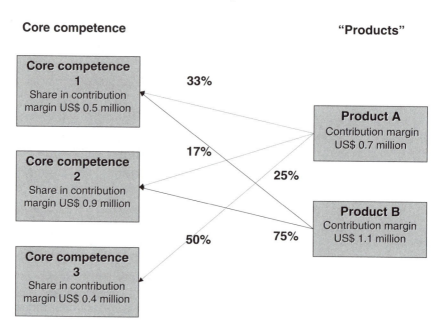

Fictional example of the allocation of contribution margins to core competencies

this for each core competence individually. As we saw in Chapter 3, there are many definitions of the useful life of intangible resources. The useful life of a core competence is as long as the competence remains core. This is equal to the number of years it will take a competitor to acquire the same competence. The sustainability test, as described in the previous section, indicates this. The method introduced a definition of useful life called *strategic life*. The strategic life of an intangible resource reflects the ability to keep ahead of the competition. The method contained a list of questions to help determine this indicator (Table 4.7). The list was based on the distinction between past, present, and future, and looked at three types of indicators that can help determine strategic life: indicators around the life cycle of products in which the core competence is used, indicators on the competition, and indicators about the extent to which a core competence can be imitated.

If we compare this definition of useful life with traditional DCF methods that are often used to value companies or products, we see a clear difference. With DCF, the period for which the cash flow is forecasted is often very long to infinite. This means that when using DCF

Table 4.7

Questions to Help Determine the Sustainability Factor			
Element	**Past**	**Present**	**Future**
Life cycle of products	What has been the life cycle of products to which this core competence has contributed?	What is the expected life cycle of the current products to which the core competence contributes?	What is the expected growth rate for expected new products?
Competition	What developments in the competitive field have, in the past, influenced the uniqueness of this competence?	Is this core competence scarce or present?	What developments in the competitive field will influence the uniqueness of this competence?
Imitation	Did it require considerable investments in time and/or money to master this competence?	Is the core competence a combination of a number of intangibles such as skills, knowledge, processes, and corporate culture?	Will it require considerable investments in time and/or money to maintain this competence, and will they be made?

we assume the economic income will be generated indefinitely, without taking into account the competitive situation of the company. This period is often divided into two periods: the explicit forecast period and the period after the explicit forecast period. This results in a total value of, for example, a company being equal to the present value of cash flow *during* a period with an explicit forecast, plus the present value of cash flow *after* a period with an explicit forecast. This last value is called the *continuing value*, and it often accounts for a large percentage of the total value of a company (Copeland et al., 1990). The assumption for the continuing value is that the cash flow will be generated forever—an assumption that is often unlikely in today's turbulent economy. We wanted to be on the safe side, keeping a close eye on the competition. That is why the weightless wealth tool kit used the concept of strategic life and looked only at the economic income that is being generated during those years that the core competence is unique.

Income Capitalization Requirement

The last problem to solve was the estimation of the discount rate to capitalize the future economic income stream. As we saw in Chapter 3, this discount rate should reflect

- The expected growth rate of the income stream generated by the subject intangible
- The cost of capital appropriate for an investment in the subject intangible
- A compensation for inflation
- The degree of risk associated with an investment in the intangible

The version of the weightless wealth tool kit that was tested did not acknowledge the need for a compensation for inflation and the cost of capital. It focused on the growth rate and on the risk of losing the core competence. The potential test described earlier reflected the growth rate. The robustness test (also described earlier) addressed the risk element of the discount rate. The method calculated a robustness factor for each core competence, based on the specific risk profile of the core competence involved. This risk reflected the chance of losing the core competence as a result of one or more possible causes. The method contained a list of questions to help determine this factor (Table 4.8). The list was based on the distinction between past, present, and future, and it looked at the three types of intangible resources that comprise a core competence.

The method contained a formula to combine all factors described earlier and to calculate the value of a core competence. It was a simplified version of a DCF formula:

$$Vcc = \left[\sum_{t=1}^{S} CM * (1+P)^t \right] * R,$$

where Vcc is the value of core competence, S is the sustainability (in years), CM is the contribution margin, P is the potential for the future (in percent), and R is the robustness (in percent). This formula concluded the second phase of the object design of the weightless wealth tool kit.

Realization Design

The realization design of the new method is shown in Figure 4.11. The process could be completed in 12 weeks. To define core

Table 4.8

Questions to Help Determine the Robustness Factor			
Element	**Past**	**Present**	**Future**
Human component: skills and tacit knowledge, values and norms	What was the turnover in personnel in the years $t - 1$, $t - 2$, and $t - 3$ of people contributing to the core competence?	What is the current size of the core competence community?	To what extent will it become more difficult/easy to recruit or maintain members of the core competence community?
Structural component: explicit knowledge and technology, processes	Have there been any incidents in the past that have affected knowledge or systems?	How much does the core competence depend on specific knowledge and systems and how vulnerable are they?	Are there any discontinuities that can affect these knowledge and systems?
Endowments	Have there been any incidents in the past that have affected the company image, the client relationships, the networks of people, and so forth?	How much does the core competence depend on a specific company image, on client relationships, on networks of people, and so forth?	Are there any discontinuities that can affect these endowments?

competencies, the method used a number of techniques. First, available documentation was analyzed, including annual reports and management reports. This information was summarized to produce a core competence report. Part of this step was to conduct interviews with a number of key people within the company using a standardized interview protocol. The information from the document analysis and interviews was used to develop initial core competence hypotheses.

During the first workshop, the project and the method were introduced. Then the core competence hypotheses were presented. Participants were asked for their reaction to the core competence hypotheses. A discussion was held that led to amendments to the hypotheses and questions for further research.

Figure 4.11

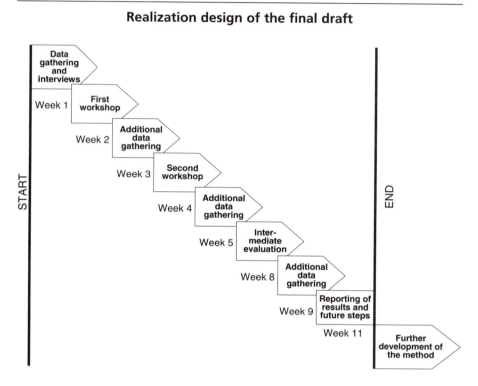

Realization design of the final draft

Then financial data were gathered on products and services using the questions presented in Table 4.5. These data were used to calculate the contribution margin of the products and services. To gather information about the potential factor, the sustainability factor, and the robustness factor, additional interviews were held. The method included a special interview protocol for this purpose. This protocol translated the questions about the potential factor (Table 4.6), the sustainability factor (Table 4.7), and the robustness factor (Table 4.8) into interview questions.

The next step was to have a second workshop with key people to collect their views on the contribution of each of the core competencies to the various products identified and to determine their views of the potential factor, the sustainability factor, and the robustness factor. This information was used to calculate the financial value of the core competencies. To test these results, an intermediary evaluation session was organized with key people. This would, in most cases, lead to the need for additional data. After some final data gathering, the supplement to the annual report was produced. This supplement was reported to the management.

This realization design concluded this version of the weightless wealth tool kit. Until now, the method has been rather abstract and it may look complicated to you. In the next chapter I describe six case studies that show how we used the tool kit in practice. These practical examples help to explain the basic mechanisms of the tool kit. The tool kit itself can be found in Appendix B. The next chapter also shows that the implementation of the tool kit was not always very successful.

Test: Trying Out the New Method

At the end of the day
It is what you do not what you say
At the end of the day
You'll be fine

At the End of the Day, Spock's Beard from the album V

On September 29, 1998, we met with the management team of Bank Ltd. This prestigious private bank occupies a majestic old building in the heart of Amsterdam, alongside the canal. We were impressed by the grandeur of the environment and the seniority of the management team. We were nervous, and we were not at all confident the bank would accept our ideas and that our method would work.

In this chapter I describe the results of this and five other consecutive case studies. Unfortunately, for reasons of confidentiality, I have to use aliases for all the companies participating in the research (Table 5.1).

We selected the first three cases—Bank Ltd., Electro Ltd. and Automotive Ltd.—as part of a study funded by the Ministry of Economic Affairs. These companies were selected because they were medium-size knowledge-intensive businesses covering various industries. Logistic Services BU was the fourth client for the new method. The management of Logistic Services BU wanted to value its core competencies. Professional Services LLP was the fifth client. It wanted to report intangible resources in its annual report. Lastly, Consulting Department was a small consulting unit within a larger financial institution. We offered them help on determining their strengths and weaknesses as part of their decision process about becoming an independent consulting firm.

Table 5.1

Overview of Case Studies			
Case Study	**Timeframe**	**Industry**	**Type of Organization**
Bank Ltd.	September 1998–February 1999	Banking	Subsidiary of listed company
Electro Ltd.	October 1998–February 1999	Engineering	Subsidiary of listed company
Automotive Ltd.	October 1998–February 1999	Automotive	Private company
Logistic Services BU	June 99	Logistics	Department of listed company
Professional Services LLP	November 1999–June 2000	Professional Services	Professional partnership
Consulting Department	January 2000	Banking	Department of subsidiary of listed company

In each case, an implementation team used the regulative cycle to plan and implement interventions (Figure 5.1). In this chapter I describe the results of these implementations following the steps of the regulative cycle. I describe the specific context of the subject company and the problem definition that actuated the use of the method. Each case study involved a particular context leading to a tailor-made design of the method. I describe the specific requirements and the specific design. I then describe the implementation process and the results.

I evaluate each case study based on the lessons learned. The evaluation focuses on the case-specific problem and context, the specific requirements and design, and the results. Each section concludes with answering three evaluation questions based on the reflective cycle described in Chapter 2:

1. Was the case part of the application domain?
2. What does this case say about the success of the method?
3. What does this case say about possible improvements to the method?

The evaluation was based on the following input:

- A meeting with the manager or the management team of the subject company after the case was finished (At this meeting the results were presented and evaluated.)

Figure 5.1

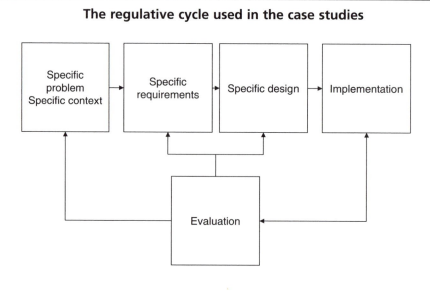

The regulative cycle used in the case studies

- An evaluation session with the implementation team after the case was finished
- Discussions with colleagues about the method
- Reflections about the success of each intervention through introspection
- In four of the six cases, a meeting with the manager of the company that took place between 1.5 and 2 years after the investigation

The lessons learned often resulted in modifications to the method. Following Weggeman (1995), I decided to distinguish between modifications that are improvements to the method (I) and those that are extensions to the method (E). I present these modifications at the end of each case study.

In addition, I evaluate the quality of the implementation process using the indicators described in Chapter 2. The purpose is to exclude the effects of the quality of the implementation from the analysis of the success of the method. In some cases it turned out that the method was not as successful as it could have been because of poor implementation by me and my implementation team.

Table 5.2 provides an overview of the data collection and analysis methods that we used during the case studies. The three main sources of data were personal interviews, structured discussions using a

Table 5.2

Summary of Data Collection and Analysis Methods	
Case Study	**Data Collection and Analysis Tools**
Bank Ltd.	Intake with management board Document analysis Three combined interviews (1.5 hours) with two informants using interview protocol; field notes used Structured workshop with two members of management board, presentation of findings by analyst, followed by discussion Document analysis Analysis of financial data Three interviews with member management board, financial controller, and accountant (1.5 hours) using interview protocol; field notes used Two unstructured interviews with audit team members; field notes used Structured workshop with 18 managers Unstructured workshop with three members of management board, presentation of the findings by implementation team, followed by discussion
Electro Ltd.	Intake with management board Document analysis Eight combined interviews (1.5 hours) each with two to three informants using interview protocol; field notes used Structured workshop with five managers, presentation of the findings by analyst, followed by discussion Document analysis Structured workshop with six managers Analysis of financial data Unstructured workshop with CEO, presentation of findings by implementation team, followed by discussion
Automotive Ltd.	Intake with management board Document analysis Six interviews (1.5 hours) with managers using interview protocol; field notes used Structured workshop with six managers, presentation of findings by analyst, followed by discussion Analysis of financial data Questionnaire
Logistic Services BU	Structured workshop with eight managers with brainstorming session Structured workshop with 11 managers Analysis of financial data Interview with financial director Unstructured workshop with general manager, financial director, and project manager, presentation of findings by implementation team, followed by discussion

Table 5.2 *continued*

Summary of Data Collection and Analysis Methods	
Case Study	**Data Collection and Analysis Tools**
Professional Services LLP	Thirty-four interviews (1.5 hours) using interview protocol; field notes used Document analysis from 37 different sources Unstructured workshop management team, presentation of findings by implementation team, followed by discussion
Consulting Department	Intake with manager Structured workshop with whole department Analysis of financial data

workshop format, and document analysis primarily focusing on financial data.

The first three cases partly took place in parallel. We developed most of the practical tools for Bank Ltd. and then used the same tools for Electro Ltd. and Automotive Ltd. When we were halfway through the Bank Ltd. case study, we added two elements to the original design, which we then implemented at both Bank Ltd. and Electro Ltd. I describe these additions as part of the case report of Bank Ltd.

Bank Ltd.

In this section I describe the results of the first case study at Bank Ltd. I portray Bank Ltd.'s specific context and the problem that triggered its management to participate. I then focus on the special realization design we used to cope with some specific operational requirements and limiting conditions. Next, I describe the implementation of the new method and present the results. After that, I go into the modifications we made to our original design because of the outcome of the second workshop. Finally, I evaluate the case study and describe the modifications we made to the design, based on the lessons learned.

This section about Bank Ltd. is more extensive than the sections about the consecutive case studies. The reason is twofold. First, this section describes each phase of the method in detail to give you an impression of how the method works in practice. Second, this case resulted in important lessons learned, leading to two major extensions to the method. I describe these modifications in detail.

Context and Problem Definition

Bank Ltd. was an independent private bank that was part of a worldwide financial institution. As a small private bank, it nurtured its independence and objectivity in serving clients. Bank Ltd. was interested in testing the new method because management faced the challenge of convincing the holding company that Bank Ltd.'s independent position within the holding and the bank's distinct style and identity were vital for its future success. Management feared that the reorganization of the holding company might threaten the position of the bank and might lead to the loss of valuable intangibles.

The specific problem they wanted to solve was how to give the holding company insight into the importance of the bank's intangible resources like corporate identity, leadership style, and values and norms. According to the management of Bank Ltd., this insight was needed to promote a "nonintervention" policy on behalf of the holding company and to secure independence in the future. As the CEO phrased it: "What is the value of our independence?" Bank Ltd. had had some previous experience with the concept of core competence. During their two-day business planning session in 1997, management had spent half a day studying the concept and applying it to the bank.

Specific Requirements and Design

1998 was a busy year for Bank Ltd. Profits grew by 36% and personnel by 18%. The time available to participate in the study was limited. We decided to arrange a limited number of interviews with six key players and to incorporate the two workshops into management meetings that had already been planned. One of the members of the management board was appointed as the contact person, and we had two additional meetings with him to report progress. We also used members of the KPMG audit team as a source of information, and they accompanied us at interviews.

The first two-hour workshop with two members of the management team took place as part of a regular board meeting. The second workshop was part of a two-day business planning session that involved 18 top managers. At that meeting we spent three hours on the topic. Three additional interviews were arranged to sort out financial data.

Finally, the results were presented during a regular meeting of the management board, at which all members of the board were present. It was during this meeting that we made a vital mistake.

Implementation and Results

This section is divided into the object recognition phase (interviews and first workshop) and the valuation phase (additional data gathering and the second workshop). The results of the case study have been reported to the client in a confidential report (KPMG, 1999b).

Object Recognition

We used the interview protocol to identify Bank Ltd.'s core competencies and underlying intangible resources. From the interviews, it became clear that people were the bank's most important intangibles. Its employees were proud of their company and created a corporate culture with a strong client and human focus in which tailor-made services were key. Important skills included the ability to work in teams and to establish networks of people inside and outside the company.

The interviews and document analysis produced an overview of intangible resources that were of strategic importance to the future success of Bank Ltd. (Table 5.3). Bank Ltd. was a nonhierarchical organization with short lines of control. This was partly the result of its relatively small size. The short lines of control enabled the company to be flexible and have a high rate of execution. The image and reputation of Bank Ltd. were strong and mostly maintained by word of mouth. The members of the management board and the key account managers had a strong network of clients and people in the financial world. These networks and the act of networking played a vital role in the bank's success. The network of clients was often the source of new clients. The networks within the financial sector helped to recruit new employees and provide useful information on investment funds. We decided to name the final report *The Intangible Resources of Bank Ltd.: The Networking Bank* (KPMG, 1999b).

From the interviews, we made four observations. First, most of the intangible resources of Bank Ltd. were human resources as opposed to structural resources. This is typical of a professional service provider. Bank Ltd.'s tacit knowledge and skills, and its human-focused corporate culture were vital to its success.

Second, most employees of Bank Ltd. could be characterized as knowledge professionals, which Tissen et al. (2000) call *smart*

Table 5.3

Overview of Intangible Resources of Bank Ltd.				
Skills and Tacit Knowledge	Values and Norms	Technology and Explicit Knowledge	Management Processes	Endowments
Social skills and networks Ability to discover talent Recruitment Coaching and training Recognizing opportunities Ability to focus Feel at ease in client circles Professional knowledge Knowledge about customers Accounting knowledge Information technology knowledge Knowledge about processes Market knowledge Research	Client focus instead of product focus Freedom to act Challenge and debate Optimism Modesty Trust Professionalism Independence Human focus Acknowledgment of expertise "Nothing is impossible" Speed	Investment policy Indexation methodology Other methodologies Trading system Handbook administrative organization	Short lines of control Teamwork Treating employees as professionals Coaching Providing freedom to act Partnerships Management by objectives Self-steering teams Job rotation Remuneration on the basis of achievement Profit sharing by personnel International Standards Organization (ISO) 9002 audits	Reputation Networks and personal relationships Customer base ISO 9002 certificate Access to low-priced money

professionals. Smart professionals have a lot of knowledge and they work according to high personal professional standards. They perform best when given a high degree of freedom to act and the opportunity to develop their talents. The leadership style within Bank Ltd. was attuned to managing smart professionals. It promoted short lines of control, working in teams, personal coaching, and the principle of (what the CEO called) "management by objectives." The small size of the company and its relative independence made it possible to apply such a leadership style.

Third, customer focus was a strong element in Bank Ltd.'s corporate culture. For a private banker this is a necessity. Private banking requires a personal touch, modesty, and servitude. Bank Ltd. combined such an attitude with flexibility and a made-to-measure approach, based on the adage that "nothing is impossible."

Fourth, in many professional services firms, most of the knowledge remains implicit. As an exception, Bank Ltd. had made some of its vital knowledge explicit by documenting its investment policy and some of its investment methods.

Based on the information acquired through the interviews, we developed four core competence hypotheses. The first core competence was the ability to provide customer-oriented tailor-made services. This is the ability to generate customer loyalty by providing customized solutions on a highly personalized basis, in which professionalism, independence, service provision, and clarity play a key role. The second core competence was the ability to leverage ideas. This is the ability to identify people with revolutionary new ideas, bind them to the organization, and leverage their ideas, giving clients access to innovative solutions. The third core competence we identified was the bank's ability to manage professionals. This is the ability to recruit the best professionals, tie them to the organization, and develop their skills, resulting in exceptional services to clients. The final core competence was the processing of orders. This is the ability to process cost-effectively large amounts of orders, enabling the provision of services to clients at high quality and low costs.

We applied the following five tests to check whether these competencies were truly core competencies:

1. Added value test: Does the competence provide added value to customers?
2. Competitiveness test: Is Bank Ltd. better in this specific competence than its competitors?
3. Potential test: Does this competence provide opportunities to create new products and services in the future?
4. Sustainability test: How difficult it is for competitors to imitate the competence?
5. Robustness test: How well is this competence anchored within the organization?

A draft assessment was based on the interviews and additional documentation. We then organized a workshop with two members of the management board to present them with the findings. In the opinion of the managers, two competencies were missing. First, they were of the opinion that the bank had the ability to invest with an above-average midterm return at a low risk. Second, they thought Bank Ltd. also had a core competence to do research and to generate objective information for clients, investors, and the media from multiple sources. As a modification to the core competencies presented by the implementation

Table 5.4

Results of Core Competence Test of Bank Ltd.					
Core Competence	Added Value Test	Competitiveness Test	Potential Test	Sustainability Test	Robustness Test
Providing customer-oriented tailor-made services	✓	✓	? → X	? → ✓	✓
Leveraging ideas	✓	?	✓	? → X	X
Managing professionals	X	?	✓ → ?	? → ✓	✓
Processing orders	X → ✓	X	X → ?	X	✓
✓, passes the test; ?, doubtful whether it passes the test; X, fails the test; →, a shift in assessment as a result of discussion during the first workshop.					

team, they suggested broadening the competence of processing of orders to include the handling and management of data in general.

The discussion about the assessment of the competencies resulted in seven modifications (Table 5.4). None of the competencies passed all tests and some did not even pass three out of five. Yet, we decided that we would continue the investigation, looking at all four core competencies and adding the two additional ones mentioned. This resulted in the following overview of core competencies of Bank Ltd. (Table 5.5).

Financial Valuation

We developed a plan for the gathering of data that we needed for the valuation of the identified core competencies. We identified who within Bank Ltd. might be able to answer questions about the contribution margin and the potential, sustainability, and robustness factor. We discovered that it not only needed to talk to a lot of people from various parts of the company, but also that most of the questions would be difficult for interviewees to answer.

For the calculation of the contribution margins, we decided to distinguish between four products:

1. Capital management
2. Brokerage
3. Special activities
4. Administrative services

Table 5.5

		Core Competencies of Bank Ltd.			
Core Competence	Skills and Tacit Knowledge	Values and Norms	Technology and Explicit Knowledge	Management Processes	Endowments
1. Providing customer-oriented tailor-made services: The ability to generate customer loyalty by providing customized solutions on a highly personalized basis, in which professionalism, independence, service provision, and clarity play a key role.	Professional knowledge Knowledge about customers Social skills Feel at ease in client circles Networking	Client focus instead of product focus Freedom to act Challenge and debate Optimism Modesty Professionalism Independence Human focus Acknowledgment of expertise	—	Treating employees as professionals Coaching Short lines of control Providing freedom to act Teamwork	Reputation Networks and personal relationships Customer base

2. Ability to invest: The ability to invest with an above-average midterm return at a low risk.	Market knowledge Research	Challenge and debate Professionalism	Investment policy Indexation methodology Other methodologies	—	—
3. Managing professionals: The ability to recruit the best professionals, binding them to the organization and developing their skills, which results in exceptional services to clients.	Ability to discover talent Recruitment Coaching and training Social skills	Freedom to act Challenge and debate Professionalism Independence Human focus Acknowledgment of expertise	—	Short lines of control Management by objectives Teamwork Partnerships Self-steering teams Job rotation Remuneration on the basis of achievement	Reputation

Table 5.5 continued

Core Competencies of Bank Ltd.

Core Competence	Skills and Tacit Knowledge	Values and Norms	Technology and Explicit Knowledge	Management Processes	Endowments
4. Research: The ability to generate objective information for clients, investors, and the media from multiple sources.	Market knowledge Knowledge about financial institutions	Challenge and debate Professionalism Speed	Various methodologies	—	—
5. Ability to leverage ideas: The ability to identify people with revolutionary new ideas, bind them to the organization, and leverage their ideas, which gives clients access to innovative solutions.	Social skills and networks Recognizing opportunities Ability to focus Professional knowledge	Freedom to act Challenge and debate Trust Professionalism	—	Short lines of control Providing freedom to act Partnerships Management by objectives	Networks and personal relationships Access to cheap money

6. Data processing and management: The ability to process and manage large amounts of data cost-effectively, which enables providing services to clients at high quality and low costs, and providing them access to information.	Knowledge of accounting Information technology knowledge Knowledge about processes	Professionalism Speed Accuracy	Handbook administrative organization	ISO 9002 audits	ISO 9002 certificate

—, not applicable.

For each product, we extracted the revenues generated in 1997 from the financial accounts. We calculated the direct costs for each of the four products by adding the labor costs of all front-office personnel working on the various products and adding a percentage of the back-office costs. This percentage was based on the share of each product in the total number of transactions processed by the back office.

The income funnel requirement demands that we isolate a portion of the contribution margin that is a fair rate of return for other assets. Bank Ltd. had limited tangible and networking capital assets. We calculated all tangible fixed assets at book value, as well as a participation in a subsidiary. The total was 12 million guilders. It used a rate of return of 5% and subtracted 0.6 million from the contribution margin as a fair rate of return for other assets. This amount was allocated corresponding to the size of the contribution margin (Table 5.6).

This resulted in a calculation of the contribution margin per product. To estimate the contribution margin per core competence, we asked the participants of the second workshop to assess the contribution of each core competence to each product, using the tool to allocate the contribution margin of the products and services to the underlying core competencies as described in the section about income allocation requirement in Chapter 4.

We soon found out it was impossible to gather the information needed to determine the potential, sustainability, and robustness factor. We decided to change the design of the method and to ask the participants during the second workshop to estimate these factors. We asked the participants to make an assessment, based on a checklist indicating various issues that affect these factors. We reviewed these

Table 5.6

Contribution Margins of Bank Ltd. (in millions of guilders)			
Product	Contribution Margin	Compensation for Other Assets	Adjusted Contribution Margin
Capital management	13.8	0.2	13.6
Brokerage	17.6	0.3	17.3
Special activities	3.4	0.1	3.3
Administrative services	2.4	0.0	2.4
Total	37.2	0.6	36.6

assessments and amended them when needed, based on expert opinion. The checklists were partly based on the valuation questions and partly based on the champagne test, as used during the Vision 2000 project. Eighteen managers of Bank Ltd. attended the three-hour workshop. They were divided into three groups, and we asked them to discuss two core competencies each. The assignment was to

- Assess the contribution of the core competence to each of the four products
- Fill in the checklists for potential, sustainability, and robustness
- Assess the potential, sustainability, and robustness factor
- Suggest ways to improve the potential, sustainability, and robustness of the core competence

None of the teams had any trouble in deciding how important a specific core competence was for a specific product. This exercise produced the results presented in Table 5.7.

We used these results to allocate the contribution margin of the products to each core competence. First, the relative share of each

Table 5.7

Product/Competence Matrix of Bank Ltd.				
Core Competence	Capital Management	Brokerage	Special Activities	Administrative Services
Providing customer-oriented tailor-made services	3	3	2	1
Ability to invest	3	3	3	2
Managing professionals	2	2	3	2
Research	2	2	1	1
Ability to leverage ideas	1	1	3	0
Data processing and management	2	2	1	3
Total	13	13	13	9

0, no contribution; 1, supporting contribution; 2, substantial contribution; 3, essential contribution.

Table 5.8

Contribution of Core Competencies to Products of Bank Ltd.				
Core Competence	Capital Management, %	Brokerage, %	Special Activities, %	Administrative Services, %
Providing customer-oriented tailor-made services	23	23	15	11
Ability to invest	23	23	23	22
Managing professionals	15	15	23	22
Research	15	15	8	11
Ability to leverage ideas	8	8	23	0
Data processing and management	15	15	8	33
Total	100	100	100	100

competence in the product was calculated using the scores in Table 5.7 (see Table 5.8).

These percentages were used to allocate the contribution margin of the products to the core competencies (Table 5.9).

It was much more difficult for the teams to assess the potential, sustainability, and robustness factor. Determining the potential factor

Table 5.9

Allocation of Contribution Margin to Core Competencies of Bank Ltd. (in millions of guilders)	
Core Competence	Allocated Adjusted Contribution Margin
Providing customer-oriented tailor-made services	7.9
Ability to invest	8.4
Managing professionals	6.0
Research	5.3
Ability to leverage ideas	3.1
Data processing and management	5.8
Total	36.6

requires an estimation of the average growth of the contribution margin of the core competence. A checklist helped the teams to determine whether this growth would be positive or negative. The checklist focuses on three factors that influence the possibility to leverage a core competence: the growth in market demand for products or services based on the competence, the possibility to leverage the competence through new products and services, and external developments that may threaten the use of the competence. However, pinpointing the exact size of the growth figure was not easy. To help the teams estimate the growth figure, we showed them a line with numbers ranging from −10 to +10%. The teams used this line to plot the potential factor.

The discussions of the teams regarding the potential of the core competencies led to interesting conclusions. It was generally felt that the main portion of future growth would be the result of the ability to provide customer-oriented tailor-made services. It was felt that the ability to manage professionals and to process data had a more supporting role. With respect to the latter, the issue was raised whether the data processing systems of the bank would be able to meet the increasing demand of customers for customized management reports.

There was not much confidence that the core competence the ability to invest would remain unique. The teams identified certain threats that would affect the potential of the core competence. The same was the case with the ability to do research and to leverage ideas. With the financial markets becoming more global and complex, the teams wondered whether in the future the relatively small research team would be able to deliver the same level of quality. The innovation process of the bank was not really institutionalized. Instead, it depended on a small number of people. The teams worried whether Bank Ltd. would be able to keep up with the speed of innovation within the sector.

Some of the estimations produced by the teams looked unrealistic, so we decided to check them using expert opinion. This resulted in a number of small changes. Table 5.10 shows for each core competence the result of the checklist (a score between −2 and +2), the team's estimation of the growth figure, the adjusted growth figure as a result of the expert review, and a justification of the adjustments made. It is clear that there is limited correlation between the results of the checklist and the teams' estimation of the potential factor.

Assessing the sustainability factor proved to be difficult too. Because the concept of core competence is rather abstract, it was difficult for the teams to gauge the number of years it would take a competitor to master the same competence. Again, the teams could express whether they thought it would be difficult, but to pin down the exact number of years turned out to be hard.

Table 5.10

Estimation of the Potential Factors of Bank Ltd.				
Core Competence	Potential Checklist, −2 to +2	Team Estimation, −10% to +10%	Expert Estimation, −10% to +10%)	Justification
Providing customer-oriented tailor-made services	2	10%	10%	—
Ability to invest	1	2%	2%	—
Managing professionals	2	5%	5%	—
Research	1	10% for capital management, 0% for brokerage	4.4%	This is a weighted average of the growth factor for capital management and brokerage (weight used = contribution margin)
Ability to leverage ideas	1	0%	5%	The checklist shows a positive score and there has been a growth of approximately 5% in recent years in related products
Data processing and management	2	2%	2%	—

We provided them with a checklist to help consider the various elements that influence sustainability. The checklist focused on the scarcity of the competence, the time and money required to master the competence, the complexity of the competence, and whether the competence can be obtained from outside sources. To help the teams estimate the sustainability further, we showed them a line with numbers ranging from 0 to 10.

The workshop participants raised serious doubts whether the ability to do data processing and management was a core competence. There was a general concern that the processes and information technology systems used by Bank Ltd. were not that sophisticated to allow a claim that Bank Ltd. was better than the competition. Consequently, the teams decided that the sustainability was zero years. The teams had the same doubts about the ability to invest. They were of the opinion that Bank Ltd.'s investment policy could be copied quite easily, although it would be more difficult for a competitor to make sure the policy is in "the veins of all the people," as one participant put it.

Furthermore, the teams were of the opinion that the ability to do research was not scarce, not unique, and could be easily copied. Here the teams made a distinction between research done by the capital management department and research done by brokerage. On capital management they were much more optimistic. The sustainability of the competence leveraging ideas produced further discussion on the uniqueness of this competence. It was felt that this competence was neither scarce nor did it require a lot of time or money to master. The teams decided that its sustainability was zero years.

These discussions produced valuable insights into the sustainability of the competencies but they also produced some inconsistencies. There was limited correlation between the results of the checklist and the estimation of the sustainability factor, especially in the case of the ability to invest, leverage ideas, and data processing. We decided to make some modifications to the estimations to bring the results of the checklist and the estimations of the sustainability factor more in line (Table 5.11).

To help the teams assess the robustness of the competencies, we developed a checklist listing threats to maintaining the competence. Most teams were able to identify risks but they found it difficult to express that risk as a percentage. They spotted a reputational risk for the core competencies managing professionals and research, and they were worried about the relatively small competence community for research and leveraging ideas. They were of the opinion that in the case of the ability to do research and to leverage ideas, the installed client base and the networks of people were vulnerable.

The results of the assessment and the modifications by our implementation team are presented in Table 5.12. There is a strong link between the results of the checklist and the team estimations, except for data processing and management. The team that reviewed this competence concluded this capability was not a core competence. Therefore, it decided the robustness of the competence was 0%. However, this is not a legitimate reason to assess the robustness of the

Table 5.11

Estimation of the Sustainability Factor of Bank Ltd.				
Core Competence	Sustainability checklist, 0–5 points	Team Estimation, 0–10 years	Expert Estimation, 0–10 years	Justification
Providing customer-oriented tailor-made services	5	5	5	—
Ability to invest	1	3	3	—
Managing professionals	4	4	4	—
Research	5 for capital management, 1 for brokerage	5 for capital management, 0 for brokerage	2	This is a rounded, weighted average of the sustainability for capital management and brokerage (weight used = contribution margin)
Ability to leverage ideas	2	0	2	The competence seems to be difficult to imitate and therefore it seems reasonable to assume a certain period of time in which Bank Ltd. can keep its advantage
Data processing and management	3	0	0	This indeed does not seem to be a true core competence

Table 5.12

Estimation of the Robustness Factor of Bank Ltd.				
Core Competence	Robustness Checklist, 0–5 points	Team Estimation, 0–100%	Expert Estimation, 0–100%	Justification
Providing customer-oriented tailor-made services	3	100%	100%	—
Ability to invest	5	100%	100%	—
Managing professionals	4	90%	80%	The fact that this ability depends strongly on the CEO was not mentioned at the workshop but is a clear reason to lower further the robustness
Research	3	80%	80%	—
Ability to leverage ideas	3	60%	60%	—
Data processing and management	4	0%	80%	Whether this is a core competence is irrelevant for assessing the robustness of the competence

competence at 0%. A competence that is not core can still have certain robustness. Therefore, we changed the estimation.

The calculation of the contribution margin and the estimation of the potential, sustainability, and robustness factor were used to calculate the value of each core competence using the formula as described in Chapter 4. Table 5.13 presents per core competence the contribution margin (CM) in year t = 0, the potential factor (P) expressing the expected yearly growth of this margin, and the sustainability factor (S) expressing the number of years this margin is included in the calculation. Then for each year the contribution margin is calculated, the total is multiplied by the robustness factor (R), resulting in the total value

Table 5.13

Intangible Value of Bank Ltd. (millions of guilders)

Competence	CM, t = 0	P, %	S, years	t = 1	t = 2	t = 3	t = 4	t = 5	R, %	Total
Providing customer-oriented tailor-made services	7.9	10	5	8.7	9.6	10.5	11.6	12.7	100	53.1
Ability to invest	8.4	2	3	8.6	8.7	8.9	—	—	100	26.2
Managing professionals	6.0	5	4	6.3	6.6	6.9	7.3	—	80	21.7
Research	5.3	4	2	5.5	5.8	—	—	—	80	9.0
Ability to leverage ideas	3.1	5	2	3.3	3.4	—	—	—	60	4.0
Data processing and management	5.8	2	0	—	—	—	—	—	80	0
Total	30.7	—	—	32.3	34.1	26.4	18.9	12.7	—	114

of each core competence and the total value of all the strategically important intangible resources of Bank Ltd. (114 million guilders).

Additions to the Design

The experiences with Bank Ltd. showed how difficult it was to derive robust measures for the potential, sustainability, and robustness factor. The data needed to support these estimations were not available or were too time-consuming to generate. The alternative—using participants of the second workshop to assess these factors and using expert opinion as a crosscheck—resulted in only a rough calculation.

The discussions that took place during the second workshop on the potential, sustainability, and robustness of the core competencies turned out to be useful. Each team produced a number of recommendations for further improvement of these factors. These recommendations were discussed at the end of the workshop and were commented on by the CEO. We decided to capture these recommendations and report them in the final report.

To accommodate these recommendations, we made three modifications to the method. First, the checklists used to facilitate the assessment of the potential, sustainability, and robustness factor were transformed into a stand-alone tool for assessing the strength of a core competence. Two more checklists, one for the added value and one for the competitiveness of a core competence, were added. The potential checklist was revised to include five items so that the score could range from 0 to 5 points.

A second extension to the method was a *value dashboard*. This dashboard is a graphical representation that summarizes the results of the strength assessment and the financial valuation. This dashboard was intended to be used as part of a supplement to the annual report (Figure 5.2).

The third extension was a management agenda. This agenda incorporates the recommendations on how to improve the added value, competitiveness, potential, sustainability, and robustness of the intangible resources of a company. It translates the results of the core competence checklists into action points for managers.

The final report to Bank Ltd. consisted of the management agenda, an introductory text explaining the background and methodology of the research, an overview of the intangible resources of Bank Ltd., an overview of core competencies including their financial value using the value dashboard, and a list of recommendations. I briefly discuss the content of the value dashboard and the management agenda of Bank Ltd. in the next two sections.

Figure 5.2

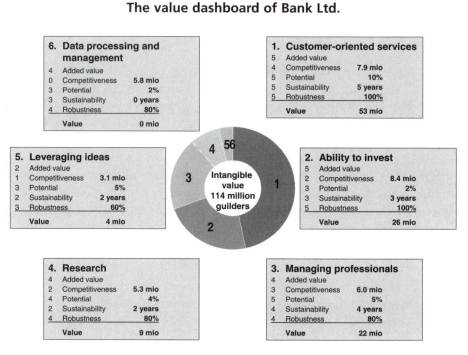

The value dashboard of Bank Ltd.

Value Dashboard

The value dashboard (see Figure 5.2) showed that the ability to provide tailor-made customer-oriented services was the most important core competence of Bank Ltd., with a value of 53 million guilders. This ability made Bank Ltd. stand out in the capital management market. In The Netherlands, the capital management market was a rapidly growing market, developing at 8% a year and attracting new service providers. Most of them were part of a large U.S.-oriented financial institution (in the year we did the case study, Merrill Lynch opened its first office in The Netherlands) offering standardized products and services that were less personal than the service of Bank Ltd. In the report to Bank Ltd., we expressed our concern regarding this competence. Although the market was growing, most of the new rich people are younger in age and have earned their fortune themselves. They often have a strong view on trading and investment, and look for a high return. It is questionable whether this group would appreciate Bank Ltd.'s personal approach. It could very well be that this group was not looking for service, but simply a high yield.

Although the ability to invest was core to Bank Ltd., it does not really distinguish Bank Ltd. from its competitors. We warned that the market for investment products would become more transparent. The rising popularity of mutual funds and the increasing possibilities to benchmark the performance of these funds is a threat to this core competence. The low score on the value dashboard of the competitiveness, potential, and sustainability factor reflect this issue. This threat affected the value of the core competence substantially. Its contribution to the contribution margin (8.4 million guilders) is the highest of all core competencies, but its value is much lower than the value of the most valuable core competence.

The ease at which Bank Ltd. recruited professionals and the low turnover of staff (in a time [1998] when there was a scarcity of professionals in the labor market) was evidence that the bank had a competence in managing professionals. Because people were the bank's most important resource, this competence played an important supporting role in generating cash flow. However, its robustness was not 100% because the competence depended largely on the leadership style of the CEO.

The value dashboard showed that the ability to do research was not that valuable, mainly because the bank was not really better at it than other banks. Given the size of the Bank's research team, this did not come as a surprise. In addition, the relatively small size of the team affected the robustness of this core competence.

Although Bank Ltd. had proved that it was able to create new and innovative products, its ability to leverage ideas suffered from a lack of competitiveness, sustainability, and robustness. The value of this core competence was therefore quite low. With respect to data processing and management, we concluded that this was not a core competence because Bank Ltd. certainly was not better at it than the competition. This resulted in a sustainability of zero years and thus a value of zero.

Management Agenda

We wrote a management agenda incorporating all recommendations on how to improve the added value, competitiveness, potential, sustainability, and robustness of the intangible resources of Bank Ltd. (Table 5.14).

Reporting to the Client

We organized a meeting with the management board of Bank Ltd. to discuss the draft version of the end report. At this meeting, we made

Table 5.14

Management Agenda of Bank Ltd.	
Factor	**Key Question**
Added value	*Does Bank Ltd. exceed customer expectations on a permanent basis?* Current customers of Bank Ltd. appreciate its personal style, its tailor-made services, and its above-average return on investment at low risk. The bank may increase its added value to customers by increasing its focus on performance, improving its customer reports and putting them online, and by putting more effort into product innovation.
Competitiveness	*Will the bank stand out from its traditional and new competitors in future times?* As a niche player, Bank Ltd. has gained a distinct position in the Dutch capital management market. Its competitiveness is, to a large extent, based on its ability to provide customer-oriented tailor-made services, its image in the marketplace, as well as its networks of clients. The number of players entering this market is growing. Bank Ltd. can stay unique by leveraging its image and its competencies in the market of new rich people.
Potential	*How can Bank Ltd. leverage its core competencies?* Bank Ltd. is not known for its ability to innovate. Current innovation is primarily the result of hiring people with new ideas. The ability to innovate can be improved by setting up innovation teams and innovation projects.
Sustainability	*Does Bank Ltd. protect its competencies against the competition?* Most of the core competencies of Bank Ltd. are embedded in its company culture and leadership style. Both are closely related to the size of the bank, its nonhierarchical structure, and its teamwork. This makes it difficult for competitors to imitate the competencies. Bank Ltd. may improve its sustainability by intensifying the coaching of personnel and by introducing a peer review mechanism.
Robustness	*Does Bank Ltd. run the risk of losing its core competencies?* Some of Bank Ltd.'s intangible resources are vulnerable because they are relying on a very small number of people. Its research teams are relatively small. The CEO plays a major role in the bank's ability to manage professionals and leverage ideas. Introducing knowledge management principles, improving the management skills of managers, and expanding existing networks can lower this vulnerability.
Source: KPMG (1999b).	

a mistake that had a big impact on the acceptance of the findings by the client. We were running out of budget. We were of the opinion that Bank Ltd. had already received more value than they could have expected from "a free ride." At the meeting, we told the management of Bank Ltd. that the draft report was the final result of the study. We would only correct major mistakes. If the bank wanted additional research, analyses, or calculations, it would have to pay.

The management team was very surprised. To their expectation, this report was merely the feedback of the results of the second workshop. It was the first time that the management team had seen the results of the valuation. They had additional questions and suggestions for improvement, and were disappointed that we did not want to do any additional analysis. They thought the results of the analysis were interesting, but the project was not yet finished. The management team wanted to feed the results back to the participants of the second workshop and to discuss a number of issues. For example, management was not satisfied with the way the report defined some of the core competencies. The managers felt that the discussion on whether the competencies were core was not yet finished. The definition of the competencies did not acknowledge some of the synergies that existed between the competencies. They also criticized the lack of supporting evidence for the estimation of the potential, sustainability, and robustness factor. They wanted to recalculate the values based on a more robust estimation of the factors using data that were more recent.

Overall, to them, this was an unfinished project. However, we decided to stick to our opinion. We agreed to make a number of changes to the final report but were not willing to do any additional analysis. A week later, we wrote Bank Ltd. a letter offering additional research, analyses, or calculations against regular fees; an offer to which the bank never responded.

The final report was not used as a supplement to the annual report of Bank Ltd. The annual report for the year 1999 did use some elements from the report. It stated that Bank Ltd. was continuously investing in its core competencies. The report continued by saying that "The bank's human capital deserves special mentioning. Knowledge, professionalism, personal touch, and team spirit are key factors in the reputation and performance of Bank Ltd." (Bank Ltd., 2000, translated by D. Andriessen). Our final report did play a supporting role in the discussion between Bank Ltd. and the holding company about the status of the bank. It was one of the documents used in the negotiations. The result of the deliberations was that Bank Ltd. would not be affected by the integration policy of the holding company and that it would keep its independent status.

Evaluation and Modifications

In this section I reflect on the steps and lessons learned from the Bank Ltd. case based on the steps of the regulative cycle: identifying the specific problem and context, developing specific requirements, implementing the method, and evaluating the outcome. I then reflect on the quality of the implementation and the way it affected the results. Finally, I summarize the modifications to the method that we made as a result of the lessons learned at Bank Ltd.

The problem at Bank Ltd. was related to external reporting. The specific problem at hand was the difficulty of convincing the holding company of Bank Ltd. to allow the bank to remain independent. This specific problem fit the application domain of the method, which could contribute to solving the problem. The method highlights intangibles that are essential to company success. It describes what factors strengthen and weaken these intangibles. This helps to predict the impact of integrating the company with other parts of the holding company, although that step was not part of the implementation at Bank Ltd.

The specific context of Bank Ltd. both limited and stimulated a successful implementation of the method. On the one hand, Bank Ltd. was an organization of professional, highly educated people, capable of understanding and using abstract concepts like core competence. It was an organization with a visionary leader who was aware of the importance of intangibles and who saw the potential added value of the method. On the other hand, there was little time available for management to—on top of their busy schedule—provide information and attend workshops. We had to adjust the realization design of the method to limit client involvement. We were also confronted with a budget constraint, leading to the decision to stop the project at a crucial stage in the process.

During the implementation, we ran into problems regarding the gathering of data supporting the valuation of the core competencies. Therefore, the final valuations were not grounded enough by evidence and lacked credibility. A second problem was the difficulty of deciding which competencies to include in the final valuations. After the first workshop, we included the competence data processing and management. During the second workshop, it became clear this was not really a core competence. Bank Ltd. was no better at this task than its competitors. Still, we included the competence in the calculations. We allocated 5.8 million guilders of the contribution margin to this competence. We assessed the sustainability of the competence to be zero years, resulting in a total value of this core competence of zero guilders. Had we excluded this competence from the calculations, then the contribution margin of 5.8 million guilders would have been allocated to the five remaining core competencies. The total value of the core competencies of Bank Ltd. would have increased by 22 million guilders. This problem pointed toward an omission in the method. The method was not specific about what to do with a core competence hypothesis that fails the core competence tests.

In the end, the success of the method was limited. The definitions of the six core competencies were not fully accepted by the board. When we produced our final report, there was still discussion on whether the competencies were truly core and whether all synergies between the intangibles had been identified. In addition, the valuations were not completely accepted. There was a demand for further supporting evidence. On the other hand, the method raised (but did not answer) important questions about the potential and robustness of some of the competencies. In addition, the report was used in the discussions between the holding company and Bank Ltd., although it played a minor role.

We compared the financial valuation with an estimation of the transactional value of Bank Ltd. to determine in what respect the valuation method produced a similar result. By adding the value of the intangible resources to the equity of the bank, we estimated the total value of Bank Ltd. The result was ten times the annual profit of the bank. Experts within KPMG were of the opinion that the transactional value of a bank is between ten and twenty times its annual profit. The following factors played a role in explaining the difference. First, a valuation from a buyer's perspective is an estimation of value using a different standard of value. The standard used is market value (Reilly and Schweihs, 1999), whereas the method used owner value. Because owner value does not take into account any of the additional gains to a buyer as a result of buying the company, it is often lower than market value. Furthermore, estimating a value of a company from a buyer's perspective often assumes the highest and best use of the company as the premise of value. The method used the premise of value in continued use as part of a going concern enterprise. This led to a lower estimate. Third, the method did not include all intangible resources; only those that were of strategic importance. Some intangibles may be missing in the equation. Lastly, the method used strategic life as useful life of the intangible resources. Strategic life is defined as the number of years it takes a competitor to master the same competence. This is, in general, substantially shorter than economic life used in most transaction-based valuations.

The quality of the implementation played a disturbing role in the testing of the method. Two of the conditions for a successful implementation presented in Chapter 2 were not fulfilled. We had not involved important players of the client system at crucial stages of the implementation, and there was lack of communication between our implementation team and the client system on the input and output of the valuation. It is difficult to separate the impact of the poor implementation on the success of the method from the impact of the method itself. When I asked the CEO of Bank Ltd. two years after the project was finished about the implementation, he showed not so much disappointment about the method and its potential results, but disappointment about the fact that the project was not finished properly. He indicated that the concept of core competencies was very important to him in making decisions on long-term investments. His investments were aimed at strengthening core competencies, not in adding additional products. The method had helped him notice core competencies he had previously overlooked. Especially, the core competence of managing professionals had surprised him. The fact that a team from KPMG considered this competence something special was interesting. He regarded putting a financial value on intangibles as very important. He indicated that the fact that the intangibles had a measured financial value helped to create awareness and management attention. He did feel that the financial valuation method required more robustness.

Based on the lessons learned, we made the following modifications to the design (E = extensions and I = improvements): The discussions on the potential, sustainability, and robustness of the core competencies proved to be interesting. To facilitate these discussions, a core competence checklist was developed to assess the strength of a core competence using five criteria: added value, competitiveness, potential, sustainability, and robustness (E). The result of this assessment is a score from 0 to 5 points. This core competence checklist added a value assessment method to the instrument, in addition to the financial valuation method.

The questions to help determine the potential, sustainability, and robustness factor (see Tables 4.6–4.8) turned out to be difficult to answer. If this is the case, the core competence checklist can be used to assess these factors in a workshop setting (E).

However, participants do not always produce consistent assessments. Therefore, an expert evaluation of the assessments was inserted into the valuation process to check the level consistency of the assessment. There needs to be a consistency between the scores on the core competence checklist and the estimation of the potential, sustainability, and robustness factor (I). If this is not the case, the analyst can adjust either the scores on the core competence checklist or the factors.

A value dashboard was added to summarize the results of the identification of intangibles, the value assessment, and the financial valuation (E). This turned out to be a useful communication tool.

The recommendations by the workshop participants on how to improve the potential, sustainability, and robustness of the core competencies proved to be relevant to management. Therefore, a management agenda was added to summarize action points for management (E). This management agenda translates the results of the project into action, making the method more action oriented and practical.

It is important to involve the client in the valuation process and to discuss each assumption and assessment. Specifically, the assessment of the potential, sustainability, and robustness factor need to be discussed extensively (I).

When the potential, sustainability, and robustness factor is assessed in a workshop, it is important to support the assessments with as much data as possible (I). This will improve client acceptance.

Electro Ltd.

Electro Ltd. had expressed an interest in having its "IQ" calculated even before the project with the Ministry of Economic Affairs started. The general manager of Electro Ltd. wanted to report the knowledge intensity of the company to external stakeholders. Electro Ltd. happily volunteered to participate in the study. In this section I describe the results of this second case study. First I describe Electro Ltd.'s specific context and problems, then I present the specific design used, the implementation of the method, and the results. Finally, I evaluate the case study and describe the modifications made to the design.

Context and Problem Definition

When we first visited Electro Ltd., it was an organization in turmoil. During the previous seven years, this electrical installation and engineering company had had five general managers, each one leaving within a year. The company was self-centered, product oriented, and lacked market focus. For the previous two years, the number of contracts won had declined rapidly. The profits from national and international projects were under severe pressure.

The newly appointed general manager was working on a turnaround, improving the market orientation and sales capability of the company, and developing a strategy focused on specific product/market combinations. He wanted to improve the structure, efficiency, and quality of the company's processes and planning and control cycle using the concept of total quality management.

The development of a new strategy was still in its infancy. The company was trying to create insight into its existing technologies and products, and into the markets it served. No decisions had yet been made, but there was a feeling that the company should transform from a low added-value company installing technical systems to a high added-value company designing complex electrical–technical systems.

At the first meeting the general manager was enthusiastic about the method and felt it could help in developing the new strategy, in setting priorities, and in determining focus. At that time, neither the general manager nor our implementation team knew there were other, much more urgent problems on the horizon.

Specific Requirements and Design

The general manager wanted to implement the method using the client collaboration mode. He considered the case study a learning opportunity for members of his staff. He appointed a project leader and established an Electro Ltd. project team that worked side by side with our implementation team during the implementation process.

The realization design consisted of a document analysis phase, a series of eight interviews with a total of 13 people, two workshops with five managers, and a closing presentation of the results to the general manager. In addition, two meetings were held with the project team of Electro Ltd. One member of this team was present at the interviews. All members were involved in gathering data.

Implementation and Results

The results of this case study have been reported to Electro Ltd. in a confidential report (KPMG, 1999c).

Object Recognition

Based on document analysis and interviews, we created an overview of strategically important intangible resources supporting a number of competencies (Table 5.15). We found mainly human-related intangible resources; people collaborating in an informal way using their personal technical skills and knowledge. An essential company value was technical excellence. Main drivers of employee behavior were the determination to provide high-quality technical solutions and to explore technological possibilities. Consequently, clients often received

Table 5.15

Overview of Intangible Resources of Electro Ltd.				
Skills and Tacit Knowledge	Values and Norms	Technology and Explicit Knowledge	Management Processes	Endowments
Knowledge of power generation, transportation, and distribution Knowledge of high-voltage technology Knowledge of technical automation Engineering knowledge High-power electronics Providing tailor-made services Experience in working in exotic places	Technical mind-set Strong personal motivation Professionalism Independence Acknowledging individual expertise Team spirit	ISO handbook Sales information system	Working in teams Using people as professionals Hierarchical management style Freedom of action ISO 9000 audits EFQM process	(Former) reputation Networks and personal relationships Relationships with large industrial companies ISO 9000 certificate

more value than they were charged for. Most technical knowledge of Electro Ltd. was implicit knowledge. The only explicit knowledge available was an ISO handbook that codified some of the procedures. We noticed a tension in the style of management. The organization established itself as a group of professionals. It savored teamwork and personal responsibility. However, this conflicted increasingly with the hierarchical style used by the general manager to implement the company's turnaround. The main endowment of the company was its strong relationship with its clients. The company had lost most of its brand recognition when it changed its name the year before.

We used two workshops to develop core competence hypotheses. We made a distinction between technical competencies and market access competencies. At the start of the first workshop, we provided the participants with a list of mainly market access competence hypotheses. The participants rejected all of them and replaced them with six technical competencies and one market access competence. It turned out to be useful to distinguish between three types of activities within Electro Ltd. One part of the company was focusing on designing technical systems, another part was focusing on installing technical systems, and the company developed technical systems, which included the whole process of designing and installing. Some technical competencies had to do with designing systems; others had to do with installing or realizing systems.

We revised the core competence definitions and presented them during a second workshop. The participants of the second workshop agreed on the following seven core competencies:

1. Designing energy conversion systems
2. Installing electrical systems
3. Realizing traffic management systems
4. Designing transmission systems
5. Realizing small-scale power generators
6. Serving the infrastructure industry
7. Designing process management systems

Designing energy conversion systems, designing transmission systems, and realizing small-scale power generators were core competencies that had their roots in the energy supply expertise that had been built up over the years. Realizing traffic management systems and designing process management systems were more recently acquired. Serving the infrastructure industry was the only nontechnical competence. It pointed toward the ability to cope with the very specific characteristics of the infrastructure industry.

Financial Valuation

For the valuation of the seven core competencies, we used the workshop assessment approach used at Bank Ltd. We organized a workshop and divided the participants into teams. Each team was asked to look at three or four core competencies and to assess the contribution of the competencies to a number of product groups. They were asked to assess the potential, sustainability, and robustness factor of the competencies as well.

We used revenue and cost figures of Electro Ltd. projects from 1996 and 1997 to create a list of 16 product groups and to calculate a contribution margin for each group. A compensation for tangible and financial assets of 1.1 million guilders was included in the calculations. The results of the workshop were used to allocate a total contribution margin of 17.7 million guilders to the seven competencies, as shown in Table 5.16.

It became clear that the low-tech, low-added value competence of installing systems was still very much a cash cow for the company. This triggered a discussion on the company's strategy. If the company

Table 5.16

Allocation of Contribution Margin to Core Competencies of Electro Ltd. (in millions of guilders)	
Core Competence	**Allocated Adjusted Contribution Margin**
Designing energy conversion systems	2.8
Designing transmission systems	2.7
Installing electrical systems	4.7
Designing process management systems	0.4
Realizing traffic management systems	3.0
Realizing small-scale power generators	2.6
Serving the infrastructure industry	1.5
Total	17.7

were to transform itself into a high-added value technical engineering company, then the installation competence would be the competence to fund this transition. This competence should not be dismantled before a new source of income was available.

We checked the results of the assessments of the potential, sustainability, and robustness factor and made alterations. These adjustments were made to bring the estimations of the potential, sustainability, and robustness factor more in line with the scores on the core competence checklists. For the sustainability factor, we decided to make this factor equal to the score on the checklist. For example, designing energy conversion systems received a score of 3 points on the sustainability checklist, so it was decided to fix the sustainability factor for this core competence at three years. At Electro Ltd. there was a high turnover in staff because of the turmoil. This created a huge risk of losing vital knowledge, expertise, and relationships with clients. Most core competence communities were small, and the new company trademark was not yet an established brand. We therefore decided to lower some of the robustness estimations. The results are presented in Tables 5.17 to 5.19.

We used these estimations to calculate the value of the core competencies. Table 5.20 shows for each core competence its contribution margin (CM) in year $t = 0$, the potential factor (P), and a sustainability factor (S). Then for each consecutive year, the contribution margin is calculated. The total is multiplied by the robustness factor (R), resulting in the total value of each core competence and the total value

Table 5.17

Estimation of the Potential Factors of Electro Ltd.			
Core Competence	Potential Checklist, 0 to 5 points	Team Estimation, −10% to +10%	Expert Estimation, −10% to +10%
Designing energy conversion systems	5	10	10
Designing transmission systems	3	2	5
Installing electrical systems	2	4	0
Designing process management systems	5	10	10
Realizing traffic management systems	3	10	5
Realizing small-scale power generators	3	6	5
Serving the infrastructure industry	3	10	5

Table 5.18

Estimation of the Sustainability Factor of Electro Ltd.			
Core Competence	Sustainability Checklist, 0–5 points	Team Estimation, 0–10 years	Expert Estimation, 0–10 years
Designing energy conversion systems	3	4	3
Designing transmission systems	2	1	2
Installing electrical systems	2	1	2
Designing process management systems	1	1	1
Realizing traffic management systems	4	3	4
Realizing small-scale power generators	2	3	2
Serving the infrastructure industry	1	1	1

Table 5.19

Estimation of the Robustness Factor of Electro Ltd.			
Core Competence	**Robustness Checklist, 0–5 points**	**Team Estimation, 0–100%**	**Expert Estimation, 0–100%**
Designing energy conversion systems	3	70	60
Designing transmission systems	3	70	60
Installing electrical systems	3	80	60
Designing process management systems	2	50	40
Realizing traffic management systems	2	70	40
Realizing small-scale power generators	3	60	60
Serving the infrastructure industry	1	50	20

of all the strategically important intangible resources of Electro Ltd. (24.4 million guilders).

Value Dashboard

The value dashboard (Figure 5.3) showed that designing energy conversion systems was the most important core competence of Electro Ltd. The competence was rooted in Electro Ltd.'s traditional expertise in energy supply. The core competence had great promise, because the conversion of energy using power electronics was creating a revolution in the energy supply market at the time. However, there were also risks involved because the competition was rapidly increasing its capabilities in this field and the core competence community within Electro Ltd. was vulnerable.

The traditional competence of installing electrical systems turned out to be of high value to the company. This was a bit of a surprise, because this competence did not completely fit with the new strategy of transforming the firm into a high-tech company. Realizing traffic management systems seemed to be a very promising competence, especially when applied abroad. Designing transmission systems had potential, but only when applied abroad because the market for this competence in The Netherlands had almost disappeared. Realizing small-scale power generators scored quite low on potential and

Table 5.20

Intangible Value of Electro Ltd. (in millions of guilders)										
Competence	CM, t = 0	P, %	S, years	t = 1	t = 2	t = 3	t = 4	t = 5	R, %	Total
Designing energy conversion systems	2.8	10	3	3.0	3.3	3.7	—	—	60	6.0
Designing transmission systems	2.7	5	2	2.9	3.0	—	—	—	60	3.5
Installing electrical systems	4.7	0	2	4.7	4.7	—	—	—	60	5.6
Designing process management systems	0.4	10	1	0.4	—	—	—	—	40	0.2
Realizing traffic management systems	3.0	5	4	3.1	3.3	3.4	3.6	—	40	5.3
Realizing small-scale power generators	2.6	5	2	2.7	2.9	—	—	—	60	3.4
Serving the infrastructure industry	1.5	5	1	1.6	—	—	—	—	20	0.3
Total	17.7	—	—	18.5	17.2	7.1	3.6	0.0	—	24.4

Figure 5.3

The value dashboard of Electro Ltd

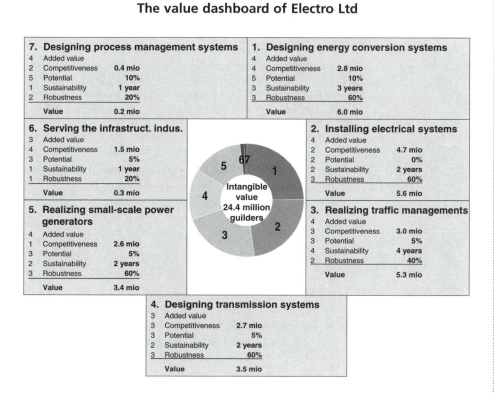

sustainability because this competence was not unique. The other two competencies, serving the infrastructure industry and designing process management systems, turned out to be low in value because they scored low on almost all criteria.

Management Agenda

We wrote a management agenda incorporating recommendations on how to improve the added value, competitiveness, potential, sustainability, and robustness of the intangible resources of Electro Ltd. (Table 5.21).

Reporting to the Client

The general manager of Electro Ltd. was pleased with the end report. He thought it contained useful information that could help create a new strategy for the company, turning it into a high-tech business. At the same time, he considered the results highly confidential

Table 5.21

Management Agenda of Electro Ltd.	
Factor	**Key Question**
Added value	*Does Electro Ltd. exceed customer expectations on a permanent basis?* Current customers see Electro Ltd. as a professional and reliable systems integrator that often adds more value than agreed. Electro Ltd. can increase its added value by improving the quality of its proposals, its customer relation management, and its project management.
Competitiveness	*Will Electro Ltd. stand out from its traditional and new competitors in the future?* Electro Ltd.'s strength is in the field of classic and modern electrical installations for the conversion and transportation of energy. A tailor-made service is what sets Electro Ltd. apart from other companies. To stay competitive in the future, it needs to focus on and excel in a limited number of technical competencies.
Potential	*How can Electro Ltd. leverage its core competencies?* Discontinuities in the market place will create opportunities, especially for the energy conversion and traffic management competence. Electro Ltd. can set up innovation teams to spot these opportunities and to create new service offerings.
Sustainability	*Does Electro Ltd. protect its competencies against the competition?* Most competencies are technical by nature. They consist mostly of tacit knowledge by individual employees. Therefore, it is vital to create employee loyalty using incentive schemes.
Robustness	*Does Electro Ltd. run the risk of losing its core competencies?* Some intangible resources are vulnerable because they depend on a limited number of people. Electro Ltd. can lower the risk of losing these resources by introducing knowledge management techniques and by improving the management capabilities of its people.
Source: KPMG (1999c).	

and stated: "In the next five to six years I will not disclose this information to the outside world" (personal communication). He asked us to write a proposal on how KPMG could help Electro Ltd. to develop its strategy, based on the case study results. The company never responded to the proposal. Six months after the project was finished the company filed for bankruptcy.

Evaluation and Modifications

The problem we addressed was an internal management problem about the creation of a new strategy for Electro Ltd. The general manager of Electro Ltd. wanted to participate because he wanted to create a new strategy for the company that was based on leveraging the company's unique knowledge in the field of electrical engineering. However, the bankruptcy proved that a lack of strategy was not the most urgent problem and that the method was not the most urgent solution (or simply came too late).

The turnaround situation created a specific context for the study. This context was both favorable and unfavorable to the implementation. On the one hand, it created a high sense of urgency. There was a clear need for the clarification of the company's strategy. On the other hand, members of the project team did not have enough time to participate because they had other, more urgent problems to address.

The general manager wanted to increase the professional standard of the middle management layer of the company, so we used the client collaboration mode to allow for client participation. This client collaboration mode worked very well. Not only did it show a number of middle managers a new way of looking at the company, the client collaboration mode also gave our implementation team better access to company data. We could use the knowledge and expertise of the middle managers during the interviews, workshops, and project meetings. In addition, we noticed a certain involvement and commitment toward the results. This commitment was missing at Bank Ltd.

One of problems during the implementation was the difficulty of deciding which competencies to include in the valuation. The core competence checklist had been developed for this purpose, but we found there is a certain ambiguity with respect to its use. On the one hand, the checklist is supposed to be a tool to help decide whether a capability can be labeled a core competence. For this purpose, the checklist needs to provide a clear yes/no decision. On the other hand, the same checklist is used to assess the strengths and weaknesses of a core competence. For this purpose, the same checklist provides a score between 0 to 5 points. At Electro Ltd., this problem was resolved by

having various discussions with the project team on the core competence hypotheses with the help of the items on the checklist. We continued the discussion until a consensus was reached regarding the core
competencies to include in the valuation.

A second problem was the difficulty assessing the potential, sustainability, and robustness factor. We made various calculations that
showed that especially the sustainability and robustness factor has a
strong impact on the outcome of the valuation. These factors are difficult for workshop participants to estimate. The lack of some sort of
benchmark can lead to extreme results. To create something to go by
when assessing these factors, we introduced an automatic correlation
between the results of the checklists and the sustainability and robustness factor (Table 5.22). In this way the outcome of the checklist determines the sustainability and robustness factor. This increases the
reliability of the method in the sense that the estimation of the sustainability and robustness factor becomes less user dependent.

This case study showed that the method was useful in creating a
company strategy. For Electro Ltd., one of the important outcomes
was the discovery that designing energy conversion systems was a
valuable and promising core competence. This result led to the emergence of a new vision for the company; a vision based on the exploitation of this core competence. The method also highlighted that the
traditional low-tech installation competence was still important for the
generation of cash flow and should therefore not be put aside too easily. The case study also showed that the method may produce results
that are too sensitive to disclose. According to the general manager, the
assessment of strengths and weaknesses of the various competencies—

Table 5.22

Automatic Link between Checklist Scores and Sustainability/Robustness Factor			
Sustainability		Robustness	
Checklist Score, points	Factor, years	Checklist Score, points	Factor, %
0	0	0	0
1	1	1	20
2	2	2	40
3	3	3	60
4	4	4	80
5	5	5	100

and especially their sustainability and robustness—were too confidential to report.

The client collaboration mode used at Electro Ltd. helped to fulfill the conditions for successful implementation as described in Chapter 2. It increased the level of involvement of the client system with the engagement, it intensified the communication between our implementation team and the client system, it produced a level of equivalence between the client system and the implementation team, and it helped to make the implementation a success.

In response to these findings, we made the following modifications to the design (E = extensions and I = improvements): It is important to reach consensus on the definitions of the core competencies before the valuation phase. For this purpose, a step was added to the method to come to a consensus on which core competencies to include. This consensus should be based on the results of the core competence checklist (I).

To cope with the difficulty of assessing the sustainability and robustness factor, an automatic relationship was introduced between the results of the core competence checklist and the sustainability and robustness factor (I).

Automotive Ltd.

In this section I describe the results of a third case study at Automotive Ltd. The specific context we encountered required modifications to the design of the method. The owner of the company and the members of his management team had little time to spend on participating in the study, so we had to limit client involvement to six interviews and one workshop. This turned out to be a special case. We were not allowed to finish it.

Context and Problem Definition

Automotive Ltd. was a supplier to the automotive industry. Over the years it had expanded its product range. It had started as a trading company but started to develop and produce its own products. It transformed from a trading house, to a manufacturer, to a knowledge-intensive innovation, manufacturing, and service company. The company's owner had led this transformation for 25 years and was still making all major decisions. He was a true entrepreneur who made decisions in an intuitive way. He induced a corporate culture of ambition, success, hard work, and combativeness.

When we first approached the company, the main contact was through the financial controller. He was interested in the concept of intangible assets from an accounting point of view. He was working hard to formalize a number of processes within the company. When the company was small, it could run its operation in a rather informal way. Now, as it grew bigger, there was a need for more transparency and rules and regulations. One of the controller's ambitions was to improve the strategic decision-making process. Until then, the owner had made all strategic decisions based on limited market research and without an explicit corporate strategy. The financial controller hoped that a discussion on intangible resources would help make the strategy process more explicit. Talking to the owner, we did not sense this need, nor did we notice that the owner was worried about any other specific problem. He was willing to cooperate, as long as it would not consume too much of his time or the time of his staff.

Specific Requirements and Design

At the introductory meeting, the owner of the company made it clear that he and his staff had little time to spend. Therefore, we decided to adjust the realization design. We decided to combine the two workshops. We also decided not to use the core competence checklist at the workshop but to turn it into a written questionnaire and send it to the participants after the workshop.

We noticed that the company culture was very pragmatic, practical, and down-to-earth. Therefore, we had some concern whether the rather abstract concepts of intangible resources and core competencies would fit the company's (and especially the owner's) sense-making process. Extra effort was spent on communicating the method in a very practical and concrete way. We had doubts regarding at what stage of the process to involve the owner. On the one hand, it might be best to involve him after the workshop and present him with draft results that would be concrete and useful to him. On the other hand, it might be better to involve him earlier in the process to get commitment for the results. In the end, this decision was taken out of our hands when the owner decided he wanted to join the workshop.

Implementation and Results

We started the case study but were never able to finish it. The six interviews went well and a comprehensive slide pack was put together for the workshop. At the workshop all members of the management team were present but one. This workshop concluded the object recognition phase. However, the valuation phase was never finished. Next I briefly describe the two phases.

Object Recognition

From the interviews and from an analysis of supporting documentation it became clear that the main strength of Automotive Ltd. was its winning mentality. The company had a strong client focus, short lines of control, and an ambitious and charismatic leader. The uniqueness of the company was a result of in-depth knowledge of the transportation market, a wide and strong network of relationships in that market, and a way of approaching customers that made them feel like kings. This approach was combined with technology that offered high added value for customers. The interviews and document analysis resulted in the following overview of intangible resources (Table 5.23).

We developed four core competence hypotheses. Two of them were labeled true core competencies. The first was the ability to acquire customer loyalty by offering value-adding solutions under all circumstances. The second was the ability to do business in a flexible way by being financially independent. The other two were labeled latent core competencies. The first was the ability to own the customer by

Table 5.23

Overview of Intangible Resources of Automotive Ltd.				
Skills and Tacit Knowledge	**Values and Norms**	**Technology and Explicit Knowledge**	**Management Processes**	**Endowments**
Entrepreneurship Ability to solve problems Ability to make decisions in a short period of time Products knowledge Market expertise Ability to recognize valuable ideas Ability to combine different capabilities Ability to establish subsidiaries in other countries	Client focus Loyalty Young, fast, and dynamic No nonsense Freedom to act Arrogance Ambitious Result oriented Focus and mission Proactive Guts Fighter's mentality Will to survive	ISO 9001 handbook Software code	Manager–owner structure Small management team Short lines of control One decision maker	Reputation Network of market relationships Customer base Financial independence Subsidiaries in 14 countries Distribution network

offering complete solutions to one client base. The second was the ability to serve foreign markets locally. The first was a latent competence because it was not yet fully anchored within the organization. The second was a latent competence because it did not stand out from the competition and was quite easy to imitate.

We designed the following agenda for the workshop. First, the purpose and process of the case study were revisited. Then a novelty was used. We presented the results of the interviews using anonymous quotes. The quotes were grouped by subject: company ambition, company strategy, corporate culture, management processes and leadership, unique endowments, economic engine, and opportunities and threats. We then introduced the concept of core competencies, the core competence checklist, and the four core competence hypotheses. We presented the results of the tests for each core competence and opened up for discussion. After the discussion, we briefly introduced the financial valuation method, the potential, sustainability, and robustness factor, and the method for allocating the contribution margin. Then the participants were asked to assess each of the factors using a dedicated scale for each factor. Finally, we asked them to assess the importance of the contribution of each core competence to the company's products.

The way participants reacted during the workshop reflected the company culture. Their response was full of self-confidence. The owner dominated the discussion. Whenever our implementation team suggested that a certain competence might not be totally competitive, sustainable, or robust, the owner made it very clear that it was. Some members of the management team did try to use the concepts of competitiveness, potential, sustainability, and robustness to trigger a strategic discussion, but the owner, through his response, made it clear he did not feel the need for such a discussion. During the discussion, one additional core competence hypothesis was suggested. To a certain extent, Automotive Ltd. was a market maker because it offered solutions for implicit problems. The solutions created a market demand that until then had not existed. Therefore, the suggestion was raised that Automotive Ltd. had the ability to create a market demand by offering new value-adding products. When it came to assessing the various factors for the valuation of the core competencies, again the self-confidence was reflected in the results. The participants felt that the expected growth rates for all competencies would be 12.5% and their sustainability would be more than 10 years (the sustainability scale provided to them ranged from 0 to 10 years). The average robustness would be 70%. At the end of the workshop, it was decided that we would work on the definition of some of the core competencies and would approach the financial controller to gather more financial data.

We had mixed feelings about the results of the workshop. On the one hand, the analysis and the resulting core competencies had been confirmed. On the other hand, assessing the various valuation factors had proved to be even more difficult than during the other two case studies. We felt that some of the assessments were a bit oversimplified. We sent out the core competence checklist to all participants to gather more supporting evidence for the estimations. The intention was to use the outcome of this questionnaire to make a final assessment of all the factors—the sustainability and robustness factor in particular—using the correlation table as shown in Table 5.22. We sent out six questionnaires. Only one was returned. We reminded the other participants several times, and in the end were told that the study did not have enough priority. Another foreign acquisition had required all of management's attention. At that point, we decided to stop the project.

Evaluation and Modifications

The premature termination of the process was the result of three factors. First, it was clear from the beginning that the key decision maker did not experience any direct problems, at least not any problems he felt could be solved by the method. Because he was clearly the person in command, his decision to give the case study no further priority was decisive. Only the financial controller had a specific problem. He wanted to improve the internal management of Automotive Ltd. by creating a more transparent strategic decision-making process. Second, the intermediary results presented at the workshop did not provide enough new insight for the owner to continue spending time on the project. Part of the reason was that the owner had a very practical mind-set. The discussions on core competencies were rather abstract for him, despite our effort to make them concrete. Therefore, they did not fit the owner's sense-making processes. Finally, the workshop discussion did not turn out the way some members of the management team had hoped. It did not evolve into a more fundamental discussion about the company's strategy, and strengths and weaknesses. This disappointed some of the members of the management team.

Although it was never finished, the case study was still very instructive. It demonstrated that without a clear problem, creating insight into the value of intangibles has less added value. This does not mean the problem needs to be clear from the start. The method itself can bring important problems to light. However, when no problems come to the surface, people with a practical mind-set, who are not intrigued by a more abstract analysis of their business, will lose interest.

Some of the conditions for successful implementation as described in Chapter 2 were not fulfilled. The level of involvement of the client system with the engagement was minimal. The communication between the implementation team and the client system was deliberately kept to a minimum in order not to take too much of the client's time. There was no equivalence between the client system and our implementation team. These factors explain part of the lack of success. My hypothesis is that the lack of a clear and urgent problem, and the very pragmatic mind-set of the owner were other important factors.

In response to these findings, we included the following modifications in the design (E = extensions and I = improvements): A new format was added to the method for the presentation of the interview findings at the first workshop, to make it more practical and compelling. The results of the interviews were presented using anonymous quotes from the interviews, grouped by subjects (I).

During situations when there is little time, the two workshops can be combined. In that case the core competence checklist can be sent out as a written questionnaire (E).

Logistic Services BU

The fourth case study was the first implementation that was not part of the study initiated by the Ministry of Economic Affairs. It provided our implementation team with a special challenge because the client wanted to have the results within two weeks.

Context and Problem Definition

Logistic Services BU was a business unit of a large multinational company in the transportation industry. The unit had been created to explore the opportunities in logistics consultancy. The unit was on the brink of a breakthrough after working more than a year on a new business model. Part of its business model was to set up an alliance with an information technology partner. The management of Logistic Services BU decided to identify and value the unit's core competencies to give insight into its potential to a possible alliance partner and to identify the competencies it would bring to the alliance. For that purpose, it contacted KPMG. The unit provided consultancy in business logistics to major customers around the world. It was still in its start-up phase and had not yet shown positive results. The mission of the unit was to become a major service provider in logistics management. It wanted to know what its existing core competencies were and how they could be strengthened.

Then the economic situation changed. The holding company was forced to reconsider the position of the business unit within the group. The management team of the unit decided to look at several alternatives, ranging from reorganization to a possible management buyout. Information about the financial value of the unit's core competencies would be useful in choosing among the alternatives. The results had to be available within two weeks because the decision needed to be made at short notice.

Specific Requirements and Design

The fact that Logistic Services BU wanted to have the results within two weeks provided a special challenge to the implementation team. There was no time to conduct any interviews to identify Logistic Services BU's intangible resources. Therefore, the team altered the design of the method in four ways.

The team replaced the interviews with a full-day workshop with eight members of the business unit. This workshop was followed by a second workshop one week later, aimed at defining and testing the core competencies. A third workshop with a limited number of people was used to assess the contribution of each core competence to the various products of Logistic Services BU.

As we saw in the first two case studies, it was difficult to determine which core competencies to include in the analysis. In the second case study, this was partly solved by including a discussion with the client on this topic, aimed at reaching a consensus. For Logistic Services BU, the implementation team decided to expand this discussion. An additional discussion about Logistic Services BU's capabilities was initiated, and then these capabilities were combined to create core competencies.

We also saw that it is difficult to assess the sustainability, potential, and robustness factor in a reliable way. The second adjustment to the method was to add more credibility to the sustainability, potential, and robustness factor. The assessments were checked with customers of Logistic Services BU and with experts in the field.

The business unit had not yet shown a real profit, so another modification was needed. The business unit was still in a startup phase, working hard on business development. There were limited data available on the contribution margin of the products. Therefore, the implementation team had to work with the financial forecasts for years t + 1 and t + 2. The forecasts showed an exponential growth in contribution margin. However, the valuation formula of the method can only cope with a linear growth as expressed by the potential factor. There are several ways to solve this problem. The implementation team decided to develop three scenarios and to calculate three different values. There is an alternative solution, which I present in the evaluation section. With hindsight, I think the alternative is more sound. At the time, the team wanted to stick to the formula and used the contribution margins for a years t, t + 1, and t + 2 to calculate three sets of values for the core competencies. The line of reasoning was that at the time of the case study, the services offered by Logistic Services BU had not been proved on the marketplace; hence, their contribution margin was quite low. Had the analysis been done one year later (scenario 1) then their contribution margin would have grown substantially, and as a result the formula would show a substantially higher value of the underlying core competencies. Had the analysis been done two years later (scenario 2) this would have been even more the case. So the implementation team presented the client with three sets of financial values for its core competencies: the value in the year of the case study, the value after one year of proven business, and the value after two years of proven business.

Implementation and Results

The results of this case study were reported to the client in a confidential report (KPMG, 1999d). I next briefly describe the object recognition, the financial valuation, the value dashboard, and the management agenda of Logistic Services BU.

Object Recognition

The first section of the first workshop was used to create an inventory of the important intangible resources of Logistic Services BU (Table 5.24).

This input was used to identify a number of capabilities for Logistic Services BU. The capabilities were combined into four core competencies (Table 5.25). The first row shows the name of the core competence. The second row presents a list of capabilities that contribute to the core competence.

Financial Valuation

During the second workshop, the implementation team used the core competence checklist to assess the added value, competitiveness,

Table 5.24

Overview of Intangible Resources of Logistic Services BU				
Skills and Tacit Knowledge	Values and Norms	Technology and Explicit Knowledge	Management Processes	Endowments
Analytical capability Innovation capability (combination of analytical, critical, and associative thinking) Implementation capability Creativity Flexibility/agility Integration capability (know-how and do-how) Integrated knowledge of logistics (theoretical), information technology, and management services (operational) Learning organization Context and delta thinking Global implementation of knowledge Implementation experiences Information technology/ logistics knowledge and skills Commercial capability	Learning organization Freedom of development of ideas Team spirit Open mind Commitment (risk sharing) Motivation Open and honest Self-respect and self-confidence Entrepreneurship Multicultural Informal communication Entrepreneurship/ take initiatives (instead of "I cannot") Learning by doing Make your own decisions (as if it is your own company) Freedom to develop ideas (in time and money) Multicultural within one organization	Various methodologies ISO 9001, business manual Logistics concepts, models, and tools Forecasting platforms Simulation of transportation and distribution structures	Coaching Democratic decision making, consensus (Caesar's Palace) Decentralized/ entrepreneurial Management by vision, objectives, and result area Competence management Relation management Financial management	Being part of a large, well-known organization No heritage Reliable image of mother company

potential, sustainability, and robustness of each of the four core competencies. In addition, the team asked the participants to estimate the potential, sustainability, and robustness factor. The results were checked with a number of customers and experts in the field.

The interviews with customers showed that the competence to develop and implement logistics concepts had a high added value to

Table 5.25

Capabilities and Core Competencies of Logistic Services BU			
Develop and Implement Concepts	Analyze and Optimize Processes	Inventively Create Opportunities	Manage Processes
The ability to develop and implement logistics concepts The capability to Implement concepts and/or develop concepts Obtain support for solutions Deliver know-how plus do-how Link theory and practice Offer a real-life concept Shorten the life cycle for strategic decisions Combine theoretical logistics knowledge with implementation	The ability to quickly analyze and optimize logistics processes The capability to Understand clients' position and processes Structure chaos Detect problems Diagnose Describe processes Analyze processes Redesign processes Optimize processes	The ability to create inventively business opportunities for clients The capability to Offer (creative) solutions Facilitate Think in processes and improvement Offer improvements Identify and realize opportunities Apply knowledge and experience in different contexts	The ability to manage logistics processes The capability to Manage logistics processes Enhance business efficiency Improve business results

customers, but experts claimed that many competitors were trying to develop the same skills. This limited the sustainability of the core competence. There also was a risk of losing this competence because it depended heavily on the image of and contacts within the holding company. Clients did appreciate the high level of logistical knowledge of Logistic Services BU, but the competence to analyze and optimize logistics processes quickly could be acquired from many other consulting companies. Therefore, the sustainability of this core competence was limited. In addition, the robustness of the core competence was low because there was a limited number of people in the core competence community. Clients considered the ability to create opportunities inventively as the best competence of Logistic Services BU. This competence was the driver for expansion. The ability to manage logistics processes required a lot of practical skills and experience. Experts felt it would be challenging to develop further Logistic Services BU's management skills. The implementation team recommended developing this competence further with the help of outside partners.

Five Logistic Services BU products were identified. For each product a contribution margin was calculated by subtracting personnel costs from the product gross revenues. Because the business unit did not have a separate balance sheet, the implementation team was not able to calculate the value of the tangible assets and networking capital used. Therefore, it was not possible to subtract a provision for a return on these assets.

During the third workshop, the team constructed the core competence–product matrix to assess the contribution of each core competence to the products (Table 5.26). This information was used to calculate the value of the core competencies in the year of the case study (Table 5.27).

Value Dashboard

The value dashboard presented the scores on the core competence checklist and the value of the core competencies (Figure 5.4).

According to the dashboard, the competence *inventively create opportunities* was the most valuable. This was consistent with its role as "top" competence as recognized by clients. The values of *manage processes*, and *analyze and optimize processes* were limited by their low sustainability. *Develop and implement concepts* had a high potential but a low value as a result of limited market penetration.

To obtain a feel for the potential of these competencies, two other sets of values were developed. The contribution margins of year t were replaced by the margins from the forecast for years t + 1 and t + 2. All other factors remained constant. The results showed that the value of

Table 5.26

Allocation of Contribution Margin to Competencies of Logistic Services BU (in millions of dollars)	
Core Competence	**Allocated Contribution Margin**
Develop and implement concepts	0.1
Analyze and optimize processes	0.2
Inventively create opportunities	0.1
Manage processes	0.5
Total	0.9

Table 5.27

Intangible Value of Logistic Services BU (in millions of dollars)

Competence	CM, t = 0	P, %	S, years	t = 1	t = 2	t = 3	t = 4	t = 5	R, %	Total
Develop and implement concepts	0.07	10	3	0.08	0.09	0.10	—	—	60	0.16
Analyze and optimize processes	0.17	8	1	0.18	—	—	—	—	80	0.15
Inventively create opportunities	0.09	10	4	0.10	0.11	0.12	0.14	—	100	0.48
Manage processes	0.52	4	1	0.54	—	—	—	—	60	0.33
Total	0.86	—	—	0.91	0.20	0.22	0.14	—	—	1.11

Figure 5.4

The value dashboard of Logistic Services BU

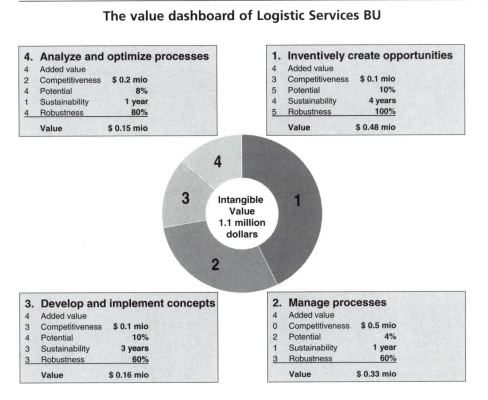

4. Analyze and optimize processes		
4	Added value	
2	Competitiveness	$ 0.2 mio
4	Potential	8%
1	Sustainability	1 year
4	Robustness	80%
	Value	**$ 0.15 mio**

1. Inventively create opportunities		
4	Added value	
3	Competitiveness	$ 0.1 mio
5	Potential	10%
4	Sustainability	4 years
5	Robustness	100%
	Value	**$ 0.48 mio**

3. Develop and implement concepts		
4	Added value	
3	Competitiveness	$ 0.1 mio
4	Potential	10%
3	Sustainability	3 years
3	Robustness	60%
	Value	**$ 0.16 mio**

2. Manage processes		
4	Added value	
0	Competitiveness	$ 0.5 mio
2	Potential	4%
1	Sustainability	1 year
3	Robustness	60%
	Value	**$ 0.33 mio**

the core competencies increases the moment the business model of Logistic Services BU has proved itself in the marketplace (Table 5.28).

Management Agenda

The implementation team wrote a management agenda incorporating the recommendations on how to improve the added value, competitiveness, potential, sustainability, and robustness of the core competencies (Table 5.29).

Reporting to the Client

The client was satisfied with the process and the results. The management of Logistic Services BU considered the method to be well structured and thought out. The method had created energy within the group. Management approved of the results and used them in their negotiations with the holding company. An agreement was reached with the holding company that allowed Logistic Services BU to prepare

Table 5.28

Alternative Scenarios for the Intangible Value of Logistic Services BU (in millions of dollars)			
Core Competence	Today	Scenario 1: One Year Proven Business	Scenario 2: Two Years Proven Business
Develop and implement concepts	0.16	0.69	2.54
Analyze and optimize processes	0.15	1.29	5.84
Inventively create opportunities	0.48	1.85	6.31
Manage processes	0.33	0.97	4.93
Total	1.12	4.80	19.62

a management buyout within a month. Unfortunately, key people within the unit decided not to join the business unit as an independent company. Therefore, the management buyout never took place and the business unit was dismantled. During the dismantling process, the results of the exercise were used to determine whether core competencies could be transferred to other business units.

Evaluation and Modifications

The specific problem of Logistic Services BU was to improve internal management. The initial idea was to improve the collaboration with alliance partners. After it became known that the business unit had to reconsider its future, the aim was to facilitate the decision-making process regarding the various options. The client specifically asked for insight into the strengths, weaknesses, and financial value of its core competencies. It was already using the concept of core competencies in its sense-making process. This contributed to the success of the implementation.

The specific context required a special realization design. The results had to be available within two weeks. An effective workshop design replaced the interviews. The workshop resulted in a comprehensive list of intangibles, collective capabilities, and core competencies. The additional step of identifying capabilities before defining core competencies speeded up the creative process and improved decision making regarding which core competencies to include.

Table 5.29

Management Agenda of Logistic Services BU	
Factor	**Key Question**
Added value	*Does Logistic Services BU exceed customer expectations on a permanent basis?* Clients appreciate the competencies of developing and implementing concepts in a creative manner. Therefore, we recommend investing in these competencies. Information technology knowledge should be obtained to be able to serve the customer better.
Competitiveness	*Will Logistic Services BU stand out from its traditional and new competitors in the future?* At this moment, Logistic Services BU does not exceed the competencies of competitors in a particular way. Logistic Services BU seeks excellence through the integrated offering of its competencies using its own specific methodology. This integrated offering can be enhanced through permanent partnering to obtain or develop new competencies.
Potential	*How can Logistic Services BU leverage its core competencies?* New opportunities can be created through the development of networking as a new core competence. This competence will enhance the integrated service offering without the need for permanent mergers.
Sustainability	*Does Logistic Services BU protect its competencies against the competition?* Logistic Services BU's specific methodology can be copied by the competition. Copying implementation skills will be more difficult. Therefore, Logistic Services BU should excel at implementation.
Robustness	*Does Logistic Services BU run the risk of losing its core competencies?* Because the knowledge of Logistic Services BU is concentrated around relatively few people, loss of employees can easily damage the competencies. Knowledge management focused at sharing and codifying this knowledge can diminish this risk. Incentives to create employee loyalty will also help to enhance the robustness. If Logistic Services BU chooses to separate from its mother company, the loss of the shared image can endanger its position.
Source: KPMG (1999d).	

The fact that the business unit was a startup indicated that there were no solid contribution margins. The forecasted contribution margins showed nonlinear growth. The implementation team chose to alter the object design and to develop additional scenarios for years t + 1 and t + 2, based on the forecasts provided by the business unit. This created two problems. First, each scenario assumes a linear growth rate, as shown by the potential factor. The valuation for year t was based on the expectation that the contribution margin of the four core competencies would grow linearly between 4 to 10%. These percentages were estimated during the workshops and were modified based on customer and expert opinion. Yet, the company's forecasts showed that the total contribution margin would grow by 311% in the year t + 1 and another 357% in the year t + 2. The implementation team did not notice this inconsistency. Second, the scenarios assume that the sustainability factor of each core competence will still be valid in year t + 1 and t + 2, even when the sustainability factor is only one year. For example, the core competence *manage processes* had a sustainability of one year, which means that it would take a fictional competitor one year to acquire the same competence. Yet, in scenario 1 (one year of proven business) the sustainability of *manage processes* was again assumed to be one year. This would only be the case if, in the meantime, no competitor had tried to imitate this competence. The same problem occurred in scenario 2 (two years of proven business). If, in the meantime, a competitor imitated the core competence, then the sustainability of that particular core competence in year t + 1 should have been zero.[1]

An alternative would be not to use the potential factors as estimated during the workshop but to use the forecasts for the contribution margin. When we assume that the relative contribution of each core competence to the generation of contribution margin remains constant, we can calculate the contribution margin of each core competence in years t + 1 and t + 2 based on the forecast. For years t + 3 (which we need for the core competencies with a sustainability that lasts longer than two years) and t + 4 (which we need for core competencies with a sustainability that lasts longer than three years), we need to calculate a contribution margin using the growth rate as estimated in workshops because we do not have a forecast for years

---

[1] However, we should keep in mind that useful life, defined as strategic life, is not the same as economic life. A competence with a strategic life of zero can still contribute to the generation of cash flow and have a positive economic life. However, it can no longer be considered a core competence, because it is no longer unique. Therefore, from a strategic life point of view, its value is zero.

t + 3 and t + 4. The results of the alternative method are included in Table 5.30.

Figure 5.5 presents a comparison of the four ways to calculate the intangible value of Logistic Services BU: the three scenarios calculated by the implementation team and the alternative way presented earlier.

The alternative method not only produces a much lower total value than scenario 2, there is also a shift in the relative importance of the core competencies. *Inventively create opportunities* is still the most important core competence, but *develop and implement concepts* is now second, followed by *analyze and optimize processes*, and *manage processes*. This reflects the impact of the sustainability factor on the valuation. *Develop and implement concepts* has a useful life of three years, whereas the other two only have a useful life of one year. *Develop and implement concepts* therefore profits much more from the strong increase in contribution margin in the alternative approach than the other two.

The new outline for the workshops used at Logistic Services BU helped to fulfill the conditions for successful implementation as described in Chapter 2. It increased the level of involvement of the client system with the engagement, it intensified the communication between the implementation team and the client system, it produced a level of equivalence between the client system and the implementation team, and it helped to make the implementation a success.

Figure 5.5

Four ways to calculate the intangible value of Logistic Services BU

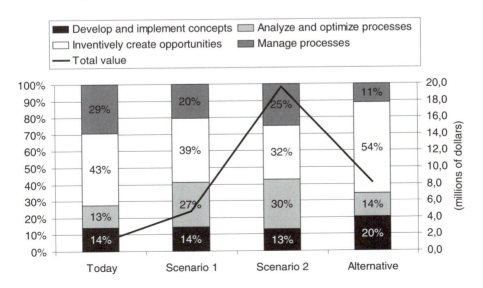

Table 5.30

Revised Intangible Value of Logistic Services BU (in millions of dollars)									
Competence	CM, t = 0	P, %	S, years	t = 1	t = 2	t = 3	t = 4	t = 5	R, %	Total
Develop and implement concepts	0.07	10	3	0.31	1.16	1.28	—	—	60	1.65
Analyze and optimize processes	0.17	8	1	1.46	—	—	—	—	80	1.17
Inventively create opportunities	0.09	10	4	0.36	1.24	1.36	1.49	—	100	4.45
Manage processes	0.52	4	1	1.56	—	—	—	—	60	0.94
Total	0.86	—	—	3.70	2.40	2.64	1.49	—	—	8.21

We included the following modifications in the design (E = extensions and I = improvements): A new workshop design was added to the method as an alternative to the interviews. This design can be used when there is not enough time to have interview meetings (E).

An additional step was added into the discussions about core competencies. During this step, an inventory of a company's collective capabilities is created. These capabilities are combined into core competencies. This helps in deciding which core competencies to include (I).

When a company is a startup company, there are no data available regarding the contribution margins of products. In this case, the potential factor cannot be used to create a forecast. As an alternative, the financial valuation can be based on forecasts produced by the company or by financial analysts (E).

Professional Services LLP

This professional services firm requested help in identifying its intangible resources. It wanted to report intangibles in its annual report. This case study presented us with the dilemmas that a company encounters when it wants to report its intangibles externally. Unfortunately, we were not able to reconcile all dilemmas, resulting in an unpleasant decision.

Context and Problem Definition

Professional Services LLP offered a wide range of consulting and auditing services to its clients. It was well aware of the transition in the global economy from an industrial economy to an intangible economy. At the end of the millennium, it wanted to express this transition in its annual report. The traditional balance sheet and profit-and-loss statement have their roots in the agricultural and industrial age. The intangible economy is the age of intangibles. Professional Services LLP had the idea that this would be a nice theme for its annual report. In addition, the company had had extensive experience in using the concept of core competencies as a strategic tool.

The idea was to analyze the intangible resources of the firm, assess their strengths and weaknesses, and use this information to report externally, proving to the outside world that the company had prepared for the future. Because Professional Services LLP was a services firm, intangible resources were the most important resources of the company. This justified special attention to the subject in the annual report. The member of the management board of Professional Services LLP who was responsible for the annual report gave us the assignment to do the study. However, a few weeks after granting the assignment, he retired. This had considerable impact.

Specific Requirements and Design

We deliberated with the client and this resulted in special requirements for the design of the method. First, the results had to be easy to communicate to the public. This meant the report should contain no jargon and complicated concepts. Instead, the results needed to be catchy, clear, and self-explanatory. Second, all results had to be grounded in fact. Every claim made needed to be supported by evidence, preferably from an independent source. Third, the company wanted to refrain from any sort of financial valuation. Although the results of the exercise would not become part of the balance sheet or profit-and-loss statement, they would still be part of the annual report and therefore subject to scrutiny. Finally, the section on intangibles would play only a supporting role in the annual report. The purpose of the section was to ornament the report. The subject should therefore not be extensive or wide ranging.

We made changes to the object design, based on these specific requirements. We developed a specific way to report core competencies. We would search for a short and catchy name for each core competence. This made the core competencies easy to communicate. This name was supported by a subtitle to add a bit of flavor to its meaning. Each core competence was accompanied by a definition and a glossary containing all the important words used (Figure 5.6) and unraveled into its supporting intangibles. A list of indicators was created as evidence. These qualitative data confirmed the claim that this competence was a core competence. These data were supplemented by quotes from the interviews. A management dashboard contained the scores on the core competence checklists marked in red (0 to 1), yellow (2 to 3) and green (4 to 5), and a list of strength and weaknesses (Figure 5.7).

We amended the interview protocol too. So far, the interview protocol had been satisfactory, except that in most interviews the protocol turned out to be too long. This was the result of the extensive list of questions regarding the various types of intangibles. We decided to create a new outline for the protocol, to skip a number of questions, and to replace some others. Questions were added that had proved to be useful in strategy assignments in which members of our implementation team had been involved. Four questions turned out to be especially revealing:

Figure 5.6

Defining the connecting capability competence of Professional Services LLP

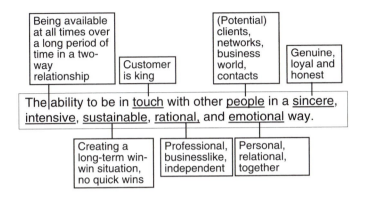

- Being available at all times over a long period of time in a two-way relationship
- Customer is king
- (Potential) clients, networks, business world, contacts
- Genuine, loyal and honest

The ability to be in <u>touch</u> with other <u>people</u> in a <u>sincere</u>, <u>intensive</u>, <u>sustainable</u>, <u>rational</u>, and <u>emotional</u> way.

- Creating a long-term win-win situation, no quick wins
- Professional, businesslike, independent
- Personal, relational, together

Figure 5.7

Reporting format for evidence used at Professional Services LLP

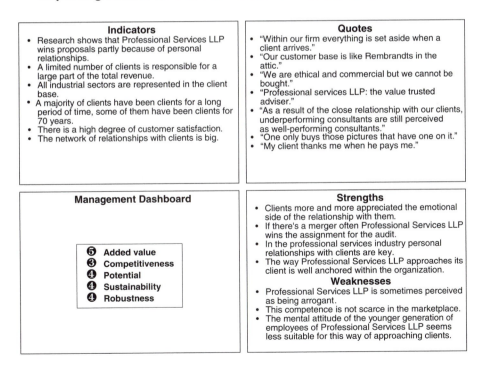

Indicators
- Research shows that Professional Services LLP wins proposals partly because of personal relationships.
- A limited number of clients is responsible for a large part of the total revenue.
- All industrial sectors are represented in the client base.
- A majority of clients have been clients for a long period of time, some of them have been clients for 70 years.
- There is a high degree of customer satisfaction.
- The network of relationships with clients is big.

Quotes
- "Within our firm everything is set aside when a client arrives."
- "Our customer base is like Rembrandts in the attic."
- "We are ethical and commercial but we cannot be bought."
- "Professional services LLP: the value trusted adviser."
- "As a result of the close relationship with our clients, underperforming consultants are still perceived as well-performing consultants."
- "One only buys those pictures that have one on it."
- "My client thanks me when he pays me."

Management Dashboard
- ❺ Added value
- ❸ Competitiveness
- ❹ Potential
- ❹ Sustainability
- ❹ Robustness

Strengths
- Clients more and more appreciated the emotional side of the relationship with them.
- If there's a merger often Professional Services LLP wins the assignment for the audit.
- In the professional services industry personal relationships with clients are key.
- The way Professional Services LLP approaches its client is well anchored within the organization.

Weaknesses
- Professional Services LLP is sometimes perceived as being arrogant.
- This competence is not scarce in the marketplace.
- The mental attitude of the younger generation of employees of Professional Services LLP seems less suitable for this way of approaching clients.

1. What is the biggest complement you can give Professional Services LLP?
2. What is your biggest complaint about Professional Services LLP?
3. What is your most important dream about Professional Services LLP?
4. What is your biggest concern regarding Professional Services LLP?

A valuation of the intangible resources of Professional Services LLP was not part of the assignment, and we removed this phase from the realization design. The design consisted of a number of interviews with members of the firm and with outside experts, and an analysis of supporting data. This information was used during a brainstorming session within our implementation team to produce a list of core competencies. We presented this list and all supporting evidence to the client using the reporting format as described earlier. After this intermediary presentation, we created a scheme on how to use the results in the annual report. At that stage, we turned the process over to a professional journalist, who wrote the text for the annual report.

Implementation and Results

The implementation of the tailor-made method included only an object recognition phase. Within six weeks our implementation team conducted 34 interviews and gathered information from 37 different sources. We then held a full-day brainstorming session to develop core competence hypotheses, assess the competencies' strengths and weaknesses, and select supporting material.

There was a lot of diversity within Professional Services LLP. Each individual business unit had its own style of working, business model, and corporate culture. We found strong core competencies that were unique for the various units. However, we decided to focus on the competencies that all units had in common. We wanted to present only those competencies in the annual report. We identified five core competencies based on a list of 40 capabilities.

During the brainstorming session we looked for a way to label each core competence in a short and meaningful way. During the process of lateral thinking, we stumbled on the Dutch word *vermogen,* which the dictionary translates as "be able to, have the power to, be in a position to" (Wolters, 1977, p. 887), but also as "fortune, wealth, richness," and "power." This term has both the connotation of ability and of wealth, which made it a very suitable word for describing a valuable core competence. I translate it into the word *capability,* knowing this

English word does not cover the richness of the Dutch meaning. We also discovered that defining each core competence required selecting the right words with precision to transmit the intended meaning. This painstaking process required juggling of words and a censorious mindset. It required discarding words that did not fit 100% and then trying to find better ones. The challenge was to find the wording for a list of core competencies that would make sense to every reader. We carefully selected each word of the core competence definition. The results are presented in Table 5.31.

To show how the reporting format works, I elaborate on the connecting capability competence. The subtitle for this competence was "Professional Services LLP's network of relationships is like Rembrandts in the attic." Its definition was "the ability to be in touch with other people in a *sincere*, *intensive*, *sustainable*, *rational*, and

Table 5.31

Core Competencies of Professional Services LLP		
Term	**Term in Dutch**	**Definition**
Connecting capability	*Relatievermogen*	The ability to be in touch with other people in a sincere, intensive, sustainable, rational, and emotional way
Branding capability	*Imagovermogen*	The ability to position Professional Services LLP continuously in all sorts of ways as reliable, excelling, innovative, and socially involved
Innovative capability	*Ontwikkelvermogen*	The ability to recognize new business opportunities and bring them to prosperity by acquiring and sustaining innovative talent, allowing it to flourish, and sponsoring and supporting it with people, money, branding, and clients
Recruiting capability	*Aantrekkingsvermogen*	The ability to acquire the attention of the right people, to recruit them, and to create employee loyalty in a variety of ways
Tolerating capability	*Tolerantievermogen*	The ability to tolerate a wide variety of talent and to bring it to value

Figure 5.8

Intangibles of connecting capability of Professional Services LLP

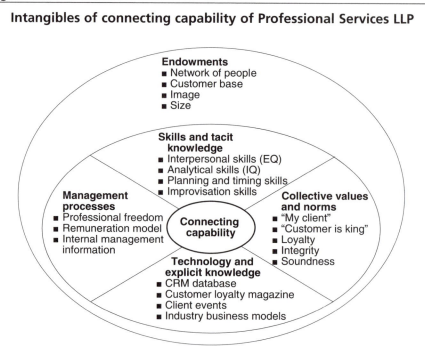

emotional way." The words in italics were defined as presented in Figure 5.6.

Several intangible resources supported this core competence, as shown by Figure 5.8. This egg shape was used as an aesthetic way to communicate intangibles. To report the supporting evidence about strengths and weaknesses, we created the management dashboard (see Figure 5.7).

The upper left corner presents all supporting indicators. Each indicator was accompanied by data using a graph or a table that supported the claim that this competence was indeed a core competence. The upper right corner shows a selection of quotes from the interviews. In the bottom left corner, we presented the outcome of the core competence checklist. This was elucidated by an overview of strengths and weaknesses in the bottom right corner.

Reporting to the Client

We presented the findings to the client using the reporting format as described earlier. The client did find the results valuable but decided to postpone its judgment until a draft text for the annual report was produced. A number of dilemmas emerged from informal discussions with the client during the period we were working with a journalist to write the text for the annual report.

The first dilemma had to do with valuation. We had already noticed that the client was very cautious about publishing valuations or financial figures. On the other hand, people from the public relations (PR) department considered the strength of the method that it could "turn soft values into hard valuations," as one of them phrased it. The PR department appreciated the PR value that this would have. The dilemma was that publishing mainly qualitative descriptions is low risk but probably generates only low exposure, whereas reporting quantitative valuations generates higher exposure but potentially evokes scrutiny and criticism.

The second dilemma had to do with benchmarking. Reporting indicators without a benchmark or other form of yardstick is low risk but conveys little meaning. Readers will not be able to judge the indicators. Comparing results with competitors will allow readers to judge the figures better. The problem is that these benchmarks are often not available or they may evoke criticism. They may even induce litigation when competitors argue that the figures are not correct. The dilemma was that reporting indicators without benchmarks is low risk but has limited meaning, whereas publishing benchmarks makes indicators much more meaningful but is more risky. Our client was reluctant to mention any competitor in its annual report.

The third dilemma focused on the desirability of not only reporting a company's strengths but also its weaknesses. We identified several weaknesses with regard to the core competencies of Professional Services LLP. Publishing some of these in the annual report would add to the credibility of the report. It could make the results of the method more meaningful because it would enable readers to judge the results better. However, the client was cautious and preferred to focus on the company's strengths. The dilemma was that telling only the good news is low risk but does not convey much meaning, whereas publishing the good news and the bad news is high risk but probably adds credibility and significance.

The fourth dilemma had to do with the confidentiality of some of the information. The client was reluctant to publish any information that would tell competitors more than strictly necessary. On the other hand, we argued that a company like Professional Services LLP should not fear its competitors and should disclose information on its intangibles and gain credibility. The dilemma was that keeping on the safe side is less risky but not very explanatory, whereas being very informative might harm future business.

Finally, we found that proper interpretation of the results required explaining the underlying method. It turned out that an extensive reading instruction was needed because the average reader of annual reports is probably not familiar with concepts like intangible resources and core competencies. For this purpose, we prepared text explaining the concept of intangible resources and their importance for a company like Professional Services LLP. The text told something about the method. The distinction between the five types of intangibles was explained. The concept of core competencies was clarified. The text concluded with a reading instruction explaining the reporting format as described earlier. The dilemma was that an elucidation like this allows the reader to interpret the results but shifts the focus from the message to the method, whereas leaving out the explanation centers the attention on the content but makes the message difficult to interpret.

These dilemmas came to light when the draft text for the annual report was discussed with the client. They had a big impact on the project. After considering all the pros and cons, the client decided *not* to use the outcome of the method in the annual report, except for some of the quotes. All results of the study remained confidential and were only reported to the management board of the company.

Evaluation and Modifications

The specific problem in this case study was the external reporting of intangibles. This problem fits the application domain of the method. The context of the study changed during the process because of a shift in management. The new management seemed less interested in reporting intangibles and preferred a low-risk profile. This influenced the decision about the use of the results in the annual report.

The case study involved specific requirements regarding making the results of the method easy to communicate and grounding them in fact. To meet these requirements, a special design of the method was created with a heavy focus on fact finding. We were fortunate that Professional Services LLP had a lot of material from market studies and employee satisfaction research available to support the findings. The specific design included a new reporting format that worked well to report results. However, we found that to explain the results to the public we needed a lot of elucidation. This turned out to be a problem. The need for elucidation influenced the decision not to use the results in the annual report.

The implementation of the design was instructive. It showed the important issues companies face when reporting intangibles. In this

case, key issues were the amount of supporting explanation necessary, the reporting of financial valuations, and the reluctance to
publishing the company's weaknesses. The method's ability to value
intangibles and turn soft factors into hard cash seemed attractive from
a PR point of view; yet, because the valuations depended on assumptions and estimations, the client was unenthusiastic to publish this
information in the annual report. It is understandable that the client
was reluctant to publish any of the identified weaknesses. Any company tries to look its best in the annual report. There is a natural
tendency to omit any criticism or negative points. The method dominated the text for the annual report and the client decided not to
publish it. The focus on the method blurred the message. It is difficult
to use the method for external reporting without adding an extensive
explanation. From this case I conclude that the method is too complicated to be self-explanatory. This had been the concern of the
Ministry of Economic Affairs (see Chapter 4). This case proved they
were right.

Did the quality of the implementation have any affect on this
disappointing result? The change in management did not help in
increasing the level of involvement of the client system with the
engagement. However, we did spend extra effort communicating the
process and intermediary results to the new manager responsible.
There was no sign of inequality between the client system and our
implementation team. I think the decision not to publish was not the
result of a lack of quality or poor implementation. In the end, management considered the risks of publishing the information too high
and the benefits too low.

The case study produced the following modifications to the method
(E = extensions and I = improvements): To improve the efficiency and
effectiveness of the interviews the interview protocol was shortened.
Some questions were replaced by questions that turned out to be more
effective (I).

To improve the communication about the results of the method, a
format was added for reporting core competencies in a clear and con-
cise way. Each core competence must have a short and catchy name.
This name must be supported by a subtitle. Each core competence
must be defined and a glossary must be added containing the important words used. Each core competence must be unraveled into its supporting intangible resources (I).

To prove the robustness of the findings, supporting evidence must be
added. These qualitative data support the claim that a competence
is indeed a core competence of the firm. These data can be supplemented by quotes from the interviews (I).

Consulting Department

Case studies 1, 2, 3, and 5 each took three months to complete. The fourth case study was finished within two weeks. This sixth case study offered a real challenge because we had only half a day to complete it.

Context and Problem Definition

Consulting Department was an internal consulting unit within a larger financial company. It offered services in the field of information management, human resources management, and organizational design. The company had merged with a large financial institution. This institution was restructuring its back and front offices, and supporting units. For Consulting Department, the continuation of the unit as a separate entity was no longer an option. Several alternatives were being investigated. The department manager was a very enterprising person and he considered the option of outsourcing the consulting unit. The idea was to turn the unit into an independent consultancy company. The former mother company would be its major client and this would guarantee work for a number of years. The manager was interested in analyzing the core competencies of his unit as part of the discussion with his team about the future. We offered to organize a half-day workshop.

Special Requirements and Design

The manager was primarily interested in a facilitated discussion with his team on the core competencies of the unit, and their strengths and weaknesses. There had not yet been an open and thorough discussion about the future of the unit. Many questions had not yet been discussed: the added value of the unit, how competitive it would be, and what its potential was. These kinds of questions needed to be debated. The manager was also interested in the value of the core competencies: "At a bank, everybody thinks in terms of money."

We created a special object design that included the identification of core competencies, an assessment of strengths and weaknesses, and a valuation based on a rough calculation of a contribution margin for each of the products. Because there was very little time available, we decided to focus the workshop on the identification of core competencies and the assessment of their importance for each of the unit's products. In a meeting with the manager, we identified the products of Consulting Department. The manager also provided the necessary financial data to calculate the contribution margin of each product.

We assessed the potential, sustainability, and robustness factor using their expert opinion, and calculated the financial value of the core competencies.

Implementation and Results

The implementation of the method consisted of organizing a half-day workshop with the total team of Consulting Department and composing a spreadsheet.

Object Recognition

The workshop started with a brief introduction of the methodology. The group was then divided into two teams. Each team was asked to brainstorm on the unique capabilities of Consulting Department and to combine them into four to six core competencies. Each team presented its results. In a plenary discussion, the results were combined. This produced a list of six core competencies. A critical factor for success was finding a compelling and catchy phrase for each core competence—a phrase that in a short and precise way would depict a rich image of a collective ability and would be easy for everybody to understand. Therefore, every core competence was phrased as a specific capability (in Dutch, *vermogen*). This resulted in the following six capabilities of Consulting Department (Table 5.32).

During a second assignment we asked the participants to assess the importance of each of the six competencies to each of the six products.

Table 5.32

Core Competencies of Consulting Department		
Term	**Term in Dutch**	**Description**
Analytical capability	*Analytisch vermogen*	The ability to analyze situations and processes
Projection capability	*Inlevingsvermogen*	The ability to identify with clients and their situation
Collaborative capability	*Samenwerkingsvermogen*	The ability to work together in teams
Organizing capability	*Organisatievermogen*	The ability to organize
Motivational capability	*Motivatievermogen*	The ability to motivate people
Learning capability	*Leervermogen*	The ability to learn from previous experiences

This resulted in the product–competence matrix shown in Table 5.33.

Financial Valuation

The manager provided information on the number of full-time equivalents each member of the team was supposed to spend on each product. An average market rate and a salary rate were used to calculate a contribution margin per full-time equivalent. This margin was used to calculate a contribution margin per product. We used the core competence checklists to assess the strengths and weaknesses of the core competencies. With the results of the checklists, the sustainability and robustness factor was estimated using the automatic correlation algorithm shown in Table 5.22. This information was summarized in a spreadsheet. This task concluded the assignment. Table 5.34 presents the results.

We were of the opinion that Consulting Department was not a particularly unique organization, except for the fact that—being an internal consulting unit—it knew its clients exceptionally well. This was reflected by the core competence projection capability and its two-year sustainability factor, which made this competence very valuable. If Consulting Department were to become independent, the bond with the mother organization would become less strong. As a result, this competence would gradually become less valuable. In that situation, this competence would have to be compensated by the ability to build relationships with other potential customers.

Reporting to the Client

The manager was very satisfied with the results. The questions raised during the workshop were exactly the kinds of questions that needed to be discussed with the team. The method proved to be an excellent way to introduce the team to the idea of becoming independent. Team members became more aware of the different contributions of each member to the team. The key message of the workshop was that every member has its strengths and weaknesses, but together the team has important capabilities.

The workshop raised the issue of product development. The Consulting Department team acknowledged that it had to make its services much more tangible and concrete. It recognized that it was very vulnerable because its most valuable competence was knowing a client that would be lost when Consulting Department became independent. This prompted the need for additional skills in acquisition

Table 5.33

Product/Competence Matrix of Consulting Department						
Core Competence	Information Analysis	Project Work	Administrative Organization Consultancy	Change Management	Strategy Development	Business Architecture
Analytical capability	3	2	3	1	2	3
Projection capability	2	2	2	3	1	2
Collaborative capability	1	3	1	2	1	1
Organizing capability	1	3	1	2	1	1
Motivational capability	0	3	0	3	2	3
Learning capability	1	1	1	1	2	2
Total	8	14	8	12	9	12

0, no contribution; 1, supporting contribution; 2, substantial contribution; 3, essential contribution.

Table 5.34

	Intangible Value of Consulting Department (in millions of guilders)								
Competence	CM, t = 0	P, %	S, years	t = 1	t = 2	t = 3	t = 4	t = 5	R, %	Total
Analytical capability	0.61	10	1	0.68	—	—	—	—	100	0.68
Projection capability	0.54	8	2	0.58	0.63	—	—	—	80	0.96
Collaborative capability	0.43	0	1	0.43	—	—	—	—	100	0.43
Organizing capability	0.43	10	1	0.47	—	—	—	—	100	0.47
Motivational capability	0.42	10	1	0.46	—	—	—	—	80	0.37
Learning capability	0.32	10	1	0.35	—	—	—	—	100	0.35
Total	2.74	—	—	2.96	0.63	—	—	—	—	3.26

and networking. The results of the workshop also helped to fill in Consulting Department's balanced scorecard.

Two years after the case study a new and independent consulting firm opened its doors. It had a contract with the mother company that guaranteed work for two years. The company employed five members of Consulting Department. The other members did not want to join this outsourced company and found new positions within the larger financial organization.

Evaluation and Modifications

The specific problem of Consulting Department was not very precise. We were asked to facilitate a discussion about the future of the unit. This falls into the class of problems about improving internal management. The specific context offered the team a special challenge. Half the method had to fit into one half-day workshop. This realization design worked surprisingly well. Within a period of four hours, a set of mutually agreed-on core competencies was developed. This initiated a strategic discussion about the future of the unit, based on a better understanding of its strengths. The results of the method signified the importance of the bond with the mother organization and of networking as a desirable core competence.

The implementation was successful because the participants were trained and skilled consultants whose core competence was the ability to analyze organizations. In addition, our implementation team knew the business of Consulting Department and its market intimately well. This case study proved that under these conditions it is possible to come to a comprehensive list of core competencies in half a day. It also reconfirmed the power of defining core competencies in a catchy and compelling way.

The realization design helped to fulfill the conditions for successful implementation as described in Chapter 2. The half-day workshop produced a high level of involvement of the client system with the engagement. It created intense communication between our implementation team and the client system, it produced a level of equivalence between the client system and the implementation team, and it helped to realize a successful implementation.

The case study produced one extension to the method. When the time to implement the method is extremely short, a workshop can be used as an alternative for interviews and brainstorming sessions. A condition for success is that the participants have the mental capability to analyze their organization using the concept of core competencies.

Result of the Tests

These six implementations helped to develop the method into a comprehensive instrument. But how well did it perform? Did it turn out to be a useful tool? And what can we learn from these tests about the valuation of intangibles in general and the weightless wealth tool kit in particular? In this section I evaluate the performance of the method. In the next chapter I summarize the lessons that we can learn from these tests. There are two elements to performance. First, the question is whether the method is able to meet all the requirements set out in Chapter 4. To answer this question I compare the final version of the method with the requirements described in Table 4.4. The numbers in the text below refer to Table 4.4. The second question is: How successful was the method in solving the problems identified?

The Method and Its Requirements

The final method consisted of five consecutive elements: the identification of intangible resources, a value assessment, a financial valuation, a management agenda, and the value dashboard. The last four elements can be included at will. This shows the method did meet the stepwise and modular requirement (3.3).

The method identified intangible resources that are strategically important to companies. It did so by identifying a company's core competencies and underlying supporting intangibles. The method prescribed the use of different perspectives when identifying core competencies. The core competencies showed how intangible resources create synergy when combined into powerful abilities. This element of the method helped to meet the identification (2.1), demarcation (2.2), and synergy (2.3) requirement. The reporting format for presenting core competencies presented the findings in a simple, compelling, and comprehensive way. This helped to meet the requirement of transparency (3.1).

The method included a value assessment that uses five criteria, incorporated into one core competence checklist: added value, competitiveness, potential, sustainability, and robustness. The assessment was performed by the analysts, acting as experts, or by members of the client organization. The results were presented as "traffic lights." This element of the method helped to meet the management assessment requirement (2.10). The method did not assess the management or stewardship of intangibles directly, but it evaluated the impact of management on the added value, competitiveness, potential, sustainability, and robustness of intangibles. This helped to find ways to improve the management of the intangible resources.

The method performed a financial valuation of core competencies. It used owner value as standard of value, and value in continued use as part of a going concern business enterprise as premise of value. This met the value definition requirement (2.4). The method used the contribution margin per product group as a measure of economic income. The income projection was based on a potential factor, indicating the growth of the income stream (2.5). It charged the income with a fair return on tangible assets and networking capital (2.6). To allocate the remaining income stream, the method looked at the contribution of each core competence to each of the product groups. It used a scoring mechanism to assign percentages to the various contributions (2.7). The method used the strategic life of a core competence as the definition of useful life. Strategic life is the sustainability of the core competence, and it is equal to the number of years it takes a competitor to acquire the same competence (2.8). The method included a robustness factor to reflect the risk of losing the core competence. This in part met the income capitalization requirement (2.9). This requirement demanded that a valuation take into account growth and risks, but also the cost of capital and inflation. However, the version of the method that was tested did not fulfill this latter part of the capitalization requirement. In Chapter 6, I suggest further improvements to tackle this problem.

The first deliverable of the method was a management agenda. This agenda reflected the implications for management of the results (cf. Mouritsen et al. [2001c] note 3). It described how management can improve the value of intangibles by raising the added value, competitiveness, potential, sustainability, and robustness of the company's core competencies. The first four aspects help to improve the uniqueness and the strategic focus of the company. The latter helps to anchor this uniqueness securely into the organization. The management agenda met the management assessment requirement (2.10).

The second deliverable was the reporting format for the final report. This report contained the value dashboard. The dashboard summarized the results from the identification of intangibles, the value assessment, and the financial valuation. It provided a bird's-eye view of the results and made them easy to explain. This helped to meet the transparency requirement (3.1).

The method could be implemented in three ways: workshop based, interview and workshop based, and interview based. When the organization is small and there is little time available, the method can be implemented by organizing between one and three workshops. When the organization is bigger and there is more time available, a combination of interviews and workshops can be used. This strategy produces more insight into the core competencies of the company, and its strengths and weaknesses. When there is little time available to organize workshops, the method can use data derived solely from interviews. In this situation, the results are expert based. During the first two situations results predominantly come from the participants, and the analyst provides a check of consistency. This modular setup of the realization design helped to meet the limitations (4). Appendix B describes the elements of the method, making it standardized and explicit (3.2).

The pilot studies indicated that the method can be used in knowledge-intensive (1.1), middle-size (1.2) companies that are either start-up companies (Logistics Services BU) or mature companies (the other five companies; 1.4). The method has not yet been tested in all industries. It is too early to conclude whether it meets the requirement of "applicable in every industry" (1.3).

The Success of the Method

The case studies resulted in important modifications to the method. However, the success of the method in solving problems was limited (Table 5.35).

In two cases the limited success was the result of poor implementation. At Bank Ltd. we stopped the implementation process before it was finished because the team ran out of budget. Although the process was never finished, the end report was used in the decision-making process about Bank Ltd.'s independence. According to the CEO, its contribution to the decision was limited. At Automotive Ltd. the manager/owner of the company stopped the process because of other priorities. We were not able to convince him otherwise.

When the implementation *was* successful, in only one case the problem was solved. Consulting Department became a successful, independent company. According to the manager, the method had been very important in facilitating the discussion about independence. It helped to make explicit important considerations for outsourcing. In three other cases, the problem was not solved. The general manager of Electro Ltd. had been very satisfied with the results at the time of the final presentation. However, circumstances beyond our control changed the situation completely. It turned out Electro Ltd. had a severe cash flow problem. This problem became urgent just after the project was finished. The cash flow problem was never solved and the

Table 5.35

Appraisal of the Success of the Method in Six Case Studies					
Problem Type	Case	Problem Definition	Successful Implementation?	Problem Solved?	Contribution of Method?
Internal management	Electro Ltd.	Develop a strategy based on available technologies and skills	Yes	Wrong problem	Not available
	Logistic Services BU	Create a future for Logistic Services BU	Yes	No	Some
	Consulting Department	Create a future for Consulting Department	Yes	Yes	Big
	Automotive BU	Improve strategy-making process	No	No	None
External reporting	Bank Ltd.	Remain independent within holding company	No	Yes	Limited
	Professional Services LLP	Report on intangibles	Yes	No	Not available

company went bankrupt. In a sense, the method was solving the wrong problem. At Logistics Services BU, a similar thing happened. The method contributed to the decision to effect a management buyout. However, in the end, key players decided not to join the new company and the buyout was canceled. According to two participants, the method contributed to the decision-making process. It created enthusiasm and energy within the group, and it helped to develop a proper business case because it created insight into the four core competencies and their strengths and weaknesses. At Professional Services LLP, all the necessary conditions for successful implementation were met. However, we discovered that the method did not produce results that could be reported easily externally. The results were not self-evident or self-explanatory. The supporting evidence was not suitable for external publication. Without the evidence, the results were not robust enough to present in the annual report. From these findings, I conclude that the method is not an appropriate tool for the external reporting of intangibles. This has been an important lesson. The next chapter presents the other important lessons that I learned that may also be helpful to you.

Lessons Learned: Contributions to Intellectual Capital Research

"There are no answers, only choices."
Solaris, Steven Soderbergh (2002)

On September 8, 1999, I started my research and now it is finished. This chapter presents the lessons that I learned. I wanted to contribute to the repertoire of the intellectual capital community by designing a method for the valuation of intangible resources. I created a new method that I named the *weightless wealth tool kit*, after the book in which its basic form was first presented (Andriessen and Tissen, 2000). The following section presents the lessons I learned about this tool kit; about its application domain, its mechanisms, and its strengths, and weaknesses. The section concludes with two additional modifications to the method that have not yet been tested. The final version of the weightless wealth tool kit is described in Appendix B.

I also wanted to contribute to the field of intellectual capital research by developing knowledge about the valuation of intangible resources. In this chapter I summarize what I found, based on the literature review and my struggle to design a proper valuation method.

A third objective of my study was to contribute to the methodology of intellectual capital research. In Chapter 2 I presented my view on reality, truth, and scientific research. I concluded that there is a need for management research practiced as a design science, to help reconcile the dilemma of rigor versus relevance. Chapter 2 presented the reflective cycle as a model that intellectual capital and other management researchers can use to design management methods in a rigorous way. This chapter reflects on this model, based on my own experiences in applying it to intellectual capital research.

I formulate my findings as hypotheses. One of the limitations of the reflective cycle is that it provides limited possibilities of generalizing results. Case study research does not allow the generalization of findings to a wider population. Furthermore, the methodology of practicing management research as a design science demands that researchers continue testing in order to accumulate supporting evidence until theoretical saturation has been reached (Van Aken, 2000). Theoretical saturation has not yet been achieved for the weightless wealth tool kit. There is much more to explore. Therefore, I end this chapter with suggestions for future intellectual capital research.

Lessons about the Method

This section summarizes the lessons I learned about the method. First, I reflect on the application domain of the method. The application domain includes the class of problems the weightless wealth tool kit addresses and the class of contexts to which it is applicable. Second, I describe the mechanisms embedded in the method that produce results. These mechanisms reflect the strengths of the method. I then describe the weaknesses of the weightless wealth tool kit. These findings result in two additional modifications. These improvements to the tool kit have not yet been tested but are included in Appendix B.

The Application Domain of the Method

As we saw in Chapter 3, methods for the valuation or measurement of intangible resources are often solutions in search of a cause. Our method has been no exception. At the start of the design process, the Ministry of Economic Affairs was looking for a reporting tool. The design team consisted primarily of consultants working in the area of knowledge management and had a special interest in improving the management of intangibles. The team wanted to address a wide range of problems and to include internal management and external reporting issues.

The findings from the case studies indicate that the method is not an appropriate tool for the external reporting of intangibles. The results of the method are not self-evident and must be accompanied by an extensive reading instruction. Interpretation of the results requires insight into the underlying method. Furthermore, clients are reluctant to publish the results. Professional Services LLP considered the reporting of financial valuations risky. In addition, supporting evidence for core competencies often includes data about competitors. Professional

Services LLP was reluctant to report these data because it might provoke criticism. The weightless wealth tool kit highlights a company's strengths but also its weaknesses. Professional Services LLP and Electro Ltd. were hesitant to report these weaknesses to the outside world. Finally, these companies considered data about their core competencies confidential information. As the CEO of Electro Ltd. put it: "I will not published this information for the next six years" (personal communication).

In three cases I found that the method was a useful tool to help improve the way a company is managed. These cases had in common that the companies were reconsidering their position. Management wanted to develop a new future for the company based on the company's intangible strength. However, the management of these companies did not know the strength of the company and wanted insight into its future potential. In this situation, it proved useful to identify the intangible resources, assess their strengths, and determine their value. Based on these findings, I formulated the following hypothesis about the class of problems the weightless wealth tool kit addresses: *The weightless wealth tool kit can help in solving problems of future orientation and strategy development, by helping to create resource-based strategies for companies that lack insight into or are insecure about the intangible resources that make these companies successful and that determine their future potential.*

A second factor that determines the application domain of a management method is the class of contexts in which the method can be used. The class of contexts is determined by the limiting conditions and by the indications and contraindications found while testing the method. The indications and contraindications highlight under what circumstances the method will and will not work.

The limiting conditions of my weightless wealth tool kit include the requirement that the method should work for knowledge-intensive, middle-size companies employing from 50 to 1,000 employees. The tests show it also works with smaller units that are part of a bigger company (Logistics Services Ltd., Consulting Department). Tests also prove it can be used with bigger companies (Professional Services LLP), provided that the analyst focuses on the core competencies of the company that various departments have in common. The method was designed to work across all industries. However, the tests only took place in the professional services, automotive, engineering, and financial industries. Further testing in other industries is needed to determine whether the method works in all industries.

The tests highlighted that the following conditions must be fulfilled to ensure a successful implementation. The company must have an issue about its future direction. If there is no clear issue, as in the case of Automotive Ltd., it is less likely that the method will produce useful results. In addition, management of the company must have a certain willingness to reflect on the organization and to review critically the organization's strengths and weaknesses. Management must have enough time to participate—at least to join in the interviews and visit the end presentation. At Automotive Ltd. these two conditions were not met, which in part explains the early termination of the project. Finally, management must have the willingness, as well as the mental ability, to look at the company from an intangible perspective. This, too, was lacking at Automotive Ltd. On the other hand, one can argue that the method should be able to translate the rather abstract concept of intangibles into the language of the client. Van Aken (1996) makes a distinction between "back-office" and "front-office" language. The designer of management methods can use back-office language among colleagues when he is designing the method. In his interactions with clients, however, he must use the language of the clients (although he may try to introduce some elements of the back-office language). Further testing must determine whether the method suffers from too much back-office language, which may hinder the application of the method at ordinary companies. These findings lead to the following hypothesis about the class of contexts of the method: *The weightless wealth tool kit is especially suited for knowledge-intensive, middle-size companies in all industries that have an issue about their future direction and whose management has the time, the mental capacity, and the willingness to review critically the company's strengths and weaknesses using an intangible perspective. The method can be used with smaller units that are part of a bigger company. It can also be used at bigger companies, provided the analyst focuses on mutual core competencies.*

The Strengths and Mechanisms of the Method

According to Van Aken (2000), it is not so important to test whether a method works but to determine what it is about the method that makes it work. What are the explaining mechanisms of the method? These mechanisms may include external, impersonal factors as well as the interpretation and reasoning of the actors involved. Mechanisms are important for translating the method to other contexts. The case studies shed light on the mechanisms of my method. The various elements of the weightless wealth tool kit, as presented in Chapter 5, each have a different set of mechanisms. I briefly discuss each element in the following paragraphs.

The first element of the method is the identification of intangible resources with the help of core competencies (see Appendix B.3). Two of the six companies had never worked with the concept of core competencies before. Three companies had experimented with the concept to a limited degree. Only one company had had extensive experience with core competencies. So in five cases the method offered members of the companies a new perspective, providing new angles for sense making. This intangible perspective is a positive perspective because it emphasizes the things that make a company unique and successful. Discovering core competencies can evoke a sense of pride and open up the mind of participants for new opportunities. The identification phase of my weightless wealth tool kit makes use of this mechanism. I hypothesize that the list of core competencies, with their definitions and glossary of terms, helps to explain why a company is successful, like it did at Bank Ltd. and at Professional Services LLP. It can install a sense of pride and boost a company's self-confidence, like at Electro Ltd. (although the confidence turned out to be a little inappropriate). It can point toward new opportunities for products and services, as it did at Electro Ltd. The list of core competencies provides a common language to the participants to discuss the future of their company in a new light. When I interviewed managers at Bank Ltd. and Consulting Department two years after the event, I still could trace elements of that new language.

The weightless wealth tool kit searches for the combined power of intangible resources. It determines the way individual intangibles contribute to a company's uniqueness and cumulative capabilities. It determines which intangibles are important and how they contribute to company success. The method also produces an inventory of individual intangible resources, but this inventory did not play a role of significance in any of the cases. Instead, participants discussed the *combined* strength of intangible resources. During the interviews, managers referred to the core competencies and not to individual resources. This underpins the hypothesis presented in Chapter 3, that individual intangibles are not interesting but their combined strength is.

These findings lead to the following hypothesis about the mechanisms that make the identification phase of the method work: *The use of core competencies in the weightless wealth tool kit to identify intangible resources provides a new and positive view on a company, and a common language that can explain the company's success, install a sense of pride, boost its self-confidence, and identify new opportunities.*

The second element of the weightless wealth tool kit is the value assessment of the core competencies using five checklists (see

Appendix B.4). This accomplishes two things. First, it helps companies to become realistic again, in case they became overly optimistic about their competencies during the identification phase. At Bank Ltd., management had to acknowledge that its data processing capability was not unique. The management of Electro Ltd. realized that its small-scale power technology was quite common in the marketplace. Managers of Logistics Services Ltd. found out the company had to improve its management skills. Members of Consulting Department concluded the department was not unique, except for its intimate knowledge about its only client. Second, the value assessment provides input for the management agenda. The assessment shows the weaknesses in the core competencies. During workshops, participants were asked to develop ways to mitigate these weaknesses. The implementation team translated these suggestions into action points.

These findings lead to the following hypothesis about the mechanisms that make the value assessment phase work: *The value assessment of the weightless wealth tool kit helps to create a realistic view on the capabilities of a company that are genuine core competencies. In addition, the assessment highlights strengths and weaknesses of core competencies. These weaknesses can be the starting point for improvement initiatives.*

The third element of the weightless wealth tool kit is the financial valuation of the core competencies (see Appendix B.5). The financial valuation highlights the *absolute* importance of intangibles. Both the CEO of Bank Ltd. and the manager of Consulting Department acknowledged the importance of the monetary value figure in conveying the significance of intangible resources to other stakeholders. The manager of Consulting Department phrased it as follows: "Within the financial services industry, people speak the language of money. If something has no monetary value attached to it, it is not considered important" (personal communication). The added value of the financial valuation of intangible resources lies in the fact that numbers attract management attention. This finding is in line with the view of Mouritsen et al. (2001b) about the importance of indicators in intellectual capital statements. They state that these indicators are especially important because they demonstrate seriousness on the part of top management.

In addition, the financial valuation shows the *relative* importance of the core competencies. The financial valuation uses money as a common denominator to compare the usefulness of the competencies. At Bank Ltd., the financial valuation showed how important the bank's competence to provide customer-oriented services was for the success of the bank. This ability was far more important than the bank's investment skills. At Electro Ltd., the financial valuation demonstrated the future potential of the company's energy conversion technology; something that had not been acknowledged before. At Consulting Department, the financial valuation illustrated how much it depended on its knowledge about its only customer. When a core competence has little value, management has two options. One is to stop investing in the competence; another is to strengthen the competence. The results of the preceding value assessment phase show how the value of a core competence can be increased by either investing in its added value, competitiveness, potential, sustainability, or robustness.

These findings lead to the following hypothesis about the mechanisms that make the financial valuation work: *The financial valuation of intangible resources that is part of the weightless wealth tool kit helps to emphasize the absolute importance of these resources to company success. This helps to attract management attention. In addition, the financial valuation shows the relative importance of the various core competencies. This can help when making decisions about investments in intangibles.*

The fourth element of the weightless wealth tool kit is the management agenda (see Appendix B.6). The management agenda reflects the implications of the findings for management. It provides an action plan on how to strengthen the company's intangible resources. The management agenda can help to make the important step from valuation to action, making the method practical and meaningful. At Bank Ltd., important issues on the management agenda were increasing innovation and decreasing vulnerability. At Electro Ltd., improving quality standards and project management skills were crucial. Logistics Services Ltd. was missing a number of skills. The management agenda suggested the use of alliance partners to fill the gaps.

These findings lead to the following hypothesis about the mechanisms that make the management agenda work: *The management agenda of the weightless wealth tool kit helps to translate the outcome of the method into action, making the method practical and meaningful.*

The fifth element of the method is the end report, which contains the value dashboard (see Appendix B.7). The comprehensiveness of the dashboard helps to convey the outcome of the method in one picture. This picture presents the value of the core competencies and the total value of the strategically important intangibles. The "traffic lights" highlight the strengths and weaknesses of the core competencies. The contribution margin and the value of the potential, sustainability, and robustness factor help to explain the financial value of each core competence. They are the value drivers of the core competencies.

As a result, the financial values are no longer the outcome of a black box.

These findings lead to the following hypothesis about the mechanisms that make the value dashboard work: *The value dashboard of the weightless wealth tool kit helps to communicate the findings of the method in an effective and comprehensive way by providing insight into the strengths, weaknesses, and value drivers of core competencies in one comprehensive picture.*

The findings of my study contribute to the core competence approach to strategy development (see Hamel and Prahalad [1994]), although that has never been my intention. The core competence approach has been criticized for a number of reasons (see Baaij et al. [1999], Leonard–Barton [1992, 1995], and Weggeman, [1997a]). Weggeman (1997a) and Baaij et al. (1999) point toward the lack of proper definitions of the term *core competence* and the difficulty identifying them. The weightless wealth tool kit offers an approach for the identification of core competencies that uses various tools and perspectives. It forces the analyst to look at core competencies from the perspective of customers, products and services, intangibles, competition, successful projects, product innovations, and strategy. My hypothesis is that by using all these perspectives simultaneously, and involving members from various parts of the organization in the workshops, reliable identification of a company's core competencies can be achieved. Leonard–Barton (1992) argues that the act of identifying core competencies increases the risk of creating core rigidities. In turbulent markets, strengths can quickly become weaknesses. Therefore, a constant flow of new knowledge is needed to create improvement and innovation. This creates a dilemma. It is not wise to stick to old competencies of the past, yet it is also unwise to throw them away until you have new ones. This is what Weggeman (1997a) calls the *competence trap*. A dominant focus on core competencies can lead to rigidities in developing new ones. One may even argue that putting a static value on core competencies increases the risk of creating core rigidities. The weightless wealth tool kit can help avoid the competence trap. It can help determine a company's core competencies and their value to determine which new ones to develop. The method highlights the strengths and weaknesses of the core competencies and their relative value. Companies can decide which new competencies to develop, confronting this information with information about trends and discontinuities in the environment.

These observations lead to the following hypothesis about the contribution of the method to the core competence approach: *The weightless wealth tool kit can help determine which core competencies a*

*company has and to determine which new ones to develop. The finan-
cial valuation and value assessment provide insight into the usefulness,
strengths, and weaknesses of the core competencies. Companies can
use this information to decide to invest in some core competencies and
to abandon others. When they confront the findings with information
on trends and discontinuities in the environment, they can decide
which new competencies to develop.*

The Weaknesses of the Method

The previous sections focused on the strengths and mechanisms
of the method. In this section I am very honest about the method's
weaknesses. I formulate hypotheses about these weaknesses based on
comparing the method with the requirements, comparing it with the
state-of-the-art in the intellectual capital field as described in Chapter
3, and based on the case study findings. In the following paragraphs I
suggest a number of improvements to the method that mitigates some
of these weak points.

The version of the weightless wealth tool kit that came out of the
last case study has certain weaknesses. First, the version lacks a diagnosis phase. The method does not include a step in which the analyst
checks whether the problems of the company fit the class of problems
for which the method was designed. The method "jumps to solutions"
(Kerssens, 1999), does not prevent pigeonholing (Perrow, 1970), or,
phrased differently, the method suffers from the "child-with-a-
hammer-syndrome."[1] It can very well be, as we saw with Electro Ltd.
and Automotive Ltd., that creating insight into the value of a company's intangible resources is not the right solution for the problems at
hand. In addition, the method does not include a check on whether the
necessary conditions are met for a successful implementation. There is
a danger that the implementation fails because the context is not right,
as we saw with Automotive Ltd. Later I suggest an intake phase as an
extension to the method that addresses these two shortcomings (see
Appendix B.2 as well).

Second, the step from creating an inventory of intangibles and
capabilities to defining core competencies is still a more or less
creative and unguided step. The personal skills of the analyst play an
important role. The existing guidelines for this step leave room for personal preferences, diminishing the reliability of the outcome. Further
research is needed to determine the reliability of the core competence
definitions and how they can be improved.

---

[1] Give a child a hammer and, to the child, suddenly everything becomes a nail.

Third, the outcome of the financial valuation is sensitive to the estimation of the sustainability and robustness factors. These factors are difficult to determine. This is caused by the definitions of useful life and risk that are used in the method. Strategic life is used as definition of useful life. Strategic life indicates the time required by a competitor to copy the same core competence. From the perspective of core competence theory, this is an appropriate definition. Strategic life reflects whether a core competence is difficult to imitate, and this is an important notion in the work of Hamel and Prahalad (1994). However, strategic life is also difficult to determine. As long as a competitor has not actually copied the core competence, there are no data available on how long this will take. Often there is not even data available on how long it took the subject company to acquire the core competence. The same applies to the robustness factor. This factor reflects the risk of losing the core competence. This risk is difficult to assess. As a result, the financial value estimations show a high degree of unreliability. The outcome of the financial valuation depends strongly on the analyst who applies the method. Later, I suggest a different definition of both useful life and risk that results in estimations that are more reliable, although from the viewpoint of core competence theory they are less appropriate.

Fourth, the results of the method are internally focused. The method describes important intangible resources of a company without looking at the environment. Roos et al. (2001) distinguish between two approaches to strategy: external analysis and the resource-based view. I agree when they state that a strategy process should combine the best of both approaches. The weightless wealth tool kit takes care of the resource-based view, identifying the valuable resources of the company. However, before a company can develop a new strategy, an external analysis of major environmental, competitive forces must be made. Further research is needed to develop this complementary approach.

These observations lead to the following hypothesis about the weaknesses of the method: *The weaknesses of the tested version of the method are the lack of a thorough diagnosis of the problem and the context, the reliability of the core competence definitions and financial valuations, and the internal focus of the outcome.*

Final Modifications to the Method

I improved the tested version of my method in two ways. I added an intake with the potential subject company to diagnose the problem and context, and I improved the financial valuation tool to make it more reliable. Appendix B describes the final version of the weightless wealth tool kit. Companies can use it as a do-it-yourself tool kit or it can be used by an (external) analyst.

The first phase in using the weightless wealth tool kit is the intake. The purpose of the intake is to determine whether the subject company falls within the application domain of the method. The intake includes a check of whether the problem at hand falls within the class of problems as described earlier in this chapter. The company must have a problem with its future positioning. It must lack a clear strategy or it must be dissatisfied with its existing strategy. It must require a clear insight into its intangible resources or be insecure about their strength and potential. The intake also checks whether the conditions for a successful implementation are met as described earlier. It checks whether the subject company is a knowledge-intensive, middle-size company. It also checks whether management of the company has the time to participate. It asks whether management has the ability to reflect on the company in abstract terms and is willing to review critically the company's strengths and weaknesses.

The second improvement is an alternative approach to the financial valuation of intangibles. This alternative approach borrows from the valuation method developed by Gu and Lev (2002). The financial valuation starts with an estimation of a company's normalized earnings, an annual weighted average of past and future earnings. The future earnings are based on forecasts by financial analysts if available, on the pattern of the firm's past sales, or on a company's own forecasts.

Next, the values of tangible and financial assets are obtained from the firm's balance sheet and footnotes, converting historical accounting costs to current values. Then a normal rate of return on tangible and financial assets is used as a fair rate of return for these assets. The tool kit recommends using the rates determined by Gu and Lev (2002), which are after-tax rates of 7% for tangible assets and 4.5% for financial assets. Subtracting the fair rate of return for assets from the normalized earnings results in the contribution of intangible resources to the enterprise's performance. Gu and Lev (2002) define this as IDEs.

Next, the three-stage valuation model is used as proposed by Gu and Lev (2002) to forecast the series of IDEs. For future years 1 through 5, a financial analyst's long-term growth forecasts or a sales-based forecast is used, through future years 6 through 10 linearly converging the forecasts to the long-term growth of the economy, like 3%. For future years 11 to infinity, the method assumes that IDEs grow annually by 3%. The forecast is based on the assumption that the intangible resources have an indefinitely useful life. This removes the sustainability factor from the equation.

Next, the forecasted income stream is capitalized using a discount rate that reflects the average weighted cost of capital of the company, a compensation for inflation, and the above-average riskiness of IDEs. This incorporates the robustness factor into the discount factor. The capitalized income stream reflects the financial value of all the intangible resources of the company.

Finally, this financial value is allocated to core competencies in two steps. The value is allocated to the various product groups of the company based on the contribution of each product group to earnings during the current year. The allocation tool (as described in Chapter 4) is then used to allocate product earnings to core competencies. The allocation tool includes a scoring mechanism to determine the contribution of each core competence to each product group. The result is the financial value of the core competencies of the company.

What are the hidden drivers behind the success of your business? Do you know where the weightless wealth of your organization lies? How can you leverage your intangible resources? What do you need to do to adapt to the intangible economy? Start experimenting with the weightless wealth tool kit and find out for yourself. Appendix B provides you with all the tools you need. Let me know what you find and share your experiences with me so I can further develop the tool kit. Go to www.weightlesswealth.com for more information.

Lessons about Valuing Intangible Resources

This section summarizes the lessons that I learned about the valuation of intangible resources on my journey to develop the weightless wealth tool kit. In this section I clarify a number of issues. Within the intellectual capital community there seems to be confusion about the following six issues, and this blocks further development in the field.

Valuing Intangibles Requires Values

In this book I have defined value as *the degree of usefulness or desirability of something, especially in comparison with other things.* The degree of usefulness or desirability depends on values. To determine value, an analyst needs to apply values as yardsticks. Valuation is a comparative assessment or measurement of something with respect to its embodiment of a certain value. As we saw in Chapter 3, 8 of 25 existing methods do not incorporate values and can therefore not be considered valuation methods. If you want to start measuring or assessing value, you need to have yardsticks.

Valuing Intangibles Requires a Beholder

Values are by definition subjective. A value reflects the concept an individual or group has regarding the useful or the desirable. The popular saying that beauty is in the eye of the beholder is also applicable to value. Any valuation requires beholders who apply their values. This is why with any financial valuation it is important to define carefully the standard of value. This standard determines "value to whom." Consequently, value is not objective; it does not reside in the material world. Therefore, the concept of truth, defined as "correspondence with reality," is not applicable to a valuation. We cannot determine the logical–positivist validity of a valuation. However, sometimes the values of the beholder can be operationalized into observable phenomenon, like client satisfaction or future cash flow. If this is the case, we can check the *reliability* of the valuation. A valuation method yields reliable results if the outcome is the same, independent from the analyst applying the method. As we saw earlier, the version of the weightless wealth tool kit that was tested in the study cases did not meet this requirement. If you want to start measuring or assessing value, you need first to define from which stakeholder's perspective you want to start valuing.

Valuing Intangible Resources Does Not Require Money

The criterion of value does not have to be money. If you *do* use money as a criterion of value, you perform a financial valuation. The advantage of using money is that it can act as a common denominator for various subject intangibles. This makes it possible to compare apples and oranges. A monetary value scale is a scale on a ratio level. This allows you to do mathematical transformations like adding values.

However, you can also use other criteria of value for the valuation of intangibles, as proved by, for example, Brooking's (1996) intellectual capital audit and Viedma's (2001b) intellectual capital benchmarking system. If you use criteria for valuation that can be measured in the outside world, you perform a value measurement. If the criteria cannot be measured, you perform a value assessment. M'Pherson and Pike (2001b) and Pike and Roos (2000) have shown that even without money as a common denominator it is possible to add apples and oranges (intangible resources) when you do a value measurement. You can combine indicators to create one overall nonfinancial indicator of value. However, if you want to do that, you must fulfill the requirements for proper multidimensional value measurement. With respect to this, researchers in the field of intellectual capital can learn a lot from measurement theory. M'Pherson and Pike (2001b) provide us with a very good summary of measurement theory.

Valuing Intangibles Requires Identification and Demarcation

One of the problems of valuing intangible resources is to identify the resources to value. How can you identify something that is hidden and not material? As we saw in Chapter 3, the intellectual capital community makes this issue even more difficult to solve because the community does not agree on a common definition of intellectual capital.

In Chapter 3, I justified my concept of intangible resources as an overall umbrella for various types of intangibles. Intangible resources include both human-based and structural intangibles. However, including human-based intangibles creates a problem of demarcation: What part of the skills and knowledge of an employee is part of the company and what part is not? In the design of the weightless wealth tool kit, I solved this problem by replacing it with the question: Which intangible resources are the most important for company success? The weightless wealth tool kit identifies only the intangible resources that are of strategic importance. It does so by looking at a company's core competencies. This has proved to be successful. The Skandia navigator and the intellectual capital index use a similar approach (albeit implicitly) because they use the concept of critical success factors to identify important intangible resource indicators (Roos et al., 1997; Skandia, 1998). The list of indicators included in the Skandia navigator and the intellectual capital index also does not include all intangible resources, only those that are part of critical success factors. With intangible resources, it is difficult to determine which resources are part of the company and which ones are not. Any method that you want to use to value intangible resources has to address and solve this problem. The weightless wealth tool kit successfully solves this problem by identifying which intangible resources are the most important for company success.

Valuing Intangibles Requires Diagnosis

The valuation of intangible resources can help to solve three types of company problems: internal management problems, external reporting problems, and transactional and statutory problems. However, you need to do a thorough diagnosis to determine the specified problem of the situation at hand. This is especially essential when your intention is to improve the internal management of your organization.

There can be many reasons why your company is performing suboptimally or poorly. There can be many ways to optimize your company's performance. This diagnosis phase is missing in all methods examined in Chapter 3. Chapter 3 showed that in many cases methods are also not very specific regarding the class of problems they address. And sometimes methods use problem definitions that are incomplete or that are based on a logical argumentation that does not hold.

It is not sufficient merely to identify the problem at hand as an internal management problem. Neither is it sufficient to apply a nonspecific problem definition like the ones presented in Table 3.5. Instead, you should analyze the specific context of your organization and diagnose its unique situation. You may find that the intangible perspective is an appropriate perspective to diagnose the problem. Using this perspective implies focusing on the intangible resources of a company, the way they are managed, their strengths and weaknesses, and their potential. However, to avoid pigeonholing, you must be aware that other perspectives may be more appropriate. Otherwise, there is a clear risk that an inappropriate or unimportant problem will be solved, thereby making a third-order mistake (De Valk, 1997). In the case of Electro Ltd., it became apparent that the most urgent problem was a cash flow problem. In this case, using a financial perspective may have been more appropriate than using an intangible perspective. To avoid solving an inappropriate or unimportant problem, you need to perform a diagnosis of the problems at hand before starting to value intangibles.

As we saw Chapter 2, problems are not entities in the real world waiting to be discovered. Problems are social constructs created by people applying certain norms or values to a particular situation. One cannot say a problem is true or untrue. However, a problem definition can be useful or unuseful in a particular situation. The degree of usefulness of a problem definition depends on whether solving that problem will contribute to achieving a higher value. In the case of Electro Ltd., lack of insight into the strategically important intangibles may have been a useful problem in the end. However, if we stipulate that the higher goal of Electro Ltd. was the sustainability of the company, then a more useful and urgent problem definition would be a problem definition about the lack of cash flow!

A problem definition can be useful or unuseful in a particular situation. Or, stated in other words, problems have value! This concept opens up a new field of management research: research into the value of problems. To determine the value of a problem definition, the researcher needs to identify a higher goal that can be used as a yardstick. This can be long-term sustainability, short-term profit, or any other organizational goal. Using this yardstick, the researcher can determine whether solving the problem as defined contributes to the higher goal, measuring or assessing the degree of usefulness of the problem definition. This is, in effect, a way to determine the value of a problem.

Valuing Intangibles Requires Methods

In Chapter 3, I presented 25 methods for the valuation of intangible resources. However, eight of them do not include values and are merely measurement methods. Five contain methodological flaws that limit their usefulness. Six methods that are often presented as methods for measuring intangibles fail to do so. They measure a different subject. Seven have a limited scope, looking only at one subcategory of intangible resources. Of the seven remaining methods, three are financial valuation methods, three are value measurement methods, and one is a value assessment method. The weightless wealth tool kit combines a financial valuation and a value assessment. These eight methods are a solid basis for the further development of methods for the valuation of intangible resources. One of them may be exactly the tool that fits your purpose, or it may contain a number of ingredients that you can use to construct your own valuation method.

Lessons about Practicing Intellectual Capital Research as a Design Science

One of my motivations for writing this book was my concern about the lack of relevance of scientific management research. I meet many Ph.D. graduates who are forced by their supervisor to do large-scale (quantitative) research with hardly any practical use. This is a waste of time, money, and effort. One of the reasons seems to be that scientists in this field have a narrow view of science. It appears that management research, including intellectual capital research, struggles to prove its status as a scientific discipline. As a result, researchers think they have to demonstrate they are good scientists by doing data-intensive number crunching. The results can be useful, but more often they are not.

It was my intention to free intellectual capital research from this straitjacket and show that it can help improve performance without letting go of scientific rigor. To do this I practiced intellectual capital research as a design science. In this section I reflect on the lessons that

I learned about this approach. I describe the methodological difficulties and limitations I encountered, but start with a plea for combining the explanatory and design approach in intellectual capital research to reconcile the rigor versus relevance dilemma. This plea is based on the epistemological and methodological premises presented in Chapter 2. This section is especially relevant for researchers in the field of management, organization, or intellectual capital who want to do scientific research but who also want to contribute to the practical improvement of the performance of businesses.

Reconciling the Rigor–Relevance Dilemma in Intellectual Capital Research

Intellectual capital research has evolved primarily from the desires of practitioners (Bontis, 2002). At the same time, it has the ambition to be an academic discipline. The former requires relevance; the latter requires rigor. Many publications in the intellectual capital field qualify as, what Van Aken (2000) calls, *Heathrow literature*—lacking justification. The question is how to improve the justification of the claims of intellectual capital research without losing relevance. This can be achieved by making sure that within the field, intellectual capital research is practiced both as an explanatory science (focusing on describing, explaining, and predicting) and as a design science (focusing on diagnosing, designing, and improving). Both methodologies have their specific advantages, difficulties, and limitations. I briefly summarize both approaches and highlight their difficulties and limitations (Table 6.1). Combining the explanatory and the design approach in intellectual capital research can help to reconcile the dilemma of rigor versus relevance.

In general, intellectual capital research practiced as an explanatory science focuses on quantitative evaluation based on statistical analyses using the empirical cycle. Its criterion of truth is contextual validity, because it checks whether observations validate the theoretical predictions. In practice, it is often difficult to operationalize the theoretical concepts (like human capital and structural capital) and to obtain the necessary data. A limitation to the approach is that the validity of the operationalization cannot be proved because the concepts are constructs applied to a constructed social world. As a result, there is a logical hole in the empirical cycle. Whether falsification of a hypothesis is the result of poor operationalization or poor theory cannot be proved beyond doubt. In general, intellectual capital research practiced as an explanatory science results in a reductionistic causal model (Van Aken, 2000) that can be generalized to a wider population based

Table 6.1

Characteristics of the Explanatory and Design Approach to Intellectual Capital Research		
Aspect	**Intellectual Capital Research Practiced as an Explanatory Science**	**Intellectual Capital Research Practiced as a Design Science**
Criterion of truth	Contextual validity	Contextual success
Main form	Quantitative evaluation	Qualitative exploration
Logic	Empirical cycle	Reflective cycle
Logical difficulties	Hole in the empirical cycle during the operationalization phase; one can never prove that falsification is the result of poor operationalization or of poor theory	Hole in the reflective cycle during the implementation phase; one can never prove that falsification is the result of poor implementation or poor design
Practical difficulties	Difficult to obtain necessary data Difficult to operationalize the abstract concepts	Difficult to find cases with the same class of problems in the same class of contexts Difficult to isolate the effects of the design
Type of results	Stochastic causal model	Context-specific heuristic rule
Nature of results	Reductionistic	Holistic
Limitation to relevance	It is uncertain whether a stochastically proved causal relationship will be present in a specific case	It is uncertain whether a context-specific heuristic rule will work in the next case
Generalizability	Wide; based on a representative sample	Limited; only conditions for success can be generalized; for heuristic rules, only accumulating supporting evidence can be obtained based on additional testing
Based in part on Van Aken (2000).		

on a representative sample. Because of the nature of the social world (see Chapter 2), these causal effects are not deterministic but stochastic. The reductionistic and stochastic nature of the explanatory results limits their practical relevance. When we want to make use of the tested causal model to design an intervention, we have no certainty (but only a certain probability) that the causal relationship is present in the situation at hand.

Intellectual capital research practiced as a design science has the same amount of difficulties and limitations, albeit in a different area.

In general, it focuses on qualitative exploration based on case study research, using the reflective cycle. Its criterion of truth is contextual success, because it checks whether a designed method is successful in providing the intended results. The method is tested in a series of problems and contexts of the same class. In practice, it is often difficult to find similar cases that fall within the same class of problems and contexts. Furthermore, many uncontrollable (and often unobservable) variables affect the results. Consequently, it is difficult to isolate the effects of the tested method. In design research, there is a hole in the logic of the reflective cycle. This hole is found during the implementation phase. The success of the implementation of a method cannot be proved decisively. As a result, it is difficult to determine whether lack of success of a method was the result of poor implementation or a poor method. However, this type of intellectual capital research does have the advantage that the researcher can ask the subject company about the implementation and try to determine the role of the quality of the implementation in the outcome. Design knowledge takes the form of heuristic rules: If you want to achieve Y in situation Z, then something like action X could help. According to Van Aken (2000), these rules are holistic: "A given intervention is applied in a certain context and all organizational and contextual factors have an impact on its outcome" (p. 9). Given their undetermined nature, heuristic rules cannot be proved conclusively. However, by testing them in multiple case studies one can accumulate supporting evidence, leading to tested heuristic rules. Each test will provide more certainty about the class of contexts and the class of problems to which the rule is applicable. Yet, we will never have certainty that the heuristic rule will work in the *next* case we study. Heuristic rules cannot be generalized. However, we can have certainty about conditions under which the method will *not* work. The necessary conditions for success identified in earlier cases are falsification factors that *can* be generalized to all cases within the application domain.

Table 6.1 summarizes the characteristics, difficulties, and limitations of both approaches. Intellectual capital research practiced as an explanatory science generates limited, reductionistic knowledge that is valid for a wide population but is of limited practical use. Intellectual capital research practiced as a design science generates more and holistic knowledge that does have practical use but that has proved to be successful in only a number of cases. The picture presented in Table 6.1 is not overly positive, but intellectual capital research needs to make due with what it has. It can do so by combining both approaches as much as possible.

Determining the Effect of the Implementation

One of the limitations of the reflective cycle is the logical hole during the implementation phase. I encountered the hole at Bank Ltd., Automotive Ltd., and Professional Service LLP. In these tests, the method was unsuccessful, yet it was difficult to determine whether this was caused by the method (either the object design or the realization design of the method) or by a poor implementation of the method.

In the analysis of the case studies, I tried to mitigate this problem by checking whether necessary conditions for success were fulfilled based on a list provided by De Caluwé and Stoppelenburg (2003). At Bank Ltd. and Automotive Ltd. this check worked well. From interviews it became clear that two conditions had not been fulfilled. The implementation team had not involved important members of the client system at crucial stages of the implementation, and there was a lack of communication. At Professional Services LLP, the results were different. Here, all conditions had been met, yet the results of the weightless wealth tool kit were never used in the annual report. The conclusion was that this was because the method is not an appropriate tool for external reporting. These findings indicate that the list of conditions for success is useful to determine the impact of the implementation on the success of the method. However, there may be other conditions that are not included in the list. Further research is needed to determine factors that influence the quality of the implementation to mitigate the hole in the reflective cycle. This leads to the following hypothesis: *De Caluwé and Stoppelenburg's (2003) necessary conditions for success can help to determine the effect of the implementation on the outcome of the tested method. If the conditions are not met, then the quality of the implementation plays an important interfering role between the method and its success. If the conditions are met, then this is an indication that the implementation plays a minor role.*

Determining the Contribution of the Method

A second limitation of the reflective cycle is the difficulty in determining the contribution of the method to the outcome. This is a problem of multicollinearity. In most situations, the outcome (success or failure) is caused by multiple factors. The question is how to isolate the contribution of the method. One way to mitigate this problem is to use one or more of the approaches offered by Phillips (2000) for isolating the effects of a consulting intervention (see Chapter 2). In this study I experimented with two methods: asking managers or asking participants involved about the impact of the method. With both methods, I found that interviewees were able to express whether they were satisfied with the way the method worked and with its outcome. However, satisfaction is not the same as effect, although it may often be a good proxy measure for the method's contribution and success. To get more evidence, it is necessary to combine more than two of the approaches Phillips (2000) proposes. These findings lead to the following hypothesis about determining the impact of the method: *To obtain sufficient evidence for the contribution of the method to the outcome of the implementation, the researcher needs to combine at least three of the approaches offered by Phillips (2000) for isolating the effects of a consulting intervention.*

The Analyst Versus the Researcher

In design studies, there can be a problem of a bias in observation. In my study, the researcher (me) and the person that designed and implemented the method (often also me) have often been the same person. It may be difficult for the researcher to keep an independent view on the process and its results. To mitigate this problem I built in two safeguards: the implementation of the method has always been a team effort, and I was not involved in all implementations. Yet, further testing of the method should take place by a third party that is not involved in the design and/or testing of the method. According to Van Aken (2000), this so-called beta testing "can counteract the 'unrecognized defences' of the originator of the method, which may blind him or her for possible flaws in its use" (p. 10). This leads to the following hypothesis about the problem of bias: *To avoid bias in their observation when testing methods, researchers need to arrange further testing of the method by a third party not involved in the design and/or previous testing of the method.*

Implications for Future Intellectual Capital Research

The trend of the growing importance of intangible resources in organizations and the economy can no longer be denied. The implications of this trend are still poorly understood. We know it creates both problems and opportunities on all levels: for individuals, for organizations, for regions, and for nations. The intangible perspective is a powerful perspective to identify these opportunities and problems, and to develop methods for improvement, but there is still a lot we need to explore.

In theory, the intellectual capital community and the accounting community are the movements that can explore this uncharted territory. However, both disciplines seem to be in a deadlock. The intellectual capital movement is moving in circles around existing models, like the Skandia navigator and the balanced scorecard. The accounting community is fighting a rearguard action regarding changes in accounting regulations.

With this book it was my intention to provide a breakthrough in many ways. Not by offering one new solution that fixes all problems, but by scrupulously examining the steps one needs to take to design a method for the valuation of intangible resources: What do we want to examine? What is the problem we are trying to solve by valuing intangibles? What are the requirements for a new method? How does the method perform in practice?

In this book I asked and answered important questions that many other books in the field fail to consider. For example, as we have seen, most existing methods are solutions in search of a cause. Many authors neglect to explain the problem they intend to solve. This book showed that this question of "Why?" is the most important question to ask. Furthermore, there is great confusion within the field about the nature of value. What is value? What constitutes valuation? What is the difference between valuation and measurement? Again, many authors do not ask these questions. This book showed there is a big difference between various types of methods: financial valuation methods, value measurement methods, value assessment methods, and so forth. It proved that many methods, including famous ones like the Skandia navigator and the balanced scorecard, do not deliver on their promises. Some we cannot consider valuation methods at all, despite claims to the contrary. Others contain serious methodological flaws. Yet others do not even value intangibles, despite their intentions.

In my view the intellectual capital community is ideally suited to discover the land of the intangible because it does not have a dominant tradition in one field and is truly multidisciplinary by nature. Now that some basics have been clarified, it is time for the intellectual capital community to move on to the next phase, or perish. Because the community is close to my heart, I would hate to see it pass away and I would like to contribute to this next phase by highlighting six topics that require further research. Three topics are more suitable for an explanatory approach to intellectual capital research; three others are more suited for a design approach (Table 6.2).

Table 6.2

Suggestions for Further Intellectual Capital Research		
Research Theme	Intellectual Capital Research Practiced as a Design Science	Intellectual Capital Research Practiced as an Explanatory Science
Diagnosing organizational problems	Designing and testing methods to diagnose organizational problems using an intellectual capital perspective	Measuring the value of intellectual capital-based problem definitions
Testing the success of methods	Further testing of the weightless wealth tool kit	Describing and explaining the level of success of existing intellectual capital methods
Researching the effects of numbers on managers, analysts, and other stakeholders	Designing and testing methods that raise awareness and stimulate management to start managing their valuable weightless wealth seriously	Describing and explaining the effect of valuation and numbers on the sense-making processes and behavior of managers, analysts, and other stakeholders

The six topics address three research themes that the intellectual capital community needs to address: the need for diagnosing problems, the need for testing the success of methods, and the need for further research into the effects of numbers on managers. I elaborate on each of the research themes.

Valuing and Improving Problem Definitions

Intellectual capital research suffers from too much focus on solutions and a lack of focus on organizational problems. There is a need to develop methods that can help diagnose organizational problems based on the intellectual capital perspective using a design approach. This can help the intellectual capital community to increase its contribution to management practice and to explain the importance of the intellectual capital perspective to the world.

The explanatory approach can focus on this problem by describing intellectual capital-based problem definitions that are used by companies to define problems and by determining the usefulness of these definitions. What is the effect on the company when it chooses an intellectual capital perspective to define its problem? Answering this question would in fact be an attempt to measure the value of problem definitions, something that would fit the value-focused intellectual capital field very well.

Explaining and Improving Success Rate

The design of the weightless wealth tool kit is not finished yet. The predominantly internal point of view of the method needs to be complemented with an analysis of the environment of the company. The weightless wealth tool kit also needs further testing, especially phases 1 and 4 of the tool kit (see Appendix B). The tool kit also needs beta testing, preferably in other industries that can provide information about the reliability of the core competence identification, among other things. This is a task for the design approach.

There is a lack of empirical evidence regarding the level of success of all existing intellectual capital methods in solving organizational problems, be they internal, external, or transactional/statutory problems. There is a task for the explanatory approach to describe and explain the level of success of existing methods.

Explaining and Improving the Impact of Numbers

One of the things I discovered in this study is that financial valuation plays a role in attracting management attention. The fact that numbers are attached to intangibles seems to make them more important. How does this mechanism work? What is the effect of financial values and numbers on the sense-making processes and behavior of management? Because valuation and measurement are so important in the intellectual capital field, it is important to answer this question to gain a better understanding of the mechanisms intellectual capital methods use to produce results. An explanatory approach to intellectual capital research should try to describe and explain these mechanisms.

Even with numbers attached to them, intangible resources are still very much overlooked in organizations. In my experience, it is difficult to get serious management attention for the proper management of intangibles like knowledge, intellectual property, or brands. Intellectual capital research practiced as a design science should develop and test methods that raise awareness about the vital importance of intangible resources. The goal of this type of intellectual capital research should be to ensure that managers finally start to make sense of their intellectual capital.

Epilogue

> Maybe it was the unaccustomed burden of Double Eddie's CDs, my music tapes, the *Meisterwerk*, and that incorrectly pigeon-holed package from Seligmanns Verlag. Whatever. The brass three-tiered plaque that received the tongue of the clasp broke free from its rotten stapled moorings, pulling open the perished mouth of the briefcase and sending four hundred unbound pages of closely reasoned, intensely researched, innovatively presented, elegantly phrased argument into the eddying tornadoes of mid-May breeze that swirled around the car-park.
>
> *Stephen Fry (1997)*

In May 1998, Tissen, Lekanne Deprez, and I published our first book on knowledge management. After the launching event, we sat together reflecting on the process we had just gone through writing the book. Prof. Tissen concluded, "Knowledge work is emotional work. It has as much to do with the heart as with the brain." Now that I have finished *this* book, I realize how much that apparent paradox is true. Knowledge workers are often deeply involved in their work. Their deliverables are very close to their heart. Their drive and commitment come from a deeply emotional source. Yet, the result is supposed to be highly rational and free of emotion.

This is especially the case with academic work. Any scientific work is the result of a deeply personal journey into the unknown. Yet, when we give an account of this journey, it is common practice to do it in a formalistic, detached way as if it has nothing to do with ourselves. This has always seemed strange to me. It is as if science needs to gain authority by using a reserved and official style. Science does not need that. Its systematic and rigorous approach gives it all the authority it needs. Official language even is counterproductive because it widens the gap between academia and practice. Therefore, I have tried to avoid official language. Although it turned out to be impossible to avoid jargon, I have stayed away from using the passive voice with the help of my Microsoft Word grammar checker ("Passive Voice, consider revising"). Moreover, I chose to write in the first-person singular.

Textbooks suggest the use of passive voice "to give your writing an objective and impersonal tone" (Oshima and Hogue, 1983, p. 191). Scientific results do not become more objective when we use the passive voice. Neither are they less objective if we use the active voice.

This is a very blue book. I do not mean a sad book that offers no hope to the intellectual capital field. On the contrary. I think the intellectual capital perspective is a very important perspective. Both companies and management researchers need this perspective to explain and act on the challenges of the intangible economy. The intellectual capital perspective offers new explanations for the changes in the economy. It provides new and positive ways for improving organizational performance. However, to take its next step, the intellectual capital community needs to conquer the hurdles that I identified in Chapter 6.

This book is blue because it refers, in a number of ways, to the blueprint paradigm of change. De Caluwé and Vermaak (1999) distinguish between five paradigms for thinking about organizational change. They give each paradigm a different color.[1] The blueprint paradigm is based on the rational design and implementation of change. This paradigm assumes that organizations can change if there are clear and measurable end goals, if there is a good implementation plan, if the various steps are monitored and controlled, and if complexity is reduced. The paradigm favors measurement, planning, control, and rationality. It believes that organizations can plan and control transformation. This book is blue because of its *subject*, its *methodology*, and its *author*, although it is also quite white.

The blueprint paradigm is clearly visible in the *subject* of this book. Many authors urge the need for valuation and measurement of intangible resources using arguments that fit the blueprint paradigm. These authors believe that companies need to measure intangibles to monitor effects from management actions or to weigh alternative strategies. They argue that measurement adds to rational decision making and reduction of complexity. Quantitative information on intangible resources will improve the diagnosis of organizational problems and the design of organizational solutions. Our search for a new method started in the same way. The design team set out to develop a method

---

[1] The *yellowprint* paradigm views organizations in terms of power, interests, and politics. The *blueprint* paradigm sees organizations as entities that can be designed, planned, and controlled. The *redprint* paradigm believes in human resource management tools like remuneration and punishment to change behavior. The *greenprint* metaphor sees organizations as learning organizations and places a heavy focus on action learning. The *whiteprint* metaphor sees organizations as complex and chaotic systems that can be changed to a limited extent.

that would help managers to gain insight into the financial value of intangibles. This insight would help them to improve the management of the stock of intangible resources. However, during the design process the method also became quite white.

According to De Caluwé and Vermaak (1999), the "whiteprint" paradigm of looking at organizational change is a reaction to the mechanistic and linear thinking of the blueprint paradigm. The whiteprint paradigm considers organizations as complex systems that are unpredictable and chaotic. Within organizations, people interact using their own individual rules, without an overall blueprint of what they should do or how they should do it. Individual processes of sense making and personal motivation determine their behavior. Changing behavior is possible only to a limited degree and only with their consent. Within the whiteprint paradigm, planning, control, and measurement have little meaning. Organizations are in a constant state of flux. Change cannot be planned or controlled. A manager or consultant can only facilitate change by removing obstacles, contributing to sense-making processes, and improving people's self-confidence.

The weightless wealth tool kit became a method to help managers make sense of their organization and its future. The focus shifted from measurement and valuation to the qualitative analysis of a company's hidden strengths. Its color shifted from blue to white. The method uses the concept of intangible resources and core competencies to contribute to the participants' sense-making process, *hoping* that they will find this new perspective beneficial. The workshops became forums to discuss the company in a new and positive light. The method turned out to be not expert driven but dependent on the input of participants. To a large degree, participants have to come up with results that are meaningful and useful to them.

There are more reasons why the method is white. I have found that the method works only when a company lacks sense about its strengths and its future strategy. And it works only if the participants want to change. When it works, it can contribute to a company's self-confidence. It can provide insight into a company's "real self" and its evolution. The financial valuation phase of the method is most related to the blueprint paradigm. However, I have found that even the effect of this part of the method is primarily white: It triggers those aspects of the sense-making process of managers that are sensitive to financial data. Because the method attaches a monetary number, the subject of intangible resources receives management attention.

The blueprint paradigm is clearly present in the *methodology* that I use in this book. The methodology of the design sciences believes that organizational problems can be solved using methods that are based on grounded and tested rules. Researchers who use this methodology carefully design the change method they want to use. The change method includes the design of the intervention and a plan for its implementation. Then the researcher tests the method in a series of case studies to develop knowledge about the application domain, mechanisms, and effectiveness of the method. This leads to modifications to the method to cope with unaccommodated contexts and unexpected results in future applications. This book describes the evolution of the weightless wealth tool kit using this design methodology. I found that the tool kit's evolution can be reconstructed into the blue methodology of the design approach. The design methodology is useful in systematically reconstructing the tool kit's design process and identifying the lessons learned and modifications made. The methodology helps specify the tool kit's strengths and weaknesses, and its application domain.

However, reality was far from blue; it was rather white. The evolution of the weightless wealth tool kit was at times quite chaotic and nonlinear. As described in Chapter 2, the tool kit's problem definition tended to shift throughout the project. As we saw, the problem definition did not become clear until the very end. The requirements for the new method did not fully crystallize until we had completely designed and tested the method. In addition, some of the cases took place in parallel and not subsequently. Therefore, we were not always able to refine completely a design based on design knowledge generated from previous cases. If you want to see how the development of the tool kit really happened, you should read this book again with the chapters in a different order. You should first read about the design (Chapter 4) and test (Chapter 5) of the method. Then you should read about the methodology (Chapter 2) and the literature review (Chapter 3). Finally, you should read about the objectives (Chapter 1) and the lessons learned (Chapter 6). This sequence reflects what actually happened in a better way than the sequence presented in the table of contents. Judging from a blueprint perspective, I believe the method's design process could have been more efficient if I did follow the design methodology from the beginning. Then I would have been able to apply more knowledge from the literature review (see Chapter 3) in the initial design. In each case, I would have been more aware of the lessons learned, leading to better and more consistent modifications. On the other hand, looking from a whiteprint perspective, I conclude that the result is what it is because I did *not* strictly follow a design methodology. For example, if the design team had known more about existing methods for the valuation of intangible resources at the start of the design process, then the team would probably not have been as original and creative. As Prof. Dr. L. van Vliet, Professor of Pattern Recognition at Delft University, said at the Dutch National Science Quiz in 2002: "Reading too much of what your colleagues have written will block your own creativity and imagination."

Did I fool the reader with my reconstruction? I do not believe I did. Remember what Kaplan (1964) said about the logic-in-use of a scientist. Prescriptive scientific methodologies are always poor reconstructions of how scientists work and their actual logic-in-use. "[A] reconstructed logic is not a description but rather an idealization of scientific practice. Not even the greatest of scientists has a cognitive style which is wholly and perfectly logical, and the most brilliant piece of research still betrays its all-too-human divagations" (p. 10). So any account of scientific research is to some extent an idealization of what really happened. In my case, what happened fit well into the idealization of management research practiced as a design science. Moreover, this reconstruction proved valuable in developing knowledge about the tool kit's strengths and weaknesses, and its application domain.

Lastly, this book is also a book by a rather blue writer. According to De Waard—van Maanen (2002), blue is the color of the "thinker": a person that is a clear thinker, that uses logical argumentation, likes to analyze situations, is loyal, prefers democratic decision making, and looks for consensus. This description fits me rather well, if I may say so myself, despite the fact that I learned from Dale Carnegie (1981) that I need to play myself down. However, because of the research described in the book I have become much more white. I learned the significance of the sense-making processes of individuals in organizations. I experienced how theory laden people's views on organizations are. I noticed how much the personal tradition of the members of the design team influenced the design of the method.

I also became aware of the difficulties in creating methods that produce predefined results. I found out that many problems are hard to define and even harder to solve. I saw how difficult it is to change people's way of thinking about the company for which they work. So let us be modest about what the intellectual capital perspective can achieve, but let us try to achieve that with all our heart.

Appendix A

Overview of
25 Valuation and
Measurement Methods

This appendix contains a review of 25 methods for the valuation and measurement of intangibles. The selection of methods is based on Sveiby (2002), Bontis (2001), Bontis et al. (1999), Petty and Guthrie (2000), and additional research. There are other methods available that I did not include in the sample, including the methods from Ernst and Young and PriceWaterhouseCoopers reported in Ministry of Economic Affairs (1999), the method developed by the Dutch KEMA (Andriessen and Tissen, 2000), the alternative Dupont model developed by Tissen and Van Son (Goldman and Hoogenboom, 1997), Edvinsson's IC Rating[1] (Lundqvist, 2000) and many others.

I have structured each review as follows: The first section describes the distinctions and definitions that the author of the method uses to identify intangibles. The second section presents the problems that the method addresses and some of their consequences. The third section includes an overview of the method itself and its results. The last section contains an evaluation of the method's strengths and weaknesses.

A.1 Balanced Scorecard

The French *tableau de bord* was probably the first tool to monitor company performance with the help of indicators. It dates back to 1932 and is often regarded as the predecessor of the balanced scorecard (Bourguignon et al., 2001). In its original form the *tableau de*

---

[1] IC Rating[TM] is described on www.intellectualcapital.se.

bord was a set of physical performance measures covering various production statistics.

When Kaplan and Norton (1992) introduced their balanced scorecard in the United States, the use of indicators to supplement accounting information became popular.

A.1.1 Distinctions and Definitions

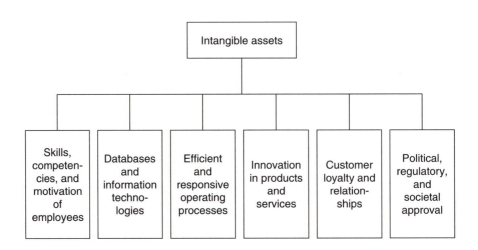

Over the years, Kaplan and Norton have made an interesting shift in vocabulary. In their early publications on the balanced scorecard they do not mention intangibles as drivers of future performance. Instead, they borrow the concept of core competencies when they state: "Companies should also attempt to identify and measure their company's core competencies, the critical technologies needed to ensure continued market leadership" (Kaplan and Norton, 1992, p. 75). Then, in their 1996 book (Kaplan and Norton, 1996a), they use the concept of intangible assets for the first time. They state that the balanced scorecard has "enabled companies to track financial results while simultaneously monitoring progress in building the capabilities and acquiring the intangible assets they would need for future growth" (p. 185).

Later, Kaplan and Norton (2001) fully adopt the intangible vocabulary. They use the term *intangible assets*, which they define as the skills, competencies, and motivation of employees; databases and information technologies; efficient and responsive operating processes; innovation in products and services; customer loyalty and relationships; and political, regulatory, and societal approval.

They distinguish between three categories of intangible assets:

1. Strategic competencies: the strategic skills and knowledge of the workforce required to support the strategy
2. Strategic technologies: the information systems, databases, tools, and network required to support the strategy
3. Climate for action: the cultural shifts needed to motivate, empower, and align the workforce behind the strategy.

However, the third category does not represent intangible assets. It describes the changes in corporate culture needed to implement the strategy. The fact that this category is included in their list reflects that Kaplan and Norton (1996) focus more on turning strategy into action than on stocks of intangible resources.

Four other distinctions play an important role in their work. First, there is the concept of the balanced scorecard (BSC): a set of measures, including financial and nonfinancial measures, that gives top managers a fast and comprehensive view of the business (Figure A.1.2).

Then there is the distinction within the balanced scorecard between four perspectives (Kaplan and Norton, 1992): The customer perspective that answers the question: How do customers see us? The internal perspective that looks at: At what must we excel? The innovation and

Figure A.1.2

The balanced scorecard

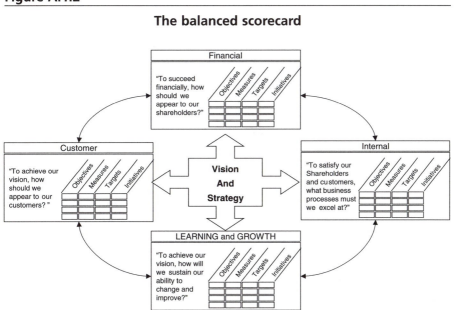

learning perspective: Can we continue to improve and create value? And the financial perspective: How do we look to shareholders? These perspectives force companies to look at themselves from the point of view of customers, figure out what to do to serve them best, and not to forget to prepare for the future. In their later work, Kaplan and Norton (2001) replace the innovation and learning perspective with the learning and growth perspective.

A third important concept introduced by Kaplan and Norton (2001) is the strategy map. According to Kaplan and Norton (2001), this map describes the chains of cause and effect that underlie a company's strategy. Nørreklit (2000) argues that strategy maps reflect finality relationships instead of causal relationships. If this is true, then a strategy map becomes similar to the concept of the "goal tree" (translated by D. Andriessen) that Kuypers (1984) has developed for describing public policy.

Each strategy map is unique, describing the distinctive strategy of a particular company. However, according to Kaplan and Norton (2001) the basic structure is always the same. It starts at the bottom with the intangible assets that are needed to enable organizational activities and customer relationships. These resources are incorporated in the bottom layer of the strategy map: the learning and growth perspective. In the second layer, internal processes (described by the internal perspective) transform these assets into customer value. Customer value is part of the third layer: the customer perspective. This layer delivers the financial results as described by the fourth layer: the financial perspective.

The fourth important concept that Kaplan and Norton (2001) introduce is the notion of strategic themes. A strategic theme is a subset of cause-and-effect relationships, grouped around a specific business issue that reflects what the management team believes must be done to succeed. The strategic map provides an overall view of a company's strategy; the strategic themes give a detailed description of the cause-and-effect relationships in subareas of management attention.

A.1.2 Problems and Consequences

The evolution of the balanced scorecard shows how the design and testing of a management method and the definition of the underlying problem interact. In their earlier work, Kaplan and Norton (1992, 1993) focused on complementing financial measures of company performance with operational measures. Their aim was to create a balanced view on both results of action already taken and drivers of future financial performance. Kaplan described this issue in his earlier work as a problem of "relevance lost": "Today's management accounting information . . . is too late, too aggregated, and too distorted to be relevant for managers' planning and control decisions" (Johnson and Kaplan, 1987, p. 1).

After working with the balanced scorecard for a couple of years, Kaplan and Norton (2001) found that the scorecard addresses a more fundamental problem: how to link a company's long-term strategy with its short-term actions. The problem shifted from measuring performance to strategy implementation. "But we learned that adopting companies used the balanced scorecard to solve a much more important problem than how to measure performance in the information era. That problem, of which we were frankly unaware when first proposing the balanced scorecard, was how to implement new strategies" (Kaplan and Norton, 2001, p. viii). According to Kaplan and Norton (2001) implementation of new strategies involves describing and communicating the strategy in a way that can be understood and acted on, focusing and aligning every resource and activity to the strategy, and establishing new organizational links.

A.1.3 Solution and Results

The solution that Kaplan and Norton (2001) propose is twofold. The first part of the solution is the creation of a strategy map that describes the causal assumptions underlying the strategy. This map illustrates the path by which *improvements* in the capabilities of intangible assets are translated into tangible customer and financial outcomes. Causal paths go from the learning and growth perspective to the internal perspective to the customer perspective to the financial perspective.

The second part of the solution is the creation of a balanced scorecard consisting of 20 to 25 measures, grouped by perspective. A measure operationalizes a particular goal that must be achieved. A proper measure meets four criteria: it must be measurable, it should reflect outputs instead of inputs, it must be something that can be influenced by the people responsible, and, most important, each measure must have a specific target attached. Targets play an essential role in the balanced scorecard, which means that the scorecard meets the definition of a value measurement method.

A.1.4 Evaluation

Kaplan and Norton have set the standard in performance measurement with their balanced scorecard. In addition, they have contributed to the field of strategy formulation with their strategy map. Yet I question whether they actually have added to the subject of the valuation of intangible resources. In their 2001 publication, they use the concept of intangible assets extensively. However, this concept is not essential in the way they define the problems they intend to solve or the solutions they propose. Leaving out intangible assets would not make any difference to their message.

Furthermore, in my view the balanced scorecard does not measure intangible resources. What is measured in the learning and growth perspective is the level of goal achievement in specific improvement areas. These improvement areas have to do with competencies, technology, and corporate climate. The scorecard measures the success in improving these three areas, which is not the same as measuring the stock or flow of these intangible assets. The scorecard does not measure the size or value of stocks of intangibles, nor does it measure flows from one type of intellectual capital to another. Even though the authors state that today's economy "calls for tools that describe knowledge-based assets" (Kaplan and Norton, 2001, p. 2), the balanced scorecard does not do that. Sveiby (2001) makes a similar point when he states that the balanced scorecard does not apply a stock flow perspective as his intangible asset monitor does.

The balanced scorecard's strong points are the simplicity of the model, which explains its widespread use, and the consequent use of targets. The strategic map is a useful tool to connect financial and non-financial measures, but we need to bear in mind that it only represents *hypotheses* about causal relationships underlying the strategy. These hypotheses have not been tested. Consequently, they cannot be used to relate changes in indicators and to draw conclusions about causes and effects. From the examples that Kaplan and Norton (2001) provide, it becomes clear that a strategy map focuses on causal relationships in areas of improvement only. Customer satisfaction and financial performance are influenced by many other causal factors that are not included in the model. This makes it impossible to test the hypothesis in practice. Another weak point of the strategy maps is that they focus on areas of *improvement*. Therefore, they don't include *risks* that may threaten performance. This makes it dangerous to manage a company by looking only at the indicators on the map.

Further weaknesses of the balanced scorecard include the fact that it is difficult to use the balanced scorecard to make trade-off decisions (Chatzkel, 2002). If we want to analyze the effect of a management decision using the balanced scorecard, we may find that two measures go up and two others go down. This does not give us much information because the question remains whether this is better or worse than if the opposite took place.

Finally, Bontis et al. (1999) criticize the rigidity of the balanced scorecard. There are only four perspectives. These perspectives drive the identification of the measures. Consequently, key success factors that are cross-perspective may be overlooked.

A.2 Calculated Intangible Value

The roots of the calculated intangible value method can be found in the work of NCI Research (Stewart, 1997), Internal Revenue Service (IRS) revenue ruling 68–609 (Luthy, 1998), and the valuation of brand premium. Calculated intangible value is similar to Lev's IDEs (Gu and Lev, 2002; see Section A.11). It is a financial valuation method.

A.2.1 Distinctions and Definitions

Intangible assets	Intellectual capital

In literature that describes the calculated intangible value method, various definitions of intangibles are used. Stewart (1997) uses the phrase *intellectual capital*, which he describes as "packaged useful knowledge." NCI Research and the IRS talk about *intangible assets*.

A.2.2 Problems and Consequences

NCI's interest in valuing intangibles comes from their aim to help new knowledge-intensive businesses acquire loans. Knowledge-intensive companies have few tangible assets as collateral. The argument is that if they could show the value of their intangibles, then this would help them secure a loan (Stewart, 1997). For this purpose NCI Research developed the calculated intangible value method. A similar method was developed by the IRS in 1920. It was used for tax purposes by breweries and distilleries to calculate the damages of

Prohibition as a result of loss in goodwill and intangible assets (Luthy, 1998).

A.2.3 Solution and Results

The calculated intangible value method is based on the assumption that the premium on a company's value is a result of its intangible assets. This can be a premium in market value, a premium compared with normalized earnings, or a premium return on assets. Calculated intangible value uses the latter method. The method calculates the present value of the premium earnings after taxes when earnings are compared with the industry average return on assets (ROA).

Steward (1997) describes the method as a seven-step process:

1. Calculate the average pretax earnings over a period of three years.
2. Calculate the average value of tangible assets over a period of three years.
3. Calculate the ROA.
4. For the same three years find the industry's average ROA.
5. Calculate the excess return for the company. Multiply the industry ROA by the value of the company's intangible assets. Subtract these from the pretax earnings. The result is the gross excess return or premium.
6. Calculate the net excess return by multiplying the excess return by the average tax rate.
7. Calculate the present value of this premium by dividing it by an appropriate discount rate.

A.2.4 Evaluation

The calculated intangible value method is an elegant method that uses publicly available accounting information to calculate a premium on tangible assets. It can be used for benchmarking to show whether an organization is fading or whether it has value not reflected in the balance sheet (Luthy, 1998). It can show stock traders when there may be a buying opportunity (Stewart, 1997).

Calculated intangible value does not reflect the value of all intangible resources. It only calculates the contribution of a stock of unidentified intangible resources to premium earnings. Intangibles that contribute to normal earnings are not included. Therefore, calculated intangible value does capture some of the value of intangibles. However, how much remains unknown. This problem surfaces once we try to calculate the calculated intangible value for a company that performs *below* industry average. In this case, calculated intangible value shows a negative value, which would indicate a negative value of its intangibles. This cannot be true.

There is also the problem of finding the right benchmarks. Using an industry based on the standard industrial classification code may not be correct. The company under investigation may have a different assets structure. In addition, the way the book value of the assets is calculated may differ.

Finally, it is doubtful whether banks will accept the calculated intangible value as a collateral for loans. Although calculated intangible value does reflect an earning potential, it does not reflect the value of an asset that can be traded by the bank in case the company fails to pay back the loan. For convincing the bank, a proper cash flow forecast may do a better job.

A.3 Citation-Weighted Patents

The citation-weighted patent method is founded in economics. The aim of the method is to act as a measure of the economic value of innovative output. Thus, it can help to explain market value. It is a measurement method. However, it is not aimed at improving the performance of a company or its external reporting.

A.3.1 Distinctions and Definitions

Hall et al. (2001) define a patent as "a temporal legal monopoly granted to investors for the commercial use of an invention" (p. 2). Citations describe the technological antecedents of the invention, including previous patents and other published material.

A.3.2 Problems and Consequences

The intention of Hall et al. (2001) is to explain the market value of firms. Their goal is to find indicators of inventive output. They assume that stock market investors hold rational expectations about the extent to which the present value of a firm's future profits (as reflected by its market value) varies with its stock of knowledge. Hall et al. (2001) test whether citation-weighted patents could be a proper indicator of this stock of knowledge.

A.3.3 Solution and Results

Hall et al. (2001) assume that patents are a proxy for inventive output, and patent citations are a proxy for knowledge flows or knowledge impact. The citation of a particular patent in other patent information provides information about the size of the technological "footprint" of the cited patent. Combining both assumptions results in the construction of a citation-weighted patent index, in which the number of patents of a firm is weighted by the number of citations. Hall et al. (2001) show that citation-weighted patents are more highly correlated with market value than patents themselves, because of the high valuation placed on firms that hold very highly cited patents. An increase of one citation per patent is associated with a 3% increase in market value.

A.3.4 Evaluation

The citation-weighted patent method is not meant to improve management but to explain market value. However, the correlation found between the index and market value can help to improve company performance. The method can indicate the value of a portfolio of patents. Companies can benchmark a citation-weighted portfolio against competitors and use this information to make investment decisions. Furthermore, Hall et al. (2001) show that patents with more than 20 cites have a strong impact on market value. This information can help management to identify individual patents with high values.

A weak point of the index is that it is limited to patents. The index does not provide information about other intangible resources. In addition, the index is not very well suited to improve external reporting. Citation-weighted patent information is only meaningful when compared with other companies. The absolute number conveys little information. In addition, a company can manipulate the number of self-citations and thereby influence the index. The biggest problem is the considerable time lag of the indicator. It can take a substantial amount of time before a patent is granted (in the sample used by Hall et al. [2001] it took on average 11 years). Then it will take time before a patent is cited (4–6 years). Using citation-weighted patents means looking far into the past.

A.4 Economic Value Added

EVA, a trademark owned by Stern Stewart and Co., is a popular method to calculate value creation in companies. It is a financial valuation method.

A.4.1 Distinctions and Definitions

Concepts like intangibles or intellectual capital do not play a role in the EVA method. There is only an indirect link between EVA and the value of intangible resources. One of the more important concepts is shareholder wealth. This is the difference between the firm's total value and the total capital that investors have committed to it (Stewart III, 1994). According to Stewart III (1994), the sole objective of companies is maximizing shareholder wealth and thus it should be measured. Key notions in measuring shareholder wealth are the concept of "cash flow," as opposed to accounting-derived earnings, and the concept of "cost of capital" (Evans, 1999).

A.4.2 Problems and Consequences

The issue the EVA method addresses is the problem of poor management decision making destroying shareholder wealth. According to Stewart III (1994), poor decision making is often a result of using the wrong indicators of wealth creation, like return on investments or ROA. The problem with most traditional indicators is that they are based on accounting-derived earnings instead of cash flow and that they do not include the cost of capital into the equation. Stewart III (1994) developed EVA to correct this.

A.4.3 Solution and Results

EVA uses market value added to measure shareholder wealth. Market value added is defined as total value minus total capital. Total value is equal to market capitalization, and total capital is equal to all capital that has been put into the company over the years.

According to Stewart III (1994), market value added also reflects the stock market's estimate of the NPV of a company as a whole. Thus, management decision making must be focused at allocating, managing, and redeploying scarce resources to maximize NPV. Stewart III (1994) developed EVA to help do this. The EVA method allows managers to calculate the NPV that results from their decisions.

In its basic form EVA is calculated by subtracting the operating expense (including tax) and the financing expense (Cost of Capital × Capital) from sales. The result is the economic value that has been added, taking into account the cost of capital needed to create that value. EVA is charged for capital at a rate that compensates investors for bearing the firm's explicit business risks. To do this it uses a weighted average cost of capital that allows different risk rates for different types of capital. EVA adjusts reported accounting results to eliminate distortions encountered in measuring true economic performance. Stewart III (1994) identified 164 possible adjustments, of which an average company will use five to ten.

Stewart III (1994) claims that EVA is a superior measure of performance. It can explain nearly 50% of changes in the market value added of companies, which is far more than traditional measures like growth in sales, growth in earnings per share, and return on equity. The evidence for the success of the method in improving company performance is less clear. Haspeslagh et al. (2001) state that half the companies that have adopted value-based management metrics like EVA have met with mediocre success. Their explanation is that implementing such a metric requires the introduction of fundamental changes to a company's culture.

A.4.4 Evaluation

It has never been the intention of the EVA method to measure the value of intangible resources. Yet, EVA is on many lists of intellectual capital measurement methods (Bontis, 2001; Bontis et al., 1999; Sveiby, 2002; Van den Berg, 2003). However, EVA is not a stock but a flow indicator. It therefore cannot be a measure of the value of intangible resources. At the most, it indicates the added value of a resource. But does it measure the added value of intangible resources?

There are two arguments in favor of this. One is what Bontis et al. (1999) call the *implicit argument*. This argument states that effective management of knowledge assets increases EVA. Therefore, EVA can be used as an indicator to measure the performance of managing knowledge assets. However, this argumentation has two limitations.

First, EVA states explicitly that the management of resources is not important, but implementing projects that create more value than their cost of capital is. In many cases the aim to create more value than the cost of capital will lead to decisions that result in low-risk cash flow in the short to medium term. These decisions may not add to the long-term sustainability of a company's knowledge assets.[2] The second limitation is that besides the management of knowledge assets there are many other factors that influence EVA. Consequently, we cannot contribute changes in EVA solely to knowledge assets.

Strassmann (1998, 1999) uses a different argument for using EVA as an indicator for the value of intangibles. His term for EVA is *knowledge value-added*. This is the value added by a firm's Knowledge Capital® (a trademark owned by Strassmann, Inc.). Strassmann (1998) defines knowledge capital as the employees' accumulated knowledge about a company.

According to Strassmann (1998), EVA is the net surplus economic value created by the firm, because the suppliers, the tax authorities, and all labor and shareholder expenses are already fully accounted for. He states:

> The creation of management value-added is something that defies the laws of conservation of energy. These laws state that the output of any system in the universe can never be greater than its input. Delivering a positive management value-added must be therefore an act of creativity that springs forth from something that is intangible, as if it were an artistic conception. The source of this creative energy is Knowledge Capital. This ephemeral element can be quantified only indirectly by observing how much management value added it yields. (Strassmann, 1998, p. 5)

To come from EVA as an indicator of knowledge value-added to the value of knowledge capital, Strassmann simply divides EVA by the price of knowledge capital (using the interest rate a firm pays for its long-term debt), because "the value-added is the interest rate earned from an accumulation of knowledge residing in the firm" (Strassmann, 1998, p. 5).

This argument is limited in three ways. First, EVA is not produced solely by intangibles. Tangible assets can also produce added value above the cost of the capital needed to acquire the assets. This is why companies that are low knowledge intensive can still create

---

[2] However, EVA does include adjustments to encourage managers to give proper considerations to the long term as well.

added value. Therefore, an unknown portion of EVA is attributable to tangible assets and not to "an act of creativity."

Second, knowledge capital is not the only form of intellectual capital. Structural and relationship capital also contribute to value added. Therefore, an unknown portion of the intangible part of EVA is attributable to structural and relational resources.

Finally, EVA is not the interest earned from a particular resource base; it is the other way around. EVA is the result of using a resource base with a certain rate of efficiency. If one wants to calculate the value of this resource base, one needs to divide the value added by a *rate of return* on these resources instead of an interest rate. This rate of return is unknown. Therefore, one cannot calculate the value of intangible resources using the EVA method.

Lev (as cited in Webber [2000]) points toward an additional weakness of the EVA method. He states that the main problem with EVA is that it is purely based on history. It is a method for accounting in the past whereas one should look at knowledge's potential for creating future earnings. An alternative would be to use EVA as a measure of economic income and to use an income approach. This implies calculating the present value of future EVA. This approach is valid, but it requires solving the problems of income funneling, income allocation, useful life estimation, and capitalization (see Chapter 4).

If we skip, for a moment, the question whether EVA can be used as a measure of value, we still need to answer the question whether EVA can be used to help guide the management of intangibles. Bontis (2001) thinks this is not the case. He emphasizes that EVA will not give managers a better understanding of the company's intangible resources and how they contribute. He describes EVA as a "black box" approach that blocks the effort to validate the value of or manage the company's intellectual capital.

Mouritsen (1998) points toward the deeper management philosophy that lies behind EVA. EVA is based on the idea of "radical empowerment." To use EVA, a firm has to reorganize into business units. The business unit manager needs only to implement projects with a positive EVA. Because of this empowerment, EVA blocks the synergy between business units. Furthermore, EVA aspires to make managers into owners who only look at cash flow. EVA tries to encapsulate all management issues into one cash flow indicator. This focus on cash flow neglects the well-being of the firm as a whole—its products, its people, its customers, and its innovative capability. In addition, EVA marginalizes the role of employees because of its emphasis on strong leaders who make tough decisions to improve shareholder value. Finally, the EVA method is not concerned with strategy. The exclusive strategic advice the method provides is to increase the return on existing assets, to invest additional capital, or to stop investing in activities that earn substandard returns. EVA does not give any indication how companies should do this. Which products should the company produce? What markets should the company enter? Which intangible resources should the company leverage? Mouritsen (1998) concludes that EVA is an "ex-post means" to evaluate actions already taken instead of a tool to make a firm progress toward an uncertain future.

A.5 Holistic Value Approach

While Edvinsson has contributed enormously to the promotion of the relevance of intellectual capital measurement, Roos has added significantly to its rigor. He is the founder of Intellectual Capital Services. He and his team, as well as his brother J. Roos, former Professor of General Management and Strategy at IMD have made several important contributions to the field.

Ever since his first major publication on intellectual capital (Roos et al., 1997), Roos has made tremendous progress in thinking about the consolidation of intellectual capital measures into one single measure. His HVA is the most advanced in the field. It combines elements of the intellectual capital—index and M'Pherson's Inclusive Value Methodology™, which will be described further on in this Appendix.

In Rylander et al. (2000) the Holistic Value Approach was named *IC*–Index. This is confusing because the HVA is substantially different from the intellectual capital—index as described by Roos et al. (1997). The most important difference is that the HVA fulfills all requirements for proper multidimensional value measurement, whereas the intellectual capital—index, version 1997, does not. HVA is a good example of a proper value measurement method.

A.5.1 Distinctions and Definitions

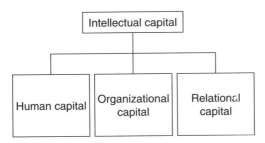

In his work, Roos stresses the importance of making proper distinctions. Roos et al. (1997) devote an entire chapter to "finding new words." This is in line with the epistemology that his brother described as "The autopoietic epistemological perspective." In this epistemology, distinctions play a vital role. "[T]he human mind does not represent the world. Rather, it brings forth, or forms the world as a domain of distinctions that are inseparable from the structure of the cognitive system" (Von Krogh and Roos, 1995, p. 53).

The distinctions Pike and Roos (2000) use within the HVA are different from those that Roos et al. (1997) use in the first book that described the intellectual capital—index, but are similar to the ones used in the 1997 article in *Long Range Planning* (Roos and Roos, 1997). Roos divides intellectual capital into human capital, organizational capital, and relational capital (Pike and Roos, 2000; Pike et al., 2002). Human capital equals the attributes of people such as intellect, skill, creativity, the way they work, attitude, competence, and intellectual agility. Organizational capital is the company-owned items such as systems, intellectual property, processes, databases, values, culture, and image. Relational capital includes external relations with customers, clients, suppliers, partners, networks, regulators, and so forth.

Roos and Roos (1997) introduce the important concepts of intellectual capital stocks, intellectual capital flows, and intellectual capital influence. The use of the metaphor of capital in the term *intellectual capital* allows them to make a distinction between intellectual capital as a stock and intellectual capital as a flow. The distinction provides interesting new insights. Roos and Roos (1997) compare measurement of intellectual capital stocks with the traditional balance sheet. Its limitation is that it provides a snapshot in time. Comparing these snapshots over time shows changes, but we do not know the causes of these changes. Furthermore, stocks of intellectual capital do not constitute value; they merely represent the potential to create value (Pike and Roos, 2000).

Intellectual capital flow measurements are like the profit-and-loss statement. They provide information on the transformation from one intellectual capital category to another. This is needed to calculate efficiency measures. When stock is used, value is created. This concept of transformation plays a vital role in Roos' work. Value is created through various "value creation paths" (Peppard and Rylander, 2001). These paths represent how managers think the organization creates value, what resources are used, how they are transformed into other resources, the relative importance of these resources and transformations, and how they are related to each other in the value creation process. Value creation paths represent the business model or business recipes (Chatzkel, 2002) of the company.

Figure A.5.2

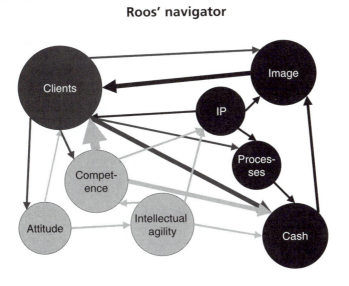

Roos' navigator

Value creation paths are visualized in one picture called a *navigator* (not to be confused with the Skandia navigator). In a navigator (Figure A.5.2) circles (the size of which reflects the importance of the resource) represent the key resources. Connecting arrows (the thickness of which reflects the importance of the transformation) represent the transformation of one type of resource to another (Chatzkel, 2002).

Pike et al. (2002) make a further distinction between flows and influence. If the aim is to measure the importance of a value creation pathway, one must measure the influence that pathway exerts on the generation of value. If the aim is to come to a relative or absolute value, one must not only quantify influence but also the size of the flow of intellectual capital. What flows is not necessarily of value, and what is influential in creating value may be a small flow of something very important.

A.5.2 Problems and Consequences

According to Pike and Roos (2000), the rapidly growing importance of intangible assets and intellectual capital has led to the need to manage companies in a new way, and to measure their performance in a new way. Companies require new tools to facilitate (internally) strategic and tactical management and to generate (externally) information needed by shareholders and investors. The internal objective of the HVA is twofold:

1. To give managers a means of translating their strategic intent into appropriate actions
2. To give feedback information showing whether these actions are working

Translating intent into action requires making trade-off decisions and being able to assess the impact of these decisions on all stakeholder groups in advance of their implementation.

The external objective of the HVA is to communicate the attributes of value to shareholders outside the company. According to Pike et al. (2002) the information asymmetry gap is growing as the proportion of company value attributable to intangible assets increases. The traditional balance sheet does not reflect some of the main sources of the firm's revenues and does not allow an accurate assessment of returns on investment in intangible resources (Rylander et al., 2000). As a result, CEOs feel that their market valuation is understated, that the volatility factor that applies to them is too high, and that money is harder to raise. Improving the information asymmetry would be beneficial to the external reputation of the company, its market valuation, its ability to raise capital, and the esteem that staff will have in the company and its management. The functional requirements for disclosure include relevance, reliability, and timeliness, while at the same time the information released must not lead to the compromise of sensitive strategic information. The authors also formulate an operational requirement: The measurement system should not impose a large measurement overhead.

A.5.3 Solution and Results

In 2002 Roos described the HVA as a third-generation intellectual capital practice (Chatzkel, 2002). The first generation is the scorecard practice, with examples like the Skandia navigator. The focus of the first generation is on identifying resources. The second-generation intellectual capital practice looks at resources as well as at transformations between various types of intellectual capital. The third-generation intellectual capital practice solves the problem of combining measures of different units into one overall measure.[3]

---

[3] It is interesting to see Roos' cumulative understanding of combining measures. In Roos et al. (1997) the label "second generation of intellectual capital practice" was given to the models that consolidate different measurements into a single index, with the intellectual capital—index as prime example. Since then, Roos realized that the 1997 version of the intellectual capital—index did not solve the consolidation

The HVA acknowledges that value by definition is subjective. Value is in the eye of the beholder. Still, value theory or axiology states that value is measurable if the preferences of the beholder are well defined. This is what Pike et al. (2002) call a *hierarchy of value*. The HVA requires that this value hierarchy be made explicit for every stakeholder for whom we want to measure value. This includes a description of the stakeholder's objectives. The HVA assumes that all stakeholders will have the same set of objectives, but that they will differ in the relative importance of each objective (Pike and Roos, 2000). For each stakeholder a set of weights is developed.

The next step is to translate the objectives into measurable attributes. Then a navigator is developed that identifies the value-creating paths within the company. It addresses the following issues (Gupta and Roos, 2001):

What tangible and intangible resources are needed to create value?
How are they transformed?
How important are the resources and the transformations?

This navigator is used to identify the relationships between the measurable attributes. The result is a model of the business as a value generator (Pike and Roos, 2000). The financial attributes are separated from the nonfinancial attributes. The financial ones can be easily combined, because they are additive by nature. The nonfinancial ones are not easily combined.

This is where the HVA needs to solve the problem of adding apples and oranges. This is how it does it. First, every measure is standardized between zero and one. This is done by defining the lowest acceptable and highest achievable value, again in the eye of the stakeholder. These values represent zero and one. Because the attributes now have the same scale, they can be combined using stakeholder-specific weights identified earlier. However, they can be combined in a number of ways, so the stakeholder needs to specify which way is the most appropriate. Attributes can simply be added, or multiplied (all attributes need to be more than zero), or any other mathematical

---

problem adequately. As we will see, the core problem of the intellectual capital—index was that the way different measures were combined did not fulfill the necessary and sufficient conditions and validity requirements set out by measurement theory (see M'Pherson and Pike [2001a,b]). The HVA does fulfill these requirements, because it combines elements of the intellectual capital—index and the Inclusive Value Methodology developed by M'Pherson and Pike (2001a). It allows for adding apples and oranges within a well-defined context.

rule can be used. The navigator will dictate how attributes are combined. This leads to a combination model, resulting in one combined intangible value (M'Pherson and Pike, 2001). The same exercise is done for the financial attributes. Then both the nonfinancial and the financial combination models are correlated into one "value space" (Chatzkel, 2002). This allows for making trade-off decisions and making calculations of the total value of intellectual capital in the eye of the beholder.

A.5.4 Evaluation

Roos[4] was the first to acknowledge that there are two fundamentally different perspectives in creating an intangible resources valuation system:

1. The *logical—positivist perspective*: value should be measured as objectively as possible
2. The *axiologist perspective*: value is always subjective and should be treated as such

Within the first school of thought, methodologies for the measurement of intangible resources tend to be judged by their logical—positivist *validity* (level of consonance with reality), *reliability* (Can results be replicated?), and *robustness* (Is the underlying theory coherent?). Within the second school of thought, validity is, by definition, not an issue because value is always subjective: Value, like beauty, is in the eye of the beholder.

The axiologists create models of the way specific stakeholders of a company define value. These models include a stakeholder's judgment of the most important value drivers, what company objectives are most desirable, and how these two relate to each other. This approach provides insight into stakeholders' mental model and their way of thinking about a company. This can be useful when, for example, considering company strategies on how to improve shareholder value, because it gives insight into what shareholders define as valuable.

The HVA is based on this axiologist perspective. The approach models the mental maps of stakeholders of a company (for example, a management team, a group of shareholders, environmental pressure groups, or public opinion). Information derived from these stakeholders is translated into a model about how these stakeholders believe value is created within the company.

---

[4] Taken from personal correspondence with the author.

Doing an exercise like this with a management team of a company can have significant added value because it gives managers insight into their own mental models. Roos phrases this as follows: "I think the issue we find is that when people come to us, they expect that the benefit will be in the outcome of the work. When they leave us, they tend to say there was as much benefit in the process as there was in the outcome" (Chatzkel, 2002, p. 110).

By measuring the underlying indicators in real life, the model can show the management team on a scale from zero to one what the value of the company is according to their own mental model. Zero means no value at all; one means optimal value. When a similar model is created for a different stakeholder (for example, a large shareholder), the results can be very different because this shareholder may value different things.

Creating a value model requires a large amount of assumptions. To measure corporate objectives like "efficiency" or "punctuality," several attributes need to be measured through operational performance indicators, which are then combined into one measurement. A typical case will consist of six to ten objectives that can each have one to five attributes, so there may be 50 or more attributes that need to be measured. Many assumptions are needed on combinatory rules to combine these attributes into one measure of value.

When the HVA is being judged from a logical—positivist perspective, it fails on the criterion of validity. A model containing so many nontestable assumptions will only provide an accurate picture of reality by pure coincidence. However, it is not fair to judge this approach on validity because it does not claim to measure value in an objective manner. It is based on an axiologist's perspective that states that value by definition is subjective. The assumptions that the approach uses describe the mental model of the stakeholder whose (subjective) view on value is being studied.

If one accepts the axiological assumptions on which the HVA is based, then the method itself has a high level of rigor. The method is especially suited to help make trade-off decisions, especially in situations in which the interests of various parties need to be considered. The downside is that the method is rather complicated to implement and companies will probably need specialist help.

I do not think the HVA has a role in external reporting of companies, unless the target audience is specific enough to define its value hierarchy. This means HVA information will not end up in general annual reports but could play a role in direct communication with specific stakeholder groups. A problem to solve here would be how to explain the meaning of the results and the way they were derived using the language of the stakeholder. As Roos and Roos (1997) put it: "The companies studied convinced us that the Intellectual Capital performance system must also be rooted in the language of the company or unit.... Intellectual Capital knowledge, then, is self referential" (p. 419). The HVA may be too complicated to accomplish this.

A.6 Human Resource Accounting

HRA, sometimes called *human resources costing and accounting*, is not a measurement method but a broad stream of thought; probably as broad as the intellectual capital movement. It has a history of more than 35 years and includes a number of methods.

A.6.1 Distinctions and Definitions

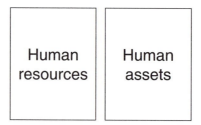

Core to HRA is the concept of "human resources." HRA has its origins in the Human Resources School, which is based on the premise that people are valuable organizational resources and therefore ought to be managed as such (Sackman et al., 1989). A similar concept used is "human assets." Authors use this term to indicate that people should be treated as important assets that are as important as tangible and financial assets. This term has evoked criticism. Authors argue against treating people as assets on ethical grounds (Johanson et al., 1999).

A.6.2 Problems and Consequences

Like the intellectual capital movement, HRA has addressed a range of different problems. Most applications of HRA seem to be motivated by the low status of human resources within companies and the equally low status of the human resources management function.

The problems addressed by HRA can be distinguished between internal management and external reporting problems. Internally

HRA has been used to improve awareness about the importance of people. Its goal was to improve decision making in the area of personnel selection, staffing choice, budget allocation, promotion, layoffs, and turnover (Sackman et al., 1989). Externally HRA has been used to influence stock investments, create financial decision ratings of a firm's potential, and make investment decisions (Sackman et al., 1989).

A.6.3 Solution and Results

Over the years, the HRA movement has developed a range of methods to measure and value human resources. Some of the methods found in the intellectual capital literature have also been developed and tested in the HRA movement. Sackman et al. (1989) distinguish between human resource cost models and human resource value models.

Cost models are monetary models for measuring human resource costs. There are various types of cost models including original cost, replacement cost, and opportunity cost models. Human resource value models can be monetary, nonmonetary, or a combination of both. Monetary models focus on measuring the economic value of human resources. A number of monetary models have been proposed, including models that calculate the value of future wages, and models that allocate a portion of discounted future earnings to human resources. Nonmonetary models use indicators to measure aspects of human resources. Models that combine the two use nonmonetary HRA measures but produce an output in monetary terms.

The evidence for the effectiveness of HRA is not clear. Sackman et al. (1989) report that in most studies on the effect of HRA on decision making, decisions were actually changed. In many cases the HRA information produced an "Aha!" reaction. However, there is doubt whether the decisions were changed because of the HRA information. It could be that any additional information would have produced a change. In addition, there is doubt whether the effect of implementing HRA is sustainable.

A.6.4 Evaluation

HRA is in many respects the predecessor of the intellectual capital movement. Of course HRA focuses on human resources only whereas intellectual capital focuses on other intangibles as well. But their aim seems to be the same. This aim is well phrased by Sackman et al. (1989): "Specifically, it can contribute to an organizational culture in which the belief that people [or intangible resources] are valuable organizational resources is actually manifested in managerial decisions and actions" (p. 261).

Other similarities can be found in the methods that have been developed. The nonmonetary models bear resemblance to the intellectual capital measurement methods like, for example, the Skandia navigator. Some of the economic value models are similar to financial valuation methods like the one described in this book.

Yet, HRA seems to have a bad reputation. It has been accused of "putting a price on people," thereby making human beings substitutable to other forms of capital (Johanson et al., 1999). This accusation is ironic, as it has been one of the main objectives of HRA to highlight the unique importance of human resources.

HRA has been accused of subjectivity, uncertainty and lack of reliability (Bontis et al., 1999). This accusation fails to acknowledge that there are many different HRA models, some of which use reliable cost or nonmonetary measures. The allegation seems to be focused on HRA methods that value human resources using an income approach. However, similar accusations are applicable to any financial valuation based on an income approach. An income approach relies on assumptions about the future (see Section A.23). Still, they are widely used, even in traditional accounting.

The popularity of HRA rose rapidly at the end of the 1960s, but in the beginning of the 1970s the movement encountered skepticism. The belief emerged that HRA was concerned with treating people as financial objects. In the beginning of the 1980s, the interest in HRA declined. With the start of the intellectual capital movement it seems there is a revival of HRA methods. The intellectual capital movement has to learn from the history of HRA to prevent becoming a similar hype.

Like intellectual capital, the concept of HRA is far from accepted. One of the lessons that can be learned from HRA is that this lack of accord was the result of the existence of multiple agendas among those who expressed an interest in the subject (Johanson et al., 1999). There is the management control interest, the capital market interest, the accounting interest, and the quality of work interest. This diversity of interests hindered the convergence of ideas into one overall framework and the acceptance by a wider audience. The same is happening in the intellectual capital movement.

There is another lesson for the intellectual capital movement to learn. The HRA movement has produced a substantial number of studies into the *effect* of HRA. Within the intellectual capital movement, these studies are practically nonexistent. I agree with Johanson et al. (1999) when they state that the future of HRA and intellectual capital may well be linked. HRA could learn from intellectual capital how to connect its efforts to business strategy. The intellectual capital movement could learn from the measures that have already been developed within the HRA framework.

A.7 Intellectual Capital Audit

Brooking is the founder and managing director of The Technology Broker, a consultancy firm in the high-technology sector.

A.7.1 Distinctions and Definitions

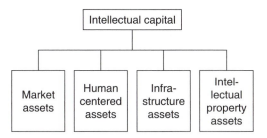

Brooking (1996) uses the term *intellectual capital,* which she defines as "the combined intangible assets, which enable the company to function" (p. 12). She separates intellectual capital into four categories:

1. Market assets are the potential an organization has as the result of market-related intangibles like brands, customers, and distribution channels.
2. Human-centered assets comprise the collective expertise, creative and problem-solving capability, leadership, and entrepreneurial and managerial skills embodied by the employees of the organization.
3. Infrastructure assets are those technologies, methodologies, and processes that enable the organization to function.
4. Intellectual property assets include know-how, trade secrets, copyrights, patents, various design rights, and trade and service marks.

This distinction tree is similar to Sveiby's (1997), although Brooking (1996) separates intellectual property from the other infrastructure assets (which Sveiby [1997] calls *internal structure*). What is striking is that Brooking (1996) includes know-how as part of intellectual property, although it is not legally protected.

A.7.2 Problems and Consequences

To gain competitive advantage, companies must balance the effective management of intangible assets with the management of cash, buildings, and machinery. However, organizations are often viewed from an accounting perspective that does not reflect the true value of an enterprise. It concerns Brooking (1996) that most enterprises do not know their intangible assets, what they're worth, or how to manage them. Brooking (1996) says it is important for companies to assess their worth to enable managers to understand where value lies, to have a metric for assessing success and growth, and to create a basis for raising a loan.

A.7.3 Solution and Results

Brooking (1996) recommends companies execute a six-step intellectual capital audit, followed by a valuation of all the different types of assets: Step one is understanding the transition the company needs to go through as well as the goal of the audit, its domain, and its constraints. The second step is to identify the company's intangibles and to determine the set of aspects of each asset. The third step is to determine the optimal state of each aspect of each asset. The optimal state functions as a yardstick for the audit. Step 4 is to choose the appropriate audit method for each type of asset. Brooking (1996) describes 30 different methods for the four types of intellectual capital. The fifth step encompasses the actual audit of each aspect of each asset. In step 6 this is documented in a database. The current state of each aspect is compared with the target value and is indexed on a scale from 0 to 5 points, with 5 points indicating the optimal state. The scores are plotted on a target (Figure A.7.2). The size of the dots (large or small) reflects the importance of the assets. This provides an instant overview of the strengths and weaknesses of intellectual capital.

This is not all, because Brooking (1996) states that "the ultimate goal is to put a financial value on every asset" (p. 119). She describes in generic terms how to put a financial value on the four types of intellectual capital and recommends the use of either a cost, a market, or an income approach.

Figure A.7.2

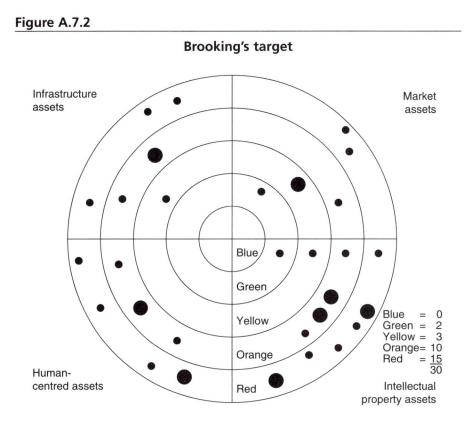

Brooking's target

A.7.4 Evaluation

Brooking's (1996) intellectual capital audit is one of the very few well-documented methods to audit various types of intangible resources. She describes 30 ways to audit various aspects of intangibles and provides 158 questions touching on a range of issues (Van den Berg, 2003). Each aspect is in fact an indicator of some kind. The audit is a value measurement approach because the method includes yardsticks for the optimal state of each aspect of each asset. The intellectual capital audit target provides a comprehensive overview of the strengths and weaknesses of all intangible resources. Brooking (1996) does not provide much help for the most difficult steps in the audit process: how to identify relevant intangibles to audit, how to determine which aspect to audit, and how to set a target for each aspect. When it comes to putting a financial value on intangibles, Brooking (1996) is very optimistic. She mentions some of the difficulties associated with the cost and market approaches, but fails to address difficulties associated with using an income approach (see Section A.23).

Therefore, her advice to value all intangibles will be difficult to put into practice.

A.8 Intellectual Capital–Index

The intellectual capital–index is the first method Roos (Roos et al., 1997) developed for measuring intangibles. He developed it as an assignment for and together with Edvinsson. In his later work, it became one of the building blocks of the HVA (see Section A.5). It is a measurement method that uses indicators but that does not include yardsticks.

A.8.1 Distinctions and Definitions

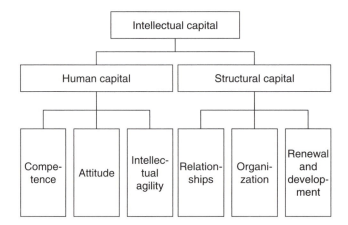

In their book *Intellectual Capital* (Roos et al., 1997), the authors start off by making a distinction between knowledge and information: Knowledge is a personal, subjective process emerging from previous experiences and current events, whereas information is objective data about the environment. They describe their view on knowledge as an "autopoietic epistemological perspective." Knowledge is always a personal thing, because the mind does not represent an objective outside world but creates a world by making distinctions. This view is in line with the epistemological view described in Chapter 2 of this book.

According to the authors, intellectual capital is knowledge based and therefore carries the same characteristics as knowledge: It takes time to build and it follows the law of increasing returns. Roos et al. (1997) describe intellectual capital in various ways without giving a precise definition. They end the discussion on the subject with "something that comes close to a definition": "the [intellectual capital] of a company is the sum of the knowledge of its members and the practical translation of this knowledge into brands, trademarks and processes" (p. 27).

They then use a distinction tree that is similar to but not exactly the same as Edvinsson and Malone's (1997) (see Section A.19). They use a distinction between structural and human capital, which they describe as the difference between nonthinking and thinking resources. The reason for making this distinction is that the two types of resources need very different management methods. This is why, contrary to, for example, Sveiby (1997) but also to Roos' earlier and later work (Roos and Roos, 1997; Pike and Roos, 2000), they consider relationship capital as part of structural capital instead of a separate third category.

The authors break down human capital into

- *Competence:* the knowledge, skills, talents, and know-how of employees
- *Attitude:* this "covers the value generated by the behavior of the employees on the workplace" (Roos et al., 1997, p. 37), which is influenced by motivation, behavior, and conduct
- *Intellectual agility:* this includes personal innovation, adaptation, and the ability to use knowledge from one context in another

In their view structural capital consists of

- *Relationships:* with customers, suppliers, alliance partners, shareholders, and other stakeholders
- *Organization:* this includes intangible infrastructure, intellectual property, processes, and culture
- *Renewal and development:* which the authors describe as "the intangible side of anything and everything that can generate value in the future . . . but has not manifested that impact yet" (Roos et al., 1997, p. 51).

A.8.2 Problems and Consequences

Roos et al. (1997) are concerned about the fact that in many companies a large part (the intangible part) is not managed properly. This is especially concerning because of the law of increasing returns. In the intangible economy, competitors can turn a small slip in efficiency into a big lead.

The authors set out to develop a measurement system because "what you can measure, you can manage, and what you want to manage, you have to measure" (Roos et al., 1997, p. 7). Their intellectual capital measurements tool "is the answer to a very practical and widespread need to manage the whole company and not just its visible part, integrating the need for a complete measurement system with the need for a holistic management strategy" (p. 24).

In their view, managing the whole company requires making tradeoff decisions. This is where the early intellectual capital models (which they referred to as *first-generation models*) like the Skandia navigator fall short. "[Intellectual capital] systems have long lists of indicators with no prioritization, thus making it impossible for managers to evaluate trade-off decisions" (Roos et al., 1997, p. 7). Another problem with the early models is that they do not clarify the relationship between intangibles and the physical and financial side of companies. In addition, most early models look only at stocks and not at flows (see the discussion about stocks and flows in Section A.5). Furthermore, early models make it difficult to carry out intercompany comparisons, and to measure and monitor the efficiency of intellectual capital.

The authors also address the subject of external reporting. They set out to develop a tool that can give stakeholders a better understanding of the real value of a company. "An [intellectual capital]–index can help the company signify to the market its hidden value creation process, and thus help the market make a better assessment of the company's value" (Roos et al., 1997, p. 91).

A.8.3 Solution and Results

The first part of the object design of the intellectual capital–index is similar to the Skandia navigator. Roos et al. (1997) create lists of nonfinancial indicators. They suggest several models for grouping these indicators to improve focus: the Skandia navigator, the Caterpillar IC Base, and Battery's Intellectual Capital System. The authors' realization design is different from Skandia's. Key to the implementation of the intellectual capital–index is that it should be deeply rooted in the strategy of the company: "Strategy has to guide the search for the appropriate indicators simply because it is the goals and direction of the company, set out in the strategy, that signify which Intellectual Capital forms are important" (Roos et al., 1997, p. 7).

The realization design starts with the company's identity and long-term goals. This is used to identify key success factors, which the authors describe as "the vital criteria that the particular strategy must meet in order to succeed" (Roos et al., 1997, p. 65). The next step is to identify the indicators that best reflect those key success factors so the company can measure the level of achievement. The choice of indicators reflects the characteristics of the company more closely and specifically than the key success factors themselves. The next step is to group the selected indicators by focus area, for example using the Skandia navigator.

There are two interesting additional elements in the object design of the intellectual capital–index. First is the consolidation of measures into one single measure. Second is the correlation of the change in intellectual capital with changes in market value.

The consolidation of indicators is done in several steps. The first step is to review critically all selected indicators, checking their precision, robustness, and relevance. The aim is to come up with a limited number of indicators for intellectual capital stocks and flows, covering all types of intellectual capital. The next step is to express each indicator as a "dimensionless number." The authors do not specify what is meant by dimensionless. Looking at the examples it seems they are looking for percentages (for example, number of training hours or total working hours) or benchmarks (for example, comparison with the closest competitor). In his later work, Roos (Pike and Roos, 2000) recognizes that what is missing in the intellectual capital–index is a *normalization* of all measures between zero and one based on a minimum and maximum value (see Section A.5). The next step is to consolidate the dimensionless numbers into one index using weights. The authors do not specify how the weights should be selected: "In the choice of the weights, the main consideration in the mind of managers has to be the relative importance each capital form has in the creation of value in the particular business of the company" (Roos et al., p. 86). The resulting intellectual capital–index can be compared over years, or separate indices can be created for various types of intellectual capital. According to the authors, this allows for comparison of alternative strategies, and for visualizing the intangible part of a company to external stakeholders.

The second additional element of the object design of the intellectual capital–index is the attempt to correlate the intellectual capital–index with market value. The authors claim that the intellectual capital–index is a self-correcting index because if changes in the index do not reflect changes of the market value, then there must be something wrong.

A.8.4 Evaluation

The authors of the intellectual capital–index clearly learned from their pioneering work on the first generation of intellectual capital models. They try to avoid the pitfall of coming up with long lists of meaningless indicators. Their solution is based on a critical selection of indicators, rooted in the company's strategy, and the combination of indicators into one single index.

One of the strengths of the approach is that it does not prescribe one reporting format. Each company can choose the format that best reflects its strategy. Roos et al. (1997) give the example of a company that grouped its indicators in four categories:

1. Human capital stock
2. Structural capital stock
3. Human to structural capital flow
4. Structural to financial capital flow

This example signifies another strength of the intellectual capital–index: its focus on both intellectual capital stocks and flows (see Section A.5).

The authors do not succeed in coming up with a methodologically sound way to consolidate indices. Their approach does not fulfill all requirements for consolidation as described by M'Pherson and Pike (2001a). The selection of indicators does not fulfill the necessary and sufficient measuring requirement that states that the total selection of indicators should be necessary and sufficient to describe the value to be measured. This means they need to be complete, distinct, independent, minimal, observable, and measurable. Furthermore, in all instances indicators are combined using the additive combinatory rule, when it could very well be that a different rule would be more appropriate. Finally, the indicators are not normalized in the correct way as described by M'Pherson and Pike (2001a, p. 8):

$$p_k = (P_k - \min P_k)/(\max P_k - \min P_k) \in [0,1],$$

where p_k is the normalized value of the kth indicator, P_k is its current operational level, and $\max P_k$ and $\min P_k$ are limits set for a feasible range of P_k.

In his work on the HVA, Pike and Roos (2000) corrected these errors with help from measurement theory and axiology.

The authors claim that the intellectual capital–index is self-correcting. If a change in the intellectual capital–index is not reflected in a change of the market value of a company, something must be wrong. The problem is that the company will not know what went wrong: the creation of the intellectual capital–index (wrong indicators, wrong weights, wrong combinatory rules) or the way the market perceives the company (the market may have a totally different view on the future potential of the company than the view expressed by the company's strategy and intellectual capital–index).

The final weakness is that the intellectual capital–index does not fulfill all functional requirements set out by Roos et al. (1997) in the beginning of their book. In theory, it is possible to make trade-off decisions and to monitor intellectual capital using this tool. However, because the tool does not include any yardsticks, it is difficult to make this monitoring data useful for decision making. Furthermore, it is difficult to use the outcome of the intellectual capital–index to compare companies unless they use exactly the same indicators. Finally, it is hard to imagine how a consolidated figure that is not normalized could help stakeholders get a better picture regarding the value of the intangible resources of the company.

A.9 Inclusive Value Methodology

M'Pherson has a background in systems engineering and has worked for many years on measurement theory before he started working on intellectual capital measurement. He is the first to apply the rigor of scientific measurement theory to the measurement of intangible value. The Inclusive Value Methodology is a good example of a value measurement method.

A.9.1 Distinctions and Definitions

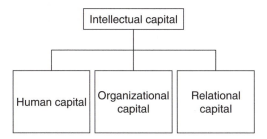

M'Pherson and Pike (2001b) make a distinction between monetary, physical, and intellectual capital, the latter being divided into human, structural, and relational capital. They make important distinctions that have to do with measurement, which they define as a way of acquiring knowledge about an object or organization of interest using a method that is based on logical axioms, and is objective, reliable, and secure. Only measurement that satisfies the axiomatic and empirical requirements is proper; the rest is "quantified opinion" (M'Pherson and Pike, 2001b, p. 246).

Within a measurement process they distinguish between

The mapping definition. This states that measurement, in essence, is a mapping of an observable manifestation of an object of interest on to a scale using a symbol—for example, the speed of atoms in the pan of boiling water using the concept of temperature on a scale of 0 to 200°C.

The primary empirical measurement. For example, the pan itself and the thermometer.

The mathematical model for multidimensional measurement. This includes a mathematical model of the processes taking place (for example, in the pan) based on theory and, when we want to measure several observable manifestations and combine them, a combination model telling us how to combine the separate measurements.

It seems M'Pherson and Pike's (2001a,b) epistemological viewpoint is that there is a social reality there waiting to be observed and measured just like temperature or pressure can be measured.

A.9.2 Problems and Consequences

M'Pherson and Pike (2001a) do not elaborate on the need for measurement of intellectual capital. They simply state: "[I]f an asset or process is to be managed properly it must be measured" (p. 1). Their contribution to the field is that they define carefully all functional requirements for proper multidimensional value measurement.

Their method is based on axiology or value theory, which states that value is measurable with respect to a well-defined context. Therefore, the first requirement is a definition of the value context. This is an explication of the objectives of the stakeholders with regard to the company. Because value is in the eye of the beholder, we need these objectives as yardsticks to measure value.

The next requirement is that these objectives be translated into attributes that can be measured. These attributes must be necessary and sufficient with respect to the objective. This implies

- *Completeness*: they cover the full meaning of the objective as understood by the stakeholder
- *Distinctness*: each attribute must carry one meaning only
- *Independence*: changes in the satisfaction of an attribute must not influence any other attributes
- *Minimality*: the attributes should be minimal sets

Furthermore, each attribute should be observable and measurable.

The next set of requirements deals with the process of combining different measurements into one measure. This includes the problem of different units and scales. To solve this problem the authors normalize all measurements by subtracting the minimal value and dividing it by the total length of the scale. The result is a number between zero and one. Zero denotes the threshold of uselessness; one signifies that the maximum value is completely achieved. In practice, this requirement means that for every indicator, a target value or maximum value needs to be defined. This target value acts as a yardstick to interpret the measure.

The authors also define rules for combining various value streams. Here the authors state that when it comes to combining value, the additive rule (1 + 1 = 2) is an exception. Much more common is the so-called *G-rule,* the goal-oriented rule that indicates that achieving a certain goal requires a trade-off between different values. When we combine indicators into one indicator we need to use the correct combinatory rule.

A.9.3 Solution and Results

The Inclusive Value Methodology meets all the requirements for proper multidimensional value measurement. The first step of the method is to create a mathematical model of the business of the company to simulate various alternative management actions. The simulation must provide output performance measures as well as cost/revenue data.

The second step is to define the objectives from the perspective of stakeholders and to translate them into measurable attributes using a "criterion hierarchy." For each attribute, the minimal and maximum values are defined. The attributes are combined using the appropriate combinatory rule. When using normalized indicators and the appropriate combinatory rules, there is no need to apply weights. Then the output performance measures are used as inputs for the criterion hierarchy to calculate the overall combined intangible value. All financial data are processed separately. Combining the financial and nonfinancial data allows for value for money analysis.

A.9.4 Evaluation

The Inclusive Value Methodology has contributed to the intellectual capital field by introducing elements of measurement theory and applying them to multidimensional intellectual capital measurement.

M'Pherson and Pike (2001ab) have made the field aware of the many functional requirements for proper measurement, thereby uncovering some bad practices.

For example, one of the biggest fallacies in the intellectual capital movement is the widespread notion that Market Value = Book Value + Intellectual Capital (see, for example, Edvinsson and Malone [1997]). M'Pherson and Pike (2001a) show that this formula is inherently incorrect for a number of reasons: the three categories all have different units and the elements are not independent as required by the equation. Book value has components that derive from cash flow, which derives from operations, which involves intellectual capital.

With the Inclusive Value Methodology there is a trade-off between rigor and relevance. Requirements for proper measurement are hard to fulfill in practice. The biggest challenges are the development of a valid mathematical model of a real organization and the development of indicators that are truly independent. The method is complex, which will make it difficult to use at the boardroom level.

A.10 Intangible Asset Monitor

Sveiby developed his interest in intangibles when he left Unilever to manage a Swedish publisher. He discovered that the tools he used at Unilever did not work in a company that was run solely on intangibles. Since then, he has made it his task to supply managers with a toolbox to help them manage knowledge-based companies. The intangible asset monitor is a measurement method to help manage knowledge-intensive companies.

A.10.1 Distinctions and Definitions

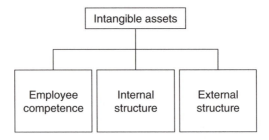

Sveiby's core concept is "intangible assets," which he uses not in the limited accounting sense but in the broad sense of "invisible assets." This includes employee competence, internal structure, and external structure. Employee competence includes the knowledge and skills of employees. Intangible internal structure includes patents, concepts, models, and computer and administrative systems. External structure includes relationships with customers and suppliers (Sveiby, 1997).

A.10.2 Problems and Consequences

Sveiby (1997) specifically focuses on a number of problems associated with the measurement of "knowledge organizations." In the field of external reporting, the problem is how to describe the company as accurately as possible so stakeholders can assess the quality of management and the reliability of the company. With regard to internal measurement, the problem for management is "to know as much as possible about the company so that it can monitor its progress and take corrective action when needed" (Sveiby, 1997, p. 163). He points to the confusing difference in the way accounting treats investments in tangible and intangible assets. And he shows that traditional financial indicators to measure yield, like return on investments or return on equity, are not very helpful for companies with large intangible assets. He claims new measurement tools are needed. "If we measure the new with the tools of the old, we won't be able to perceive the new" (Sveiby, 1997, p. 155).

Sveiby's (1997) ultimate goal is to provide managers with a toolbox to manage their knowledge organizations. Measurement is a means to focus managers on intangible assets and to allow them to monitor their assets. Sveiby (1997) explicitly states that he is not looking for another system to control subordinates. Instead, he is looking for a system that complements the accounting system with a new language for the dialog of peers—a dialog on the best way of managing knowledge organizations (Sveiby, 2000).

A.10.3 Solution and Results

Sveiby's (1997) intangible asset monitor is a framework for indicators that measures both levels and trends. He rejects the idea of using money as a common denominator. "Still there exists no comprehensive system for measuring intangible assets that uses money as the common denominator and at the same time is practical and useful for managers. Depending on the purpose for measuring, I do not think such a system is necessary, either. Knowledge flows and intangible assets are essentially non-financial. We need new proxies." (Sveiby, 1997, p. 156).

His framework consists of a three-by-three matrix (Table A.1). For each type of intangible asset, there should be indicators of growth and renewal, efficiency, and stability. Management should select one or two indicators for each cell.

Sveiby (1997) brings special attention to the issue of comparison. "As in all measurement systems, it is the comparisons that are interesting. A measurement tells nothing at all unless it is compared against a yardstick of some kind: another company, a previous year, or a budget, for example" (p. 164). This is why he recommends measuring intangibles for at least three measurement cycles before attempting to evaluate the results.

A.10.4 Evaluation

The intangible asset monitor is a comprehensive framework that allows for customization. One of its strong points is that it focuses on risks and sustainability, as did the work of the Konrad group. Also important is the emphasis on comparison to make the indicators meaningful. However, because the indicators are company specific, in most cases the only comparison available will be previous years.

The intangible asset monitor is one framework for both internal management and external reporting. This makes the monitor less tailor made to specific external stakeholders. However, it can still lead

Table A.1

Example of Sveiby's Indicators of Intangible Assets			
Perspective	**Competence**	**Internal Structure**	**External Structure**
Growth and renewal	Number of years in the profession	Investment in information processing systems	Profitability per customer
Efficiency	Proportion of professionals in the company	Sales per support person	Satisfied customer index
Stability	Average age	Rookie ratio	Proportion of big customers
Source: Sveiby (1997).			

to interesting results, as proved by the case of the Swedish company WM-data (Sveiby, 1997).

A.11 Intangibles Scoreboard

Lev is Professor of Accounting and Finance with the Stern School of Business at New York University. He is an outspoken critic of traditional accounting and a strong advocate of new, knowledge-based approaches to bookkeeping. Over the years he has developed a number of proposals to improve financial disclosure on intangibles:

1. The knowledge capital scoreboard (Lev, 1999), which was renamed *the intangibles scoreboard*
2. The intangibles scoreboard (Gu and Lev, 2002), also known as *intangible capital*
3. The comprehensive capitalization of intangible investments (Lev and Zarowin, 1999), an improved version of which was renamed *the improved GAAP*
4. The improved GAAP (Lev, 2000, 2001)
5. The restated financial report (Lev and Zarowin, 1999)
6. The economic asset-based accounting system (Lev, 2000)
7. Path matrices (Lev, 2000), of which an improved version was renamed into the *value chain scoreboard*
8. The value chain scoreboard (Lev, 2001), which was renamed the *value chain blueprint*
9. The value chain blueprint (Lev, 2003). I use the name *value chain scoreboard*.

In this appendix I focus on the intangibles scoreboard (no. 2), which is a financial valuation method to value intangibles, and the value chain scoreboard (no. 8), which is a measurement method for measuring intangibles (see Section A.25). Nos. 3 and 4 are both proposals to recognize more intangibles within the GAAP. No. 5 is a proposal to restate systematically previous financial reports the moment some major change affects the quality of the reported financial information (like deregulation or a significant drug development). No. 6 is a new way of accounting that adopts an economic definition of an asset without any reliability restrictions. Within this system, which is supposed to work next to the existing GAAP, all investments in intangibles are recognized as assets and are treated accordingly.

A.11.1 Distinctions and Definitions

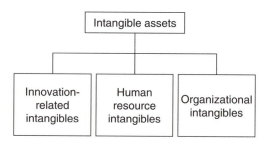

Lev (2001) defines an intangible asset as a claim to future benefits that does not have a physical or financial embodiment. He distinguishes between innovation-related intangibles, human resource intangibles, and organizational intangibles (Lev, 2001). He states that the economics of intangibles is somewhat different from the economics of physical and financial assets:

Intangibles are nonrival assets. They can be deployed at the same time in multiple uses. Although an airplane can be used during a given time period on one route only, its reservations system can serve, at the same time, a potentially unlimited number of customers.

In general they are characterized by large fixed costs and minimal marginal costs. The development of a software program often requires heavy investment, but distributing and selling it costs very little. Therefore, intangibles are often characterized by increasing returns of scale instead of decreasing returns.

Intangibles often profit from network effects. The usefulness of, for example, a computer operating system increases with the number of users.

The other side of the matter is that it is often difficult to secure ownership of intangibles, as the widespread violation of copyrights shows. As a result, others may benefit from intangible investments.

Innovations in intangibles are often highly risky. R&D, training, and acquiring technologies are often the first steps in the development of new products and services, and therefore are more risky than investments in the later stages of the development process.

Often there is no market for intangibles. They cannot be traded. Markets provide information about the value of goods and services, and this is vital to optimal resource allocation.

A.11.2 Problems and Consequences

Lev focuses on the problem of financial reporting. "The problem ... is that the systems of accounting and financial reporting that are being used today date back more than 500 years. These systems are not only part of the old economy, they are part of the old, old economy. . . . The old lens cannot capture the new economy, in which value is created by intangible assets: ideas, brands, ways of working, and franchises" (Webber, 2000, p. 217).

For example, R&D investment in product and process innovation is immediately expensed in financial reports as if no long-term benefits are expected from it. This interferes with the accounting concept of periodically matching costs with revenues. This concept is crucial in measuring income and assets in a reliable way. As a result, it becomes impossible to compare investments in R&D with their outcomes.

Investments in other intangibles such as training, brand enhancement, or information technologies are not even visible in most financial statements, which results in a complete lack of transparency. The consequence is an information deficiency. There is information asymmetry between the general public and those that do have access to information on investments and returns regarding intangibles. According to Lev (2001) this asymmetry leads to

- Abnormal gains to informed investors
- Increased volatility of market values resulting in a lack of confidence of investors
- An increase in the bid–ask securities spread (Traders quote this price differential for buying or selling a security. This may result in the market to shut down.)
- An increasing cost of capital

A.11.3 Solution and Results

Lev has developed both a top-down approach (the intangibles scorecard) and a bottom-up approach (the value chain scoreboard; see Section A.25). The intangibles scoreboard is based on looking at the past and the future. The purpose of the method is to come to an estimation of the financial value of the intangible capital of a firm based on publicly available data. The ultimate aim is to analyze the economic consequences of investment in intangible assets.

The scorecard calculates earnings created by intangible assets and it uses these IDEs to calculate intangible capital (Gu and Lev, 2002). The

method starts by looking at company earnings. Because earnings tend
to fluctuate over time and only reflect the past, Gu and Lev (2002) calculate an average, based on three years of historical data plus earnings
forecasts for one, two, and three years. The result is an estimate of
annual normalized earnings.

To come from these normalized earnings to IDEs, Gu and Lev
(2002) calculate the expected rates of return on tangible and financial
assets. Using a normal rate of return (7% for physical capital and
4.5% for financial capital) and the current value of these assets (based
on adjusted book values), they calculate the earnings linked to tangible and financial assets. Subtracting them from normalized earnings
results in IDEs.

Lastly, they forecasts the series of IDEs over three future periods
based on a three-stage valuation model. For future years 1 through 5,
they use financial analysts' growth forecasts. For the next five years,
they converge this forecast into the long-term growth of the economy
(3%), and from year 11 to infinity, they use a 3% growth rate. They
then use a discount rate that reflects the above-average risk of these
earnings to calculate the present value of these earnings: the value of
intangible capital.

These calculations open the way for a number of new financial
ratios (Lev, 1999):

- Intangible capital margin (IDEs/sales)
- Intangible capital operating margin (IDEs/operating income)
- The ratio of intangible capital to book capital, to indicate the
  degree to which a company is knowledge based
- The intangible capital margin (intangible capital/sales)
- The comprehensive value (Intangible Capital + Book Value)
- Market-to-comprehensive value (A 1:1 ratio would indicate that
  market value is mostly derived from past performance and short-
  term earnings forecasts.)
- The return on investment of R&D (intangible capital/investments
  in R&D)

Gu and Lev (2002) have statistically tested some of these metrics,
with very promising results:

- Comprehensive value (Intangible Capital + Book Value) is very
  close to market value.

- IDEs are associated significantly with the value drivers: advertising, R&D, and capital expenditure.

- IDEs and intangible capital are associated significantly with brand value, and this association even gets stronger if capitalized R&D is subtracted from intangible capital, leaving the value of intangibles other than R&D.

- Investments in human resources and information technology have a significant effect on the creation of valuable intangibles.

- IDEs turn out to be highly relevant in explaining annual stock returns, outperforming earnings, and operating cash flow. This indicates that intangible-based measures contain more useful information to investors.

- The comprehensive value-to-market ratio is a better predictor of short-term and long-term investor returns than book-to-market ratios. It can effectively distinguish between overvalued and undervalued stocks.

A.11.4 Evaluation

Lev's drive to create new, meaningful measures based on publicly available data has added tremendously to the field. He is a well-respected member of the accounting community and his comments and findings have helped to create awareness about the problem of traditional reporting. His analysis of the causes and consequences of the problem are very insightful (see Chapter 3). They provide clear starting points for improvement.

The intangibles scoreboard is based on the idea that tangible, financial, and intangible resources produce earnings. IDEs are the residual after a fair return for tangible and financial capital has been subtracted. This is common practice in financial valuation literature (see, for example, Reilly and Schweihs [1999]). I referred to this procedure in Chapter 4 as *income funneling*. The same approach is used by Strassmann (1999) to calculate knowledge capital (see Section A.4). It is interesting that Lev (1999) uses the result to develop seven additional ratios that can help to shed light on the knowledge intensity and efficiency of companies.

However, there are two limitations to this approach. First, Gu and Lev (2002) calculate a fair return on the tangible and financial resources used. This is not the same as the contribution of these resources to earnings. The actual contribution can be lower or higher. More troublesome is that earnings are the result of the synergy between tangible, financial, and intangible assets. This synergy produces value. Therefore, it is difficult to funnel part of the earnings to each of the capital types.

One of Lev's (1999) findings suggests that the intangibles scoreboard tends to underestimate the contribution of tangible resources to earnings. Lev (1999) found that the largest chemical and pharmaceutical companies tend to accumulate relatively more knowledge assets than the smallest companies. This finding could also be the result of an increase in the underestimation of the importance of tangible assets. Bigger companies have a bigger base of tangible assets. Because of economies of scale, the contribution of these tangibles to earnings may be relatively high. However, because Gu and Lev (2002) do not measure this contribution directly, but instead calculate an average fair return, their contribution could be underestimated.

However, their thorough statistical analyses show that IDEs and intangible capital are superior measures in explaining company performance. These measures can be calculated using publicly available data, and they allow for comparison across industries and over time. They can be used to distinguish between overvalued and undervalued stocks and therefore may become new and powerful tools for investors and managers.

A.12 Intellectual Capital Benchmarking System

Prof. Viedma is a Professor of Business Management at the UBC Polytechnic University of Catalonia. He is one of the intellectual capital pioneers in the Spanish-speaking countries and a long defender of the importance of benchmarking. His approaches include benchmarking systems for assessing intellectual capital in operational processes, intellectual capital in innovation processes, and social capital in clusters. His intellectual capital benchmarking system is a value assessment method.

A.12.1 Distinctions and Definitions

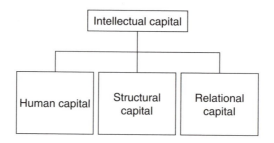

In his work, Viedma (1999, 2001b) draws heavily on resource-based theory. In his view, intellectual capital is equal to a company's core competencies, which consist of human capital, structural capital, and relational capital. A further distinction he makes is between operations processes and innovation processes. The operations process is made up of manufacturing, marketing, and after-sale service. The innovation process is made up of product design and product development (Viedma, 2001a). An interesting new concept that Viedma (2002) introduces to the intellectual capital field is the concept of social capital, which he describes as the sum of the resources and capabilities that belong to the network of organizations that a company has built to compete successfully.

A.12.2 Problems and Consequences

Viedma's (2001a) primary concern is the competitive gap that exists between a company and its world-class competitor. He states: "Knowing the causes that produce the competitive gap between the company and the international market leaders in the same business activity is the key issue in order to increase company competitiveness" (p. 5). This gap exists for every business unit. Each business unit will have a different world-class company against which to benchmark. By benchmarking each business activity, Viedma (2001a) tries to understand how to manage intellectual capital in an efficient way and how to facilitate the process of learning from the best competitors.

A.12.3 Solution and Results

The intellectual capital benchmarking system method uses a general model of business excellence to identify factors to benchmark. This general model is a normative model describing "the foundations which all companies inevitably have to rely upon if they want to achieve high standards in that extraordinary competitive context of today's global markets" (Viedma, 1999, p. 7). There is a general model for operational processes, for innovation processes, and one for social capital.

From this general model, Viedma (1999) creates specific models for the specific business units of a company. These models include normative criteria for excellent performance. From these models, a set of questions is developed to measure whether these criteria apply to the company under investigation and to the world-class competitor. The criteria are measured on a scale from -5 to $+5$, indicating whether the company is doing worse or better than a competitor. All questions on the questionnaire have a response precision box that is used to indicate the accuracy of each answer using a scale from 0 to 100 points. This information is consolidated into an overall reliability index of the assessment. The results are presented as a balance sheet. Under the Assets heading, all factors are placed on which the company is doing better than the competitor. The Liabilities heading includes all factors on which the company scores worse. The factors are weighted and added, creating a weighted average.

The intellectual capital benchmarking system benchmarks operational processes. The innovation capability benchmarking system uses the same approach to benchmark innovation processes. In addition, the social capital benchmarking system uses this approach to benchmark clusters or territories where a company is located. This last system can be used to identify the best cluster locations for a particular company.

A.12.4 Evaluation

Viedma is a pioneer in the field of benchmarking intellectual capital. In addition, he is one of the first to use the concept of core competencies as a unit of analysis for intellectual capital. He has done groundbreaking work in operationalizing normative models of excellent performance. His methods are methods for the value assessment of intellectual capital using the world-class competitor as a yardstick. The competitor functions as the yardstick on a 10-point scale.

A weak point is that the method depends solely on the judgment of an assessor, as does the weighing of the various factors. This has a strong impact on the outcome of the assessment. In addition, it is doubtful whether it is possible to develop a general model of business excellence that is valid in all industries and all contexts. The model Viedma uses in the intellectual capital benchmarking system reflects a rather arbitrary selection of normative management theories, ranging from Kanter's "change masters" to Posternack and Viscio's "centerless corporation" (Viedma, 1999).

A.13 Intellectual Capital Dynamic Value

Prof. Bounfour is a professor at the University of Marne La Valleé in France and works on R&D, innovation, and intangible resources management. This review of his intellectual capital dynamic value method is based on his work (Bounfour, 2002).

A.13.1 Distinctions and Definitions

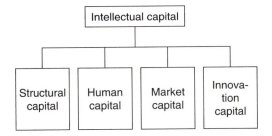

Bounfour (2002) uses intellectual capital, intangibles, intangible capital, and intangible assets interchangeably. He distinguishes between four components of intellectual capital:

1. *Human capital:* the set of all tacit knowledge and routines in the minds of employees
2. *Structural capital:* all intangible items that are separable from tacit knowledge
3. *Market capital:* the organization's endowments related to its relationships with the outside world (According to Bounfour, this includes databases, market share, reputation, new products, and new services.)
4. *Innovation capital:* the innovation capabilities of the organization

He also identifies four perspectives for analyzing, reporting, and managing intangibles:

1. The input perspective, which focuses on investments in intangibles
2. The output perspective, which focuses on valuing the output generated by intangibles
3. The internal–managerial perspective, which focuses on creating company-specific metrics to measure intangibles
4. The external perspective, which focuses on universal applicable accounting and financially based metrics.

A.13.2 Problems and Consequences

It is Bounfour's (2002) aim to integrate these four perspectives into one framework. He wants to establish a link between inputs, processes, the build-up of intangible assets, and company performance. According to Bounfour (2002), this process needs to be improved, and creating a link between the financial value of assets and the internal performance of companies can help to do this. This is a dynamic process, hence the name of the tool "dynamic value of intellectual capital."

A.13.3 Solution and Results

The intellectual capital dynamic value approach is based on indicators in three areas:

1. Performance indicators for resources
2. Performance indicators for processes
3. Performance indicators for outputs

These are combined into one overall index of performance. How the individual indicators are combined is not clear, except for the fact that a relative weighting is given to the three categories and that the overall index is between zero and one. The overall index of performance is multiplied by the market value of the company to calculate the dynamic value of the intangible capital of the company. In a separate calculation, the market value is divided into three components of intellectual capital: human capital, structural capital, and market capital.

A.13.4 Evaluation

A more detailed description of the intellectual capital dynamic value approach is needed to determine the strengths and weaknesses of the method. However, a few weaknesses can be mentioned. From the paper (Bounfour, 2002), it is not clear the exact problem the method tries to solve. It is unclear what the indicators stand for, how they are combined, and whether this meets the requirements for proper multidimensional value measurement. Bounfour (2002) does not explain how the overall indicator should be interpreted and why it is multiplied by the market value.

Multiplying the overall indicator by the market value would indicate that for a company with an overall indicator value of almost one (which according to Bounfour would be a company that is "best in class for 20 distinct criteria of performance" [2002, p.17]), its market value would represent the dynamic value of its intellectual capital. This seems to be a dissatisfying result. It is also unclear how the value of human, structural, and market capital is calculated, and why they add up to the total market value of the company.

A.14 Intellectual Capital Statement

Mouritsen is a Professor of Management Control at the Copenhagen Business School in Denmark. He focuses on empirical research into the role and effects of numbers in organizations. He has been involved with the project organized by the Danish Agency for Trade and Industry to construct intellectual capital statements for

17 Danish firms. This three-year project produced a *Guideline for Intellectual Capital Statements: A Key to Knowledge Management* (Danish Agency for Trade and Industry, 2003). The project involved cooperation between academic researchers and a consulting firm. Mouritsen's role (Mouritsen et al., 2001a) was to provide feedback on what the 17 firms were doing, how the activities of the firms could be rationalized, where the differences between the firms lay, and how their next challenge could be defined. The result was a measurement method named the *intellectual capital statement*.

A.14.1 Distinctions and Definitions

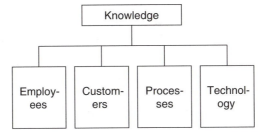

The distinctions and definitions Mouritsen et al. (2002) use in their work are new and different from other authors in the field. The first distinction is about knowledge. In their view knowledge is never something by itself—a "thing" or an "asset." Knowledge does not exist in the abstract but only in relation to a practice, a purpose (Mouritsen et al., 2002). Knowledge is not a stand-alone "finding," but is part of a wider set of processes related to the marketing, dissemination, and use of knowledge. It is, in fact, a social activity (Mouritsen et al., 2001a).

Consequently, intellectual capital statements (like the ones published by Skandia) do not represent the size or value of the knowledge of the firm. This would be impossible because knowledge is constituted by a network of elements. More importantly, it is not only impossible but also not useful to report the size or value of knowledge. According to Mouritsen et al. (2001a), the purpose of intellectual capital statements is to track the management activities that are put to work to organize the knowledge resources of the firm. The authors call these management activities *knowledge management*, which they define as follows: "Knowledge management is about aligning all the firm's knowledge resources, which implies a form of coordinated effort to bring employees, technologies, processes and customers together" (Mouritsen et al., 2001a, p. 38).

To describe knowledge, the purpose of knowledge, and knowledge management, Mouritsen et al. (2002) use narratives. "A narrative is a plot about a certain phenomenon. It shows the sequence of a set of events, it dramatizes the linkages between these events, and it points out not only the 'good' things that characterize the phenomenon but also the crucial 'bad' elements that have to be avoided to make the point of the narrative succeed" (p. 14).

An important point in the work of Mouritsen et al. (2001c) is their critique on the three-way split of intellectual capital into human, organizational, and customer capital. They claim this classification is problematic because the three categories are related and even integral to each other. People work through technology and customers get services from people. In addition, the classification does not provide any guidelines for handling intellectual capital or solving problems. Finally, the mere fact that an indicator is classified into one of the three types of intellectual capital does not mean it refers to or measures that type of intellectual capital. This conclusion is supported by the fact that the same indicator can sometimes fall into two categories at the same time—for example, employee training in technology (human capital or structural capital?), or customer satisfaction with employees' service (relationship capital or human capital?).

A.14.2 Problems and Consequences

Mouritsen et al. (2001c) address the problem of how to manage knowledge to create value. The intangible economy requires companies to develop their knowledge resources. Their idea is that an intellectual capital statement will help companies to apply knowledge management techniques systematically and comprehensively. The guideline for intellectual capital statements produced by the Danish Agency for Trade and Industry (2003), describes seven benefits of intellectual capital statements:

1. Preparing an intellectual capital statement forces companies to work out a strategy for knowledge management.
2. The statement helps to structure and assign priorities to knowledge management efforts.
3. Preparing an intellectual capital statement can help to create a culture of knowledge sharing.
4. It can add to the creation of a common identity.
5. The statement can improve communication to both internal and external stakeholders.
6. It can help to attract new employees.
7. It can help to improve communication between the company and its customers.

Note that the majority of the benefits are the result of the act of preparing an intellectual capital statement. Only the last three benefits are the result of the statement itself.

A.14.3 Solution and Results

Mouritsen et al. (2001c) have set out to develop an intellectual capital statement that describes the actions and activities that managers put in place in the name of knowledge. Such activities are complex sets of interventions that cannot be captured easily. Therefore, it is necessary to combine numbers with narratives and visualizations.

The intellectual capital statement consists of three elements. The first is the knowledge narrative that tells how the company's products and services help the customer and how the company has organized its resources to produce these products. It shows those areas at which the company and its employees must excel to create value. It also describes the company's ambition to make a difference through knowledge management.

The second element is the management challenge. Management challenges are the series of challenges within knowledge management that the company has to overcome to implement the knowledge narrative. These challenges are translated into concrete actions. The actions are aimed at four types of resources: employees, customers, processes, and technology. There are three possible types of management actions (Mouritsen et al., 2001c):

1. Portfolio management, aimed at strengthening the portfolio of resources
2. Qualification management, aimed at putting mechanisms in place to create value from the resources
3. Monitoring effects, aimed at creating insight into the effects of those mechanisms

The final element of the intellectual capital statement is a set of indicators. Mouritsen et al. (2001c) call this set an *intellectual capital accounting system*. This system consists of indicators for each of the four types of resources. There are three types of indicators: indicators describing the resources themselves, indicators describing qualifying activities, and indicators describing their effects (Figure A.4).

The complete intellectual capital statement is a combination of narratives (also named *stories*), indicators, and sketches. "Indicators create seriousness because they are published. Stories create

Figure A.14.2

Intellectual capital accounting system of Mouritsen et al. (2001c)

Management arena	Monitoring of effects	Qualification management	Portfolio management
Modality	Competencies	Qualifying activities	Portfolio
Domain \ Areas	Effects	Activities	Resources
Employees	:	:	:
Customers	:	:	:
Process	:	:	:
Technology	:	:	:

comprehensiveness of the strategy proposed although it cannot be defined in its details. Sketches, which visualize the relations in the story, produce and suggest the connectivity in the indicators reported" (Mouritsen et al., 2001b, p. 418).

The role of the indicators is interesting. Because there's no standardized way of interpreting intellectual capital indicators (like there is for financial statements), Mouritsen et al. (2001c) claim the indicators can only be interpreted as part of the wider intellectual capital statement, including the knowledge narrative and the visualizations. The narrative and visualizations act as justification for the numbers. Furthermore, measurement is useful only when aimed at management. "Therefore the measurement system needed to probe into Intellectual Capital has to be part of an idea of intervention around managing knowledge" (Mouritsen et al., 2001c, p. 360).

The indicators help to monitor the development and implementation of the firm's knowledge narrative. They visualize the path toward realizing the knowledge narrative. But why use numbers? Why not simply stick to a story line? According to Mouritsen et al. (2001b) there are two reasons. Although they believe that the numbers in an intellectual capital statement do not bring "reality" forth, they still think numbers are important. Numbers demonstrate seriousness on the part of top management. They allow inquiry into whether management is sincere about implementing the strategy (Mouritsen et al., 2001b). Numbers also help to make the fuzzy concept of knowledge management clear. "The clarity emanating from actually numbering certain efforts and practices makes the referent of the statement very precise" (Mouritsen et al., 2002, p. 12). The authors put it even stronger: "[I]t is by counting the development of these aspects that knowledge management activities get a form—and a practice. Only when attached to numbers is it possible to identify and communicate, in a reasonable form, what knowledge is all about" (p. 19).

A.14.4 Evaluation

Mouritsen et al. have taken the concept of intellectual capital measurement and reporting a step forward. Building on the Scandinavian tradition and experiences in intellectual capital measurement, they have created focus and have produced a very practical method for reporting intangibles. An important step forward is the way they focus measurement on concrete management activities aimed at improving the performance of resources. This focus not only clarifies the purpose of the intellectual capital statement but also makes the statement action oriented. The result of creating the statement is a practical management agenda of issues.

In addition, Mouritsen et al. put measurement in the wider context of a company's story line. This helps the reader to understand the numbers and to form an opinion. Intellectual capital measurement is more than numbers; it is a story line, a narrative. Equally important is their attempt to clarify why numbers are important. They argue that numbers make the narrative clear, precise, and serious.

Mouritsen is among the few authors that acknowledge that the process of creating an intellectual capital statement is as important as the statement itself. The process of thinking and of communicating that takes place while preparing a statement can create clarity about the company's vision, mission, strategy, identity, and priorities. It can help create awareness about the importance of knowledge sharing.

Yet, the method contains also a number of weaknesses. First, the model is not new. A proper balanced scorecard implementation will take the same steps described earlier: defining the vision, mission, and strategy (cf. knowledge narrative); identifying critical success factors or "do wells" (cf. management challenges); and selecting indicators. The only difference is that the intellectual capital statement focuses on knowledge resources and knowledge management, whereas the balanced scorecard is aimed at management in general. This difference is mitigated if we take into account that Mouritsen et al. (2001a) define knowledge management as broad as "an effort to bring employees, technologies, processes and customers together" (p. 38).

Second, the method does not completely solve the yardstick problem. Without a goal or yardstick, it is difficult to give meaning to the measure. Is it good or is it bad? It is truly a step forward that the indicators are made an integrated part of a narrative about the strategy of the company, but this is not enough. Yardsticks are still missing. The method remains merely a measurement method.

Furthermore, there is a clear danger of manipulation on the part of the company publishing an intellectual capital statement. Companies are allowed to select indicators that support the story line and omit others. But Mouritsen et al. (2001c) seem to acknowledge this when they state: "This does not mean that the [intellectual capital] Statement is necessarily correct. However, it may allow readers to form their own opinions about the value of the firm" (p. 380). Whether this opinion is grounded remains to be seen.

Finally, their argument to justify the need for numbers is not totally convincing. Numbers as such are not sufficient to produce the clarity, precision, and seriousness the authors wish the intellectual capital statement to provide. Numbers need to be relevant, reliable, clear, important, and neutral to provide insightful information. Most of all, numbers must be meaningful, which requires that they can be compared with a yardstick and that differences can be explained.

A.15 iValuing Factor

Standfield is a member of the International Knowledge Certification Standards Board, Australia. His iValuing factor method is a financial valuation method to measure the value of intangibles.

A.15.1 Distinctions and Definitions

Intangible
assets

Standfield (2001) does not precisely define his key distinctions. He uses the terms *intellectual assets, intellectual capital,* and *intangible assets* interchangeably. He also uses the term *intangibles,* which "include intangible assets, intangible liabilities, intangible revenue, intangible expenses and intangible capital" (Standfield, 2001, p. 317). He uses a definition of intangible assets that "is much wider [than intellectual property] and includes reference to human interactions, knowledge, quality, cycle time and more" (Standfield, 2001, p. 317).

A.15.2 Problems and Consequences

Standfield's (2001) motivation for measuring intangibles is summarized as follows: "As intellectual assets are the most important assets within any business, they must be measured and managed according to the most objective means possible" (p. 316). Standfield wants to improve management decision making and to include market value risks in the decision-making process.

A.15.3 Solution and Results

Stanfield (2001) uses his iValuing factor to create decision risk ranges. "A decision risk range establishes the potential downside risk and upside benefit of an executive decision" (p. 319). The iValuing factor is determined by taking the ratio of book value to share price. This ratio is used to estimate a market value risk associated with a specific management decision. Stanfield (2001) gives the example of a $200,000 cost savings. This figure is multiplied by the iValuing factor to create a decision risk range of plus/minus the estimated figure. The basic idea is that a management decision can have a positive or a negative impact on market value. The size of this impact depends on the intangibility of the company as determined by the iValuing factor.

A.15.4 Evaluation

The iValuing factor contains a number of weak points. It is based on comparing the difference between book value and market value. However, from the article (Standfield, 2001) it remains unclear why this difference is a predictor for the impact of a management decision on share price. In addition, Standfield does not explain how the calculation of the iValuing factor should influence management decisions.

A.16 Konrad Group

It took several years before the groundbreaking work of the Konrad group was recognized within the intellectual capital community. The Konrad group was one of the first groups to focus on other forms of capital besides traditional financial and tangible capital, and the first group to introduce the concept of structural capital. The method the group proposes is a measurement method.

A.16.1 Distinctions and Definitions

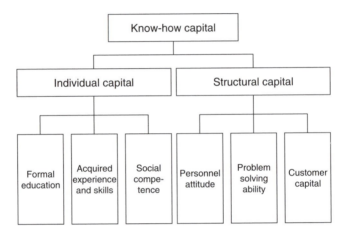

The work produced by the Swedish Konrad group focuses specifically on companies that sell know-how. These so-called "know-how companies" are a special type of service company whose people sell knowledge. Examples are consultancy organizations, advertising agencies, and audit firms.

The group distinguishes between two types of capital in a know-how company: traditional financial capital and know-how capital. The latter is divided into individual capital and structural capital (Sveiby et al., 1989). Individual capital is the "formal education, acquired experience and skills, social competence and ability to turn it all into action" (p. 23). The three cornerstones of structural capital are

1. People's attitude toward the company, the organization of the company, and the way people were recruited and retained
2. The problem-solving ability sold to the client, including the ability to create, package, and refine products

3. Customer capital, which is described as "the company's combined position in the market and with its customers" (Sveiby et al., 1989, p. 37).

A.16.2 Problems and Consequences

The key concern of the Konrad group is the external reporting of know-how companies. These companies have a different business model and risk profile and "do not really know how to report their operations so that external stakeholders . . . can get their answers" (Sveiby et al., 1989, p. 11). The group is especially concerned about the lack of information on personnel.

A.16.3 Solution and Results

The Konrad group proposes a list of 35 indicators to be reported externally by know-how companies, grouped into four categories:

1. Know-how capital, which includes mainly human resource indicators
2. The return on know-how capital, which includes indicators focusing on value added and profit per employee
3. The stability of the business, which includes indicators focusing on potential risks around business stability
4. Financial stability, which includes indicators on solvability, interest cover, and liquidity

A.16.4 Evaluation

The Swedish Konrad group was one of the first to search for other forms of capital besides traditional financial and tangible capital, and to introduce the concept of structural capital. Their set of distinctions is not as sophisticated as, for example, the one used by Edvinsson and Malone (1997). Their use of the term *structural capital* is much broader than Edvinsson and Malone's (1997) definition of structural capital, but at the same time it is more ambiguous. There seems to be an overlap between the concept of individual and structural capital, because experience and skills fall in the individual capital category whereas attitudes fall in the structural capital category.

The problem definition of the Konrad group is limited to the problem of the external reporting of know-how companies. The indicators they suggest are especially suited for an advisory type of business model. A strong point is their focus on risk and sustainability, because these issues are of core interest to the investment community. However, most indicators lack a clear yardstick, which makes them difficult to interpret.

A.17 Market-to-Book Ratio

Within the literature on intangibles, one can find the widespread statement that the difference between book value and market value represents intangibles or intellectual capital (see, for example, Edvinsson and Malone [1997], Stewart [1997, 2001b], Sveiby [1997], and Roos et al. [1997]). Stewart (1997) lists market-to-book ratio as a quick, easy, and reasonable indicator of intellectual capital.

A.17.1 Distinctions and Definitions

Market value is defined as the most probable price that a company would bring in a competitive and open market under all conditions requisite to a fair sale. It is equal to price per share multiplied by total numbers of shares outstanding. Book value is the reported stockholders' equity of the company, less the liquidating value of any preferred shares. According to White et al. (1998), book value equals neither the market value of the firm nor the fair value of its net assets. It is an accumulation of accounting entries and adjustments over the lifetime of the company. It contains the following elements:

- Original capital used to start the firm, plus proceeds from any additional shares issued, less the cost of shares repurchased
- Retained earnings accumulated over the firm's life
- Accounting adjustments

A.17.2 Problems and Consequences

Stewart (1997) includes the market-to-book ratio in his list of measurement tools because he thinks there is a need for tools to improve the management of intellectual capital. "Ultimately managing Intellectual Capital depends on finding rigorous ways to track it, which correlate with financial results. The data we want should, first, allow management to evaluate year-to-year performance—to measure progress towards goals—and, second, but more difficult, permit company-to-company comparisons" (pp. 222–223).

A.17.3 Solution and Results

The formula of this method is very simple: Market Value – Book Value = Value of Intangibles. The rational behind this formula is that "everything left in the market value after accounting for the fixed assets must be intangible assets" (Stewart, 1997, p. 224).

A.17.4 Evaluation

Andriessen (2002) states that subtracting market value and book value is not a good method to calculate the value of intangibles because it is like comparing apples and oranges. Book value is the reported stockholders' equity (less the liquidating value of any preferred shares), which represents the difference between assets and liabilities, both of which are most often valued at historical costs. Market value is equal to the perceived present value of the future cash flow of the company.

Pike et al. (2002) add another argument by stressing the fact that all resources of a company combine and interact with each other. The equation Market Value = Book Value + Intellectual Capital is incorrect because the variables are not separable, as required by the equation. For example, book value depends partly on retained earnings, which derive from operations, which involves intellectual capital (M'Pherson and Pike, 2002).

Mouritsen et al. (2001b) add two more arguments. First, the formula is a poor identification of intellectual capital by merely saying what it is not. The residual between market value and book value is anything. It has been claimed for intellectual capital, for reputation, for brand valuation, and competitive position. Second, the ratio changes when a change in accounting rules occurs.

That the residual between market value and book value is not only intellectual capital becomes clear when we look at the underlying theory of the market-to-book ratio. According to White et al. (1998), in theory they are the same. Market value equals the sum of the discounted expected cash flows. For an infinite and constant cash flow this is

$$Value = \frac{CF}{r},$$

where CF is the cash flow and r is the expected rate of return.

$$CF = r^* B,$$

where B is the book value of the firm and r^* is the actual rate of return. If we assume that the firm earns the required rate of return r ($r^* = r$), then CF is rB and $Value = B$.

If we assume that the actual rate of return does *not* equal the required rate of return, the equation can be transformed into

$$Value = B + \frac{(r^*-r)}{r} B$$

The component

$$\frac{(r^*-r)}{r} B$$

is a measure of the firm's economic goodwill, the excess of market value over book value. Firms with growth opportunities will have an actual rate of return that is bigger than the expected rate of return. Their market value will be higher than their book value. So the difference between market value and book value is in part the result of expected growth opportunities and not only of intellectual capital.

Another problem with the market-to-book ratio is that book values most often are valued at a historical cost basis. This poses a problem when we want to subtract market value and book value. When we want to subtract market value and book value, we need to reduce both types of value to the same denominator. But in so doing we must be careful not to be caught in a circular approach. Subtracting book value and market value means the need to transform the book value of the assets and liabilities into a type of value equal to a value that comes out of a market valuation. This means we need to revalue each asset and liability using a new definition of value—a definition in line with a definition of value of the company as a whole as determined through the stock market. This definition includes a proper premise of value and standard of value (see Chapter 4). The market value of a company is the value under the premise of "value in continued use." This means the assets and liabilities on the balance sheet need to be reappraised under the premise of value of "value in continuous use, as part of a going concern business enterprise." The proper standard of value to adopt is market value, which Reilly and Schweihs (1999) define as "the most probable (or most likely) price that an asset would bring in a competitive and open market under all conditions requisite to a fair sale, including the condition that the buyer and seller are each acting prudently and knowledgeably, and assuming the price is not affected by undue stimulus" (p. 60). If we ignore the problem that this definition of value is still quite dissimilar from value as determined by the stock market (because that market also includes buyers and sellers who are not acting prudently and knowledgeably), then it is still difficult to estimate market value for all assets and liabilities. It becomes even more difficult if we then add the requisite of applying the correct premise of value. This implies we need to appraise all assets and liabilities at market value under the premises of continued use. This means we cannot use, for example, the market price of a piece of machinery. Instead we need to determine the "price" of that piece of machinery as it is in use as part of the business enterprise. There is only one market that can give us such a price and that is the stock market. So to revalue all assets and liabilities at market value, we need to use the stock market value of the company as a whole and subtract all intangible value (the value not related to the assets and liabilities). But we can't do this because the intangible value was what we were looking for in the first place. Therefore, we are caught in a circular approach.

A.18 Options Approach

The options approach is a refined version of the income approach (see Section A.23). It is often listed separately as an approach to valuing intangibles (see, for example, Van den Berg [2003]).

A.18.1 Distinctions and Definitions

Options

The central theme in the literature about real options is the idea of an investment as an opportunity. Option theory uses the analogy with financial options to calculate the value of an investment opportunity. Option theory has no direct relationship with intangible resources, but the theory may be used as an improved version of DCF valuation.

A.18.2 Problems and Consequences

Option theory tries to deal with the following problem: "How should a corporate manager facing uncertainty over future market conditions decide whether to invest in a new project?" (Dixit and Pindyck, 1998, p. 325). Traditionally, a DCF calculation is made comparing the NPV of the expected stream of cash that the investment will generate with the NPV of the stream of expenditures required to undertake the project. If the resulting NPV is greater than zero, the investments should be made.

The problem is that this method assumes that the investment decision cannot be deferred. The possibility of deferral creates two additional sources of value (Luerman, 1998a):

1. If we can pay later, we can earn the time value of money on the deferred expenditure.
2. While waiting, the world can change and the value of the investment may go up (or down).

Furthermore, the decision to make an irreversible investment means we cannot put this money into other possible investments. Options are lost, which is an opportunity cost that must be included as part of the cost of the investment. The value of creating other options should also be taken into consideration. An investment may look uneconomical but may create other options in the future that are valuable.

A.18.3 Solution and Results

To incorporate these sources of value in decision making, option theory draws from the research on the valuation of financial options. Option theory adds an additional metric to the NPV matrix, which Luerman (1998b) calls the *volatility metric*. This metric includes the uncertainty of the future value of the asset in question and how long a decision can be deferred. If we then allow investment options to influence other future options, we can use "nests" of options upon options to depict investment strategies and to calculate their value.

A.18.4 Evaluation

Option theory is an interesting method to overcome some of the shortcomings of the traditional DCF method. It can only be used when there is a decision to be made regarding an investment. Under these circumstances, it can help to improve decision making about investments in intangible resources. If there is no investment option or the investment decision can no longer be deferred, then the conventional NPV and the option value are identical.

A.19 Skandia Navigator

Edvinsson was appointed the world's first corporate director of intellectual capital at Skandia in 1991. He calls himself a *global knowledge nomad*, as he travels the world to spread the word of intellectual capital. He is CEO of Universal Networking Intellectual Capital, he is adjunct professor of intellectual capital at Lund University and winner of the prestigious Brain of the Year Award for 1998. His well-known Skandia navigator is a measurement method for measuring intellectual capital.

A.19.1 Distinctions and Definitions

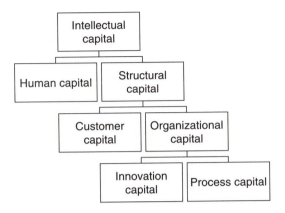

Edvinsson (Edvinsson and Malone, 1997) defines intellectual capital as the possession of the knowledge, applied experience, organizational technology, customer relationships, and professional skills that provide a company with a competitive edge in the market. In his book, written with Malone, he offers a list of synonyms for intellectual capital that includes knowledge capital, immaterial assets, and invisible assets. So, according to Edvinsson, all invisible assets of a company are intellectual by nature. In his later work, Edvinsson defines IC as derived main (head) insights about future earnings capabilities.[5]

Intellectual capital is broken down into two components. Human capital is the combined knowledge, skill, innovativeness, and ability of the company's individual employees to meet the tasks. Structural capital is the hardware, software, databases, organizational structure, patents, trademarks, and everything else of organizational capability that supports the employees' productivity. The relationship between human capital, structural capital and intellectual capital is described as Human Capital + Structural Capital = Intellectual Capital. In his book *Corporate Longitude,* Edvinsson (2002a) describes it as Human Capital × Structural Capital = Intellectual Capital, thereby acknowledging the existing synergies between the two factors, a point also made by Pike et al. (2002). Structural capital is further broken down. Edvinsson places a heavy focus on the intellectual capacity of human beings. He is a strong advocate of transforming human capital into structural capital. Structural capital can be owned and traded, and is therefore (in the eyes of the shareholder) comparatively stable, which

---

[5] Taken from personal correspondence between the author and Edvinsson.

will add to the market value of a company. According to Edvinsson, "the role of leadership is the transformation of human capital into structural capital to add to the organization's strength" (Edvinsson and Malone, 1997, p. 46). "It is a refined approach . . . focused on the packaging of knowledge into multiplicative recipes to be shared globally and rapidly" (Edvinsson, 2002a, p. 93).

A.19.2 Problems and Consequences

Edvinsson's main concern is the long-term future of companies and nations. He compares the intellectual capital of a company with the roots of a tree. The trunk, branches, and leaves are the company, as it is known in the marketplace. For the tree to flourish and bear fruit, strong and healthy roots must nourish the tree (Edvinsson and Malone, 1997).

Edvinsson addresses his concern at three levels. At the level of internal management it is his goal to add to the long-term sustainability of the organization and to nurture the roots of sustainable cash flow generation. For this, managers need more than traditional accounting measures. They need to know what forces create value, they need information on their strengths and weaknesses, and they need new perspectives on how the business works. Managers are "flying blindly in a hurricane depending on instruments that measure the wrong things" (Edvinsson and Malone, 1997, p. 13). A new tool is needed for measuring the value of intellectual capital because "[w]e become what we measure" (Edvinsson, 2002a, p. 71). So he sets out to develop a report of intellectual capital that is "a living, dynamic, human document that not only must have relevant indicators but also present those in a manner that is intuitively understandable, applicable, and even comparable between diverse enterprises" (Edvinsson and Malone, 1997, p. 39).

On the level of external reporting, Edvinsson notices that traditional financial data as presented in the annual report are no longer leading indicators of future financial performance. They do not show the real value of companies. This leads to a misallocation of capital. "As a result, too many deserving companies are underoptimized and undercapitalized, and thus sometimes are unable to complete their destiny. Meanwhile, other, troubled firms are artificially propped up until they collapse, pulling down shareholders and investors with them" (Edvinsson and Malone, 1997, p. 8). The lack of transparency in intellectual capital also results in information asymmetry between professional investors and small private investors. The misallocation of capital, in the end, produces social costs like unemployment, reduced productivity, and diminished national competitiveness.

This brings us to the third level of concern: the wealth of nations. In his more recent work, Edvinsson (2002a,b) transposes his ideas about intellectual capital to regions and nations. His aim is to create insight into the dynamics of intangibles at work on a national scale. National measurement and reporting systems overlook the contribution of intangibles. For example, public sector activities are undervalued because their contribution is not measured. His aim is to help develop a new political leadership agenda by visualizing the knowledge capital of nations. He wants to help governments to capitalize on knowledge capital and to increase the collective wealth of nations.

A.19.3 Solution and Results

To describe the purpose of the Skandia navigator, Edvinsson (2002a) uses the analogy of navigation. The Skandia navigator "provides a 3-D compass for charting a course towards tomorrow as well as a map of yesterday. The Navigator is a versatile strategic leadership tool for planning, management and follow-up" (p. 84). It is also meant as a diagnostic tool. "Moreover, it can be used as a diagnostic tool to trace overheating, fatigue, health, stress or illness in the corporate body (and individual bodies as well)" (Edvinsson, 2002a, p. 84).

The navigator consists of five groups of indicators, each focusing on a different area of attention (Figure A.19.2). The financial focus records the financial results of the company and looks at the past. The customer, human, and process focuses look at the present, whereas the renewal and development focus looks at the future.

Figure A.19.2

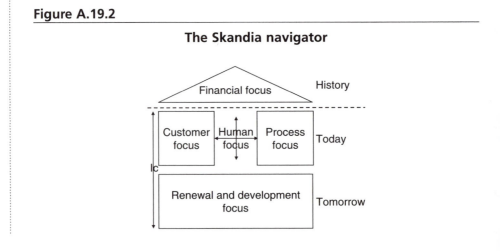

The Skandia navigator

Within each area, companies need to develop their own intellectual capital metrics. When working at Skandia, Edvinsson used a process model to develop these metrics. Starting with the objectives and vision of the business units, critical success factors were identified. The metrics were based on success factors and grouped according to focus area. Then concrete action plans were developed (Skandia, 1998).

Edvinsson and Malone (1997) use four types of indicators:

1. *Cumulative:* direct measures, usually in monetary terms (for example, market value)
2. *Competitive:* measures that compare the company with its industry, typically as a percentage or index (for example, loss ratio compared with market average)
3. *Comparative:* measures that include two company-based variables (for example, value added per employee)
4. *Combined:* measures that combine more than two company-based variables (for example, return on net assets resulting from a new business expense)

Indicators come in three shapes: direct counts, dollar amounts, and percentages.

Edvinsson and Malone (1997) present a list of indicators used at Skandia consisting of more than 160 indicators. They then slim it down to a list of 111 universal indicators, which they claim are applicable to any profit and non-profit organization. Then they combine a selection of these indicators into one intellectual capital yardstick for comparing value creation. They combine 21 dollar-amount indicators into the value of intellectual capital in dollars, C, and nine percentage indicators into a coefficient of efficiency, i. This leads to the formula Organizational Intellectual Capital = iC. In addition, Edvinsson has developed the concept of the IC-multiplier (Edvinsson, 2002a) which is the ratio between human capital and structural capital. He states that transforming human capital into structural capital is crucial for value creation. Looking at the IC multiplier will enable managers to forecast the growth of IC.

Mouritsen et al. (2001b) point toward the fact that the Skandia navigator is only one of the elements of Skandia's intellectual capital statements. The seven intellectual capital supplements to the annual reports Skandia has published over the years consist of indicators, stories and sketches. "Indicators create seriousness because they are published. Stories create comprehensiveness of the strategy proposed although it cannot be defined in its details. Sketches, which visualize the relations in the story, produce and suggest the connectivity in the indicators reported" (Mouritsen et al., 2001b, p. 418).

In addition, Skandia has released two CD-ROMS, two videos, and several books and papers. According to Mouritsen et al. (2001b), these statements do not attempt to value intellectual capital as such but they attempt to describe the way value is created. Together the statements tell the Skandia story of "valuing." "Here 'valuing' refers to identifying the mechanisms by which (net present) value is created and transformed, rather than accounting for how the (net present) value of the firm is to be represented by one number" (p. 404). The Skandia story is aimed at an external audience as well as an internal one "to persuade them about the (new) roles and obligations in the firm, and how they (should) contribute to value creation. This communication talks to 'sentiments' more than to 'reason'" (p. 400).

A.19.4 Evaluation

Edvinsson's work has been by no doubt the biggest contribution to the field of intellectual capital measurement. The Skandia navigator is probably the most widely cited example of an intellectual capital measurement method. The method has added significantly to the general awareness about the importance of intangible resources and the shortcomings of traditional reporting. Edvinsson and Malone (1997) admit that the navigator "is but the first systematic attempt to uncover these factors and to establish the key indicators for establishing their metrics" (p. 20). However, they claim, "[t]he Skandia Navigator has already proven to be so effective that it will likely be the basis for most future [intellectual capital] navigation tools" (p. 68). Edvinsson tries to solve a broad range of problems: the internal management of intellectual capital, the external reporting to stakeholders, and problems concerning the wealth of nations. He has found that the concept of the navigator can be translated from the corporate to the national environment.

Yet when we look at the more than 160 Skandia indicators and look at some of the data they produce (as presented, for example, in the supplement to Skandia's 1996 interim report [Skandia, 1996]), it is difficult to see how the navigator can help improve decision making by management, stakeholders, and governments. There are three reasons for this.

The navigator is intended to be a navigational tool, to direct the course of the company. However, the indicators may show you where you are, but they do not show you where you need to go. They provide no help setting out a business strategy. As such, the navigator is more like a global positioning system than a tool to plot a route. It is more like the navigator on a ship who has the job of recording and controlling the course than the captain, who has the job of telling where to go.

Furthermore, the navigator was designed as a diagnostic tool. Yet it includes no yardsticks to compare the measurements and so it does not help in diagnosing the situation. Edvinsson's IC Rating does include yardsticks that can help identify improvement areas.

In addition, the tool provides no insight into cause-and-effect relationships between indicators. Although indicators are grouped into various focus areas, it is not clear which indicators are causes and which are effects. So if a measurement would indicate illness because it deviates from a yardstick, we still do not know the causes of the illness. The diagnosis is not complete. The IC-Index (see A.8), to which Edvinsson has contributed extensively, does look at cause and effect relationships.

The problem with the overall formula Organizational Intellectual Capital = iC is that it combines various indicators that have different units and skills. This leads to problems of comparability and commensurability (M'Pherson and Pike, 2001).

In defense of the Skandia navigator, Mouritsen et al. (2001b) state that the indicators are only one part of a more comprehensive approach to telling the story of Skandia. In their opinion the stories and sketches are equally important. The indicators are only there to show that top management is serious about implementing the strategy.

> There is no exhaustive list of indicators in Skandia's Navigator. They are never interpreted in the Supplements as sets of statistics that can bring "reality" forth in a set of ratios. Indeed, there is hardly any mentioning of indicators in the stories given. They are always lying in the back of the Supplements. This does not mean they are not important, however. They are there to demonstrate seriousness on the part of top-management (Mouritsen et al., 2001b, p. 419).

A.20 Sullivan's Work

Sullivan is founder of and senior partner at Intellectual Capital Management Group, Inc. Before that he was a testifying expert specializing in intellectual property valuations and litigation expert testimony. Sullivan (1998a,b,c, 2000) developed a financial valuation method for determining a purchase price for an acquired company and a financial valuation method for determining the market value of a company.

A.20.1 Distinctions and Definitions

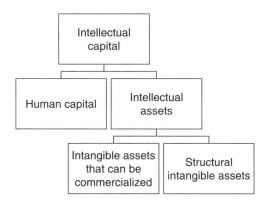

Sullivan's prime interest in intellectual capital is in commercializing intellectual assets such as intellectual property. This is a process he calls *value extraction* (Sullivan, 1998c). He makes a distinction between the economic paradigm of intellectual capital and the social paradigm. According to Sullivan (1998c), the social paradigm focuses on knowledge creation as "essentially a human and social activity where the value of particular knowledge is determined by the culture and values of the group" (p. 9). The economic paradigm focuses on the ownership of knowledge, creating knowledge for future commercialization, and extracting current profits from existing knowledge value creation and value extraction.

Given his interest in value extraction, it comes as no surprise that Sullivan (1998a) focuses on the economic paradigm, stressing the importance of the codification of tacit knowledge. "With increasing size it becomes ever more important for knowledge firms to motivate their human capital resources to codify their knowledge and know-how, thereby creating intellectual assets" (p. 23).

Edvinsson, with whom he cofounded the Intellectual Capital Management Group in 1995, inspired Sullivan's model. Sullivan (1998c) defines intellectual capital as "knowledge that can be converted into profits" (p. 4) comprising two elements: human capital and intellectual assets. He uses the term *human capital* in three different ways: In one definition he describes it as the following: "Human capital consists of a company's individual employees, each of whom has skills, abilities, knowledge and know-how" (Sullivan, 1998c, p. 5). In another publication (Sullivan, 1998a), he also includes the capabilities of contractors, suppliers, and other company-related people. In an article with Westberg, he makes a distinction between human capital at an individual level and at the firm level. At the firm level it "consists of the firm's know-how and institutional memory about topics important to its business" (Westberg and Sullivan, 1998, p. 67).

Sullivan (1998a) describes intellectual assets as follows: "Intellectual assets are the codified, tangible, or physical descriptions of specific knowledge to which the company can assert ownership rights. . . . Intellectual assets that receive legal protection are intellectual property" (p. 23). He separates intellectual assets that can be commercialized from structural intellectual assets. The latter include intangibles like organization and structure, customer capital, operational methods and procedures, managerial methods and analysis, and the way of doing business (Sullivan, 1998b).

Sullivan (1998a) also uses the term *structural capital,* but in a way that is totally different from authors like Edvinsson (2002a), Stewart (2001b), and Bontis (2002). For Sullivan (1998a), this includes all supporting infrastructure and includes all tangible assets of the firm. Sullivan (1998a) uses this distinction to draw attention to the tangible complementary business assets that often are needed to commercialize intellectual assets.

A.20.2 Problems and Consequences

Sullivan (1998a,b,c) uses value measurements of intellectual capital to improve decision making—for example, the decision whether to invest further in developing an intangible, to continue holding it, or to sell it. In a more recent publication, Sullivan (2000) also addresses the problem of determining the purchase price for a business acquisition as well as three problems related to the market value of a company:

1. The problem of describing the relationship between stock price and intellectual capital
2. The problem of companies wishing to convey information that fully informs about their value
3. The problem of companies wishing to affect stock price positively

A.20.3 Solutions and Results

Sullivan (2000) introduces a method for determining a purchase price for an acquired company. This price should reflect the value that the acquired intellectual assets of this company will bring for the buyer. The method involves four steps:

1. Definition of assets of interest for an acquisition
2. Determination of how acquired assets are expected to be used
3. Determination of the amount of value created by acquired assets
4. Determination of purchase price for acquired assets

The crucial step is obviously step 3. This step requires a forecast of additional revenues that can be attributed to the acquired assets. Unfortunately, Sullivan (2000) provides no solution for how to forecast these revenues.

Sullivan (2000) also presents a method for determining the market value of a company. According to Sullivan (2000), the market value of a going concern enterprise is equal to the value of the firm's tangible assets and the value of the DCFs the firm is expected to generate. "Market capitalization reflects the market's view of two things. First, it reflects the market's understanding of the value of the firm's fixed assets, those found on the company's balance sheet. Second, it reflects the market's intuition or perception of both the amounts of (a company's) Intellectual Capital as well as its ability to leverage that Intellectual Capital in its market place" (Sullivan, 2000, pp. 119–120). Sullivan's method distinguishes between three earnings streams:

1. Earnings from intellectual capital
2. Earnings from complementary business assets
3. Earnings from generic structural capital

Unfortunately, he does not explain how these individual earnings can be separated and calculated.

A.20.4 Evaluation

Sullivan (1998a) made an important contribution to the intellectual capital field by emphasizing the relative nature of value. "The value of an item depends primarily on the needs of the person or organization that will be using it" (p. 33). The value of an individual intangible strongly depends on a company's vision and strategy. Sullivan does not provide a practical method for valuing intangibles. His approaches do not provide any suggestions regarding how to handle the practical problems associated with a DCF method. The two approaches he proposes draw heavily on the notion that Market Value = Tangible Assets

+ Intellectual Capital.[6] As we saw in Section A.17, this is not automatically the case.

A.21 Technology Factor

Khoury is senior intangible assets appraiser at The Dow Chemical Company. Dow has been a pioneer in the management and exploitation of intellectual property. The technology factor method became known because of its application at Dow but was authored by Arthur D. Little, an American consulting firm.

A.21.1 Distinctions and Definitions

Intangible assets	Complementary intangible assets
• Copyrights • Patents, propriety know-how and technology • Service marks • Trademarks • Computer software	• Assembled workforce • Culture and management • Customer lists • Etc.

Khoury (1998) uses the term *intangible assets,* which covers copyrights, patents, proprietary know-how and technology, service marks, trademarks, and computer software. He uses the term *complementary intangible assets* to cover assets like assembled workforce, culture and management practices, and customer lists.

A.21.2 Problems and Consequences

It is Dow's commitment "to build on its existing technology competencies and to maximize their value through the leveraging of its

---

[6] Although he seems to deny this: "We must be careful to point out that it is not true that a company's value is equal to the sum of the value of the tangible assets and intellectual capital. It is true that a knowledge firm's value is the sum of its tangible assets and the discounted value of the cash flow that is generated largely by the firm's intellectual capital" (Sullivan, 2000, p. 121). However, elsewhere he states that the discounted future stream of benefits is the economic measure of value (1998c). Combining the two statements leads to the conclusion that the discounted value of the cash flow generated by intellectual capital equals the value of intellectual capital.

intellectual assets" (Khoury, 1994, p. iii). Businesses within Dow are encouraged to look at ways of exploiting technology. To make decisions on technology exploitation, it is necessary to value technology at every stage of its development. The technology factor method was designed to do this.

A.21.3 Solution and Results

The technology factor method attempts to calculate the fair market value of a specific technology. This can be a group of patents, individual patents, know-how, copyright, or trade secret. It uses a DCF approach to calculate the NPV of the incremental cash flow derived from the practice of a specific technology within a specific business.

The technology factor method consists of two parts. Part 1 is the calculation of the NPV of the incremental business. This is a straightforward income approach to valuation (see also Section A.23). Part 2 is the estimation of a technology factor between 0 to 100% that approximates how much of the total incremental cash flow can be attributed to the specific technology.

The technology factor is based on a qualitative assessment by a multidisciplinary team of experts. This team looks at utility issues and competitive advantage issues. The utility issues include

- Usefulness of the technology to Dow
- Usefulness of the technology to others
- Capital required for implementation
- Time required for implementation
- Useful life of the technology
- Other

The competitive issues include questions like

Does the technology allow competitive differentiation?
Are there alternative technologies?
What is its legal strength?
What is the anticipated competitive response?

Each issue is assessed using −, 0, or +; − signals negative impact on value and + signals creation of value. Then for the utility issues and the competitive issues, an overall assessment is made resulting in a low, medium, or high value for the technology factor range (low, 0–30%; medium, 30–50%; high, 50–75%). Then both assessments are combined into an overall range, and an overall technology factor score is estimated. This score is multiplied with the NPV to calculate the value of the technology.

Khoury (1998) claims this method is not only useful for internal decision making on exploitation and investment but also for litigation infringement, out-license/sell decision making, in-license/purchase decision making, as well as for collateral for financing, joint ventures, and minority equity positions and taxation purposes.

The method uses several scenarios depending on the maturity of the technology. If the technology is in its early stage and there is not yet a real application available, a scenario is developed for a model enterprise. When the technology is more mature, a specific Dow business or an external company may function as the basis for a scenario.

A.21.4 Evaluation

The technology factor method is a straightforward income approach to valuation. The method separates elements of the income approach (see Section A.23) and incorporates them into one technology factor. In theory, this factor calculates the part of the NPV that can be attributed to the specific technology. As such, it tries to solve the problem of income funneling and income allocation (see Section A.23).

However, when we look at the various issues listed under utility and competitive advantage, we see that these issues address other elements of the income approach as well. For example, the issue of "usefulness" is an issue that has already been covered when solving the income projection problem to calculate the NPV. The issue of "capital required for implementation" has been estimated when calculating projected cash flow. The issue of "useful life of the technology" was incorporated in the useful life estimation, which is also part of the NPV calculation. The issue of "legal strength" was incorporated as a risk component in the discount factor. So some of the issues are addressed twice: as part of the calculation of NPV and again as part of the technology factor. Probably this results in a lower total value. Surprisingly, the problems of income funneling and income allocation are not addressed in the checklist. The technology factor does not calculate which part of the cash flow can be attributed to the technology. To summarize, the technology factor solves problems that (should) have been resolved when calculating the NPV and, at the same time, it does not address the problems that it should address.

A.22 Tobin's Q

In 1981, the U.S. economist James Tobin (1918–2002) received the Nobel Prize for his analysis of financial markets. He is probably most famous for introducing the concept of Tobin's Q.

A.22.1 Distinctions and Definitions

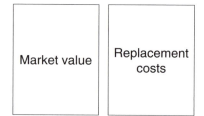

Tobin's Q is the ratio between the market value of an asset and its replacement cost. Market value is the most probable price that an asset would bring in a competitive and open market under all conditions requisite to a fair sale. Replacement cost contemplates the cost to recreate the utility of the subject asset (Reilly and Schweihs, 1999).

A.22.2 Problems and Consequences

Tobin developed Q as part of his research into capital investment. He wanted to know what elements affect investment decisions. He did not develop Q with the intent to measure intangibles. According to Stewart (1997), Tobin's Q is a good measure of intellectual capital and an improvement to market-to-book ratios (see Section A.17).

A.22.3 Solution and Results

Tobin introduced the concept of Tobin's Q as a measure to predict whether capital investments would increase or decrease. If an asset's Q is less than one, a new investment in a similar asset is not profitable. According to Stewart (1997), Q has a wider application because Q is a measure of "monopoly rent." This is a company's ability to get unusually high profits because it has something no one else has. "That's not a bad definition of the manifest power of Intellectual

Capital: You and your competitors presumably have similar fixed assets, but one of you has something uniquely its own—people, systems, customers—that allows it to make more money" (Stewart, 1997, p. 226). Stewart (1997) suggests the use of Tobin's Q as a measure of intellectual capital.

A.22.4 Evaluation

The use of Tobin's Q as a measure of intellectual capital is based on the same assumptions as the use of the market-to-book ratio. The advantage of Q is that it neutralizes the depreciation policies of companies because it uses replacement costs instead of book value. However, the other problems associated with the market-to-book ratio as measure of intellectual capital also apply to Tobin's Q (see Section A.17).

A.23 Valuation Approaches

In the literature on valuation methods, one can find three approaches to financial valuation (Lee, 1996; Reilly and Schweihs, 1999; Smith and Parr, 1994):

1. Cost approach
2. Market approach
3. Income approach

These methods are often not directly applicable to the problem of valuing intangible resources. However, I include them in this overview because many of the other methods derive from these fundamental financial valuation methods.

A.23.1 Distinctions and Definitions

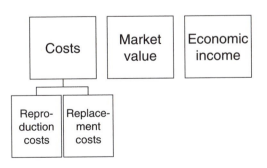

According to Reilly and Schweihs (1999), two types of costs are related to the *cost approach*: reproduction cost and replacement cost. Reproduction cost is the estimated cost to construct, at current prices, an exact replica of the subject intangible. Replacement cost is the estimated cost to construct, at current prices, an intangible asset with equivalent utility to the subject asset.

A core concept in the *market approach* is market value. This is the most probable price that an asset would bring in a competitive and open market under all conditions requisite to a fair sale (Reilly and Schweihs, 1999). The *income approach* is based on the concept of economic income. There are numerous measures of economic income, including gross or net revenues, gross income, and net operating income.

A.23.2 Problems and Consequences

Many problems require an intangible resource appraisal (adapted from Reilly and Schweihs [1999]):

- Transaction pricing and structuring, for the sale, purchase, or license of an intangible asset

- Financing securitization and collateralization, for both cash flow-based financing and asset-based financing

- Taxation planning and compliance, with regard to all sorts of possible deductions, tax compliance, and estate planning

- Management information and planning, including investment planning and strategic decision making

- Bankruptcy and reorganization, including the value of the estate in bankruptcy and the assessment of the impact of proposed reorganization plans

- Litigation support and dispute resolution, including infringement of intellectual property rights and breach of contract

- Bookkeeping and goodwill impairment testing, including the impairment testing of goodwill according to the new FASB guidelines for goodwill (FASB, 2001a)

- External reporting and accounting, including the reporting of fair value estimates in notes to the annual report

Each purpose requires a specific valuation approach. For example, the sale of an intangible asset (like a patent) to a specific buyer would result in the "acquisition value" of that asset. Reilly and Schweihs

(1999) define acquisition value as "[t]he price that a particular, specifically identified buyer would be expected to pay for an intangible asset with consideration given to any and all unique benefits of the intangible asset to the identified buyer" (p. 60). This value can be substantially different from, for example, its "owner value." Reilly and Schweihs (1999) define owner value as "[t]he value of an intangible asset to its current owner, given that owner's current use of the intangible asset and current resources and capabilities for commercially exploiting the intangible asset" (p. 60). The conclusion is that the same intangible resource can have many different values.

A.23.3 Solution and Results

The *cost approach* is based on the economic principles of substitution and price equilibrium. These principles assert that an investor will pay no more for an investment than the cost to obtain an investment of equal utility (Reilly and Schweihs, 1999). Thus, the price of a new resource is commensurate with the economic value of the service that that resource can provide during its life.

The *market approach* is based on the economic principles of competition and equilibrium. These principles assert that in a free and unrestricted market, supply and demand factors will drive the price of any good to a point of equilibrium. In the market approach, an analysis is made of similar resources that have recently been sold or licensed. These market data are used to estimate a market value.

The *income approach* is based on the economic principle of anticipation. The value of intangible resources is the value of the expected economic income generated by these resources.

Using an income approach we have the following requirements to fulfill:

- Income projection requirement
- Income funnel requirement
- Income allocation requirement
- Useful life estimation requirement
- Income capitalization requirement

A.23.3.1 Income Projection Requirement

The income approach is based on a projection of economic income and thereby on somehow predicting the future. Therefore, it always contains a level of uncertainty and subjectivity. "All income approach analyses are based on the premise that the analyst can project economic income with a reasonable degree of certainty. . . . The term reasonable degree of certainty is, by its very nature, subjective" (Reilly and Schweihs, 1999, p. 182).

A.23.3.2 Income Funnel Requirement

Intangible resources generate not all the income produced by a business enterprise. Tangible resources and networking capital also contribute to the income. The problem is how to assign the overall enterprise income to the constituent components of the business enterprise, including all tangible and intangible resources. This requirement is referred to as

> a funnel of income adjustment because all of the income that is generated by a business enterprise can be analogized to the top (or wide) end of a funnel. For analytical purposes, we are only interested in that portion of the total enterprise income that gets down to the bottom (or narrow) end of the funnel—that is, that relates directly to the subject intangible asset. The adjustment is often necessary in order to avoid double-counting or overestimating intangible asset values (Reilly and Schweihs, 1999, p. 177).

This adjustment should include a fair return on the investment of all the resources that are used in the production of economic income, especially investments in tangible assets and networking capital.

A.23.3.3 Income Allocation Requirement

The economic income that is left after the funnel of income adjustments can be attributed to the intangible resources of the business enterprise. The next problem is how to allocate this income among the various (bundles of) intangible resources. This allocation should take into account the synergy of the combined intangible resources within the company.

A.23.3.4 Useful Life Estimation Requirement

Crucial to any income approach analysis is the estimation of the remaining useful life of the intangible resources. This is also referred to as the *forecast period* (Copeland et al., 1990), the *projection period* (Reilly and Schweihs, 1999), or the *cash flow duration* (Smith and

Parr, 1994). There are at least eight different ways to look at the remaining useful life of intangible resources (Reilly and Schweihs, 1999):

1. Economic life, depending on the ability to provide a fair rate of return
2. Functional life, depending on the ability to continue to perform
3. Technological life, depending on changes in technology
4. Legal or statutory life
5. Contractual life
6. Judicial life, as a result of a court rule
7. Physical life
8. Analytical life, as a result of an analysis of similar intangible resources

A.23.3.5 Income Capitalization Requirement

To come to a value of future income, the economic income generated by the subject intangible is divided by an appropriate rate of return. This discount rate reflects

- The expected growth rate of the income stream generated by the subject intangible
- The cost of capital appropriate for an investment in the subject intangible
- A compensation for inflation
- The degree of risk associated with an investment in the intangible

Applications of the income approach can be found in Sections A.2, A.4, A.6, A.15, and A.21.

A.23.4 Evaluation

The problem with the *cost approach* is that in many cases cost is not a good indication of value. Many of the important factors that drive value are not reflected in the cost approach. These factors include (Smith and Parr, 1994):

- The amount of benefits associated with the resource
- The trend of the economic benefits (increasing or diminishing)
- The duration over which the economic benefits will be enjoyed

- The risks associated with receiving the expected economic benefits

Furthermore, all relevant forms of obsolescence of the subject resource have to be identified, quantified, and subtracted from the cost of the resource to estimate the value. The cost approach is appropriate to value intangible resources when setting transfer prices, royalty rates, or when estimating the amount of damages suffered by the resource owner in an infringement or other type of litigation.

The *market approach* can be used only if data are available regarding the transaction of intangible resources that are similar to the subject resources. When the subject resources are unique, which is often the case, this approach is not appropriate.

The *income approach* is often the best alternative but requires many assumptions on income projection, income funneling, income allocation, useful life estimation, and income capitalization. According to option theory, the problem with the income approach is that it assumes that the investment decision cannot be deferred. The possibility of deferral creates two additional sources of value (Luerman, 1998a):

1. If we can pay later, we can earn the time value of money on the deferred expenditure.
2. While waiting, the world can change and the value of the investment may go up (or down).

Furthermore, the decision to make an irreversible investment means we cannot put this money into other possible investments. Options are lost, which is an opportunity cost that must be included as part of the cost of the investment. In addition, the value of creating other options should be taken into consideration. An investment may look uneconomical but may create other options in the future that are valuable.

A.24 Value-Added Intellectual Coefficient

Pulic is Professor of Economics at the University of Zagreb and the University of Graz. He is best known for the development of the VAIC, which he has used to measure the efficiency of key resources in companies. Lately he has applied this approach to measure the efficiency of regions in Croatia (IBEC, 2003). VAIC is a financial valuation method.

A.24.1 Distinctions and Definitions

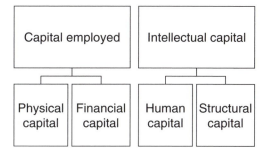

Pulic (IBEC, 2003) states that two key resources create value added in companies: capital employed and intellectual capital. Capital employed consists of physical and financial capital. Intellectual capital consists of human and structural capital. Value added is the output minus the input of a firm. Output is sales revenue; input is everything that comes from outside the company.

A.24.2 Problems and Consequences

Traditional accounting focuses on controlling costs. Instead, Pulic (2000b) focuses on value creation. He states that to manage value creation we need to measure it. For him, a measurement tool must monitor the efficiency of resources in creating value. His aim is to develop a method that can measure resource efficiency for listed and unlisted companies as well as for regions and countries.

A.24.3 Solution and Results

The main assumption of the VAIC method is that labor expense is an asset, not a cost. The consequences of this assumption are fourfold: In calculating the value added of a firm, Pulic (2000b) excludes all labor expenses:

$$VA = GM - sgaExp. + LExp.,$$

where *VA* is value added; *GM* is gross margin; *sgaExp.* is selling, general, and administrative expenses; and *LExp.* is labor expenses.

Labor expenses are treated as an asset that Pulic (2000b) calls *human capital*. The value of human capital can be expressed by the expenditures for employees. It is possible to calculate the efficiency of this asset by computing how much value added one unit that is spent on employees creates. Labor expense should no longer be an item on the profit-and-loss statement, instead, it should be recognized as an asset on the balance sheet (Pulic, 2002).

The first step of the VAIC method is to calculate the value added of a firm by subtracting input from output, whereby labor expenses are not included in the input. In financial terms, this is equal to

$$VA = GM - sgaExp. + LExp.$$

This is equal to

$$VA = OperatingIncome + LExp.$$

The next step is to calculate the value of human capital. According to Pulic (2000b), this can be expressed by the labor expense

$$HC = LExp.,$$

where HC is human capital.

The third step is to calculate the value of structural capital. According to Pulic (2000b), Structural Capital = Intellectual Capital − Human Capital. From this, Pulic concludes that structure capital must be equal to

$$SC = VA - HC,$$

where SC is structural capital.

The next step is to calculate capital employed. This is equal to the book value of the net assets of the firm (Firer and Williams, 2003).

We now have four indicators:

1. $HC = LExp.$
2. $VA = OperatingIncome + HC$
3. $SC = VA - HC$
4. $CE = BookValueofNetAssets$, where CE is capital employed

Pulic (2002) then sets out to calculate the ratio between each of the three forms of capital and value added: CEE, HCE, and SCE:

$$CEE = \frac{VA}{CE}$$

$$HCE = \frac{VA}{HC}$$

His approach for structural capital is different. He states that human capital and structural capital are reciprocal. The lesser human capital participates, the more structural capital is involved. To achieve this effect mathematically Pulic (2000b) defines SCE as

$$SCE = \frac{VA}{\dfrac{1}{SC}} = \frac{SC}{VA}$$

To come to an overall measure of efficiency, Pulic (2000b) adds the three efficiency measures:

$$VAIC = HCE + SCE + CEE$$

This indicates the corporate value creation efficiency or "intellectual ability" of the company. The VAIC software allows for real-time tracking of the four indicators, not only for the company as a whole but also on the level of individual processes and functions.

The VAIC indicator has been tested a number of occasions to determine whether it correlates with aspects of company performance. Williams (2001) found no relationship between the VAIC and the extent of intellectual capital disclosure in annual reports. Pulic (2000a) found a correlation with market value. Without the use of any control variables, the VAIC was able to explain 19% of the variance in market value. Firer and Williams (2003) tested the VAIC against profitability, productivity, and market value, and found small negative correlations between VAIC, and productivity and market value. This result was unexpected.

A.24.4 Evaluation

Pulic has been a great promoter of intellectual capital in both Austria and Croatia. His recent study on the VAIC in 21 regions of Croatia is a major achievement and a great contribution to the awareness of the importance of intellectual capital in regional economies. The VAIC method is applied increasingly as an indicator of intellectual capital performance in statistical analysis, because it uses data that are publicly available.

Yet, I have difficulty with its basic assumptions. These assumptions have a big influence on the method and its outcome. These difficulties may explain the disappointing results of using the VAIC as an indicator for explaining company performance.

First, the VAIC method does not properly separate expenses from assets. An asset is a claim by the enterprise to an expected benefit (Lev, 2000), whereas an expense is not expected to provide any benefits beyond the accounting period. Labor expenses may include expenses that provide future benefits (like training expenses or labor used for R&D). However, a large part of labor expenses provide immediate benefits, and this part should *not* be treated as an asset. To treat all labor expenses as an asset means overstating their future benefits. If we were to treat them as an asset, we would have to look at the required depreciation rate of these assets. We would probably discover that a large part of these capitalized expenditures would need to be amortized within the same accounting period because they do not provide benefits beyond that account. This depreciation would bring these expenses back to the profit-and-loss statement.

Second, the method confuses stocks and flows. Value added is a flow indicator for the return on assets like capital employed, human capital, and structural capital (which are stock indicators). Labor expense is a flow indicator, but within the VAIC method, labor expense is treated as a stock. If we were to accept that labor expenses yield future benefits, we then still would have to treat it as a flow—in this case, as an *investment* into human capital, not as the value of human capital itself. An investment is a contribution to an asset that produces future benefits. Often assets accumulate because of a series of investments over the years (like investments in R&D). The value of the stock of human capital is the result of an accumulation of yearly labor expenses. It is this *stock* value of human capital we need to relate to value added to calculate the efficiency rate, not the investment in a particular year. Another example of confusing flows and stocks is the calculation of structural capital. Structural capital is a stock, but within the VAIC method, it is calculated as the residual of two flows: value added and human capital. At the most, this residual is a *return* on structural capital, not the value of structural capital itself. This error results in peculiar results. For example, if the operating income of a company is negative, structural capital becomes negative.

Third, the aim of the VAIC method is to calculate the efficiency of capital employed, human capital, and structural capital. The report on the VAIC of Croatia phrases this as follows: "if the analysis indicates that Human Capital Efficiency is 2.5, it means that each $/E invested in employees creates $/E 2.5 of new value" (IBEC, 2003). Unfortunately, the VAIC does not calculate efficiency. HCE is calculated by dividing value added by human capital. This ratio does not provide information about the *contribution* of human capital to value creation. Human capital, structural capital, and capital employed all contribute to value added, but simply calculating their ratios does not show you which one produces how much. What is needed is insight into the causal relationship between these types of capital and value added. Only by measuring this causal relationship, one can determine efficiency.

Fourth, the assumption that the effect of structural capital is the inverse from the effect of human capital yields strange results. HCE is defined as value added divided by human capital, whereas SCE is defined as structural capital divided by value added. Let us consider the example of British Telecom (Table A.2). The first row of the table was reported by Pulic (2000a). Scenario 1 describes the situation in which British Telecom has equal amounts of human capital and structural capital. You would expect them to have equal efficiency rates. However, the score for the efficiency of HCE is four times bigger than SCE, indicating that a unit invested in human capital would result in four times as much value added.

If we rewrite the formulas for HCE and SCE, it becomes clear why, in fact, HCE is usually bigger than SCE:

$$HCE = \frac{VA}{HC} = \frac{OperatingIncome + HC}{HC} = \frac{OperatingIncome}{HC} + 1$$

So except when OperatingIncome is less than zero, HCE is more than one.

$$SCE = \frac{SC}{VA} = \frac{VA - HC}{VA} = \frac{OperatingIncome + HC - HC}{VA}$$
$$= \frac{OperatingIncome}{VA}$$

Because VA is more than OperatingIncome, SCE is less than one (except when VA is less than zero). If VA is more than zero and OperatingIncome is less than zero, SCE is less than zero. So SCE can only be bigger than HCE if VA is less than zero (see Table A.2, scenario 2), which is a dissatisfying result. Knowing this, it comes as no surprise that Firer and Williams (2003) found that all values of HCE in their sample were bigger than SCE. Wrongly, they concluded: "The sample firms were generally more effective in generating value from its human resource assets than . . . structural assets" (p. 14). This result was simply the effect of the mathematics of the formula.

Fifth, the method ignores the fact that value added is not only produced by human capital, structural capital, and capital employed

Table A.2

Scenarios for the VAIC of British Telecom

Scenario	VA	Operating Income	HC	SC	CE	HCE	SCE	CEE	VAIC
British Telecom (1999)	11,380	7,499	3,881	7,499	19,933	2.93	0.66	0.57	4.16
Scenario 1, HC = SC	11,380	5,690	5,690	5,690	19,933	2.00	0.50	0.57	3.07
Scenario 2 negative VA	−100	−3,981	3,881	−3,981	19,933	−0.03	39.81	−0.01	39.78
Scenario 3, limited CE	11,380	7,499	3,881	7,499	100	2.93	0.66	113.80	117.39

Based on Pulic (2000a). VA, value added; HC, human capital; SC, structural capital; CE, capital employed.

individually, but it is also the result of the synergies between these three. An analysis of the contribution of human capital, structural capital, and capital employed should therefore be extended to include the contribution of human capital/structural capital, human capital/ capital employed, structural capital/capital employed, and human capital/structural capital/capital employed. This is a another reason why the assumption that the relation between human capital and structural capital is reciprocal is incorrect. This assumption ignores synergistic effects. This mistake is a direct consequence of the postulation that Structural Capital = Intellectual Capital − Human Capital. This postulation is false because these types of capital are *non*additive in nature (M'Pherson and Pike, 2001a).

Finally, the solution to add all efficiency indicators to come to one overall indicator is an interesting idea but produces dissatisfying results. Consider for example scenario 3 (see Table A.2), in which British Telecom has little net assets (for example, because of some big liabilities). Capital employed would be small to zero, and as a result CEE and VAIC become very big. So big liabilities can result in very positive VAIC scores, which is another rambling result.

I sympathize with Pulic's (2000b) argument that we should not treat labor simply as an expense. I admire the work he and his team have done in creating awareness of the importance of intellectual capital in regional and national economies, but I think the VAIC method is based on assumptions that can be seriously questioned. Consequently, the method produces dissatisfying results.

A.25 Value Chain Scoreboard

Lev (2001) has developed both a top-down approach (the intangibles scorecard, see Section A.11) and a bottom-up approach: the value chain scoreboard (Lev, 2001). The value chain scoreboard is a measurement method. In a later publication, Lev (2003) renamed it the *value chain blueprint,* but I refer to it as the value chain scoreboard.

A.25.1 Distinctions and Definitions

Lev (2001) uses the same distinctions and definitions as those used in Section A.11.

A.25.2 Problems and Consequences

Lev (2001) proposes a value chain scoreboard to facilitate "the democratization and the externalization of decision-making processes both within organizations and in capital markets" (p. 107). Democratization points toward the increasing role of individual investors in capital markets. They have less access to inside information than analysts and investment funds. This creates an uneven playing field. Externalization points toward the fact that increasingly important decisions that managers need to make are shared with entities residing outside the company itself. This increases the scope of the information required. The objective of the value chain scoreboard is "to provide the needs of the emerging constituencies—primarily individual investors and the myriad partners to the networked corporations—enabling these constituencies to make and execute decisions at the level of professional investors and managers" (Lev, 2001, p. 109).

A.25.3 Solution and Results

According to Lev (2001), the information that is most relevant to decision makers concerns the value chain (or business model) of the enterprise. He describes this value chain as a process of innovation, starting with discovery and learning, through implementation, culminating in the commercialization of new products and services. For each of these three phases of the value chain, Lev (2001) proposes three boxes of indicators (Figure A.25.1).

This model represents a broad cross-section of industries. Specific companies will use specific subsets of indicators (Figure A.25.1).

During the discovery and learning phase, the three boxes represent the three sources of innovation: internal renewal, acquired capabilities, and networking. During the implementation phase, the focus is on evidence of technological feasibility. This can be the granting of a patent or the passing of a drug test. These milestones are important to investors because they reduce the risk associated with R&D investments. The final phase of the value chain signifies the commercialization of the innovation process. Lev (2001) distinguishes between information on customers, performance indicators not included in GAAP (this box includes the concept of IDEs, see Section A.11), and forward-looking information. For each of the boxes, Lev (2001) provides several examples of indicators. These include both input and output indicators, like investments in R&D and number of patents granted.

Specific scoreboard indicators should satisfy three criteria:

1. They should be quantitative.
2. They should be standardized to allow for comparison across firms.

Figure A.25.1

The value chain scoreboard

Discovery and learning	Implementation	Commercialization
1. Internal renewal • Research and development • Work force training and development • Organizational capital, processes	**4. Intellectual property** • Patents, trademarks and copyright • Licensing agreements • Coded know-how	**7. Customers** • Marketing alliances • Brand values • Customer churn and value • On-line sales
2. Acquired capabilities • Technology purchase • Spillover utilization • Capital expenditures	**5. Technological feasibility** • Clinical tests, food and drug administration • Beta tests, working pilots • First mover	**8. Performance** • Revenues, earnings and market share • Innovation revenues • Patent and know-how royalties • Intangibles-based earnings
3. Networking • Research and development alliances and joint ventures • Supplier and customer integration • Communities of practice	**6. Internet** • Threshold traffic • On-line purchases • Major internet alliances	**9. Growth prospect** • Product pipeline dates • Expected efficiency savings • Planned initiatives • Expected break even and cash burn rate

3. They should be confirmed by empirical evidence as relevant to users.

A significant statistical association between the measures and indicators of corporate value is an example of such empirical evidence. Some of Lev's own research provides some good examples (Aboody and Lev, 1998; Amir and Lev, 1996; Gu and Lev, 2002; Lev and Sougiannis, 1996).

The scoreboard is aimed at both internal and external decision making. The difference is in the level of detail provided. For internal purposes, measures are provided at business unit level. For external purposes, aggregated measures are used.

A.25.4 Evaluation

Lev's value chain scoreboard is based on a thorough analysis of the problems of current corporate disclosure. The value chain scoreboard incorporates the result of research into the needs of investors and analysts for additional information. The scoreboard focuses on

Figure A.25.2

The value chain scoreboard for a biotechnology company

Discovery and learning	Implementation	Commercialization
1. Internal renewal • Investment in research and development classified by type (basic, applied) • Investment in IT • # of employees who are star scientists	**4. Intellectual property** • # of patents granted, citations to patents (self- and other) • Cross licensing • Royalty income from patent licensing	**7. Customers** • Marketing alliances • Brand values • Customer churn and value • On-line sales
2. Acquired capabilities • Investment in acquired IT • In-licensing	**5. Technological feasibility** • Results of clinical tests • Food and drug administration approvals	**8. Performance** • Innovation revenues • Revenues form alliances, joint-ventures and patent licensing
3. Networking • Investment in alliances and joint ventures • Total number of alliances, classification of active and dormant ventures	**6. Internet**	**9. Growth prospect** • Product pipeline, expected launch dates of new products • Cash burn rate • Expected market potential for new products

innovation, which is one of the most important drivers of growth and one of the most important variables explaining market-to-book ratios (Lev and Sougiannis, 1999). The framework is easy to understand. It creates a logical (although not causal) relationship between groups of indicators, similar to the four perspectives of a balanced scorecard.

Another strong point is the statistical association that is required between an indicator and a corporate value. This prevents the scoreboard from becoming cluttered with meaningless indicators. A nice example of this is the use in the biotechnology sector of the number of employees who are star scientists as an indicator. There is a statistical association between star scientists and the value of biotechnology companies.

The framework does need some additional fine-tuning. For example, it is not clear why box 6, Internet, is in the implementation phase. The Internet can be a source of renewal (when used as a channel for receiving customer feedback), in which case it is part of the discovery and learning phase. It can also be the channel for commercialization or a means to increase brand value, in which case it is part of the commercialization phase. This may be the reason why On-line Sales is in box 7, Customers, and not in box 6. Further testing of the framework is needed to determine whether it is generic enough to cover all industries. In the financial services industry, for example, intellectual property and technological feasibility play a minor role, leaving the implementation phase almost blank. It may be necessary to expand box 6 to include more indicators that show how service-oriented companies turn innovation into value. A final comment is that, as with any measurement method, the value chain scoreboard does not include yardsticks. This makes it difficult for the user of the information to interpret the results.

Appendix B

Weightless Wealth Tool Kit

B.1 How to Use the Tool Kit

Using the weightless wealth tool kit is all about asking new questions. The tool kit offers a set of questions to help managers operate successfully in the intangible economy. The tool kit consists of

- *Steps:* A plan incorporating 20 steps that can help you in your expedition
- *Questions:* Suggestions for questions you can ask on the way
- *Exercises:* Exercises you can do alone or with others
- *Checklists:* Checklists to help you assess value and determine your core competencies' strengths and weaknesses
- *Calculations:* A method to help you calculate the financial value of your intangibles

You can use the tool kit alone, but the results are better if you involve others in your expedition. You should think of involving employees, customers, partners, and perhaps shareholders and financial analysts. A workshop is a good idea for certain steps, particularly when determining and assessing your core competencies. Such workshops also provide you with the opportunity to start a dialog with your colleagues and employees about the position of your company and its future. Not only will this help develop a sense of involvement among your staff, it will also help strengthen the links within your company and promote a common feeling of identity, purpose, and vision.

B.2 Phase One: Do Intake

The weightless wealth tool kit is a method that can help companies develop strategies to cope with the intangible economy. It is especially suited for companies that are uncertain about their future and do not know how they can adapt to an economy that is based on knowledge, image, and other intangibles. It can help companies that lack self-confidence about their strengths and uniqueness; companies that have difficulty recognizing why they are successful or unsuccessful. This first phase determines whether the weightless wealth tool kit can be useful for your company. You also need to check whether the right conditions are in place to guarantee a successful implementation.

Step 1: Diagnosing Usefulness

Check the items on the following checklist (Figure B.1). The more questions you answer positively, the more likely it is that the weightless wealth tool kit will be a useful tool for you to use.

Step 2: Checking Conditions for Success

To safeguard a successful implementation, the right conditions have to be in place. Check the following items on the checklist (Figure B.2). Do not start implementing the weightless wealth tool kit until you can answer all questions positively.

B.3 Phase Two: Identify Intangible Resources

Step 3: Gathering Basic Information

Questions Regarding General Information

What was your turnover and results during the last three years?
In what branch is your company active?
How well-known is your company and your brand?
How would you describe your position in the market?
How old is your company? At which stage of the life cycle is it?

Questions Regarding Customer Groups and Needs

What groups of customers do you serve?
What percentage of your turnover is generated by each of these groups?

Figure B.1

Checklist for assessing the usefulness of the tool kit

Item	Yes/No
1. Are you reconsidering your company's future or developing a new corporate strategy?	
2. Are you insecure about how to respond to the intangible economy?	
3. Do you have difficulty deciding in which elements of your company to invest?	
4. Are you insecure about your company's strong points and future potential?	
5. Are you insecure about what makes your company successful and unique?	
6. Are you insecure about the most important intangible resources your company uses?	
7. Are you insecure about whether you are managing your intangible resources properly?	
8. Are you dissatisfied about the attention management gives to managing intangible resources?	
9. Are you insecure about what capabilities your company needs to have to achieve its strategic objectives?	
10. For those questions you have answered yes, are these issues relatively urgent?	

Which customer need does your company fulfill for each of these customer groups?

Questions Regarding Market and Competition

Who are your company's competitors in today's market?
What developments are taking place in the market?
Which (type of) companies are likely to enter your market as newcomers?

Questions Regarding Products and Services

Which products or services do you offer?
What is the turnover per product/service?
What percentage is this of the total turnover?
What is the gross profit per product/service?

Figure B.2

Checklist for assessing the conditions for success

Item	Yes/No
1. Are you a knowledge-intensive company (do more than 20% of your employees have a higher education)?	
2. Are you a small or middle-size company (1–1,000 employees)?[1]	
3. Is management willing to spend time on the weightless wealth tool kit?	
4. Does management have the necessary skills to look at the company in a more abstract way?	
5. Is management willing to look at the company in a judgmental and critical way?	
6. Is management willing to look at some of the company's weaknesses?	
7. Is management willing to think about how the weak points can be improved?	
8. Is your company's corporate culture open enough to allow discussions about your company's weak points?	
9. Do you have access to the skills necessary to conduct interviews and to facilitate workshops?	
10. Do people from various departments have time to provide the necessary information?	

Questions Regarding Organization and Staff

How many people work in what functions?
Which people are essential for the continuity of your company?
What does the organizational chart look like?

Exercise: Analyze the Company Processes

Describe in broad terms the processes in your company. This is very important because it helps show in which part of the value chain the core competencies can be found. What's more, thinking about processes helps you turn a complex reality into something abstract. You should think "from the outside in." In other words, think from the

---

[1] If your company employs more than 1,000 employees, you can still use the tool kit. However, you may need to focus your analysis on the core competencies that are common across the company.

product back through the processes that lead up to that product. Try to combine as many subprocesses as possible into one main process or steps in the total process. Should several main processes exist (in practice there are rarely more than five) in the company, you should devise a process description for each of these. It is important that a survey be conducted of all the major processes within the company. It is not necessary to be complete and detailed. When describing the processes, the following points are of importance:

What is the output of the company divisions?
Which main processes are required for this output?
What are the steps/stages in these processes?
What input (knowledge, material, time) is necessary for this process?
Which quantities can you allocate to the process (for example, turnover, costs, throughput time, number of staff, number of products)?
Which relationships or dependencies are essential for this process?
What are the essential functions (management, systems, knowledge, skills)?
How are the processes controlled?
Which management processes (for example, planning and control processes) are crucial for the company?

Questions Regarding Success Factors

What makes the company successful?
What does the company do better than other companies in the market area?
What factors are essential for the future success of the company?

Exercise: Interview Your Employees

People on the work floor often know a lot more about a company than management. So go talk with ten employees and ask them about things such as

What are we doing right?
What are we doing wrong?
What complaints do our customers make?
What is the greatest compliment you would give to our company?
What is your major complaint?
What is your dream for the future of our company?
What warning would you give our company?

Step 4: Creating Ideas

Questions Regarding Looking at Your Customers

Why do customers like your company?

Why do they come to you rather than choose the products or services of one of your competitors?

What benefits do you offer to your customers that other companies apparently do not offer?

What fundamental advantages set you apart from the rest of the field?

Which new advantages would you like to offer your customers?

Which competencies and skills will you need to acquire to offer these advantages successfully and continuously?

Exercise: Interview Your Customers

Ask your customers directly, preferably in a one-on-one interview situation, exactly what they think the strong points of your company are. Ask what they think should be improved. Ask what skills they perceive your company possessing. Ask them where you score better than the competition, and where the competition scores better than you. Make sure the interview is carried out in an open and honest manner. Ask the interviewee to be honest. Listen carefully; not only to what they do say, but also to what they don't say, which is often just as illuminating.

Questions Regarding Looking at Your Products and Services

Do your products and services have added value?

What advantages and benefits do your customers enjoy once they have purchased them or made use of them?

Do your products or services add value for your customers and help them enjoy something that they would not otherwise enjoy?

What are the specific requirements you need to manufacture your product or to offer your service?

Are their any special skills and technologies that are demanded?

Does the product or service require specialized knowledge?

When you are recruiting new employees, is there a specific type of person you need?

Do they have to have special knowledge, a specific skill, or a certain mentality?

What are the essentials you require them to have to do the job properly?

If one of your most important stakeholders were to call you and ask you to improve your product or service, what would be the one thing you would try to improve?

Exercise: Identify Important Intangibles

We know that there are many intangibles in any company. But do you really know the ones that make the difference in your own? Ask yourself what they are. List them under the following five categories:

1. Endowments
   What are the unique assets of your company? Think about things you have inherited from the past that have made the company what it is (customer relationships, brand awareness, and so forth).
   What value do these have in the eyes of your customer?
   How important are they to the success of the company?

2. Skills and tacit knowledge
   What are the unique areas of knowledge and skills in your market? In this context, unique means differentiating.
   What value does the client get from them?

3. Collective values and norms
   What are the core values shared throughout your company?
   What norms are derived from them? (For example, the value is perfection in presentation; the norm is that any piece of correspondence is free of grammatical and typographical errors). Concentrate on the essentials and try to describe the values at the highest level of abstraction possible and try to show how various concrete norms contribute to this value. Consider the company as a whole and place the company in its proper context with its surroundings.
   How much of this is noticed by the customer?
   How would you describe the style of management?
   What does management consider its prime objective?

4. Technology and explicit knowledge
   What systems and technologies does your company have that allows it to supply its products and services?
   What handbooks and procedures are used within your company?

5. Primary and management processes
   Which primary processes are essential?
   Which management processes (for example, planning and control processes) are crucial for the company?

Exercise: Brief a New Employee

You should also ask yourself which of these intangibles are essential within your specific branch. There is a good way of determining which of these are of primary importance. Imagine that you have employed a highly skilled professional from a different branch of industry. You have to tell her those things that are vital within your company—all the pieces of corporate wisdom and technical expertise that everybody in the company needs to know to remain successful. What would you tell your new employee? When you tell her, which topics would be open for discussion? Which of the gems of wisdom have become folk-lore and have little or no significance under the current circumstances? Which of these ideals could lose their relevance in the future?

Questions Regarding Looking at Your Competition

Using the five categories already mentioned, what are the intangibles that make your competitor unique?

Will the competition be able to offer products and services that are the same as yours?

Will they be able to catch up or even overtake you?

How can you improve your existing product or service offering to maintain your competitive edge?

Exercise: Winners and Losers

Make a list of fundamental factors that distinguish your market's winners from its losers. Again, be honest with yourself and look at your company's current position. Draw up plans to eliminate the losing factors and increase the winning factors.

Exercise: Collision Course

List the three most dangerous courses of action your competition could take to win market share from you. Be creative and be honest. Consider all possibilities—even those that may currently seem to belong to the world of fantasy. Then, once you have listed these three strategic threats, plan actions that you could take to thwart them. A further possibility here is, of course, that you come up with ideas that could be of strategic importance to you and give you an even greater lead over your competition!

Exercise: Switch Jobs

Imagine that your leading competitor offered you the job of CEO. What actions would you take in your new job to attack your previous (in other words, your current) company? Such a scenario helps expose strategic weaknesses in your current company and can help you devise improvement programs to rectify the situation before you come under attack.

Exercise: Look at Successful Products and Services

Analyze successful products and services and determine what makes them successful:

What makes a product a success?
Is it because of technology?
Customer appeal?
Added benefits?

Exercise: Look at Successful Projects in Your Company's Past

What contributed to that success?
What aspects need to be continued in the future, and what aspects need to be relegated to the past?

Exercise: List Recent Landmarks in Your Company's Success

What factors have contributed to these successes?
Are they the result of the development of a new technology?
The creative use of an existing skill?
Were they the result of an acquisition?
Or because you recently increased your pool of talented employees?

Exercise: Look at Your Current Innovations

What new products and services are in the pipeline?
Are they very new developments or are they a reaction to the success of a competitor?
Do these imminent innovations add value to your company and to the way your customers benefit from using your products or services?

Exercise: Armageddon: Look at Your Future

Imagine that in the coming ten years your company's prospects become so bad that there is only a 10% chance that things could get any worse. You have almost hit rock bottom. Can you describe that future? Can you list internal and external causes for such a doomsday scenario? Be honest. Look failure in the face and describe the causes of that failure.

Exercise: Conquest

Imagine that in the coming ten years your company's prospects improve to such a degree that there is only a 10% chance that things will improve even further. Can you describe that future? Can you list all the external causes and internal measures that created such a rosy future? Again, be honest. Look success in the face and describe the reasons for that success.

Step 5: Defining a Number of Core Competencies

You have completed all the preparatory work. You now have a better view of your company. You know all the forces working in your market—customers, innovation, and competition. You have listed intangible resources that you believe are essential for success. You know where you stand in comparison with your main competitors. Now is the time to define a number of core competencies.

Exercise: Define Core Competencies

1. Start with "the ability to. . . ." Your company may have a unique ability to do something that sets you apart from the rest of the competition. Try to define this uniqueness.
2. Think of a combination of skills, knowledge, processes, and culture that together form a unique competence.
3. Always think of a customer benefit. You work for your customer, and a core competence should always reflect a benefit for your customer.
4. Give your core competence a catchy name.
5. Write down a very precise description of the core competence. The uniqueness of your company is probably founded in very subtle things. Catching this subtlety in a definition is the most important step in determining your core competencies. If you fail to do so, others will perceive your competencies as platitudes, clichés, or trivialities that are applicable to any other company. To force yourself to be very precise you should provide definitions and synonyms for every important word in your core competence description.

Step 6: Breaking Down Your Competence into Intangible Resources

Exercise: Break Down Core Competencies

Break down each of the preliminary core competencies into the underlying intangibles. When you are satisfied with the result, you can move on to the next stage: testing for strengths and weaknesses. The result could be that a core competence scores poorly on the majority of test questions. This could mean that you return to this stage to reassess your core competencies.

B.4 Phase Three: Conduct Value Assessments

I developed five checklists to help you execute a value assessment of your core competencies. The checklists identify strengths and weaknesses. The results of applying the checklists to each of your core competencies will be a score between 0 to 5 points. The checklists will show

- Added value
- Competitiveness
- Potential
- Sustainability
- Robustness

It is often beneficial to use these checklists in a workshop and have your managers discuss each item, either plenary or in teams. Ask them how they would score each of the core competencies on the items of the checklist. Then ask them if they can come up with measures that will help improve the score. Record all suggestions carefully because you will need them when writing the management agenda.

Step 7: Testing for Added Value

The factual data used for answering the questions of the added value checklist (Figure B.3) often comes from customer satisfaction surveys and from additional market analyses.

Step 8: Testing for Competitiveness

The essential data for answering the questions of the competitiveness checklist (Figure B.4) is largely derived from competitive research together with any further business intelligence.

Step 9: Testing for Potential

The fundamental data for answering the potential checklist (Figure B.5) is gathered through market research, together with additional research into economic and social developments.

Figure B.3

Added value checklist

Added Value	Score (1 = yes, 0 = no)
The core competence offers a substantial benefit for your customers or a substantial cost saving for your company.	
Customers demand this specific benefit or cost saving.	
This benefit is important for a large number of customers; it goes further than just "nice to have."	
Customers will continue expecting this benefit in the near future; it is not simply a passing fancy.	
Leadership in this core competence makes customers think you are different from the competition, rather than just better.	
Total score added value	

Figure B.4

Competitiveness checklist

Competitiveness	Score (1 = yes, 0 = no)
Fewer than five of your competitors share this particular competence.	
You are superior to your competitors in most aspects of this particular competence.	
You invest substantially more time and money in this competence than your competitors.	
Your customers choose your products or services largely because you have this competence.	
Your leadership in this competence is generally recognized and can be illustrated by articles in trade journals, patents, and so on.	
Total score competitiveness	

Step 10: Testing for Sustainability

The fundamental data for answering the sustainability checklist (Figure B.6) is gathered through market research, together with additional business intelligence.

Figure B.5

Potential checklist

Potential	Score (1 = yes, 0 = no)
There is an increasing demand for products/services that can be provided thanks to this core competence.	
The core competence allows the development of new products and services in the future.	
The core competence allows new markets to be entered in the future.	
There are no economic threats (customers, suppliers, competitors) that will adversely affect the use of this competence.	
There are no social threats (regulatory and social) that will adversely affect the use of this competence.	
Total score potential	

Figure B.6

Sustainability checklist

Sustainability	Score (1 = yes, 0 = no)
This core competence is scarce in your branch.	
It would require considerable investments in time and/or money for competitors to master this competence.	
Patents, trademarks, and other legal measures protect components of the competence.	
This competence is a combination of a number of intangibles such as skills, knowledge, processes, and corporate culture, thus making it difficult to copy.	
This competence cannot be obtained through acquisition or from other outside sources.	
Total score sustainability	

Step 11: Testing for Robustness

The fundamental data for answering the robustness checklist (Figure B.7) is gathered through organizational research. The following checklist deals with the vulnerability of the intangibles that

Figure B.7

Robustness checklist

Robustness	Score (1 = yes, 0 = no)
The group of people that possess the skills and knowledge crucial for this competence is vulnerable.	
The values and norms on which this competence is built are under pressure.	
The technology and information technology systems that form part of this competence are vulnerable.	
The primary and management processes that this competence uses are unreliable.	
The endowments on which this core competence depends (like the corporate image or the installed client base) are vulnerable.	
Total = A	
Total score robustness	5 – A =

contribute to the core competence. If you answer yes to a question, then there is a degree of vulnerability. To achieve a robustness score between 0 to 5 points, you must subtract the result achieved at the end (marked "A") from 5 points.

You have now completed a value assessment of your company's core competencies. The next step is to start calculating their value using a financial valuation.

B.5 Phase Four: Perform Financial Valuation

To calculate the financial value of your core competencies, you require information about your company's past core earnings and future earnings. The value is then calculated in five steps using this and other information. It is useful, when making the calculations, to use a computer spreadsheet program. The calculation method is partly based on Gu and Lev (2002).

Step 12: Determining Earnings: Calculating Normalized Earnings

First you calculate your company's earnings over a number of years. Earnings are the result of revenues minus costs, excluding all unusual and extraordinary items. The purpose is to come to an estimate of future earnings, but we also include past earnings to validate the likelihood of future earnings.

Gather information on your company's past earnings for the past three to five years. Then gather information on the expected earnings for the next three to five years. You can do this by looking at consensus earnings forecasts by analysts if available. If these earnings are not available, use your company's financial forecasts or develop your own forecasts based on the pattern of the company's past sales. Use these six to ten earnings numbers to calculate an average, which we will call *normalized earnings*. You now have defined your company's enterprise performance.

Step 13: Calculating a Fair Return for Tangible and Financial Assets

Earnings are the result of combining tangible, financial, and intangible resources. You need to make sure financial and intangible resources receive a fair return from the normalized earnings. To do this you first need to obtain the book value of all tangible and financial assets from your balance sheet. Then you calculate a fair return for these assets by applying a fair return rate. Use a rate of 7% for your tangible assets and a rate of 4.5% for your financial assets. Subtract the returns for these assets from your normalized earnings. What remains is the contribution of intangible resources to your normalized earnings. Gu and Lev (2002) call these *intangibles-driven earnings*.

Step 14: Forecasting Intangibles-Driven Earnings

Now you need to forecast these IDEs for a number of years. You do this for three periods: years 1 through 5, years 6 through 10, and year 11 to infinity. It is useful to use a spreadsheet program like Microsoft Excel. Name the cell in row 1, column B, Now. Name columns C to M: Year 1, Year 2, . . . Year 11. Use the next row to type in the number of each consecutive year. We need these numbers later. So name row 2, column A, Year. Type in column C to M the numbers 1 to 11.

Name the cell in row 3, column A, Growth rate. Name the cell in row 4, column A, IDE. Put the IDEs that you have calculated in step 13 in the second column (cell B4). Now calculate the average growth rate of your company's earnings based on the forecasts for the first three to five years (see step 12). Put this growth rate in row 3, columns C to G. Use this growth rate to forecast the IDEs from year 1 to year 5 and put these numbers in row 4, columns C to G. In Microsoft Excel you can do this by entering the formula = B4 * (1 + C3) into cell C3 and copying this formula to the other cells. This concludes the forecast for the first period.

Now put the long-term growth rate of the economy (3%) into cell M3, underneath the column Year 11. We will assume that from year 11 to infinity your IDEs will grow with the long-term growth rate of the economy. Now calculate the difference between the growth rate as used in the first period and the long-term growth rate of the economy. Divide this difference by five and you will know how much the growth rate will need to become bigger or smaller each year to converge linearly into the long-term growth rate.

For example, let us assume the growth rate of your IDE was 8%. The long-term growth rate is 3%. The difference is 5%. This means the growth rate needs to diminish 1% a year to converge to 3%. For year 6 it will be 7%, for year 7 it will be 6%, for year 8 it will be 5%, for year 9 it will be 4%, and for year 10 it will be 3%. You can use a formula to calculate this growth rate. For year 6 (cell H3) this formula will be = $M3 + (10 − H2) * ($G3 − $M3)/5. Copy this formula to cells I3 to L3. Apply these growth rates in your spreadsheet to calculate IDEs for years 6 through 10. You can simply copy the formula that you used for the first period in cell G4 to cells H4 to L4. This concludes the forecast for the second period.

For the third period, we will assume that the IDEs will grow by 3% a year. More on this later.

Step 15: Calculating the Financial Value of Intangible Resources

You have now gathered all the information you need to calculate the value of your intangible resources. It may sound complicated, but the value of your intangible resources is equal to the net present value of the IDEs. To turn IDEs into a present value we use a discount factor that reflects three things: the rate of inflation, your cost of capital, and a risk factor that reflects the risk associated with these earnings.

You can calculate the present value of the IDE using the following general formula:

$$V = \frac{IDE1}{(1+i)} + \frac{IDE2}{(1+i)^2} + \frac{IDE3}{(1+i)^3} + etc.,$$

where V is the value of intangible resources, $IDEn$ is the IDE in year n, and i is the discount rate.

Use your spreadsheet again. In cell A5 type "Discount rate" and in cell A6 type "Present value." In cell B5 type the discount rate you are going to use (for example, 18%). In cell C5 calculate the discount factor for year 1 by entering the formula = 1/POWER((1 + $B5);C2). Copy this formula to cells D5 to L5. Use row 6 to calculate the present value of the IDE for each year by simply multiplying the IDE by the discount factor. You can do this by entering the formula = C4*C5 into cell C6 and copying it to cells D6 to L6.

Now you only need to calculate the present value of the IDE for year 11 to infinity. To do this we use the following formula:

$$V = pvIDE10\frac{(1+g)}{i-g},$$

where V is the value of intangible resources, $pvIDE10$ is the present value of the IDE in year 10, g is the growth rate, and i is the discount rate. Enter the following formula in cell M6: = L6 * (1 + M3)/ (B5 − M3).

To calculate the discounted value of the expected IDE, sum the values of the individual years. You can do this by entering in cell B6 the formula = SUM(C6 : M6).

For example, let us assume a toy manufacturing company has IDEs of $8 million. Its average growth rate for the first five years is 8%. The discount factor is 18%. The spreadsheet will look like the one presented in Figure B.8.

Step 16: Allocating the Financial Value to Core Competencies

Exercise: Identify Products and Services

Determining the value of the core competencies starts with an analysis of the products to which the core competencies make a contribution. For convenience, you should make a list of three to seven products or product groups. Your list should be so designed to allow

- As broad a spread over the core competencies as possible, so that not all core competencies contribute to every product
- It to be understandable and informative
- It to match as far as possible the structure of the figures produced by your financial group

Figure B.8

Example of the spreadsheet for a toy manufacturing company

	A	B	C	D	E	F	G	H	I	J	K	L	M
		Now	Year 1	Year 2	Year 3	Year 4	Year 5	Year 6	Year 7	Year 8	Year 9	Year 10	Year 11
1													
2	Year		1	2	3	4	5	6	7	8	9	10	11
3	Growth rate		8,0%	8,0%	8,0%	8,0%	8,0%	7,0%	6,0%	5,0%	4,0%	3,0%	3,0%
4	IDE	8,0	8,7	9,3	10,1	10,9	11,8	12,6	13,3	14,0	14,6	15,0	
5	Discount rate	18%	84,7%	71,8%	60,9%	51,6%	43,7%	37,0%	31,4%	26,6%	22,5%	19,1%	
6	Present value	69,4	7,3	6,7	6,1	5,6	5,1	4,7	4,2	3,7	3,3	2,9	19,7

Gather information about the earnings per product group from last years' financial data. Use these data to calculate the relative share of each product group in the total earnings of your company.

Calculation: Calculate Intangible-Driven Earnings Per Product

You need to know what part of the value of your intangible resources can be attributed to which product group. Use the relative share of each group in the total earnings to allocate the value of your intangibles to the product groups that you have identified.

Exercise: Create a Core Competence–Product Matrix

The contribution of a core competence to the realization of a product always varies. The core competence can make an essential, substantial, or supporting contribution, but may also make no contribution at all. The contribution is essential if the core competence constitutes the core of the product. It is substantial if the core competence contributes to the success of the product. It is supporting if the core competence supports the realization of the product. This is shown in the competence–product matrix.

Construct a matrix in, for example, a spreadsheet, showing along the top the products, and on the left the core competencies. Indicate in each cell of the matrix the contribution each competence makes to the product, using the following: 0, no contribution; 1, supporting contribution; 2, substantial contribution; and 3, essential contribution. Add the various columns and calculate the relative weights (in percent).

Calculation: Allocate Intangible-Driven Earnings

Use a spreadsheet to show the relative share each competence has in the product using the previous scores. Use these percentages to allocate the IDEs of the products to the core competencies. This results in a total value of each core competence.

For example, let us assume our toy manufacturing company produces four products with the help of three core competencies. In this case, the spreadsheet may look like the one presented in Figure B.9.

This step concludes the financial valuation of your company's core competencies. Now you need to start drawing some conclusions.

Figure B.9

Example of the value of core competencies for a toy manufacturing company

Products:	Jigsaw Puzzles	Puzzle books	Board games	Computer games	Total	
Earnings	2.9	1.6	0.3	3.2	8.0	
Share in earnings	36%	20%	4%	39%	100%	
Share in intangible value	25.0	14.2	2.8	27.4	69.4	
Core competencies:						
Printing and die-cutting	60%	0%	29%	0%		
Graphic design	20%	33%	29%	50%		
Intellectual entertainment	20%	67%	42%	50%		
Total	100%	100%	100%	100%		
Value of core competencies:						
Printing and die-cutting	15.0	-	0.8	-	15.8	23%
Graphic design	5.0	4.7	0.8	13.7	24.2	35%
Intellectual entertainment	5.0	9.5	1.2	13.7	29.4	42%
Total	25.0	14.2	2.8	27.4	69.4	100%

B.6 Phase Five: Develop Management Agenda

You have now gathered information about your core competencies, their strengths and weaknesses, and their financial value. Next you need to create a management agenda. The management agenda reflects the implication for management of the results. It describes how you can improve the value of your core competencies by raising their added value, competitiveness, potential, sustainability, and robustness.

Step 17: Gathering All Weaknesses

Exercise: Find All Weak Spots

In steps 1 through 16 you discovered a number of your company's weaknesses. These are evident from the interviews, exercises, and the core competence checklists. Gather this information and analyze it. Determine whether each of the weak points fits into one of the following areas:

- Issues related to your company's added value to customers
- Things that diminish your competitiveness
- Problems that block your future potential
- Elements that make that your competencies easily copied and thus reducing their sustainability
- Issues of robustness concerning the way your competencies are anchored within the organization

Step 18: Developing Solutions and Writing a Management Agenda

Exercise: Develop Solutions

Group all issues into the areas identified in step 17 and create a table. In the left column define, as clearly as possible, all problems you have discovered. In the right column, record all suggestions you have gathered to solve these problems.

Exercise: Summarize the Results

Now summarize these results in the following format presented in Figure B.10.

Figure B.10

Format for the management agenda

Added value *Key question: Is [name of the company] delivering added value beyond customer's expectations on a continuing basis?* Answer Solutions
Competitiveness *Key question: Will [name of the company] continue to stay unique compared with its competitors?* Answer Solutions
Potential *Key question: How can [name of the company] create new opportunities using its core competencies?* Answer Solutions
Sustainability *Key question: Does [name of the company] protect its core competencies from the competition?* Answer Solutions
Robustness *Key question: Will [name of the company] run the risk of losing its core competencies?* Answer Solutions

B.7 Phase Six: Report Value Dashboard

Finally, summarize all findings into one comprehensive report. I designed a format for this report to communicate the essence and implications of your findings. At the center of the report there is a value dashboard that gives the main results at a glance. It shows your company's core competencies, their scores on the core competence checklist with the use of "traffic lights," and the financial value of the competencies.

Step 19: Drawing the Value Dashboard

Exercise: Practice Your Drawing Skills

You can draw the value dashboard using a presentation program like Microsoft's PowerPoint. PowerPoint has a feature to insert doughnut-

Figure B.11

Example of a value dashboard

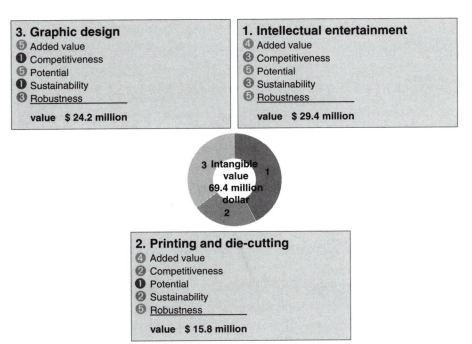

shaped graphs that are useful to show the relative value of each core competence. The result may look like the one presented in Figure B.11.

Step 20: Writing the Report

Now it is time to put all your findings onto paper. Write a brief report that has the following structure:

- Front page
- Name of the company
- Title: The Intangible Resources of [name of the company]
- Subtitle describing the essentials of the findings in one sentence
- Management agenda: This section contains the management agenda created in step 18.
- Introduction: This section contains a summary of the purpose of the investigation and the way you conducted it. It also shows the structure of the report.

Table B.1

Format for the Overview of Intangible Resources				
Skills and Tacit Knowledge	Collective Values and Norms	Technology and Knowledge Explicit	Primary and Management Processes	Endowments

- Overview of intangible resources: This section contains a summary of the most important intangible resources. It includes Table B.1.

- Overview of core competencies: This section describes the core competencies of your company. It also describes the results of the core competence checklist.

- Value dashboard: Include the value dashboard you created in step 19.

- Recommendations: Include recommendations based on the information you gathered. Each recommendation describes a specific action that management could take to improve the management of the intangible resources of the company. This section translates the management agenda into concrete actions.

Congratulations! You have now finished the implementation of the weightless wealth tool kit.

List of Figures

List of Tables

Glossary of Terms

Abstract theory   Theory that neither provides explanation nor can be used to develop practical methods

Added value test   A test designed to assess the extent to which a core competence delivers customer value

Book value   The reported stockholders' equity (less the liquidating value of any preferred shares), which represents the difference between assets and liabilities, both of which are most often valued at historical costs

Collective values and norms   The collective definition within an organization of good and bad and right and wrong

Competitiveness test   A test designed to assess the extent to which a core competence is competitively unique

Core competence   A bundle of intangible resources that enables a company to provide a particular benefit to customers

Correspondence theory of truth   Theory that states that the criterion for truth is "correspondence with reality"

Cost approach   Approach to valuation that uses costs to determine value

Deduction   The act of determining something from general principles in relation to a particular thing

Design   A representation of a system or process to be realized

Design cycle   A series of steps used to craft an initial design of a new method

Design objective   Answering the question as posed by the design problem by creating a design or method that helps solve the problem

Design problem   A question that asks how a system or process can be realized that helps solve a specific problem

Design science   A way of practicing science with the primary goal of diagnosing situations, defining problems, and improving situations

Developing multiple case studies A scientific methodology aimed at refining a method that is being designed as a result of the design knowledge generated in sequential cases

Diagnosis An assessment of a situation with the intention to define a problem and to assess its causes

Distinction A combination of words used to separate a phenomenon from its background

Empirical claim The extent to which a set of distinctions is able to provide explanations and predictions

Empirical cycle The scientific process used to test the validity of empirical propositions

Empirical method A consistent set of steps to achieve a certain goal based on tested and grounded means—end relationships

Empirical proposition A proposition that describes, explains, or predicts reality

Empirical theory A set of interconnected general and specific statements, of which at least some are statements predicting certain events under certain conditions

Endowments Intangible resources that a company has inherited from the past

Evaluation Comparison between the results of an observation and the expectations

Explanation Set of causal relationships able to create insight into the question of why a phenomenon occurred

Explanatory science A way of practicing science with the primary goal of describing, explaining, and predicting phenomena

Financial resources Monetary resources that are able to produce future benefits for an organization

Financial valuation A comparative measurement of something with respect to its embodiment of a certain value that uses money as a denominator of value

Functional requirements Requirements that define the results a method needs to produce

Goodwill The excess of the cost of an acquired company over the sum of identifiable net assets

Grounded theory Theory that has been tested for validity and was not rejected

Guidelines Rules or suggestions on how to improve a situation with regard to the defined problem of that situation

Human assets   See human resources

Human resources   The people employed by a company

Hypothesis   Tentative prediction about the occurrence of phenomena and their causal relationships

Implementation   The realization of a designed method through a series of interventions

Income approach   An approach to valuation that uses future income to determine value

Induction   The act of determining general principles from a particular situation

Insight   Deeper understanding as a result of a process of sense making

Intangible asset   A claim to future benefits that does not have a physical or financial embodiment

Intangible economy   A description of the economy that stresses the growing importance of intangible resources in creating added value

Intangible perspective   A way of looking at phenomena like the economy or organizations that highlights and emphasizes the importance of intangible resources

Intangible resources   Nonmonetary resources without physical substance that in combination are able to produce future benefits for an organization

Intangibles   See intangible resources

Intellectual capital   A subset of intangible resources that includes all resources that are based on intellectual capabilities and activities

Interpretation   To assign meaning to a set of words

Inventorying multiple case studies   A scientific methodology aimed at testing the same method several times in different cases

Knowledge management scan   A tool to assess the quality of the way a company manages knowledge

Knowledge value chain   A model of the way knowledge flows from input to output

Limitations   Boundaries for finding solutions to the design problem

Limiting conditions   Requirements the contexts place on the method when applied

Management   The process of allocating, and in the case of intangible resources also nurturing, resources; involves sense making, decision making, and communicating

Management and primary processes Chains of continued sets of actions performed intentionally to manage an organization and to produce products and services

Management research The scientific discipline that studies organizations with the purpose of either explaining or improving their performance; done in a rigorous way that involves testing of empirical and/or practical propositions

Market approach Approach to valuation that uses market price to determine value

Market value The most probable price that a company would bring in a competitive and open market under all conditions requisite to a fair sale

Meaning The idea that is the result of applying a set of distinctions in a specific situation

Measurement The process of assigning scaled numbers to items in such a way that the relationships that exist in reality between the possible states of a variable are reflected in the relationships between the numbers on the scale

Method A consistent set of steps to achieve a certain goal

Methodology A set of rules about the process of scientific inquiry

Natural sciences Sciences that study the physical world

Object design The design of an intervention or artifact

Operational requirements Requirements that define the ease of use of the method as defined by the contexts in which the method needs to be successful

Operationalization The translation of variables into observable entities

Organization A group of people involved in a network of inter-subjectively shared meanings that are sustained through the development and use of common language and everyday social interaction, producing goods, and/or services by combining financial, tangible, and intangible resources

Physical world The array of physical phenomena

Potential test A test designed to assess the extent to which a core competence can produce new and promising products and services in the future

Practical claim The extent to which a set of distinctions is able to provide diagnosis of a situation and guidelines for improvement

Practical method A consistent set of steps to achieve improvement in a particular situation or to solve a problem

Practical proposition A proposition that diagnoses or "problemizes" reality or provides guidelines for improvement

Practical relevance The contribution of research to the capability of solving a specific problem

Practical theory Tested and grounded means—end relationships that can be used to create a consistent set of steps to achieve a certain goal

Pragmatic theory of truth Theory of truth that states that the criterion of truth is "everything that works in practice"

Prediction Tentative statement about the occurrence of a phenomenon (not necessarily in the future)

Problem Discrepancy between the actual and the desired situation

Process design The method used to design the solution to the problem

Realization design The plan for the realization of the intervention or for the actual building of the artifact

Reconciliation A process of being ourselves but yet seeing and understanding how the other's perspective can help our own

Reconstructed logic An idealization of scientific practice

Reflective cycle The scientific process used to test a practical proposition

Regulative cycle Steps undertaken to solve a problem; consists roughly of defining the problem out of its "messy" context, planning the intervention, applying the intervention, and evaluating

Reliability The extent to which a procedure produces a stable result, independent of random variables like the person who is applying the procedure

Requirements Demands for the characteristics and abilities of a practical method

Robustness test A test designed to assess the extent to which a core competence is securely anchored in the organization

Science A specific way of making sense that follows a rigorous set of rules

Scientific relevance The contribution of research to the knowledge of the subject under investigation

Sense making   The process of using language to create distinctions with regard to the world that give us insight, allow us to make predictions, and are the basis for our actions

Skills and tacit knowledge   The abilities and knowledge that reside within the heads and hearts of employees

Social constructions   Phenomena in the social world created by a combination of words used to separate it from its background

Social world   The array of nonphysical phenomena produced by interacting human beings who are constantly involved in a process of sense making

Solution   Something that solves a problem

Strategic knowledge map   A map of all knowledge domains that are important for the future success of a company

Success   The extent to which a method produces the desired results

Sustainability test   A test designed to assess the extent to which a core competence is difficult to imitate

Tangible resources   Nonmonetary resources with physical substance that are able to produce future benefits for an organization

Technology and explicit knowledge   Industrial methods and knowledge that have been embedded or codified in processes, procedures, databases, and other nonhuman means of storage

Test   An inquiry into the validity of a theory or the success of a method

Theory   A set of interconnected general and specific statements, of which at least some are statements predicting certain events under certain conditions

Truth, conditional success criterion   The situation in which action based on a practical proposition leads to success as defined by that proposition

Truth, conditional validity criterion   The situation in which observations based on an empirical proposition validate predictions derived from that proposition

Validity, logical—positivist view   The extent to which a proposition corresponds with reality

Valuation   A comparative assessment or measurement of something with respect to its embodiment of a certain value

Value   The degree of usefulness or desirability of something, especially in comparison with other things

Value assessment A comparative assessment or measurement of something with respect to its embodiment of a certain value that uses a nonobservable criterion of value

Value measurement A comparative assessment or measurement of something with respect to its embodiment of a certain value that uses a nonmonetary but observable criterion for value

References

Aboody, D., and Lev, B. (1998) "The value–relevance of intangibles: the case of software capitalization." *Journal of Accounting Research Supplement*, (36):161–191.

Adams, Douglas. (1979) *The hitch hiker's guide to the galaxy.* London: Pan Books.

American Institute of Certified Public Accountants (AICPA). (1994) *Improving business reporting: a customer focus.* New York: AICPA.

Amir, E., and Lev, B. (1996) "Value–relevance of non-financial information: the wireless communications industry." *Journal of Accounting and Economics*, (22):3–30.

Andriessen, D. (2001) "Weightless wealth: four modifications to standard IC theory." *Journal of Intellectual Capital*, 2(3):204–214.

Andriessen, D. (2002a, December) "Measuring intangibles: selecting the right tools for the job." In: *Finance & Management.* Monthly newsletter of the Institute of Chartered Accountants in England and Wales: 6–8.

Andriessen, D. (2002b) *The financial value of intangibles: searching for the Holy Grail.* Presented at the 5th World Congress on Intellectual Capital, McMaster University, Hamilton, Ontario, Canada.

Andriessen, D., and Tissen, R. (2000) *Weightless wealth: find your real value in a future of intangibles assets.* London: Financial Times Prentice Hall.

Arthur, W. B. (1996, July–August) "Increasing returns and the new world of business." *Harvard Business Review*, 100–109.

Baaij, M., Lekkerkerk, P., van der en Weert, N. (1999) "Kerncompetentiesbenenadering Prahalad en Hamel slechts beperkt uitvoerbaar." *Holland Management Review*, 67:24–29.

Bank Ltd. (2000), Annual report 1999.

Barnard, C. I. (1938). *The functions of the executive.* Cambridge: Harvard University Press.

Barth, M. E., Clement, M. B., Foster, G., and Kasznik, R. (2003) "Brand values and capital market valuation." In: Hand, J., and Lev, B., eds. *Intangible assets: values, measures, and risks.* New York: Oxford University Press, 153–184.

Batchelor, A. (1999, February) "Is the balance sheet outdated." *Accountancy*, Institute of Chartered Accountants in England & Wales.

Bedrijfskunde, Tijdschrift voor modern management, (1996) Jaargang 68/2.

Bedrijfskunde, Tijdschrift voor modern management, (1994) Jaargang 66/1.

Biemans, W. G., and van der Meer–Kooistra, J. (1994) "Case research voor bedrijfskundig onderzoek." *Bedrijfskunde*, jaargang 66/1:51–56.

Blair, M. M., and Wallman, S. M. (2001) *Unseen wealth.* New York: The Brookings Institution.

Bontis, N. (2002) "Managing organizational knowledge by diagnosing Intellectual Capital: framing and advancing the state of the field." In: Bontis, N., ed. *World Congress on intellectual capital readings.* Boston: Butterworth Heinemann, 621–642.

Bontis, N. (2001) "Assessing knowledge assets: a review of the models used to measure intellectual capital." *International Journal of Management Reviews*, 3(1):41–60.

Bontis, N., Dragonetti, N. C., Jacobsen, K., and Roos, G. (1999) "The Knowledge Toolbox: a review of the tools available to measure and manage intangible resources." *European Management Journal*, 17(4):391–401.

Bounfour, A. (2002) *How to measure Intellectual Capital's dynamic value: the IC-dVAL approach.* Presented at the 5th World Congress on Intellectual Capital, McMaster University, Hamilton, Ontario, Canada.

Bourguignon, A., Malleret, V., and Nørreklit, H. (2001). Available at: http://netec.mcc.ac.uk/WoPEc/data/Papers/ebgheccah0724.html.

Brooking, A. (1996) *Intellectual capital: core asset for the third millennium.* London: International Thomson Business Press.

Caddy, I. (2000) "Intellectual Capital: recognizing both assets and liabilities." *Journal of Intellectual Capital*, 1(2):129–146.

Cañibano, L., Ayuso Covarsí, M. G., and Sánchez, M. P. (1999) *The value relevance and managerial implications of intangibles: a literature review.* Presented at the OECD symposium measuring and reporting intellectual capital; experiences, issues and prospects, Amsterdam.

Carnegie, D. (1981) *Quick and easy way to effective speaking.* Pocket Books.

Chatzkel, J. (2002) "A conversation with Göran Roos." *Journal of Intellectual Capital*, 3(2):97–113.

Copeland, T., Koller, T., and Murrin, J. (1990) *Valuation: measuring and managing the value of companies.* New York: John Wiley & Sons.

Crosby, A. (1997) *The measure of reality: quantification and western society, 1250–1600.* Cambridge: Cambridge University Press.

Danish Agency for Trade and Industry. (2003) *A guideline for intellectual capital statements.* Available at: www.efs.dk/icaccounts

Davenport, T. H., and Prusak, L. (1998) *Information ecology.* New York: Oxford University Press.

David, S., and Meyer, C. (1998) *Blur*. New York: Capstone Publishing.

De Caluwé, L., and Stoppelenburg, A. (2003) "Organisatieadvies bij de Rijksoverheid; kwaliteit onderzocht." *Tijdschrift voor Management en Organisatie*, 57e jaargang 1:25–52.

De Caluwé, L., and Vermaak, H. (1999) *Leren Veranderen: Een Handboek voor de Veranderkundige*. Samsom: Alphen aan den Rijn.

Deng, Z., Lev. B., and Narin, F. (2003) "Science and technology as predictors of stock performance." In: Hand, J., and Lev, B., eds. *Intangible assets: values, measures, and risks*. New York: Oxford University Press, 207–227.

De Valk, W. (1997) *Het Milieu tot Besluit; Een Evaluatie van de Nederlandse Regeling Milieu-effectrapportage*. Ph.D. Thesis. Amsterdam: Vrije Universiteit Amsterdam.

De Waard–van Maanen, E. (2002) *De Veldheer en de Danseres: Omgaan Met Je Levensverhaal*. Apeldoorn: Garant.

Dixit, A. K., and Pindyck, R. S. (1998) "The options approach to capital investment." In: Neef, D., Siesfeld, A., and Cefola, J., eds. *The economic impact of knowledge*. Boston: Butterworth Heinemann, 325–340.

Drucker, P. (1993) *Post-capitalist society*. New York: Harper Business.

Eccles, R. G. (1991) "The performance measurement manifesto." In: *Harvard business review on measuring corporate performance*. Boston: Harvard Business School Press, 25–46.

Edvinsson, L. (2002a) *Corporate longitude: what you need to know to navigate the knowledge economy*. London: Financial Times Prentice Hall.

Edvinsson, L. (2002b, April) "The knowledge capital of nations." *Knowledge Management*, 27-30.

Edvinsson, L. (2000) "Some perspectives on intangibles and Intellectual Capital 2000." *Journal of Intellectual Capital,* 1(1):12–16.

Edvinsson, L., and Malone, M. S. (1997) *Intellectual capital: realizing your company's true value by finding its hidden brainpower*. New York: Harper Business.

Evans, M. H. (1999) *Creating value through financial management*. Available at: http://www.exinfm.com/training/pdfiles/course08.pdf

Feyerabend, P. (1993) *Against method*. London: Verso Books.

Financial Accounting Standard Board. (2001a) *Statement no. 142: goodwill and other intangible assets*. Available at: www.fasb.org

Financial Accounting Standard Board. (2001b) *Improving business reporting: insights into enhancing voluntary disclosures*. Available at: www.fasb.org

Financial Accounting Standard Board. (1999) *Proposed statement of financial accounting standards: business combinations and intangible assets— accounting for goodwill*. Available at: www.fasb.org

Firer, S., and Williams, S. M. (2003) *IC and traditional measures of corporate performances.* Presented at the 6th World Congress on Intellectual Capital, McMaster University, Hamilton, Ontario, Canada.

Fry, Stephen. (1997) *Making history.* London: Arrow Books.

Gable, G. G. (1996) "A multidimensional model of client success when engaging external consultants." *Management Science*, 42(8):1175–1198.

Goldman, S. E., and Hoogenboom, D. (1997) *No brains, no value: Over de Waardebepaling van Kennis in Ondernemingen.* Breukelen: KPMG Knowledge Management/Nijenrode University.

Gröjer, J. E., and Johanson, U. (2000) *Accounting for intangibles at the accounting court.* Work in progress. Available at: http://www.ktm.fi/1/aineeton/seminar/johanback.htm

Gu, F., and Lev, B. (2002) *Intangible assets: measurement, drivers, usefulness.* Available at: www.stern.nyu.edu/~blev/

Gupta, O., and Roos, G. (2001) "Mergers and acquisitions through an intellectual capital perspective." *Journal of Intellectual Capital*, 2(3):297–309.

Hall, B. H., Jaffe, A., and Trajtenberg, M. (2001) *Market value and patent citations: a first look.* University of California at Berkley working papers, Department of Economics. Available at: http://repositories.cdlib.org/iber/econ/E01-304

Hamel, G. (1994) "The concept of core competence." In: Hamel, G., and Heene, A., eds. *Competence-based competition.* New York: John Wiley & Sons, 11–34.

Hamel, G., and Prahalad, C. K. (1994) *Competing for the future.* Boston: Harvard Business School Press.

Hand, J., and Lev, B. (2003) "Introduction and overview." In: Hand, J., and Lev, B., eds. *Intangible assets: values, measures, and risks.* New York: Oxford University Press, 1–8.

Haspeslagh, P., Noda, T. and Boulos, F. (2001) "Managing for value: it's not just about the numbers." *Harvard Business Review*, 79(7):64–73.

Houghton, J., and Sheehan, P. (2000) *A primer on the knowledge economy.* Melbourne: Centre for Strategic Economic Studies, Victoria University.

Hudson, W. (1993) *Intellectual capital: how to build it, enhance it, use it.* New York: John Wiley & Sons.

International Business Efficiency Consulting (IBEC). (2003) *Intellectual capital: efficiency in Croatian economy.* London: IBEC.

International Accounting Standards Committee. (1998) *IAS 38 intangible assets.* Available at: http://www.iasc.org.uk.

Isaacs, W. (1999) *Dialogue and the art of thinking together.* New York: Currency Doubleday.

Jacobs, D. (1999) *Het Kennisoffensief.* Samsom, Deventer.

Johanson, U., Eklov, G., Holmgren, M., and Mårtensson, M. (1999) *Human resource costing and accounting versus the balanced scorecard: a literature survey of experience with the concepts.* Working paper. Stockholm: Stockholm University, School of Business.

Johnson, H. T., and Kaplan, R. S. (1987) *Relevance lost.* Boston: Harvard Business School Press.

Kaplan, A. (1964) *The Conduct of inquiry.* Scranton: Chandler Publishing.

Kaplan, R., and Norton, D. (2001) *The strategy focused organization.* Boston: Harvard Business School Press.

Kaplan, R., and Norton, D. (1996a) *The balanced scorecard.* Boston: Harvard Business School Press.

Kaplan, R., and Norton, D. (1996b) "Using the balanced scorecard as a strategic management system." In: *Harvard business review on measuring corporate performance.* Boston: Harvard Business School Press, 183–211.

Kaplan, R., and Norton, D. (1993) "Putting the balanced scorecard to work." In: *Harvard business review on measuring corporate performance.* Boston: Harvard Business School Press, 147–181.

Kaplan, R., and Norton, D. (1992) "The balanced scorecard: measures that drive performance." In: *Harvard business review on measuring corporate performance.* Boston: Harvard Business School Press, 123–145.

Kerssens, I. C. (1999) *Systematic design of R&D performance measuring systems.* Thesis. Enschede: University of Twente.

Khoury, S. (1998) "Valuing intellectual properties." In: Sullivan, P. H., ed. *Profiting from intellectual capital: extracting value from innovation.* New York: John Wiley & Sons, 335–356.

Khoury, S. (1994) *Valuing intellectual properties.* The Dow Chemical Company.

Koningsveld, H. (1976) *Het Verschijnsel Wetenschap.* Amsterdam: Boom Meppel.

KPMG. (1999a) Report KPMG. In: *Ministry of Economic Affairs, intangible assets: balancing accounts with knowledge.* The Hague: Information Department of the Ministry of Economic Affairs.

KPMG. (1999b) *The intangible resources of Bank Ltd: the networking bank.* Confidential report. Amsterdam: KPMG.

KPMG. (1999c) *The intangible resources of Electro Ltd: the energy conversion company.* Confidential report. Amsterdam: KPMG.

KPMG. (1999d) *The core competencies of Logistic Services BU.* Confidential report. Amsterdam: KPMG.

KPMG. (1998) *Waardevolle kennis; voorstel voor een pilot-project waardering immateriële productiemiddelen bij vijf middelgrote ondernemingen.* Amstelveen: KPMG.

Kuypers, G. (1984) *Beginselen van Beleidsontwikkeling.* Muiderberg: Coutinho.

Kuypers, G. (1982) *ABC van een Onderzoeksopzet.* Muiderberg: Coutinho.

Leadbetter, C. (2000) *New measures for the new economy.* London: Institute of Chartered Accountants in England & Wales.

Lee, T. (1996) *Income and value measurement.* London: International Thomson Business Press.

Lekanne Deprez, F., and Tissen, R. (2002) *Zero space, moving beyond organizational limits.* San Francisco: Berrett-Koehler Publishers.

Leonard–Barton, D. (1995) *Wellsprings of knowledge: building and sustaining the sources of innovation.* Boston: Harvard Business School Press.

Leonard–Barton, D. (1992) "Core capabilities and core rigidities: a paradox in managing new product development." *Strategic Management Journal,* 13:111–125.

Lev, B. (2003) "What then must we do?" In: Hand, J., and Lev, B., eds. *Intangible assets: values, measures, and risks.* New York: Oxford University Press, 511–524.

Lev, B. (2001) *Intangibles: management, measurement and reporting.* Washington, DC: The Brookings Institution.

Lev, B. (2000) *New accounting for the new economy.* Available at: www.stern.nyu.edu/~blev/.

Lev, B. (1999, February) "Seeing is believing: a better approach to estimating knowledge capital." *CFO Magazine,* Available at: www.stern.nyu.edu/~blev/.

Lev, B., and Sougiannis, T. (1999) "Penetrating the book-to-market black box: the R&D effect." *Journal of Business Finance and Accounting,* 26:419–449.

Lev, B., and Sougiannis, T. (1996) "The capitalization, amortization, and value–relevance of R&D." *Journal of Accounting and Economics,* 21:107–138.

Lev, B., and Zarowin, P. (1999) *The boundaries of financial reporting and how to extend them.* Available at: www.stern.nyu.edu/~blev/

Lewin, K. (1945) "The research centre for group dynamics at Massachusetts Institute of Technology." *Sociometry,* American Sociological Association. (9):126–136.

Liebowitz, J., and Suen, C. Y. (2000) "Developing knowledge management metrics for measuring Intellectual Capital." *Journal of Intellectual Capital,* 1(1):54–67.

Lim, L. L. K., and Dallimore, P. (2002) "To the public-listed companies, from the investment community." *Journal of Intellectual Capital,* 3(3):262–276.

Lindgren, Astrid. (1977) *Pippi in the south seas*. New York: Puffin Books.

Luerman, T. (1998a, July–August) "Investment opportunities as real options: getting started on the numbers." *Harvard Business Review*, 51–67.

Luerman, T. (1998b, September–October) "Strategy as a portfolio of real options." *Harvard Business Review*, 89–99.

Lundqvist, J. (2000), "Intellectual Capital in Information Technology Companies", Available at: www.intellectualcapital.se.

Luthy, D. H. (1998) "Intellectual Capital and its measurement." In: Proceedings of the Asian Pacific Interdisciplinary Research in Accounting Conference (APIRA), Osaka, Japan. Available at: http://www3.bus.osaka-cu.ac.jp/apira98/archives/htmls/25.htm

Luu, N., Wykes, J., and Williams, P. (2001) *Invisible value: the case for measuring and reporting intellectual capital*. Canberra, Australia: Department of Industry, Science and Resources.

Maister, D. (1993) *Managing the professional service firm*. New York: Free Press.

Maturana, H. R., and Varela, F. J. (1987) *The tree of knowledge: the biological roots of human understanding*. London: Shambhala Publications.

Mavrinac, S., and Siesfeld, G. A. (1998) "Measures that matter: an exploratory investigation of investors' information needs and value priorities." In: Neef, D., Siesfeld, A., and Cefola, J., eds. *The economic impact of knowledge*. Boston: Butterworth Heinemann, 273–293.

Ministry of Economic Affairs. (1999) *Intangible assets: balancing accounts with knowledge*. The Hague: Information Department of the Ministry of Economic Affairs.

Ministry of Economic Affairs. (1998a) *Waardering van Immateriële Activa* [letter]. Brief aan de Tweede Kamer.

Ministry of Economic Affairs. (1998b) *Oproep voor deelname aan EZ-pilot-project waardering immateriële productiemiddelen*. EZ, Den Haag.

Morgan, G. (1986) *Images of organizations*. Beverly Hills: Sage Publications.

Mouritsen, J. (1998, December) "Driving growth: economic value added versus Intellectual Capital." *Management Accounting Research*, 461–482.

Mouritsen, J., Bukh, P. N., Larsen, H. T., and Johansen, M. R. (2002) "Developing and managing knowledge through Intellectual Capital statements." *Journal of Intellectual Capital*, 3(1):10–29.

Mouritsen, J., Larsen, H. T., and Bukh, P. N. (2001a) "Intellectual capital and the 'capable firm': narrating, visualizing and numbering for managing knowledge." *Accounting, Organization and Society*, (7/8): 735-762.

Mouritsen, J., Larsen, H. T., and Bukh, P. N. (2001b) "Valuing the future: Intellectual Capital supplements at Skandia." *Accounting, Auditing and Accountability Journal*, 14(14):399–422.

Mouritsen, J., Larsen, H. T., Bukh, P. N., and Johansen, M. R. (2001c) "Reading an Intellectual Capital statement: describing and prescribing knowledge management strategies." *Journal of Intellectual Capital*, 2(4):359–383.

M'Pherson, P. K., and Pike, S. (2001a) *Accounting, empirical measurement and Intellectual Capital.* Presented at the 4th World Congress on the Management of Intellectual Capital, McMaster University, Hamilton, Ontario, Canada.

M'Pherson, P. K., and Pike, S. (2001b) "Accounting, empirical measurement and Intellectual Capital." *Journal of Intellectual Capital*, 2(3):246–260.

Nakamura, L. (2003) "A trillion dollar a year investment and the New Economy." In: Hand, J., and Lev, B., eds. *Intangible assets: values, measures, and risks.* New York: Oxford University Press, 19–47.

Nasar, S. (1999) *A beautiful mind.* New York: Simon & Schuster.

Nørreklit, H. (2000) "The balance on the Balanced Scorecard: a critical analysis of some of its assumptions." *Management Accounting Research*, 11:65–88.

Oshima, A., and Hogue, A. (1983) *Writing academic English.* New York: Addison Wesley.

Peppard, J., and Rylander, A. (2001) "Leveraging Intellectual Capital at ApiON." *Journal of Intellectual Capital*, 2(3):225–235.

Perrow, C. (1970) *Organizational analysis: a sociological review.* Belmont: Wadsworth Publications.

Petty, R., and Guthrie, J. (2000) "Intellectual capital literature overview: measurement, reporting and management." *Journal of Intellectual Capital*, 1(2):155–176.

Phillips, J. (2000) *The consultant's scorecard.* New York: McGraw Hill.

Pike, S., and Roos, G. (2000) "Intellectual capital measurement and holistic value approach (HVA)." *Works Institute Journal (Japan)*, 42.

Pike, S., Rylander, A., and Roos, G. (2002) "Intellectual capital management and disclosure." In: Bontis, N., and Choo, C. W., eds. *The strategic management of intellectual capital and organizational knowledge.* New York: Oxford University Press, 657–671.

Pike, S., Rylander, A., and Roos, G. (2001) *Intellectual capital management and disclosure.* Presented at the 4th World Congress on Intellectual Capital, McMaster University, Hamilton, Ontario, Canada.

Pirsig, Robert M. (1975) *Zen and the art of motorcycle maintenance: an inquiry into values.* New York: Bantam Books.

Procter, P. (1978) *Longman Dictionary of Contemporary English.* Essex: Longman Group Ltd.

Pulic, A. (2002) *Do we know if we create or destroy value?* Available at: www.vaic-on.net

Pulic, A. (2000a) *MVA and VAIC^TM analysis of randomly selected companies from FTSE 250.* Available at: www.vaic-on.net

Pulic, A. (2000b) *VAIC^TM: an accounting tool for IC management.* Available at: www.vaic-on.net

Reilly, R., and Schweihs, R. (1999) *Valuing intangible assets.* New York: McGraw-Hill.

Reneman, D. (1998) *Self reference and policy success: an exploration into the role of self-referential conduct of organizations in the effectiveness of policies.* Ph.D. thesis. Amsterdam: Free University.

Rescher, N. (1969) *Introduction to value theory.* Englewood Cliffs, NJ: Prentice-Hall.

Roos, G., Bainbridge, A., and Jacobsen, K. (2001) "Intellectual capital analysis as a strategic tool." *Strategy and Leadership Journal*, 29(3):21–26.

Roos, G., and Roos, J. (1997) "Measuring your company's intellectual performance. *Long Range Planning*, 30:413–426.

Roos, G., Roos, J., Dragonetti, N., and Edvinsson, L. (1997) *Intellectual capital: navigating in the new business landscape.* New York: New York University Press.

Rorty, R. (1989) *Contingency, irony and solidarity.* New York: Cambridge University Press.

Rutledge, J. (1997, April) "You are a fool if you buy into this." *Forbes ASAP.* Available at: http://www.versaggi.net/ecommerce/articles/intlcapital.htm

Rylander, A., Jacobsen K., and Roos G. (2000) "Towards improved information disclosure on Intellectual Capital." *International Journal of Technology Management*, 20:715–742.

Sackman, S., Flamholz, E., and Bullen, M. (1989) "Human resource accounting. A state of the art review." *Journal of Accounting Literature*, 8:235–264.

Schön, D. A. (1983) *The reflective practitioner.* New York: Basic Books.

Seethamraju, C. (2003) "The value relevance of trademarks." In: Hand, J., and Lev, B., eds. *Intangible assets: values, measures, and risks.* New York: Oxford University Press, 228–247.

Skandia. (1998) *Annual report.* Skandia.

Skandia. (1996) *Power of Innovation.* Supplement. Skandia

Skandia. (1995) *Visualizing intellectual capital in Skandia.* Supplement.

Smith, G., and Parr, R. (1994) *Valuation of intellectual property and intangible assets.* New York: John Wiley & Sons.

Soete, L., and Ter Weel, B. (1999) *Innovation, knowledge creation and technology policy in Europe*. Available at: www.soete.nl

Standfield, K. (2001) "Time capital and intangible accounting: new approaches to Intellectual Capital." In: Malhotra, Y., ed. *Knowledge management and business model innovation*. Hershey, PA: Idea Group Publishing, 316–324.

Stewart III, G. B. (1994) "EVA: fact and fantasy." *Journal of Applied Corporate Finance*, 7:71–84.

Stewart, T. A. (2001a, May 28) "Intellectual capital: ten years later, how far we've come." *Fortune*: 106-107.

Stewart, T. A. (2001b) *The wealth of knowledge: intellectual capital and the twenty-first century organization*. New York: Doubleday/Currency.

Stewart, T. A. (1997) *Intellectual capital: the new wealth of organizations*. New York: Doubleday/Currency.

Stewart, T. A. (1994, October 3) "Your company's most valuable asset: Intellectual Capital." *Fortune*: 28-33.

Stewart, T. A. (1991, June 3) "Brainpower." *Fortune*. Available at: http://www.fortune.com/fortune/print/0,15935,372049,00.html.

Strassmann, P. A. (1998) "The value of knowledge capital." *American Programmer*, 11(3):3–10.

Strassmann, P. A. (1999) *Calculating knowledge capital*. Available at: files.strassmann.com/pubs/km/1999-10.php

Strikwerda, J. (1994) *Organisatie-Advisering: Wetenschap en Pragmatiek*. Delft: Eburon.

Sullivan, P. H. (2000) *Value driven intellectual capital: how to convert intangible corporate assets into market value*. New York: John Wiley & Sons.

Sullivan, P. H. (1998a) "Basic definitions and concepts." In: Sullivan, P. H., ed. *Profiting from intellectual capital: extracting value from innovation*. New York: John Wiley & Sons, 19–34.

Sullivan, P. H. (1998b) "Extracting value from intellectual assets." In: Sullivan, P. H., ed. *Profiting from intellectual capital: extracting value from innovation*. New York: John Wiley & Sons, 173–185.

Sullivan, P. H. (1998c) "Introduction to Intellectual Capital management." In: Sullivan, P. H., ed. *Profiting from intellectual capital: extracting value from innovation*. New York: John Wiley & Sons, 3–18.

Sveiby, K. E. (1997) *The new organizational wealth: managing & measuring knowledge-based assets*. San Francisco: Berrett-Koehler Publishers.

Sveiby, K. E. (2002) *Methods for measuring intangible assets*. Available at: http://www.sveiby.com/articles/IntangibleMethods.htm

Sveiby, K. E. (2001) *The Balanced Score Card (BSC) and the Intangible Assets Monitor—a comparison*. Available at: http://www.sveiby.com/articles/BSCandIAM.html

Sveiby, K. E. (2000) "Measuring intangible assets—an emerging standard." Available at: http://www.sveiby.com.au/articles/EmergingStandard.html

Sveiby, K. E., et al. (1989) *The invisible balance sheet*. Available at: http://www.sveiby.com/articles/IntangAss/DenOsynliga.pdf

Sveiby, K., Linard, K., and Dvorsky, L. (2002) *Building a knowledge-based strategy: a system dynamic model for allocating value adding capacity*. Working paper. Available at: http://www.sveiby.com/articles/sdmodelkstrategy.pdf

Swanborn, P. G. (1981) *Methoden van sociaal-wetenschappelijk onderzoek*. Amsterdam: Boom Meppel.

Teece, D. J. (2000) *Managing intellectual capital*. Oxford: Oxford University Press.

Tissen, R. (1991) *Mensen Beter Managen in Theorie en Praktijk*. Deventer: Kluwer Bedrijfswetenschappen.

Tissen, R., Andriessen, D., and Lekanne Deprez, F. (2000) *The knowledge dividend: creating high-performance companies through value-based knowledge management*. London: Financial Times Prentice Hall.

Tissen, R., Andriessen, D., and Lekanne Deprez, F. (1998) *Value-based knowledge management: creating the 21st century company: knowledge intensive, people rich*. Amsterdam: Addison-Wesley Longman.

Trompenaars, F., and Hampden–Turner, C. (1997) *Riding the waves of culture*. London: Nicholas Brealey Publishing.

Upton, W. S. (2001) *Business and financial reporting: challenges from the new economy*. Norwalk, CT: FASB.

Van Aken, J. E. (2000, September 26) *Management research based on the paradigm of the design sciences: the quest for tested and grounded technological rules*. Available cut: www.tm.tue.nl/ecis

Van Aken, J. E. (1996) "Methodologische vraagstukken bij het ontwerpen van bedrijfskundige systemen." *Bedrijfskunde*, jaargang 68/2:14–22.

Van den Berg, H. (2003) *Models of Intellectual Capital valuation: a comparative evaluation*. Presented at the 6th World Congress on the Management of Intellectual Capital, McMaster University, Hamilton, Ontario, Canada.

Varela, F. J. (1979) *Principles of biological autonomy*. Amsterdam: Elsevier.

Viedma, J. M. (2002) *SCBS social capital benchmarking system*. Presented at the 5th World Congress on Intellectual Capital, McMaster University, Hamilton, Ontario, Canada.

Viedma, J. M. (2001a) "ICBS innovation capability benchmarking system." In: Bontis, N., ed. *World Congress on intellectual capital readings*. Boston: Butterworth Heinemann, 243–265.

Viedma, J. M. (2001b) "ICBS intellectual capital benchmarking system." *Journal of Intellectual Capital*, 2(2):148–164.

Viedma, J. M. (1999) *ICBS intellectual capital benchmarking system.* Presented at the 3rd World Congress on Intellectual Capital, McMaster University, Hamilton, Ontario, Canada.

Von Böhm–Bawerk, E. (1959) *Capital and interest.* Libertarian Press.

Von Krogh, G., and Roos, J. (1995) *Organizational epistemology.* London: Macmillan Press.

Walsh, J. P., and Ungson, G. R. (1991) "Organizational memory." *Academy of Management Review,* 16:57–91.

Webber, A. M. (2000, January/February) "New math for a new economy." *Fast Company,* 214–224.

Weggeman, M. (1997a) *Kennismanagement: Inrichting en Besturing van Kennisintensieve Organisaties.* Schiedam: Scriptum Management.

Weggeman, M. (1997b) *Organiseren met Kennis.* Schiedam: Inaugurele rede Technische Universiteit Eindhoven. Scriptum Management.

Weggeman, M. (1995) *Creatieve Ambitie Ontwikkeling.* Ph.D. thesis. Tilburg: Tilburg University Press.

Weggeman, M. (1992) *Leidinggeven aan Professionals.* Deventer: Kluwer Bedrijfswetenschappen.

Weick, K. E. (1995) *Sense-making in organizations.* London: Sage Publications.

Westberg, P. B., and Sullivan, P. H. (1998) "In search of a paradigm." In: Sullivan, P. H., ed. *Profiting from intellectual capital: extracting value from innovation.* New York: John Wiley & Sons, 59–75.

White, G. I., Sondhi, A. C., and Fried, D. (1997) *The analysis and use of financial statements.* New York: John Wiley and Sons.

Williams, S. M. (2001) *Are companies' Intellectual Capital performance and Intellectual Capital disclosure practices related?* Presented at the 4th World Congress on Intellectual Capital, McMaster University, Hamilton, Ontario, Canada.

Wolters. (1977) Wolters' Woordenboek Nederlands / Engels. Groningen: Wolters-Noordhoff.

Zucker, L. G., Darby, M. R., and Brewer, M. B. (2003) "Intellectual human capital and the birth of US biotechnology enterprises." In: Hand, J., and Lev, B., eds. *Intangible assets: values, measures, and risks.* New York: Oxford University Press, 185–206.

About the Author

Dr. Daniel Andriessen is Professor of Intellectual Capital at INHOLLAND University of Professional Education, The Netherlands, and director of the Centre of Applied Research in Intellectual Capital, a research group set up to study the impact of the intangible economy on people and organizations (www.inholland.com).

Through his research group he offers help to companies, governmental and educational organizations, academics, and students on the subject of knowledge management and intellectual capital valuation and measurement. He is a popular speaker at conferences and likes to do guest lectures, presentations, and training sessions on a variety of subjects related to the growing importance of intangibles.

Before joining INHOLLAND, Dr. Andriessen worked as a management consultant for KPMG for more than 12 years. He was founder of KPMG's Knowledge Advisory Services Group in 1997, together with Prof. Dr. René Tissen. Together they have grown this group from 2 to 30 people, servicing clients all over the world in the field of knowledge management and intellectual capital valuation.

Daniel received his Ph.D. degree at Nyenrode University in The Netherlands (the first thesis on intellectual capital) and he holds a masters degree in political and administrative science at the Free University, Amsterdam. His publications include the groundbreaking, full-color book *Value-Based Knowledge Management: Creating the 21st Century Company: Knowledge Intensive, People Rich* (Addison-Wesley, 1998), which he wrote with his former KPMG colleagues Prof. Dr. René Tissen and Frank Lekanne Deprez. This book was updated and published by Financial Times Prentice Hall in 2000 as *The Knowledge Dividend: Creating High-Performance Companies through Value-Based Knowledge Management.* Together with Prof. Dr. René Tissen he wrote *Weightless Wealth: Find Your Real Value in a Future of Intangible Assets* (Financial Times Prentice Hall, 2000).

The notion of multiple perspectives on reality plays a leading role in his life. There is no such thing as the absolute truth. In his work and private life, Daniel tries to make room for different opinions, and he champions respect. He has a special interest in the management of diversity, intercultural management, and the science of knowledge (epistemology).

Daniel loves to listen to and play rock music, but it has to be melodic, harmonic, and complex. Spock's Beard, Dream Theater, Steely Dan, and YES are among his favorite bands. If you like good music, he recommends looking at www.radiantrecords.com. Daniel is married and is the father of two girls. He likes to cook, take his girls cycling, and go with them to the playground or the swimming pool.

He suggests you check out his Web site (www.weightlesswealth.com) and mail him your feedback.

Index